Torn between America and China

The **Institute of Southeast Asian Studies (ISEAS)** was established as an autonomous organization in 1968. It is a regional centre dedicated to the study of socio-political, security and economic trends and developments in Southeast Asia and its wider geostrategic and economic environment. The Institute's research programmes are the Regional Economic Studies (RES, including ASEAN and APEC), Regional Strategic and Political Studies (RSPS), and Regional Social and Cultural Studies (RSCS).

ISEAS Publishing, an established academic press, has issued more than 2,000 books and journals. It is the largest scholarly publisher of research about Southeast Asia from within the region. ISEAS Publishing works with many other academic and trade publishers and distributors to disseminate important research and analyses from and about Southeast Asia to the rest of the world.

Torn between America and China

ELITE PERCEPTIONS AND INDONESIAN FOREIGN POLICY

DANIEL NOVOTNY

LSEAS

INSTITUTE OF SOUTHEAST ASIAN STUDIES
Singapore

First published in Singapore in 2010 by
ISEAS Publishing
Institute of Southeast Asian Studies
30 Heng Mui Keng Terrace, Pasir Panjang
Singapore 119614

E-mail: publish@iseas.edu.sg • *Website*: bookshop.iseas.edu.sg

ISEAS Library Cataloguing-in-Publication Data

Novotny, Daniel.
    Torn between America and China : elite perceptions and Indonesian foreign policy.
    1. Indonesia—Foreign relations.
    2. Elite (Social sciences)—Indonesia—Attitudes.
    3. United States—Foreign public opinion, Indonesian.
    4. China—Foreign public opinion, Indonesian.
    I. Title
JZ1743 N94   2010

ISBN   978-981-4279-59-8 (soft cover)
ISBN   978-981-4279-61-1 (E-Book PDF)

Typeset by International Typesetters Pte Ltd
Printed in Singapore by

Torn between America and China

ELITE PERCEPTIONS AND INDONESIAN FOREIGN POLICY

DANIEL NOVOTNY

ISEAS

INSTITUTE OF SOUTHEAST ASIAN STUDIES
Singapore

First published in Singapore in 2010 by
ISEAS Publishing
Institute of Southeast Asian Studies
30 Heng Mui Keng Terrace, Pasir Panjang
Singapore 119614

E-mail: publish@iseas.edu.sg • *Website*: bookshop.iseas.edu.sg

ISEAS Library Cataloguing-in-Publication Data

Novotny, Daniel.
    Torn between America and China : elite perceptions and Indonesian foreign policy.
    1. Indonesia—Foreign relations.
    2. Elite (Social sciences)—Indonesia—Attitudes.
    3. United States—Foreign public opinion, Indonesian.
    4. China—Foreign public opinion, Indonesian.
    I. Title
JZ1743 N94   2010

ISBN   978-981-4279-59-8 (soft cover)
ISBN   978-981-4279-61-1 (E-Book PDF)

Typeset by International Typesetters Pte Ltd
Printed in Singapore by

To the five Angels of my life —
Ludmila, Marie, Dewi, Daniela, and Devita

CONTENTS

Foreword   xi

Preface   xv

List of Figures   xix

Acknowledgements   xxi

PART I: THE CONTEXT

1. Introduction   3
       Introduction   3
       Book's Structure   8

2. The Power of Perceptions   16
       Introduction   16
       Realism and Balance-of-Power Concept   21
       The Concept of "Threat Perception"   31
       Balance-of-Threat Theory   36
       Enhancing Explanatory Power of the Balance-of-Threat   41
          Theory
       Conclusion   48

3. The Foreign Policy Elite and Indonesia's National Interest   61
       Introduction   61
       Elite Perceptions and the Conception of National Interests   62
          and Security
       Foreign Policy Elite: The Definition and Research Method   65
       Elite Heterogeneity and Division: The Roots   68
       Elite Heterogeneity: The Key Factors   73

The Foreign Policy Elite: Survey Research in Indonesia   83
Conclusion   90

PART II: THE PERCEPTIONS "ANTARA DUA KARANG"

4.   Elite Perceptions of the United States   103
     Introduction   103
     Elite's Attitudes towards the United States: Historical   105
        Context
     The Love-Hate Attitude to the United States   116
     The Changing Dynamics of the Elite's Attitude to the 121
        United States
     The War on Terrorism: Elite versus Public Perceptions 136
     Other Non-Traditional Sources of Threat   145
     Anti-Americanism as an Issue-Based Occurrence   153
     Conclusion   160

5.   Elite Perceptions of China   174
     Introduction
     Post-Suharto Period: Change and Continuity of the   175
        "China Threat" Perception
     The Missing "Love" Aspect in the Elite's Attitude to China 180
     The Elite Images behind the "China Threat"   181
     The "China Threat" Phenomenon in a Historical Context 188
     New Order, Suharto, and "China Threat"   191
     The Ethnic Chinese as a "Trojan Horse" Inside Indonesia 200
     The Elite's Ambivalence About China's Rise   211
     Conclusion   228

PART III: ELITE CONSENSUS AND POLICY OUTCOMES

6.   The Bigger Picture: Elite Perceptions of Other Powers 247
     Introduction   247
     Australia   250
     Japan   265
     India (Versus China Juxtaposition)   279
     ASEAN Countries   281
     Conclusion   288

7. The Indonesian Elite Facing a Changing World   299
    Introduction   299
    "*Mendayung Antara Dua Karang*": The Elite's "Balance-of-   300
        Threat" Mode of Thinking
    The Indonesian Elite's Long-Term Threat Assessment   306
    China: Long-Term Threat Assessment   309
    The United States: Long-Term Threat Assessment   316
    Factor No. 1: "Geographic Proximity"   320
    Factor No. 2: "Religion"   329
    Conclusion: The Question of the Elite Consensus   335

8. Conclusion   346
    The Summary of Findings   346
    The Findings and Indonesia's Future Foreign Relations   349

Glossary   353

Abbreviations   357

Bibliography   361

Index   387

Note on the Author   401

FOREWORD

Many countries will be "torn between" in the 21st century — called on to modulate their relations between the United States and China. Daniel Novotny's book stands as a work of foresight and imagination, attempting to understand the pressures that policy-makers face as the world moves into a new age of two great powers after the collapse of the Soviet system and a generation of unchallengeable U.S. dominance.

Novotny's book has a number of qualities to recommend it. First, there is the focus on how an Asian country and the world's largest Muslim country (yet with a powerful Chinese minority) finds its way between the United States, its friend since the 1960s, and a growingly powerful China, keen to assert its ascendancy in its region. Readers curious about China, Islam, and Southeast Asia need this book.

Second, Novotny raises teasing questions about how "foreign policy" is made. To what extent are the policies of modern states dictated by their material facts of life — their geographic boundaries, the richness of their economies, the ethnicities of their people? Or, do foreign policies get made by small elites who constantly balance their own interests, prejudices, and long-term judgements against the pressures of domestic politics?

Novotny makes an important contribution by trying to get at "the mind" of a bureaucracy and a state's elite as they formulate policy towards the world outside their political boundaries. His diligent interviewing highlights the qualities that scholarship can bring to the study of contemporary affairs: a journalist might do an interview here and there; Novotny, the scholar, had a hit-list of more than forty interviewees whose views he sought systematically and relentlessly.

This relentless interviewing highlights another aspect of the book. Novotny brings to his research the multiple lenses of a widely travelled European, highlighted by his own remarkable linguistic talent. He is a Czech who is fluent in three European languages and Indonesian. (He used to speak passable Spanish and Russian but says he has forgotten them through lack of use.) He has lived and worked throughout Europe, travelled widely in northern Africa and Southeast Asia, lived in Indonesia with his Balinese wife and their children and had much of his academic experience in Australia. As a professional photographer in another life, he brings to his scholarship the idea that different lenses and different angles produce different pictures.

At the level of information-gathering and story-telling, the book also has much to offer. Indonesia is a country too often ignored. Japan made the economic big time two generations ago; China is the hot story of the twenty-first century; and India's recent rapid growth has business pages breathless. But Indonesia, the fourth largest country in the world, with a population of 230 million (100 million more than Japan's), and the largest Muslim country, falls off the mental maps of many observers of world affairs. Indeed, awareness of the transformations of Indonesia since the fall of Suharto in 1997 is remarkably limited. Indonesia is a different country, a democracy, struggling to create reliable institutions. It has embarked on an unpredictable voyage of social and political change, which for the past ten years has been largely constructive and peaceful.

In redressing the world's picture of Indonesia, Novotny's book plays an important part. We learn about Indonesia's elites — some of whom have been Novotny's informants — and their views of their country's position and global potential. Though the book focuses on China and the United States, Indonesia's relations with its ASEAN partners can never be ignored, because as the largest country in ASEAN, Indonesia has the potential to exert greater influence in world affairs. One of the tests for its policy-makers is to make this advantage work effectively, both to enhance Indonesia's national interests and those of Southeast Asia and ASEAN generally. The book also has to deal with Indonesia's two other day-to-day relationships: with Japan and Australia. Australia maintains its largest diplomatic mission in Jakarta, and the two countries interact daily along their long maritime frontiers. Japan has been a major investor, though the passion has waned in the past ten years. And both Australia and Japan will seek to influence Indonesian responses to the new China.

As well as diligent fact-finding and reporting, Novotny aims to place Indonesian experience in the theory-building that goes on in Big-I, Big-R International Relations. He notes that the peculiarities and complexities of the Indonesian experiment have tended to be overlooked, save for Weinstein's *Indonesian Foreign Policy and the Dilemma of Dependence* (1976), Michael Leifer's *Indonesia's Foreign Policy* (1983) and Rizal Sukma's *Indonesia and*

China (1999). He takes up Weinstein's ideas of the threat perceptions of Indonesian elites in what they regarded in the 1960s and 1970s as a hostile world. Novotny finds that the world continues to look threatening from an Indonesian perspective but that elites are more divided than they once were about where the most serious threats come from. There is agreement, however, that internal disarray, encouraged by outside ill-wishers, rather than outright attack on the country's borders, poses the greatest threat.

Novotny's skills, fascinations, and perspective have enabled him to produce a book that will engage a number of audiences. It helps to refine views of 21st-century Indonesia; it contributes to our understanding of how "foreign policy" is made; and it provides readers with a remarkable perspective, through the eyes of a European whose feet and heart are in Southeast Asia, on how the world's fourth largest country views itself, Asia, and the world.

Robin Jeffrey
Institute of South Asian Studies
Singapore
May 2010

PREFACE

The origins of this book can perhaps be found somewhere inside the extensive maze of narrow corridors or in the State Rooms of the "Office of the President" that is located within the splendid Prague Castle perched on top of the hill in the heart of Prague, the capital city of the Czech Republic. As an intern and later an aide in the Political Department during President Václav Havel's tenure, I enjoyed the privilege of watching closely the "human dimension" behind foreign policy-making. I was often taken aback when I saw how much impact the President's, senior diplomats' and policy-makers' personal idiosyncrasies (shaped by past experiences), their personal perceptions, attitudes and preferences would have on the dynamics and actual outcomes of a state's foreign relations. One of the main arguments underlying the discussion in this book is the idea that policy-makers' perceptions are as important as realities, in that they shape their real actions.

This book was written for many thousands of people — students, academics, professional diplomats, as well as a general audience who are interested in and want to learn more about foreign policy-making in general and the important role Indonesian policy-makers' threat perceptions play in shaping the country's foreign policy in particular. I spent more than four years researching this topic — including countless hours of interviews with present and former Indonesian presidents, cabinet ministers and senior diplomats (and days spent at the library) — and, finally, wrote this book out of passion and curiosity. "International relations" and "foreign policy" are fascinating objects of study. However, most texts on foreign policy formation tend to use mostly narrative, descriptive and *atheoretical* approaches and generally seem to downplay the important role of decision-makers' threat perceptions in explaining foreign policy outcomes. Their limitation stems from the failure to use a theoretical framework to organize and assess empirical findings. While this book brings a theoretical perspective based on the balance-of-threat concept to bear on the study of foreign policy elite perceptions, it puts a special emphasis on the elite's state-based security concerns. The balance-of-threat theory is employed here as a predictor about how Indonesia will behave and whether it will implement policies intended to prevent other countries from endangering Indonesia's national interests and security.

Indonesia is used here as a case study to explore the subject matter. This book constitutes a comprehensive perceptive account of Indonesian foreign policy — it analyses the perceptions of the country's foreign policy elite about other states, with a special attention devoted to Indonesia's triangular relationship with the United States and China, and the manner in which these shape the decision-making process and determine policy outcomes. I sought to find answers particularly to these questions: What are some of the most important factors in forming the Indonesian elite's threat perceptions? Is there a causal relationship between elite perceptions and policy outcomes? Moreover, with a special reference to the United States and China, will a particular threat perception remain the same through a long period of time, or will it change with time? And last but not the least, to what extent have all of the diverse sections of the Indonesian elite agreed on the nature and urgency of the threat posed, respectively, by the United States and China, to their country's national interests?

Like virtually any academic study in the field of social sciences, also this book is not capable of covering all aspects, qualities and eventualities of the subject matter under consideration. This limitation ought to be even more accentuated given the character of this study, which is concerned with the phenomenon of elite perceptions. Among the sheer variety of possible factors affecting foreign policy elite perceptions, in terms of the policy-makers' background, I chose to focus primarily on the factors of religion and education and to a lesser extent on their party or professional affiliation. Because of their non-material, subjective and effectively elusive character, the description and evaluation of human perceptions completely depends on the quality of the person's recollection and the accuracy of his or her narrative. In this context, this book does not aspire to offer a substantial elaboration on the psychological mechanisms at work in threat perceptions. While admittedly the existing literature on threat perceptions tends to be agnostic about the role of emotion, as well as affective and cognitive processes in generating perceptions and images about international environment, I do not consider myself as being academically equipped to carry out a fruitful research in the field of psychology or physiology.

There have been only a few studies of Indonesia, or non-Western countries more generally, that have employed a systematic approach within a theoretical framework to explain the correlation between elite perceptions and foreign policy outcomes. In broad terms, this book is a kind of "update" of Weinstein's major 1976 study on Indonesian elite's perceptions titled *Indonesian Foreign Policy and the Dilemma of Dependence: From Sukarno to Soeharto*. Within these pages I will set out on a journey through the minds of Indonesian presidents, cabinet ministers, senior diplomats and high-ranking army officers during the present plural democratic system of government in the post-Suharto period to find what they see when they view the outside world. The comparison with the earlier Suharto and Sukarno-dominated regimes, as discussed in Weinstein's book, will reveal some dramatic changes and surprising continuities — notably the enduring perception of Indonesia as having to constantly deal with position fraught with dilemmas within the "tricky" and "perilous" international system.

LIST OF FIGURES

Figure 2.1	The Most Effective Approaches to Peace and Security in Southeast Asia	20
Figure 2.2.	Transformation Process from the Projection of the Reality to the Elite Perception	35
Figure 3.1	The Religious Make-Up of the Interviewed Members of the Indonesian Elite	82
Figure 4.1	Views of a Changing World 2003; War with Iraq Further Divides Global Publics	133
Figure 4.2	Views of a Changing World, June 2003; The Pew Global Attitudes Project	137
Figure 4.3	Support for the U.S.-led War on Terrorism; The Pew Global Attitudes Project	154
Figure 4.4	Sources of Anti-American Sentiment; The Pew Global Attitudes Project	155
Figure 4.5	Dramatic Drop in Support for Global Terrorists among Indonesians since Tsunami	157
Figure 4.6	Tsunami Relief Boosts U.S. Image; The Pew Global Attitudes Project	157
Figure 4.7	Does U.S. Foreign Policy Consider Others' Interest?; The Pew Global Attitudes Project	158
Figure 5.1	Better If Another Rivalled U.S. Military Power?; The Pew Global Attitudes Project	178
Figure 5.2	Views of China; The Pew Global Attitudes Project	178
Figure 5.3	Need for Caution in Dealings with China?	185
Figure 5.4	Did "China Threat" Exist during the New Order?	194
Figure 5.5	China in the Future Goes Hegemonic?	212

Figure 5.6   The "Pretty Maiden" Analogy, Based on the Research   216
               Data Evaluation

Figure 6.1   Degree of Urgency: External versus Internal Threats,   261
               Based on the Research Data Evaluation

Figure 7.1   Long-Term Threat Assessment; Based on the Research   309
               Data Evaluation

Figure 7.2   Attitude to the Future Involvement of External   322
               Powers in Southeast Asia; Based on the Research
               Data Evaluation

Figure 7.3   The Greatest Present External Threat to Indonesia: 333
               Muslim versus Non-Muslim Dichotomy; Based on
               the Research Data Evaluation

Figure 7.4   The Elite Future, Long-Term Threat Assessment: 334
               Muslim versus Non-Muslim Dichotomy; Based on
               the Research Data Evaluation

ACKNOWLEDGEMENTS

While this book is the most evident product of the five-year-long journey made up of research, collecting data, interviewing policy-makers, library visits and writing-up, by no means less important is its not-so-obvious human dimension — the support, inspiration and motivation given to me by many people. The journey has certainly been much easier because I could travel together with the following people:

The first person to whom I would like to express my gratitude is my first main supervisor A/Prof David Reeve. He has stood on my side from the very beginning till the end of my Ph.D. candidature, both during good and difficult times. David Reeve has been my "guru", colleague and closest advisor, an indispensable source of ideas and inspiration, as well as motivation when I felt let down by the lack of progress. Being a brilliant scholar, I have enjoyed the privilege of "tapping" into the bottomless pool of David Reeve's knowledge about Indonesia. Besides of being an excellent supervisor, I dare to say that David has been as close as a relative and a friend. I deeply value his never-ending empathy and understanding of my complicated family situation when I had to "fairly" divide the time between the research and my newly born baby girl.

I would also like to thank my co-supervisor Dr Liz Thurbon who guided me through the abstract world of international relations theory, introducing me to new ways of how to effectively use the theories to explore and better understand the complexities of Indonesian foreign policy. Moreover, I also owe lots of gratitude to Prof John Ingleson who kept an eye on the progress of my work and always was available when I needed his valuable comments. John especially helped me in finding the right words to explain some complicated phenomena with regards to Indonesian elite perceptions and in streamlining the text in this book.

Another credit goes to the University of New South Wales (UNSW) for offering me the UPRS/UPRS scholarship without which I would not have been able to commence this research. But the UNSW did not give me only the valuable experience of studying (and tutoring/lecturing) at one of the best universities in the Asia-Pacific — it was at the UNSW campus where I met my future wife, herself a UNSW graduate. After all, a university campus is not only a place where research and experiments are carried out but also a place where new friendships and partnerships come into being. My colleagues from the School of Modern Languages all gave me the feeling of being at home at work.

Thanks are also due to other colleagues and academics with whom I have had the opportunity to discuss my research and who have thus in one way or the other helped to shape my ideas: A/Prof Jean Gelman Taylor, Dr Charles Coppel, Dr Angus McIntyre, Dr Richard Chauvel, Dr Thomas Reuter and others. I am particularly grateful to Prof Peter Reeves and Prof Robin Jeffrey and their wives Noelene and Lesley for their useful advice, warm friendship and unforgettable hospitality during my research-related stays in Singapore and Melbourne. For the same reason, I would like to send lots of thanks to Singapore to my friend Dr Jan Mrázek and his family.

This book would never have become a reality if it were not for the enormous support and cooperation from all the members of Indonesian foreign policy elite whom I had the opportunity to interview. Whether it was a career diplomat, an academic or a government minister or a former president, all of them put their work aside and reserved some time to discuss with a young scholar their perceptions, views and opinions. Since the university policy does not permit to reveal the respondents' identities, unfortunately, I can only express my gratitude to the interviewed leaders collectively while keeping their names in anonymity.

The Habibie Centre in Jakarta also substantially contributed to the development of this work by providing me with a base and useful contacts during the fieldwork. I would also like to thank to the ISEAS Library and the Institute of Defence and Strategic Studies (IDSS) in Singapore where I conducted my research twice as a Visiting Research Fellow. Among all colleagues and friends at the IDSS, I would like to thank namely to Dr Ralf Emmers, A/Prof Leonard Sebastian, Dr Adam Dolnik and Nita Prawindarti for extensive discussions and their valuable comments. On the European front, I also thank my former lecturers from Prague-based Charles University, namely Dr Blanka Knotkova, A/Prof Alena Miskova and Prof Lenka Rovná for giving me the initial stimulation to pursue further studies in Australia. Encouragement and tacit support came from several friends and colleagues from the Prague-based Association for International Affairs (AMO).

Special credit goes to the Institute of Southeast Asian Studies (ISEAS) in Singapore for offering me a Visiting Research Fellowship Programme that enabled me to concentrate on the final draft of the manuscript. I very much appreciated the friendly, inspiring and thought-provoking atmosphere in a community of scholars from all around the world. I would especially like to thank the ISEAS Director, Ambassador K. Kesavapany, the Head of the Publications Unit, Mrs Triena Ong, Head of Administration, Mrs Y.L. Lee, and my colleagues, fellow researchers, Dr Aris Ananta, Dr Theresa W. Devasahayam, Dr Arun Balasubramaniam, Dr Bernhard Platzdasch, Dr Michael J. Montesano, and others.

I feel a deep sense of gratitude to my mother and father who formed an important part of my character and attitudes and thus stirred me towards one of the best decisions of my life — to pursue a Ph.D. I am also grateful to my brother Radek and other members of our family, namely Lída and Iva, Olga, Amálka and Alžběta, for all their support that they gave me during the course of my research. Additional energy and inspiration for this research was provided by my extended Balinese family. Thanks to my wife's parents, Odah and Pekak Pande, and all nine of her brothers and sisters with their families, I learned a lot — as an insider — about the Indonesian way of life.

I am very grateful to my wife Dewi for her love and patience during the entire Ph.D. period. She patiently endured my late-night arrivals at home from the campus and the long months of separation. I also appreciate her great help with the technical aspect of this book. The account of the human dimension underlying this thesis would not be complete without mentioning perhaps the best experience that we lived through in this period — the birth of our first daughter Daniela Putu. It was she who supplied us with an additional joyful element to our life mission and provided me with yet another reason to strive to complete the research. And it was also the birth of my second daughter Devita Madey that has given me the ultimate impetus to complete the final draft of the manuscript for this book.

Finally, not to leave the chain of my gratitude incomplete, I would like to extend many thanks to my two late grandfathers, my late father-in-law, Pekak, and my beloved grandmother for their spiritual guidance.

PART I

The Context

1

INTRODUCTION

INTRODUCTION

Post-Cold War international relations have been marked by far-reaching shifts in the balance of power with the perhaps most widely known example being the challenge rising China poses to the predominance of the United States. It has been increasingly apparent that many smaller states are forced to respond to this trend by carefully manoeuvring between these two major powers. A case in point is Southeast Asian states' growing difficulty in effectively managing their relationship with the incumbent and the rising superpower. To this end, there has been much debate about the present dynamics and possible future direction of Indonesia's foreign policy — of particular interest is Indonesia's approach to its relations with the United States and China. From the perspective of many Indonesians and other Southeast Asians, both at the elite level and public at large, this relationship can be viewed in a triangular form.[1] Here, referring to this "triangular" relationship, Dewi Fortuna Anwar has aptly expressed the question that many people nowadays ask in the title of her authoritative article, "Indonesia's Foreign Relations: Going West or East?".[2]

How can a developing, democratic and the world's most populous Muslim country like Indonesia manage its foreign relations, while facing a myriad of security concerns (which are often multi-layered and multi-sourced in nature) and dilemmas in the increasingly complex situation of the post-Cold War international politics, without compromising its national interests and sacrificing its independence? Approaching this problem from the vantage point of the Indonesian elite, this study explores the influence of (and the complex interactions between) Indonesian foreign policy elite's threat

3

perceptions on the decision-making process behind the country's foreign policy. To illustrate the ways in which contemporary Indonesian leaders' perceptions, with a special emphasis on the United States and China, have affected the country's participation in the post-Cold War international affairs, this book presents a graphic picture of what members of the Indonesian elite see when they view the outside world and Indonesia's dilemmatic position within the "tricky" and "perilous" international system, while systematically seeking out the sources of the leaders' perceptions. We will examine the relationship between elite perceptions and foreign policy outcomes particularly in the post-Suharto period and offer an illuminating comparison of the perceptive and motivational bases of foreign policy during the democratic and plural system of government with the earlier Suharto and Sukarno-dominated regimes, revealing some dramatic changes and surprising continuities.

Initially, we should note that since attaining its independence in 1949, many in the West have considered Indonesia's foreign relations as often irrational and ambiguous.[3] In fact, Western analyses of international relations in the Third World generally tend to portray foreign policies of developing countries as irrelevant to the nations' real interests.[4] But also Indonesian international relations experts have pointed to the "lack of policy substance", characterizing the country's foreign policy as "haphazard" and "sporadic without clear direction, subject to regional and international events".[5] Moreover, several leaders interviewed for this book have posed the question as to whether Indonesia actually has any foreign policy.[6]

In part, Indonesian foreign policy has been considered "irrational" and "inconsistent" owing to the fact that its dynamics have not been in line with the principles laid down by the Western-originated realist paradigm and its prominent balance-of-power theory.[7] The theory posits the argument that material distribution of power determines whether states will pursue a balancing strategy. Kenneth Waltz's classic book on international relations stipulates that countries will strive to balance against the most powerful state or rising hegemonic power trying to upset the status quo in the interstate system.[8] Yet, international relations in Asia can be said to have challenged these neo-realist assumptions. In particular, Indonesia has presented this neo-realist orthodoxy with some difficult paradoxes and inconsistencies.

This scepticism primarily stems from what can be characterized as the Indonesian reality not matching the assumptions stipulated by the "Western" realist theory. Indonesia under President Suharto hardly displayed, contrary to realist expectations, any balancing behaviour directed against the United States — the Cold War era's most powerful country. Also, in contrast to what is seen as continuous quest for the balance of power on the European continent over the past four centuries, instead of pursuing balancing strategy against the progressively rising might of China, Indonesia and other Southeast Asian nations rather seek to engage or even bandwagon Beijing.[9] Whilst originally arguing that under normal circumstances the smaller states should "work to right the balance", even Kenneth Waltz himself later acknowledged that "the present condition of international politics is unnatural."[10]

The disputation both among academics and practitioners about what theoretical approach would most adequately explain Indonesian foreign relations persists in the post-Cold War era.[11] Contemporary Indonesia's approach to its relations with the United States can be characterized as dichotomous and ambiguous. On the one hand, the predominantly Muslim Indonesia has appeared to be, particularly during the George W. Bush Presidency, one of the main outposts of anti-American sentiments. According to the Pew Global Attitudes survey, the percentage of Indonesians who held a favourable view of the U.S. plummeted from 75 per cent in 2000 to only 15 per cent in 2003.[12] The mass anti-American rallies that have swept through many parts of Indonesia, frequently accompanied by high-level pronouncements denouncing U.S. policies at times calling for severing diplomatic ties with Washington, are widely seen as evidence of a gradual decline of the U.S. influence in the region. This tendency seems to be supported by the fact that Washington has not been invited to participate in the embryonic East Asian Community (EAC).

Yet, on the other, the relationship between Indonesia and America remains as strong and solid as ever. The Indonesian Government has ignored pressures from some groups for Indonesia to sever ties with the United States and did not respond by changing the direction of its foreign policy. Instead, a number of Indonesian leaders have repeatedly voiced their commitment to building strong partnership with Washington and the desirability of the continuing U.S. engagement in the region because it is one of "the fundamental interests of the nation and [its] people."[13] Despite vigorous domestic opposition to the U.S. invasion of Iraq, Indonesian Government has maintained close cooperation with Washington in the areas of intelligence and defence, including granting overflight rights to the U.S. military.[14] In 2008, Barack Obama's election as the first African-American President was greeted with considerable enthusiasm throughout the world. This was particularly true in Indonesia where Obama was seen as embodying a radical break with the George W. Bush Administration's aggressive and unilateralist stance and also owing to Obama's personal connection to

Indonesia. In Indonesia, America was hailed as a "great nation" and Obama greatly admired because he "brought back America to the people" around the world.[15] All in all, contrary to the realist view, the ubiquitous predominance of the United States underscored by unilateralism during the Bush presidency has not provoked an expected reaction – the establishment of an alliance to restore a balance of power.[16]

The present situation invites a comparison with Indonesia-U.S. relations during the Cold War. During the Sukarno presidency, both Indonesian public and some political leaders displayed in the late 1950s and early 1960s strong anti-American and anti-Western sentiments. The demonstrations condemning "imperialist America"and high-level anti-Western pronouncements were matched by Jakarta's attempt to build an alliance with the Communist China at the expense of its relations with Washington. Conversely, during Suharto's presidency, the anti-Chinese pogroms and anti-communist sentiments among the broader population were reflected in Indonesia-Sino diplomatic ties being frozen, while the relations with Washington became increasingly close and strategically important. The comparison of the present situation with Indonesia-U.S. relations during the Cold War raises some questions. In contrast with the post-Cold War period, anti-American sentiments among the general population during the Sukarno presidency were reflected in a fundamental shift in the Indonesia-U.S. relationship. In particular, we can question why the recent wave of high-profile anti-American expressions has not equally translated into a major change in Indonesian approach to its relations with Washington.

In contrast to its ambiguous attitude to the United States, Indonesia's relations with China in the early 21st century have displayed an overall upward tendency. While a decade ago an Indonesian leader asserted that "if [the Chinese] see you as being weak, they'll eat you alive",[17] the "China threat" is conspicuously missing in the contemporary Indonesian political discourse. Since the diplomatic relations between the two countries were re-established in 1990, Jakarta has sought increasingly close economic, political and military ties with Beijing.[18] Accordingly, the signing of the "strategic partnership" agreement between Indonesia and China on the sidelines of the Asian-African Summit in Bandung in April 2005 was hailed in Jakarta as a "really very significant ... opportunity to engage China and initiate a strategic cooperation."[19]

Inasmuch as China's ascendancy and expanding influence in Southeast Asia has been a relatively smooth process that has not caused much alarm among the regional states, it has been called "a thing of beauty".[20] This situation deserves some attention. First, it is because the rise of China's clout in Southeast Asia has not been balanced by the regional states — a move anticipated by the proponents of realist international relations theory. Second, we can consequently question whether Indonesian and other Southeast Asian elites have chosen to embrace Asia's past hierarchical order centred on the "Middle Kingdom".[21] Stuart-Fox even argues that, if faced with a militarily aggressive China, Southeast Asian states would likely "ensure their security by enrolling as good tributaries in the Chinese order" rather than strive to maintain a balance of power.[22]

Yet, some developments in Indonesian foreign policy defy this "*Asia's Past Will Be Its Future*" argument.[23] For example, in stark contrast to Beijing's view, Jakarta insisted on a more inclusive conception of the proposed East Asian Community (EAC), not defined by geography, which would also include Australia, New Zealand and India. This is because, as Anwar emphasizes, "it is unlikely that Indonesia will tie itself exclusively to China."[24] We can thus question here whether this attitude can be interpreted as that China's inexorable rise has awoken the traditional Indonesian concern about the hegemonic and expansionist intentions of the "Middle Kingdom".[25]

This book seeks to shed light on this conundrum or, in other words, the roots of the seeming ambiguity, dichotomy and "haphazard nature" that have characterized Indonesian foreign policy particularly during the post-Suharto period. By drawing on interviews with forty-five members of the Indonesian foreign policy elite that reveal great details about their perceptions about security threats facing the country, the following chapters present a substantial and comprehensive perceptive account of Indonesian foreign policy. The focal point here is how ideas, which we define as perceptions held by a state's foreign policy elite, help to explain foreign policy outcomes. While the study is based on the assumption that Indonesian policy-makers' perceptions are the leading determinant of the country's foreign policy formation, it focuses on the correlations among elite perceptions, the conception of national interests and foreign policy outcomes.[26]

Indonesia's foreign relations are shaped by the constant effort to eliminate various security threats and thus maintain a sufficient space for manoeuvring and a favourable position for Indonesia vis-à-vis other states. "Threat" is defined here in very broad, comprehensive terms, going well beyond the traditional military dimension.[27] An analysis of elite threat perceptions provides us with a better understanding about the kind of thinking, motivations and considerations which lie beneath contemporary Indonesian foreign relations. Threat perceptions have a real effect on policymakers' decision-making and, as Muthiah Alagappa contends, perceptions are "crucial to the security thinking and behaviour of Asian governments and must therefore feature in their explanation."[28] The foreign policy elite's threat perceptions are as important as realities, insofar as they shape their real actions.

BOOK'S STRUCTURE

Chapter 2 provides an overview of the relevant theoretical literature and establishes the theoretical and conceptual framework of the study — the balance-of-threat theory. It analyses the concept's main assumptions and outlines how the central research question is going to be examined in terms of this theoretical framework employed. The text argues that the past dynamics of Indonesian foreign relations cannot be explained and their future direction cannot be predicted in terms of the key realist balance-of-power theory, which has frequently been used as a tool of analysis in the study of Indonesian foreign policy. However, this study shows that we can understand the Indonesian foreign policy dynamics in terms of threat perceptions held by the country's foreign policy elite. The balance-of-threat theory is employed here as an analytical tool to examine the elite perceptions about other state actors and how these perceptions in turn inform the foreign policy decision-making process. Thus, the analysis brings the elite's historical knowledge to bear on contemporary issues. The balance-of-threat theory is used here as a predictor about how countries will behave and, in particular, whether they will implement policies designed to prevent other countries from developing power that could threaten their national interests and security.

Whilst probing the significance of elite threat perceptions as a foremost explanatory variable, this study makes a novel analytical approach by bringing the balance-of-threat theory into this framework of analysis. The balance-of-threat theory put forward by Stephen M. Walt in his 1990 study titled *Origins of Alliances* postulates that states seek to diffuse power wielded by other states, which is by the foreign policy elite perceived as the most threatening. However, this study argues for the necessity to enhance the explanatory power of the balance-of-threat theory to encompass the issue of *elite consensus*. The analysis thus extends the theory's scope beyond the elite threat perceptions by putting more emphasis on the degree of elite consensus about what constitutes present and future security threat to the nation.

This approach has become especially important in the post-Cold War period that is marked by increasing salience of various non-conventional, non-military, trans-national and trans-border threats. It is demonstrated throughout this book that the ambiguities of Indonesia's foreign policy need to be seen partially in the context of the increasingly complex security challenges that have become ever more multi-sourced, multi-dimensional and multi-layered in nature. In short, the Indonesian elite is now forced to deal with complex security challenges on all fronts: both internal and external in origins and traditional and non-traditional in nature.

Chapter 3 draws attention to the concept of "Indonesian foreign policy elite" whose perceptions are the focal point of the leader-centric, decision-making approach used in this study. In contrast to the earlier Sukarno and Suharto regimes, contemporary Indonesian foreign policy-making is determined by democratic political processes with the direct and indirect participation of a variety of stakeholders who are involved in constant mixed-motive bargaining. This discussion also highlights the inherently ambiguous nature of the concepts of "national interests" and "national security". It is argued that the Indonesian elite encompass a variety of diverging views over what constitutes and how to defend Indonesia's national interests.

Another key theme here is the historical roots of the elite's heterogeneity. The inquiry first focuses on the *priyayi* origins of the contemporary elite and then deals with the emergence of the first modern Indonesian elite during the decades leading up to the establishment of independent Indonesia. The chapter then discusses in turn the elite educational background and religious beliefs as leading sources of internal divisions and the resultant diversity of views and attitudes among the Indonesian leadership. The text presents an argument that the elite has been subject to a diversity of ideational influences, which produced a plurality of disparate views and attitudes among the Indonesian leadership. Finally, it outlines the approach and methodology used for the survey research in Indonesia. The series of interviews with forty-five members of the Indonesian foreign policy elite serves as the primary source of data about the contemporary elite and its perceptions.

Much like at the theoretical level that draws on the relatively well-established balance-of-threat theory, also the empirical level of this study builds on an established body of scholarship, namely Weinstein's major study on Indonesian elite's perceptions. *Indonesian Foreign Policy and the Dilemma of Dependence: From Sukarno to Soeharto*, a study conducted in the late 1960s and early 1970s, introduced the ideas of "hostile world" images and "Pretty Girl Analogy".[29] They refer to the elite's quite distinct worldview in the context of the Cold War, during which Indonesia was faced with numerous threats coming from what was regarded as an exploitative and hostile world. This book makes important new contributions to the findings in Weinstein's study: it reveals that some thirty years after Weinstein conducted his study, the Indonesian leaders' perceptions continue to be substantially shaped by 'hostile world' images, while the elite worldview is characterized by a higher degree of ambivalence about dangers coming from the perilous outside world.

To this end, Chapter 4 is concerned with the Indonesian elite perceptions of the United States and Chapter 5 examines the leaders' perceptions of China. This makes it possible to juxtapose elite perceptions and also pinpoint the main differences in the policy-makers' attitudes toward these two major powers. The inquiry mainly focuses on the unilateral policies of the United States and the uncertainties of the rise of China. It is because, as the series of interviews conducted in Jakarta revealed, Indonesian leaders generally believe that in the future the archipelagic nation will increasingly have to "*mendayung antara dua karang*" or "row between two reefs" — meaning the United States and China.[30] "*Mendayung antara dua karang*" refers to the Indonesian elite's belief that in the future the island nation will increasingly have to manoeuvre between two rival powers. In other words, Indonesian relations with Washington and Beijing have proven to be the elite's highest concern.

The discussion here aims to establish which of these two states under consideration is perceived as the present and which one as the future principal malign factor negatively affecting Indonesia's national interests and security. The study demonstrates that while the elite's attitude towards the West and particularly the United States can be described as "love-hate", the elite perceptions of China are also ambivalent but conspicuously lack the "love" aspect. To put it differently, while the United States is generally regarded as a benevolent superpower with the anti-American sentiments being rather superficial and issue-based, the elite perceptions of China, though at present increasingly positive, tend to be much more deep-rooted owing to the long history of mutual interaction and also China's geographic proximity. Correspondingly, whilst regarding the United States as currently the main security threat to Indonesia, the elite expects that China will be in the next twenty to thirty years the principal malign factor negatively affecting Indonesia's national interests and security.

We need to see the ambiguity that is characteristic of contemporary Indonesian foreign policy in the context of this basic dichotomy and ambivalence in the elite threat perceptions. Significantly, this state of the elite perceptions has in turn affected the dynamics of Indonesian foreign relations. On the one hand, many Indonesian leaders now welcome the rise of China because it can serve as a check on the U.S. unilateralism and curb some of the malign tendencies of America's hegemony. Yet, on the other, despite the present "strategic partnership" with Beijing, China remains to be perceived, based on the elite's long-term strategic threat assessment, as a greater danger than the United States. Consequently, in line with the balance-of-threat logic, Indonesian elite considers China as the main malign factor that needs to be balanced with the United States seen in this context as "the last guarantee".[31]

The main theme in the Chapter 6 is the Indonesian foreign policy elite perceptions of other important regional and extraterritorial states, namely Australia, Japan, India and the ASEAN countries. It demonstrates that the elite is convinced of the necessity to expand Indonesia's relationship with these countries, which will in turn enable it to maintain a favourable position vis-à-vis an equidistant balance between the United States and China. The Chapter is divided into four main parts, whereby each of them is concerned with the Indonesian elite's perceptions of one of the above mentioned countries.

The first part shows that, in contrast to the situation in the 1970s, Australia is at present one of the highest concerns among the elite. The Australian military involvement in East Timor in 1999 was the turning point that significantly changed the Indonesian foreign policy elite's perceptions of its southern neighbour. The fact that Australia is considered as the second most serious state-based threat to Indonesia, it is argued, is a reflection of three particular images that are largely shared by the Indonesian leaders. First, Australia is the main ally or "deputy sheriff" of the U.S. in the region; second, Australia has (territorial) designs on West Papua; and, third, Australians consider Indonesia as a major security threat to their country. However, the discussion argues that the persistent diplomatic efforts by Jakarta to improve the Indonesia-Australia relationship can also be seen as a vital part of its hedging strategy aimed at eliminating potentially unfavourable implications of the growing influence of China in the region.

The second part outlines the change in the elite's perceptions of Japan from an "ambiguous threat" in the 1970s and 1980s to the present awareness that Japan is an indispensable part of Indonesia's long-term national security strategy. It highlights the phenomenon that although Japan has in the last few years implemented a more assertive foreign policy, it has been seen in

Jakarta as a lesser threat than previously when Tokyo still adhered to its pacifist Constitution. It is argued here that Japan's increasingly assertive foreign policy is welcomed by the elite insofar as Japan is considered as an important counterweight to China's expanding influence. In the third part, the key theme is the growing importance of India in the Indonesian foreign policy elite's long-term national security considerations. It is demonstrated that, owing to largely peaceful economic and cultural interaction between these two countries, the Indonesian leaders' comfort level with India is higher than with China.

The fourth part looks at the sources of the elite's negative perceptions of Indonesia's neighbours. In particular, the data evaluation has shown that the leaders consider Singapore as no. 4 and Malaysia as no. 5 security threats to the country. In terms of the factors that influence the elite's images of other Southeast Asian states, we can identify four categories of perceptions: essentially conspiracy theories, sense of vulnerability to military invasion, religion-driven suspicions, and the "economic threat". Yet, the respondents simultaneously expressed a strong conviction that the countries in ASEAN need to overcome mutual suspicion and disagreements in order to create a common identity and the ensuing common threat perception, which will in turn strengthen their position vis-à-vis the major powers.

Chapter 7 highlights and elaborates on the well-established idea among the Indonesian elite of the necessity to maintain a (perceived) balance among different state actors in the interstate system. It also discusses the considerable disparity between the elite present and future, long-term threat assessment and assess the degree of influence of several factors on the leaders' perceptions and, in turn, their foreign policy preferences. The text argues here that the dichotomy and ambiguity, which has become a hallmark of Indonesia's foreign relations in the post-Cold War era, is substantially caused by the following two factors: first, the existence of diversity of ideational influences that has generated a plurality of disparate views among contemporary Indonesian elite about what constitutes Indonesia's national interest and how to defend it; and, second, an increasing complexity of international system that gives rise to perceived multiple threats facing the nation. The analysis also illustrates that, on the whole, the main concern among the Indonesian elite is not the traditional military threat but rather a variety of non-conventional security challenges.

These two factors in turn produce a considerable lack of the elite consensus about the security threats facing the nation which is revealed in two aspects: first, a relatively low level of the elite's consensus about how to rank the external threats according to their urgency; and, second, a significant disparity between the elite's present and the future, long-term threat assessment. At this point, this study essentially dismisses the official version and policy of the country's consecutive administrations that the Indonesian leaders are unanimous in their threat perceptions. This chapter ultimately aims to demonstrate that, owing to the lack of elite consensus, the Indonesian leadership is fundamentally divided in its worldview and basic perceptions regarding the security threats facing the nation.

Notes

1   Irman Lanti, "Indonesia in Triangular Relations with China and the United States", in *China, the United States, and Southeast Asia: Contending Perspectives on Politics, Security, and Economics*, edited by Evelyn Goh and Sheldon W. Simon (New York: Routledge, 2008), pp. 128–41.

2   Dewi Fortuna Anwar, "Indonesia's Foreign Relations: Going West or East", in *Indonesia at Large: Collected Writings on ASEAN, Foreign Policy, Security and Democratization* (Jakarta: The Habibie Center, 2005), pp. 85–92.

3   Karim Najjarine, "Australian Policy towards Indonesia 1965–72: An Archival Study" (Ph.D. dissertation, University of Western Sydney, 2004).

4   Franklin B. Weinstein, "The Uses of Foreign Policy in Indonesia: An Approach to the Analysis of Foreign Policy in the Less Developed Countries", *World Politics: A Quarterly Journal of International Relations* XXIV, no. 3 (April 1972).

5   Meidyatama Suryodiningrat, "RI Foreign Policy Faulted as Haphazard, Lacking Priorities", *The Jakarta Post*, 9 September 2006; "Indonesian Foreign Policy: Losing Its Focus in 2000" in Dewi Fortuna Anwar, *Indonesia at Large: Collected Writings on ASEAN, Foreign Policy, Security and Democratization* (Jakarta: The Habibie Centre, 2005).

6   This question was raised by members of the Indonesian foreign policy elite interviewed during the author; also discussed during the seminar: Daniel Novotný, "Indonesian Elite and the Power of Foreign Policy Perceptions", SISC seminar (Sydney, 29 July 2005).

7   This view broadly fits Edward Said's "Orientalist" thesis. Said argues that Western writings about the Orient portray Asian realities as irrational, weak, feminised "Other" when juxtaposed with the rational, strong and masculine West; for more on this, see: Edward W. Said, *Orientalism* (London: Penguin, 2003).

8   Kenneth W. Waltz, *Theory of International Politics: Reading* (M.A.: Addison-Wesley, 1979).

9   Kuik Cheng-Chwee, "The Essence of Hedging: Malaysia and Singapore's Response to a Rising China", *Contemporary Southeast Asia* 30, no. 2 (2008).

10   Kenneth W. Waltz, "Globalization and American Power", *The National Interest*, Spring 2000, pp. 55–56.

11   David Capie, "Southeast Asia and the United States", in "Betwixt and Between: Southeast Asian Strategic Relations with the U.S. and China", IDSS Monograph no. 7, edited by Evelyn Goh (Singapore: Institute of Defence and Strategic Studies, 2005), pp. 109–17.

12   "Views of a Changing World, June 2003", *The Pew Global Attitudes Project*, The Pew Research Centre (June 2003).

13   "RI Ties with U.S. in Nation's Interest: Ministers", *The Jakarta Post*, 11 October 2001.

14   Capie, *Betwixt and Between*, p. 117; Evelyn Goh, "Meeting the China Challenge: The U.S. in Southeast Asian Regional Security Strategies", Policy Studies 16 (Washington: East-West Centre, 2005).

15   Wimar Witoelar, "Nobel Prize for Obama shows Indonesia the way forward", *The Jakarta Post*, 13 October 2009.

16   For more ideas on this controversial issue, see John G. Ikenberry, ed., *America Unrivalled: The Future of the Balance of Power* (Ithaca, New York: Cornell University Press, 2002).

17   "Talking Back to China: Editorial", *The Wall Street Journal*, 21 August 1996.

18   "Yudhoyono Jalin Kemitraan RI-Cina", *Kompas*, 27 July 2005; "Indonesia Itu Penting", *Kompas*, 24 January 2004.

19   "Spirit Bangkit", *Media Indonesia*, 27 April 2005.

20   "China-Indonesia Relations and Implications for the United States", USINDO Report, presented at the USINDO-GWU joint conference (Washington, D.C., 7 November 2003).

21   David C. Kang, "Getting Asia Wrong: the Need for New Analytical Frameworks", *International Security* 27, no. 4 (Spring 2003): 220–21; also discussed in Daniel Novotný, "Threat Assessment: Indonesian Elite Facing the Changing World", *Perspectives* (Sydney: ABC Radio National, 14 October 2005).

22   Martin Stuart-Fox, "Southeast Asia and China: The Role of History and Culture in Shaping Future Relations", *Contemporary Southeast Asia* 26, no. 1 (April 2004): 133.

23   Amitav Acharya, "Will Asia's Past Be Its Future?", *International Security* 28, no. 3 (Winter 2003/04).

24   Anwar, "Indonesia's Foreign Relations: Going West or East", p. 92.

25   Irman G. Lanti, "Indonesia", in "Betwixt and Between: Southeast Asian Strategic Relations with the U.S. and China", IDSS Monograph no. 7, edited by Evelyn Goh (Singapore: Institute of Defence and Strategic Studies, 2005), pp. 31–32.

26   Case studies can be associated with both theory generation and theory testing. For more on the importance of case studies and the so-called inductive analytical tradition of the relationship between theory and research, see: Alan Bryman, *Social Research Methods* (London: Oxford University Press, 2004), p. 51.

27 Department of Defence of the Republic of Indonesia, "Mempertahankan Tanah Air Memasuki Abad 21" [Defending the Land and Water at the Start of the 21st Century], *Indonesia's Defence White Paper 2003* (Jakarta, 2003).

28 Muthiah Alagappa, ed., *Asian Security Practice: Material and Ideational Influences* (Stanford: Stanford University Press, 1998), p. 649.

29 Franklin B. Weinstein, *Indonesian Foreign Policy and the Dilemma of Dependence: From Sukarno to Soeharto* (Ithaca, N.Y.: Cornell University Press, 1976).

30 Muhammad Hatta, *Mendayung Antara Dua Karang* (Jakarta: NV Bulan Bintang, 1988).

31 Interview with a former high-ranking officer from the Indonesian Navy, Jakarta, 14 February 2005.

2

THE POWER OF PERCEPTIONS

INTRODUCTION

In this chapter, we are going to establish the theoretical and conceptual framework underpinning the study. The text introduces the balance-of-threat theory, outlines its main attributes and explains why it is a useful analytical tool for understanding the dynamics of Indonesian foreign policy. The discussion is carried out in the context of, first, the debate over the utility of Western-designed international relations theories in explaining dynamics of interstate relations in Asia and, second, the polemics over the virtues of a particular analytical approach to the exclusion of others — here the chapter points out limitations of the realist theory and the balance-of-power concept.

There have been a number of books that look at how domestic factors have influenced Indonesia's role in international affairs. Studies examining Indonesian foreign policy in the Sukarno and Suharto era were dominated by a leader-centric approach that emphasized the important foreign policy roles of these two leaders. This approach was sensible because both Sukarno and Suharto as ironhanded leaders exercised control and overriding influence over the foreign policy-making process and thus virtually dictated the foreign policy orientation. Yet, for much of the post-WWII period up to the 1990s, these studies offered, by and large, mostly a narrative, descriptive and atheoretical account of how Jakarta's foreign policy was designed and influenced by some domestic considerations.[1] The limitation of these texts stems from their failure to use a theoretical framework to organize and assess empirical findings. Only very few studies of Indonesia, or non-Western countries generally, employ a systematic approach within a theoretical framework to explain the correlation between external and internal and between material and non-material factors, and the process in which these shape their foreign relations.[2]

Not only scholars, in general, but also some foreign diplomats posted in Indonesia seem to find it difficult to establish a sort of "road map" by which to comprehend the pattern of foreign relations of this "big amorphous mass".[3] Keith Shann, former Australian Ambassador to this country, remarked in November 1965 that

> ... prediction in Indonesia is a form of lunacy, unless one predicts that the outcome will be untidy, illogical, messy, unsatisfactory and thoroughly Indonesian. It is not enough to suggest that the Indonesians already produced a great deal for which we have to be thankful. The point is that they are very unlikely to produce a long-term situation with which we can comfortably live.[4]

To this end, this study of Indonesian foreign policy is set apart from the mainly narrative and atheoretical texts of other similar academic works. The island nation's foreign relations appear to be made up of an intriguing maze of events sometimes combined with seemingly illogical actions of its political elite. The foreign policy elite is even by insiders considered as being involved in behind-the-scene manoeuvrings and subject to bewildering influences of religion and ideological predisposition.[5] These puzzling complexities of the Indonesian political scene may well have discouraged scholars from putting their analyses of Indonesian foreign policy within a clear theoretical framework.

Asia's Future Europe's Past?

Generally, theories are abstract concepts, which order observations or, in other words, establish "road maps" to enable us navigating through a particular set of events. Moreover, theories can provide explanations of phenomena that, at first glance, look rather puzzling and illogical. Walt argues that "there is an inescapable link between the abstract world of theory and the real world of policy" and suggests that "we need theories to make sense of the blizzard of information that bombards us daily."[6] It might have been precisely because of what appears as inconsistent and erratic dynamics of Indonesian and generally other Asian countries' foreign policies that so far no non-Western international relations theory or grand theoretical framework has been created.[7]

International relations theories, concepts and assumptions that are largely derived from the European and later North American experience tend to make universal claims that their precepts apply to both Western and non-Western entities. On the other hand, it has been argued that realist theory of international relations cannot adequately explain behaviour of Asian states because its main propositions were derived predominantly from European history.[8] This controversy has dominated the academic discourse within the discipline of international relations during the 1990s and the early 21st century.[9] Similar situation can be found in the field of economics: for example, Boeke's argument that modern economic theory cannot be applied in Asian countries has given rise to a controversy among scholars until today. He observed that the Eastern man's basic attitudes ran counter to the main premise of the Western-designed *economic theory*. In other words, while Westerners aimed in their economic activities at achieving the maximum profit, Asian people placed a greater importance on the expenditure of least energy.[10] Similarly, in the field of political science, the Western-originated *democratic theory* postulates that the middle class tends to be the harbinger of democracy. Yet, with the interests of the middle class in Southeast Asia being extremely varied, sometimes favouring more authoritarian forms of government over a liberal-democratic system, this theory may be "too steeped in the European historical experience" to be able to apply it to other parts of the world.[11]

In the field of international relations, it is argued that major historical and cultural differences between Asia and Europe need to be taken into account in any application of the realist paradigm to foreign policies of East and Southeast Asian states. In contrast to Europe, psychological factors, notably deep historical mistrust among regional actors, are said to constitute an important aspect of the dynamics driving interstate relations in Southeast Asia. For example, one analysis concluded that "the study of historical experience can greatly benefit the study of national security problems in the contemporary world. ... the experience of past societies in dealing with similar problems goes unnoticed."[12] Therefore, the analysis argued for employing "diverse ways of bringing historical knowledge to bear on contemporary issues".[13] Also Huntington, who famously pointed to cultural values as "the fundamental source of ... divisions among humankind and the dominating source of conflict," sees culture as a key factor determining the dynamics of relations between states coming from different cultural groups.[14] In short, the application of Europe-bred international relations theories to Asia is supposed to deliver doubtful results, thereby explaining why some view it as rather problematic.[15]

The scepticism among scholars stems in part from what is considered as the Asian reality not matching the ominous and dire expectations predicted by the realist theory. The end of the bi-polar Cold War was seen as ushering Asia into the era of instability and chaos, making the region "ripe for rivalry".[16] Owing to Asia's deficiency in stability-enhancing mechanisms that have transformed the war-torn European continent into the "abode of peace" spanning the last half-a-century, "Asia's future" was envisaged as resembling "Europe's past" underscored by stringent "realist" power politics.[17] Yet, other scholars did not share his pessimistic views. As Kang observed, Asia has not on the whole followed Europe's past; it has rather followed its own past, which is bent on ensuring Asia's future peace and stability. He anticipates Asian international relations shaped not by realist thinking but more likely returning to its past hierarchical order. As the realist logic predicts, Asian states should be expected to display a balancing behaviour much as the Cold War alliances formed by the United States to balance the Soviet Union. However, Kang argues that Asians are not balancing the rising China, but are *bandwagoning* it — contrary to realist assumptions and also in contrast to Continental Europe whose political entities have at least from the 17th century sought to uphold a perceived balance of power among themselves. This makes Kang call for adjusting international relations theories to Asian realities because "the Chinese experience of the past two decades poses a challenge to realist theories."[18]

Moreover, contrary to the realist view, the ubiquitous predominance of the United States underscored by Washington's unilateral policies has not provoked an expected reaction — the establishment of an alliance to restore a balance of power.[19] When faced with what was perceived as Bush Administration's aggressive, unilateralist policies and confronted recently by the waves of anti-American sentiments that engulfed large sections of the Indonesian population, by and large, the Indonesian Government was not willing to respond by changing the direction of the country's foreign policy. Instead, Jakarta has repeatedly articulated the desirability of continued U.S. engagement in the region. We can thus question whether Indonesia's response to the unilateralist policies and predominance of the United States and the rise of China of the past two decades pose a challenge to the assumptions inherent in the realist international relations theory.

Ideological Predisposition of the Elite

Complicating the whole picture have been *liberal-idealist* policies that have brought Indonesia to participate in various multilateral security arrangements, such as ASEAN, ARF, ASEAN+3 or EAC. Indonesian leaders have repeatedly stated that the promotion of multilateralism and cooperative security, as well as various confidence-building measures, is the priority of the country's foreign affairs. During the interviews, senior diplomats ostentatiously emphasized that the realist balance-of-power thinking is not the principle guiding Indonesian foreign policy-formulation. One of the explanations was that "we do not have the habit of designating, say, country A is the country we have to be wary of [and this is why] we have to be having some kind of balance of power against [this country]. It is not the way we think…"[20] Another respondent also affirmed that "we do not subscribe to the balance-of-power argument. … Academics think we are playing this balance of power but in practice it has more nuances than that."[21]

The evaluation of all interviews conducted for this book revealed the Indonesian leaders' overwhelming preference for liberal approaches to peace and security in Southeast Asia. As Figure 2.1 shows, between 75.6 and 91.1 per cent of all respondents considered the liberal approaches, whereas only between 8.9 and 37.8 per cent of them deemed the realist approaches suggested in the questionnaire to be an effective strategy to maintain peace and security in the region. While the research data show the Indonesian leaders' overwhelming preference for liberal approaches[22] over realist

FIGURE 2.1
The Most Effective Approaches to Peace and Security in Southeast Asia

	Approaches	%
Liberal	Better communication and understanding among policy-makers and ordinary people from different nations	91.1
	Increasing economic interdependence	91.1
	Narrowing the gap between rich and poor nations	75.6
Realist	Constant political effort to maintain a balance of power within Southeast Asia and between the world's biggest powers involved in the religion	37.8
	Closer military cooperation of ASEAN states	31.1
	Military superiority of the United States in the region	31.1
	Collective security through alliances	8.9

Source: "The Most Effective Approaches to Peace and Security in Southeast Asia"; How many per cent of the interviewed leaders consider each of the listed liberal and realist approaches effective to maintenance of peace and security in Southeast Asia?

approaches[23] as a means to safeguard Indonesia's national security, we will see in the following chapters that the liberal disposition of the Indonesian foreign policy elite constitutes more a form than a substance. In other words, the frequently evoked "multilateralism" and "confidence-building measures" are only secondary motivating factors. In the following chapters, we will find that the official rhetoric, which highlights multilateralism and other liberal-idealist approaches to security, exerts only a marginal influence on the foreign policy direction. In other words, rather than being informed by the belief in *liberal-idealist* approaches to security, the foreign policy-making process is principally shaped by the Indonesian elite's *realist* considerations for the (perceived) balance of power in the interstate system in the context of the leaders' threat perceptions.

REALISM AND BALANCE-OF-POWER CONCEPT

Realism is the oldest and most prominent theoretical paradigm in the study of international relations that has dominated European and, more broadly, Western thinking about international relations since the Treaty of Westphalia in 1648.[24] However, realist thinking has been pursued in relations among different polities and later states for millennia, stretching back as far as to the ancient China, India and Greece, and as an academic discipline has dominated the arena of international relations inquiry for most of the 20th century. It portrays international relations as a struggle for power among self-interested states and its hallmark is overt pessimism about future prospects for peaceful coexistence of world's nations. Realism views self-centred human nature as the prime cause of the "cutthroat" state of international relations. Although neorealism, or structural realism, is also sceptical about future peaceful evolution of the interstate system, it rather emphasizes the distribution of power within the anarchical interstate system.

Realism and neo-realism revolve around the key concept of "power". The realist paradigm rests on exertion of hard sources of hard power, such as those derived from coercion and strength, including military force, economic power, alignment and alliances, geopolitics, and, importantly, the balance of power. It stands in sharp contrast to *soft power*, which relies on intangible, non-material sources of power, such as ideology, culture, information spread by media and state's credibility. In short, while hard power rests on coercion, soft power rests on the ability to attract. Whereas with the hard power it is possible "to get other states to do what you want", with soft power "you make others want what you want."[25] Referring to the key realist concept of power, Morgenthau, one of the founders of the realist school, claims that in order

... to improve the world one must work with those forces, not against them. This being inherently a world of opposing interests and of conflict among them, moral principles can never be fully realized, but must at best be approximated through the ever temporary balancing of interests and the ever-precarious settlement of conflicts. [26]

It is thus obvious that at the core of realist thinking is a continuous struggle for the equilibrium of the system. If states want to preserve their own interests and, ultimately, their independence, they have to constantly seek to maintain a balance of power.

Balance-of-power, the key realist concept, is one of the most contentious topics in the scholarly discourse in international relations. Notwithstanding a considerable deal of scepticism that is often voiced by academics involved in the research of various IR-related topics, the balance-of-power concept has been widely employed as a tool of analysis in the study of international politics.[27] Importantly, balance-of-power theory has been readily utilized in a majority of studies on Indonesian foreign policy. The concept refers to stability within a system comprising a number of independent forces. Balance of power is regarded as "a particular manifestation of a general social principle".[28] This argument again refers to the human factor in realist paradigm. As in a society comprised of human beings, of whom some tend to enjoy an upward, while others downward social mobility, also the relative strengths of world's nations never remains constant. It is due to the unbalanced level of economic growth and technological and organizational development in different societies, a process which in turn provides one state with a relatively greater power and leverage than another.[29]

In the realist theory, the concept also signifies relatively equal power capabilities among a number of independent states or alliances. Here, opposing and inherently rival forces balance each other out in a process which smoothes the path to the system's stability. Sovereign states are regarded as the principal actors participating in the process of maintaining power equilibrium, whereby some of them strive to maintain, while the others to challenge, the immediate status quo. In the traditional realist theory, the chief objective of the status quo powers is to uphold the existing balance of power, for

> ... without a state of equilibrium among them one element will gain
> ascendency over the others, encroach upon their interests and rights, and
> may ultimately destroy them. Consequently, it is the purpose of all such
> equilibriums to maintain the stability of the system without destroying
> the multiplicity of the elements composing it.[30]

In the context of the Cold War, for instance, the United States' actions in Southeast Asia are generally portrayed as having been aimed at maintaining the existing balance of power. President Eisenhower believed that if the expanding sphere of influence of the communist states were left unchecked, it would directly impact on the power equilibrium in Asia-Pacific and thus it would then be "difficult to see how Thailand, Burma and Indonesia could be kept out of Communist hands. ... [Consequently,] threat to Malaya, Australia and New Zealand would be direct."[31]

Limitations of Realism in Explaining International Relations in Asia

Underlying the earlier outlined debate over the applicability of IR theories in the study of Asian international relations is the scholarly polemics over the advantages and shortcomings of different analytical perspectives or, in other words, over the virtues of a particular analytical approach to the exclusion of others. The proponents of the so-called *paradigmatic exclusivism* have argued for the indispensability of parsimony in analytical approaches in the study of international relations. Academic studies have been criticized for employing analytical approaches that mingled realist perspective with some of what realists consider competing and mutually incompatible theories — an idea succinctly expressed in the article titled "Is Anybody Still a Realist?"[32]

Conversely, scholars specializing in Asian international relations and politics have called for greater flexibility in using analytical approaches and "enriching" the otherwise dominant realist approach ad hoc with propositions adopted from competing theoretical perspectives. The rationale of this view is simple. If the sheer complexity of dynamic underlying contemporary international relations is to be understood, the implementation of an analytical eclecticism is vital because "no single approach can capture all the complexity of contemporary world politics."[33] Moreover, instead of approach-driven analysis, which is a commonplace method in the study of international relations, the problem-driven research would draw selectively on different paradigms.[34]

Among different theoretical approaches, realism has been the most disputed paradigm. It was challenged mainly for its inability to take into account in its analysis other, often non-material, factors that may prompt states to behave contrary to realist predictions. The proposition that "foreign policy is a phase of domestic policy"[35] is relevant in particular in the case of Third World nations. Realist analysis has, for example, little to say about deeply entrenched historical mistrust against certain extraterritorial powers, which include historical legacy of colonial experience and external dependence, the role of religious beliefs or the impact of public opinion engulfed in a wave of anti-Americanism on the direction of foreign policy.[36] Dupont points out that the balance of power between states, military-based power and mutual security dilemma are the main concerns of both contemporary neo-realists and classical realists and argues that "this characterisation of the security problematique is too narrowly conceived and Western-centred to encompass and make sense of the trans-national challenge to global security, especially in East Asia."[37]

Further diminishing the explanatory power of the realist theory in the Indonesian case was the distinct nature of its authoritarian system of government. Since the state's foreign affairs management was principally in the hands of one autocratic ruler, Presidents Sukarno and Suharto infused into Indonesia's foreign relations a great deal of their respective idiosyncrasies, along with their personal ambitions and prejudices. The reality is, however, that the realist theory does not account for leaders' personal characteristics, the elite's threat perceptions and the way these shape foreign policy direction. As the first Indonesian Vice-President Mohammad Hatta pointedly noted, "[Western international relations theories] cannot penetrate completely into the thought processes and feelings of the people. These can only be fully portrayed by Indonesians themselves."[38] Another contending perspective argues that there is no single "theory of realism', which can be tested, confirmed, or refuted. Mastanduno explains that "realism is a research program that contains a core set of assumptions from which a variety of theories and explanations can be developed."[39] According to Waltz, realism means different things to different scholars. One of realism's main limitations is inherent in the fact that it is only capable of explaining the dynamics of interstate relations at the system level using the distribution of power as its primary explanatory variable. Realism as a theoretical framework, it is argued, cannot be employed at the decision-makers' level to explain the actions of participants in the international system.[40]

"Non-Realist" Foundations of Realism

Although it describes the reality in international relations largely in material terms, realist paradigm's main premise rests on non-material logic. Realists believe that international relations are driven by basic laws of human nature and behaviour, for "there exists a fundamental identity between the human mind and the laws which govern the world."[41] Traditional realist approach rested on the assumption that human beings tend to be selfish, egocentric and act only from self-interests.[42] Hence, the realists believe that it is people themselves who determine whether relations between states will be peaceful or their disputes resolved by war. While classical realists, such as Hobbes, Machiavelli, as well as Carr and Morgenthau, attributed the nature of power politics in the main to human nature and a natural human urge to dominate others,[43] neorealism, which is sometimes referred to as structural realism, focuses on the anarchy. Whereas the realists in their studies of international relations emphasized the importance of various perceptions of human nature, the proponents of the neorealist perspective were concerned with the anarchy and distribution of power within a "structure" of the international system of states.

Here, Waltz has provided two different explanations of the causal powers of anarchy. Originally, his neorealist perspective, much like classical realism, postulated that the egocentric, selfish and essentially unpredictable condition of the human mind stands behind the anarchy. It is the human factor within the realm of domestic politics that determines the state's actions within the structure.[44] The anarchy is essentially spawned by the fact that a state's human mind is not capable of reading another state's policy-maker's mind and thus predict the latter state's future actions. In such a perilous environment, all states in the international relations, neorealists believe, have only one eternal, invariable single identity. Due to the very unpredictability of the human element, all actors in international politics are self-interested states that rely only on self-help. Later, however, Waltz reversed the logic of anarchy in the international system of states. He claimed that it is not a natural human urge for power, but the anarchical structure by itself that forces states to pursue the power struggle as a means by which to search for security.[45] Mearsheimer also omits the casual link between the human nature and the anarchy within the power structure. However, whereas Waltz believes that states' search for power and security has its limits, Mearsheimer claims that it is limitless. When viewed from the "human mind" perspective, while the latter holds human behaviour as a constant because "states are never satisfied",[46] the former admits that sensible policy-makers strive only for an "appropriate" amount of power, whereby this is determined by their security needs.[47]

At this point, Waltz effectively departs from his former thesis that human nature is not a factor behind the anarchical structure of international relations and lets social-constructivist explanation subsume his "structural realism". The main attribute of "sensible policy-makers" is essentially an ability to perceive through their senses how much of the "appropriate" amount of power one's state needs to provide for its security. Consequently, it could be assumed that the "appropriate" amount of power a state amasses reflects not only power distribution in the system, but is also subject to the "sensible decision-makers" subjective perceptions of the power. Here, both classical realism and Waltz-pioneered neorealist theory can be questioned, because of the pessimistic theory of human nature in the former and the lack for consideration for the human dimension in the latter. Classical realist theory is imbedded in a pessimistic assumption about human nature. It opposes the idealist notion of self-interested and egoistic human nature as being an exception rather than a rule among human beings. If it is the human mind, as realists rightly hold it, which stands at the core of realist paradigm, it is then disputable that human nature constitutes an eternal and never changing constant in the international relations. Holsti makes a point: "If human nature explains war and conflict, what accounts for peace and cooperation?"[48]

If the pessimistic assumption about the unchanging and constant self-interest-driven human mind were valid, what would then explain, for instance, major shifts in Indonesia's foreign policy during the last fifty years? Was the self-interest of Indonesia's first President and the nation's founding father Sukarno identical with those of the succeeding President, a lifetime military officer, Suharto? And even if foreign policies implemented by either Indonesian leader had been grounded in the self-interest, how can we account for their strikingly different outcomes? As it is assumed, part of the explanation lies in the fact that the conceptions of self-interest of either Indonesian leader were fundamentally different, for they were constructed under markedly different circumstances. To risk simplifying, statesmen's conception of self-interest is led by their varied priorities, such as a quest for national unification, advancement of an ideology, attempt at increasing one's leverage on domestic political scene or a response to the pressure of public opinion.

Waltz's neorealism does not, on the other hand, refer to human nature but emphasizes the distribution of power within the anarchy-ruled structure of the interstate system. However, if this thesis is valid, how can we then substantiate the fact that, in the post-Cold War era, the U.S. policies in Southeast Asia have had strikingly different significance for Indonesia than for Singapore or the Philippines, even though these three neighbour states have a roughly similar "structural" position? While there has been a growing rift in the late 1990s between Jakarta and Washington over various U.S. policies, both Singapore and Manila have on the whole remained staunch supporters of Washington, providing the U.S. regional military deployment with naval facilities.[49]

To sum up, we can see from the preceding analysis of the limitations of realism that although the distribution of power always to a degree shapes states' foreign policies, structural realism falls short of including non-material, discursive factors as another main variable in states' calculations. A particular condition in the distribution of power in the system is likely to affect foreign polices of different states in a different fashion. How states' calculations are affected depends on the intersubjective set of ideas, identities and norms, understandings and expectations, as well as on the "distribution of knowledge", which in turn constructs the perception of one's self-interest and other's interests.[50] Hence, it can be argued that the "neorealist" conception of structure is subjectively constructed by human mind, which thus constitutes not a constant but a variable. Consequently, it is the constantly mutating conception of self-interest in the human mind that shapes the structure, which in turn organize our and through us the states' actions.[51]

The Subjectivity of Power Assessment

Power, a central theoretical concept of neo-realism, can be said to constitute another limitation of the realist perspective. Power comprises anything that institutes and sustains control and influence over other people and their actions. Realism considers hard or material power, both military and economic, as the single most important source of a state's influence in the international politics. Realism of the 16th and 17th centuries believed that power is needed to keep human beings honest, whereby claiming that morality is the product of power.[52] Later, in the mid-20th century, Carr remarked that morality and power are two conflicting sides of human nature and this is why "political action must be based on a co-ordination of morality and power".[53] In either case, for realists, the concept of power constitutes the single most important determinant in international politics. The statesmen and policy-makers operating in such a "realist" world are bent to design foreign policy with the main imperative in mind — their interests are defined in terms of power. In this rather anarchical world, in which a number of political units interact, "the gains of one state are at the expense of others, and no state can afford to rely on others for its security and welfare."[54]

The realist theory of balance-of-power is based on the fundamental assumption that it is a state's power that functions as the most effective check on the power of other states. Consequently, foreign policy based on balance of power considerations inevitably involves calculation of power relation between a state and its rivals. It is essential that any realist analysis utilizing this concept has to be concerned with the elements of a nation's power.

According to Morgenthau, the main sources of national power derive from its geographical, political, economic and socio-cultural characteristics, as well as from the quality of its population, government, diplomacy and military.[55] In the traditional realist view, the military force constitutes the pivotal and decisive aspect of national power. Accordingly, all-powerful states are those wielding mighty armed forces. Powerful nations shape the rules of the game and the weak nations are usually subject to the dictate of the former for, as the realists believe, "the strong do what they can and the weak suffer what they must."[56]

Due to its multiple meaning, "power" is an exceedingly broad concept. Apart from the military capabilities, an obvious source of a country's power is the strength of its economic power. Sunardi observed that "the stronger the economy of a country, the more power and leverage it has in shaping the dynamics of its strategic relations."[57] However, the foundations of power, or its ability to exercise control and influence, have changed — they have been moving away from the emphasis on military capabilities.[58] Particularly since the end of the Cold War, scholars have identified and taken into account in their analyses new forms of power. Among the most frequently discussed are various trans-national networks[59] or the influence of various social, normative, and ideological factors.

Here, the phenomenon of "information" has attracted a great deal of attention as many scholars consider it as perhaps the most important source of power in international relations.[60] The power inherent in a piece of "information" is generated substantially by its ability to have a direct impact on a country's credibility and the degree of the country's benign or, conversely, threatening appearance. As Keohane and Nye note, "… credibility is the crucial resource, and asymmetrical credibility is a key source of power."[61] In the situation, in which nations are increasingly tightly linked through omnipresent influence of media and modern communications, a state's perceived aggressive intentions or an overt military conflict will immediately find their way on TV screens and computer monitors around the globe. Information can generate an instant change in states' threat perceptions — attempts at solving disputes by military means have thus become very costly, often prompting immediate opposition from other state actors.[62] Nye emphasizes that "information is power and today a much larger part of the world's population has access to it." Therefore, as he observed,

> politics have become a contest about credibility. Whereas the world
> of traditional power politics is typically defined by whose military or

economy wins, politics in an information age is about whose story wins. Governments compete with each other and with other organizations to enhance their own credibility and weaken that of their opponents.[63]

This makes the information an important source of soft power that is an increasingly crucial factor in international relations.

There is yet another case that highlights the increasingly important aspect of *soft power* and the subjectivity of measuring a state's power. It is the long-disputed question of what factors determine *great power status* in the international system. Is it the country's economic wealth, military capabilities, the size of its population or perhaps its prestige? Interestingly, a recent study points to the weak correlation between a state's *hard power* and its prestige. The explanation for this disparity lies with the fact that the great power status is *a socially constructed idea* shared by a large number of people.[64] Whether or not a state is considered a great power depends only to a rather small degree on the traditional measurements of its hard power.[65] In Nye's words, "... soft power is not simply the reflection of hard power."[66] To this end, the controversial outcome of U.S. foreign policy in Indochina during the Cold War demonstrates exactly that any assessment and measurement of national power is quite problematic. Bull claims that "... overall power ... cannot be precisely quantified: the relative importance of strategic, economic and politico-psychological ingredients in national power ... is both uncertain and changing."[67] According to the realist assumption, it would not have been too difficult for the United States with its superior armed forces to defeat the backward armed forces of the Northern Vietnam. Yet, the world's most powerful state was eventually in 1973 forced to withdraw its armed forces out of Indochina and stand by two years later when the North Vietnamese troops occupied Saigon.[68]

One of the main arguments that run through this analysis is the idea that power generally depends on the context in which it is measured. Modern history of international relations bears witness to many, often-fateful cases of incorrect assessment of a state's power due to the failure to look beyond its pure "realist" material dimension. The ill-fated U.S. involvement in Vietnam during the Cold War, as one of the most obvious examples, points to the subjectivity of a power's appraisal. Then, consecutive U.S. Administrations consistently underestimated the power of opinion among the war-weary public in the United States in combination with the aggregate power of Communist North Vietnam, which was considered to be, in line with the realist paradigm, considerably weaker than that of the United States. "I think the Americans greatly underestimate the determination of the Vietnamese people," Ho Chi Minh, the North Vietnamese leader, remarked in 1962.[69] As to the eventual "defeat" of the world's most powerful armed forces by poorly equipped guerrilla fighters, Buttinger pointedly explains:

> ... ignorance of Vietnamese history was one of the reasons the United States pursued a policy which, in its complete disregard of the political realities of contemporary Vietnam, was doomed to fail. It was bad enough not to take into consideration that the Vietnamese people had struggled for over two thousand years against being absorbed by China, and had for almost one hundred years fought against colonial rule in order to regain independence. ... how this inhumane, politically erroneous and in the last analysis stupid course could be pursued for many years by a country so rich in knowledgeable people, high intelligence and good will [?][70]

This case defies the realist theory in that the show or use of force does not inevitably constitute the decisive aspect of national power. Moreover, it shows that human errors and biases of national leaders, as well as their misperceptions and disregard for the strength of public opinion can gravely distort a state's calculation of power relations.

The limitation of balance-of-power theory and the power calculation involved also stems from the fact that it generally cannot explain the occurrence when states do not balance against a hegemonic and rising power seeking to disrupt the status quo.[71] This can be illustrated for instance by the response of the world's most powerful nations to the constant and steady rise of the United States at least since the early 19th century. The original thirteen colonies along the east coast gradually expanded throughout the 19th century to eventually take up a substantial section of the Northern American continent, while U.S. troops and navy were allowed in the 20th century to develop into the mightiest military in the world. If viewed through the lens of the balance-of-power theory, the major European powers along with Japan would be expected to have proceeded against the growing U.S. power and challenged the increasing capability to project its economic, political and military might throughout the world. The reality was, however, that these nations failed to balance against this newly emerging superpower.

All in all, the cases discussed above attest to the inherent and irrefutable difficulties with any assessment of a state's power. Power, much like gravity and electricity, makes its existence apparent to us through its effects. Therefore, it is much easier described in terms of its consequences than to identify its nature and basis.[72] Barnes points out that "... power is manifest in behavior.

Particular behaviours are routinely taken as signs or indications of the existence and operation of power [and] means of measuring the magnitude of power."[73] In short, *power* is a vague and broad concept — we can recognize many forms of power — military, political, economic, ideological and others.[74] A state's "power is not essential — important is how [its] power is perceived."[75] Or, in Nye's words, "power always depends on context."[76] The relative power always depends on someone's subjective judgement, based on which, as Spykman claims, "each state always feels that the other one needs balancing."[77] A question that naturally arises is whether and how we can measure the power of, for instance, a multinational corporation or a non-governmental organization operating in Indonesia. How can we evaluate the power of a travel advisory issued by Western governments that discourages potential visitors from going to Indonesia? This piece of information has the power to directly hurt the country's tourist industry and put off future investors, while the weakened Indonesian economy is bound to negatively affect Indonesian national security interests.

THE CONCEPT OF "THREAT PERCEPTION"

This study puts forward the concept of *threat perception* as alternative means to express a state's power while concurrently taking into account its subjective nature. To be able to capture all dimensions of power and the inherent subjectivity of its measurement, we need to use a sufficiently narrow concept. It could be reasonably argued that *threat* is a much narrower concept than *power*. This sort of common denominator can be deemed capable of expressing the nature of any kind of power and its potential effect on other state actors. The phenomenon of *threat perception* is suggested here as the common denominator by which to evaluate the impact of a particular kind of power on policy-makers' decisions.

For the purpose of this study, "threat" signifies the degree to which the power of a state or non-state actor is perceived by the elite as a malign factor affecting one's country's national interests and security. "Perception" can be defined as a concept that describes the construction of reality in the eyes of an individual involved in foreign policy decision-making. For example, a study on the impact of media coverage on public opinion and foreign policy direction concluded that "actual events themselves had no significant impact on opinion, but rather the media's interpretation of the events mattered. ... threatening events by themselves matter less than how events are interpreted."[78] A power perceived as threatening may prompt the foreign policy elite to change in some way the course of the state's foreign relations in attempt to neutralize and eliminate what is deemed as an external malign factor. Thus, the question we have to ask here is how is power perceived by a particular state, namely its elite? To risk simplifying, the elite's perception of a particular power, be it in the form of a state, an organization involved in illicit arms trafficking, or perhaps a news report, can range anywhere from benign to neutral to threatening. A country whose policies are viewed by others as benign is likely to be dealt with differently than a state whose actions are seen as aggressive and threatening others' interests. It is not the power per se but the perceptions of a particular power, e.g. its nature, which generates a response in the form of changed dynamics of a state's foreign policy.[79]

There have been few efforts to test the assumption that elite threat perceptions are closely related to policy choices in foreign policy-making and that perceptions could serve as an independent variable by which to predict policy choices.[80] Spiegel, for example, argues that philosophy and core perceptions, such as images of the opponent, of key foreign policy-makers are the most important variables affecting policy choices.[81] This view goes contrary to one of the main assumptions of realism that "most state behavior can be interpreted as rational or at least intelligent activity."[82]

Emotions in International Relations

There is a relative paucity of attention devoted to the human actors in the realm of international relations. This is despite the fact, as Tomaka and other scholars acknowledge, that "… even though in the natural world some 'threats' seem obvious, much of what is considered 'threatening' in the social world is cognitively processed and socially constructed."[83] Not only realist theory[84] but also theories of international relations and security in general essentially depend on assumptions about human actors' emotions, which may not be completely correct. Even though the phenomenon of emotion — such as love and hate, empathy and fear — is an inseparable part of theories of world politics, the systematic analysis of its effects on leaders' perceptions and, in turn, policy choices may provide for a better understanding of foreign policy decision-making. The study of emotions is an important part of foreign policy analysis because, as Crawford argues, "the perceptions of others and the attribution of their motives will depend on actors' preexisting emotions, and emotional relationships among actors."[85] One's emotions fundamentally rest on the individual's experiences that have physiological, intersubjective, and cultural components. The main categories of emotional relationships range from empathy to antipathy to hostility. The pre-existing, deep-rooted emotions may influence the attributions of intentions and motives to others' behaviour and thus are especially vital for determining who should be considered a friend and who a threat.[86]

Goldstein distinguishes three types of beliefs: worldviews, principled beliefs and causal belief. It is particularly the worldviews, which are greatly shaped by religious beliefs, underpinned by deep emotions and loyalties, what determines the way people conceive of their respective identities.[87] Moreover, these emotions in turn influence the conception of national security that is by nature an "ambiguous symbol". As Buzan notes, the concept of national security "combines a powerful emotional and political appeal with an enormous possible range of substantive meanings."[88] Leaders' emotions can also exacerbate their apprehension of other countries and thus make their fear more irrational.[89] As President Sukarno affirmed in his 1955 speech,

> Yes, we are living in a world of fear. The life of man today is corroded and made bitter by fear: fear of the future, fear of the hydrogen bomb, fear of ideologies. Perhaps this fear is a greater danger than the danger itself, because it is fear, which drives men to act thoughtlessly, to act dangerously.[90]

Crawford suggests that concentration of authority in the hands of a small group of decision-makers, especially if these are to make a very critical decision, may produce a concentration of pressure that intensifies anxiety. If taking emotions into account, she argues that "one would expect better decision-making in democracies or highly bureaucratized states, where there is an effective division of labor, rather than in monarchies, oligarchies, and authoritarian states."[91]

Present human emotions and actions are greatly determined by historical knowledge and past experience that have been accumulated and "stored" in one's mind. Images of the past and fears arising from these images are "important and dangerous companions," distinguished Indonesian scholar and humanist Soedjatmoko observed.[92] The historical knowledge gives rise to the decision-maker's worldview, ideas, ideological predisposition and conception of identity, all of which function as a kind of filter through which the diplomat's or politician's immediate thoughts and considerations are channelled. Thus, policy-maker's actions are shaped by a constant flow of accumulated historical knowledge, some of which are less and some others more entrenched in his or her mind — it is mainly the latter that are likely to influence the policy-maker's perceptions and actions over a long period of time. As a Muslim politician aptly pointed out, "to understand Indonesian foreign policy, you have to understand the man from *Cendana* [Suharto's home address]."[93]

When faced with a particular state of affairs or dilemma, the process of making choices and reaching conclusions will automatically be subject to the constant subconscious evaluation in terms of the leader's social constructions of the past. Crawford claims that "we remember what happened to us in the past, how this thing has affected us and what we did about it. Then we imagine how it will affect us this time and estimate whether it will be harmful."[94] It has also been argued that "the [elite's] domains of [historical] knowledge, expressed in social constructions of the past, are brought into the arenas of political struggle. The politics of society becomes the politics of knowledge...."[95] Consequently, because "the past shapes the way [these] actors understand their present situation,"[96] it is of paramount importance to look at the worldview and ideological predisposition of those individuals with the utmost influence on foreign policy formulation.

Elite Perceptions as a Variable

Morgenthau, one of the main advocates of classical realism, downplayed the study of elite motivations and perceptions, not because these were not important variables, but rather because they were indecipherable and could not be evaluated by serious academic research.[97] Yet, other scholars emphasize the importance of the systematic analysis of elite perceptions because of their potency to shape policy outcomes. The existence of diverging elite perceptions contribute to the fact that different decision-makers perceive a particular situation differently and, therefore, not all decision-makers in one country respond the same way to a given situation.[98] In other words, there is no such phenomenon — in line with the realist assumption — as rational policy-makers who see a given situation accurately. As Dewi Fortuna Anwar affirms, "in discussion about international relations, especially if it concern about perception, there are no right perception or wrong, every body is entitled to his or her perceptions and how he or she construct the external environment...."[99] Hence, as Wendt notes, the realist analysis faces an insoluble problem, which is making sure that the decision-makers in country "A" perceive other actors, and other actors perceive of country "A", correctly.[100]

It is deemed quite unfeasible to determine which factor features as the most dominant underlying force shaping the elite's perceptions. On the other hand, it is quite possible to establish a set of several most important factors that have a salient effect on the formation of elite members' views, beliefs and perceptions. The transformation process in the collective mind of an individual, in which the reality is transformed by one's senses into a perception, is influenced by a number of factors. As Figure 2.2. shows, Tilman identifies five factors affecting the transformation process: structural, geopolitical, historical, socio-cultural and economic.[101] First, the structural dimension of the transformation process revolves around the question "Who makes the foreign policy?" It takes into account the structure of the state's political and bureaucratic system through which foreign policy is formulated and executed. With respect to the structural dimension, later in this chapter, we will emphasize the importance of including the factor of *elite consensus* about the nature and urgency of the threat into a foreign policy analysis based on the balance-of-threat theory.[102]

Second, the geopolitical dimension encompasses the geographic proximity thesis (discussed in detail in Chapter 7), which also constitutes an important aspect of the balance-of-threat concept. Its underlying principle is simple: policy-makers tend to be more sensitive to dangers that are nearby, seeing them more threatening than threats from far away. Third, referring to the historical dimension, Tilman writes: "Policy-makers have had unique historical experiences that affect their perceptions, and in countries with strong oral traditions these personal historical experiences may continue through several or many generations."[103] Fourth is the socio-cultural dimension, which takes into consideration the ethnic, cultural, and religious make-up of a particular country and its foreign policy elite. We will see in the following chapters that these factors can significantly shape the decision-makers' foreign policy preferences. Finally, the economic dimension is concerned with the issue

FIGURE 2.2
Transformation Process from the Projection of the Reality to the Elite Perception

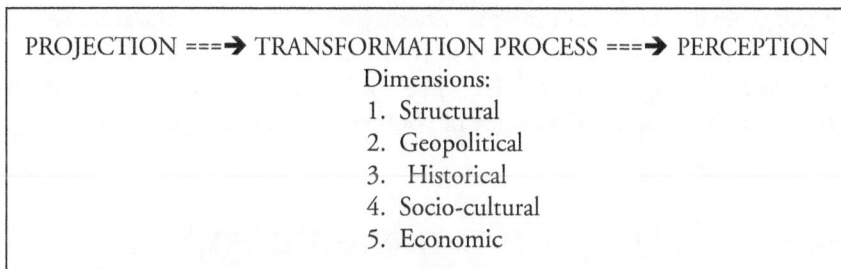

PROJECTION ===➜ TRANSFORMATION PROCESS ===➜ PERCEPTION
Dimensions:
1. Structural
2. Geopolitical
3. Historical
4. Socio-cultural
5. Economic

Source: Robert O. Tilman, The Enemy Beyond: External Threat Perceptions in the ASEAN Region, p. 2.

of corruption. It can be assumed that (not only) in the case of Indonesia, there have been policies formulated and executed for the sake of personal or family gain, rather than with the national interest in mind. However, since any analysis concerning the effects of corruption on foreign policy-making would be tantamount to speculation, this issue is only mentioned here and not further discussed in detail.[104]

Brecher along with other scholars put forward a model of foreign policy behaviour that distinguished the psychological from the operational environment and demonstrated how the former affects the latter. The psychological environment consists of two key elements termed as "attitudinal prism" and "elite image". The attitudinal prism refers to psychological predisposition of policy-makers, which is in turn shaped by societal and personality factors, namely idiosyncratic qualities of the policy-makers.[105] Rosenau argues here that "idiosyncratic sources are the most important influence on foreign policy formation in an underdeveloped country like Indonesia."[106] According to Brecher et al., leaders' idiosyncrasies are deemed as important because of their role as "the screen or prism through which elite perceptions of operational environment are filtered." The elite image, on the other hand, points to the critical role of decision-makers' perception of the external environment in that "decision-makers act in accordance with their perception of reality, not in response to reality itself."[107]

With regards to the elite images, Steinbruner introduced the concept of "uncommitted thinkers". He argued that, on the whole, leaders do not hold strong views on foreign policy and, as a result, they tend to evoke various images in a temporary fashion and formulate an inconsistent selection of policies. Conversely, the so-called "theoretical thinkers" are constantly committed to a particular perspective that unceasingly shapes the decision-makers' present policy choices.[108] Fiske's and Taylor's work on social cognition supported the "uncommitted thinkers" assumption when it concluded that people simplify reality because they tend to interpret specific instance in light of the general case.[109] For example, whether or not another state is perceived as an enemy could depend on the decision-makers' simplified image of reality: the decision-makers either "like" or "dislike" that country based on their basic belief about the degree of conflict between the other country and their own.[110]

BALANCE-OF-THREAT THEORY

Balance-of-power, the central concept of the realist and neo-realist theory, argues that the paramount concern of every state is to maintain favourable and "safe" power equilibrium between itself and other states and, consequently, is inclined to balance against a stronger or rising power. As we have seen, this theory is not capable of explaining completely and satisfactorily states' behaviour — states' behaviour does not always follow the balance-of-power logic. Many "realists" seem to underestimate or disregard, whether inadvertently or deliberately, the prime importance of decision-makers' threat perceptions in understanding the dynamics of foreign policy formation. This was for instance revealed in a recent academic disputation about the future of interstate relations in Asia. In response to Kang's argument that, by realist standards, rising China should be provoking balancing behaviour,[111] Acharya pointed out that his "analysis ignores insights from Walt's *balance-of-threat* theory, which shows that states balance against threats and not simply against power."[112] Yet, Kang, in his reaction to Acharya's critique, fails to recognize the potential of balance-of-threat thesis' explanatory power and asks once again in his next article as to "why Asian states are not necessarily balancing China in the same way that the United States balanced the Soviet Union [?]"[113]

Theoretical Foundations of the Concept

In response to the limitations of balance-of-power theory, Walt's study *The Origins of Alliances* brings forward the balance-of-threat concept.[114] One of the principal themes discussed in Walt's study is the fact that states do not necessarily always balance against the most powerful or rising hegemonic nation. He demonstrates that during the Cold War, there was actually a sizable imbalance in power in favour of the U.S. and its allies. Walt then examines his theory by using the case study of the alliance formation in the Middle East from 1955 to 1979. He argues that, in line with the balance-of-threat theory, the imbalance in power was brought about by the situation, in which the United States was more powerful but the Soviet Union appeared more threatening.

This brings him to argue that balance-of-threat thesis possesses a greater explanatory power in examining alliance formation in the Middle East than variables of political penetration, foreign aid, and ideology. Here Walt's theory challenges the traditional balance-of-power theory, as it seeks to demonstrate that states do not balance against other states' power per se, but against *perceived threats* poised by the latter. States choose their allies with the aim of balancing against the most serious threat. Importantly, the balance-of-threat concept constitutes "a refinement of traditional balance-of-power theory"[115] in that it defines "power" as something subjective and thus makes an attempt to go beyond the narrow "confines" of (neo)realism. Walt's theory subsumes and thus is superior to the balance-of-power theory — aggregate power is an important, though not the only aspect of threat.

According to Walt, this concept is informed by *threat*, which is derived from the combination of a state's aggregate power, its geographic proximity, its offensive capability, and the aggressiveness of its intentions, as perceived by other states. Walt's theory can be employed in a situation which couldn't previously be explained by means of the balance-of-power theory. A case in point is the earlier mentioned steady rise of the United States at least since the early 19th century and the response of the world's most powerful nations to it. The inertness on the part of the European powers, which during much of the 19th century clearly possessed the capability to prevent the U.S. from eclipsing their own predominance, could be explained by utilizing the balance-of-threat theory. One of the concept's main assumptions is that, in accordance with the geographic proximity factor, a nation tends to consider its neighbours to be a far bigger threat to its security than any distant superpower.[116] Hence, although the European powers have in the 19th and 20th century been concerned with the growing strength of the U.S., they were far more preoccupied with the strength of their immediate neighbours.[117]

The advantage of Walt's theory is that it can shed light, unlike the neo-realist approach, on how the Soviet threat was constructed in different places and, therefore, provide an explanation for the "lopsided" balance of power in the bipolar Cold War international relations. He argues that the Soviet Union was, due to its geographic size and proximity, perceived by practically all its numerous neighbouring states as posing a major threat to their national security. By contrast, the United States, which is separated by two oceans to its East and West, had amiable relations with its two weak neighbours. The balance-of-threat theory explains that, in line with the geographic proximity thesis, since the U.S. did not appear threatening, many countries were predisposed, or in the light of the perceived "Communist threat" compelled, to align with it.[118] In other words, Moscow's intentions were perceived as more threatening when compared with Washington's policies.

Referring to the realist central theme of gaining and maintaining power, Machiavelli writes: "… if you have to make a choice, to be feared is much safer than to be loved."[119] Yet, Machiavelli's statement goes against the main premise of balance-of-threat theory. This study challenges the key realist assumption by an argument that could be succinctly expressed as a paraphrased version of Machiavelli's statement: "If you have to make a choice, to be loved is much safer than to be feared." If you are perceived as a threat, you will most likely be faced with defensive and hostile policies from other states. Walt concludes that *threat perceptions* constitute one of the most important forces in international politics. A *threat perception* is a salient determinant, which shapes the direction of a state's foreign policy, thus contributing significantly to the formation of international alliances.[120]

Originally, Walt's study tested the balance-of-threat theory's main propositions in the case of the interstate relations of the Middle East region against the backdrop of the Cold War. The international relations shaped by the bi-polar, big power rivalry were then dominated by "hard power" — the politics of alliances and military firepower. Walt's study was mainly concerned with perceptions of threat generated by other state's offensive military capabilities. We can question whether the balance-of-threat theory can be efficiently utilized in the post-Cold War era which is marked by increasing prominence of "soft" sources of state's power and a variety of non-traditional and trans-border threats.[121]

Traditionally, the exclusive power and authority in international relations rested with states. Today, with the new sources and altered quality of power, potential threats to a state's national security are more varied and no longer restricted by geographical and political boundaries.[122] This situation has wreaked havoc the traditional conception of national security and brought about new ways of thinking about how to achieve it. *The Origins of Alliances* only briefly diverts its attention from the "hard power"-dominated Middle Eastern politics as it mentions the potency of ideological threat. Although Walt asserts that "a challenge to the ruler's legitimacy could easily be a more potent threat than any enemy army",[123] he largely fails to elaborate on the problem of non-traditional, non-military sources of threat in the foreign policy elite's calculations. This book makes an attempt to fit within the balance-of-threat theoretical framework this increasing complexity and scope of power relations and the changing conception of national security in the contemporary international arena.

Balance-of-Threat Theory and Social Construction of Subjectivity

Balance-of-threat, unlike the balance-of-power theory, is rightly based on the assumption that any assessment of power by the elite responsible for a state's foreign policy entails subjective considerations. Traces of social-constructivist thinking in international relations have occasionally appeared in scholarly debate about the viability of realist paradigm, in particular that dealing with the balance-of-power theory. Underlying realism are, for example, gloomy and pessimistic assumptions about basic laws of human nature and their impact on relations among states. "The condition of man ... is a condition of war of everyone against everyone,"[124] wrote Hobbes in the mid-17th century. Similarly, balance-of-power concept has been disputed for it was found as "meaningless and a figment of the imagination", whereby its substance constantly changes depending "upon the circumstances of the time".[125] Bull admits that the very existence of a balance of power rests on the "subjective element of belief in it".[126]

However, the rhetoric about non-material qualities of realist paradigm has not on the whole moved beyond the neorealist premise that international politics is entrenched within a set of constant, universal laws that operate across space and time. An assumption about the egoist and cutthroat human nature has in part served as a rationale for the neo-realist concepts of security dilemma, anarchy and "self-help" nature of the international system.[127] Academic debate over the condition of balance-of-power theory and neo-realist paradigm has for a long time largely failed to grapple with and examine thoroughly the mutable condition of "human nature" and "subjectivity" aspects of international relations.

Balance-of-threat concept recognizes the very subjectivity of power assessment and thus constitutes one of a handful of serious attempts at moving on beyond the "confines" of classical realism. Walt's theory effectively renounces "power" as a concept measurable in precise terms. It moves the realist analysis away from that focusing solely on a state's aggregate power to a more sophisticated one complemented by regard for non-material factors. Balance-of-threat, unlike balance-of-power theory, acknowledges that the "scope" of a state's power depends on who carries out its subjective appraisal. The degree to which a state's elite finds other country's power threatening does not depend only on the distribution of material power in the system but also on the elite's perceptions, shaped by an intersubjective set of culture, knowledge, ideas and norms.[128]

At the time of its creation, balance-of-threat was conceived as a theory befitting the neo-realist paradigm. It explains alliance formation as a function of changes on the level of external threat, which arises from the distribution of power within the interstate system. Yet, while being primarily concerned with external sources of threat, Walt falls short of recognizing the implicit constructivist dimension of balance-of-threat theory. He concludes that "a state will ally with the side it believes is least dangerous",[129] whereby the degree to which the state feels threatened is the product of, among other factors, the aggressiveness of the other state's intentions. Perceived intentions, as a source of threat, cannot be established a priori based on numerical and factual calculation — this necessitates an analysis of how particular perceptions have been constructed. The frequent use of the words "perceive", "appear" or "believe" with reference to a state's threat perceptions in Walt's study implies that the neorealist credentials of balance-of-threat theory are susceptible to a constructivist complement.[130] In other words, one of the main tacit contributions of Walt's theory is the idea that it is essentially human beings who are behind power calculations in the interstate system. Hopf goes here even as far as invoking "a theory of threat perception".[131]

Several international relations scholars have pointed to balance-of-threat theory as a rare effort in realist literature to draw attention to non-material, discursive sources of power in interstate relations.[132] For Foot, the constructivist element enables greater attention and greater explanatory weight to be given to certain features of particular societies and thus establish the domestic domain as an independent variable.[133] Peou views balance-of-threat theory as a medium, in which constructivism has incorporated realism into its security analysis, and, consequently, it is why the theory "is not as 'realist' as its proponents claim it to be."[134] Mastanduno argues that since "perceived intentions" are included as one of the key aspects of threat, the analysis based on the balance-of-threat theory is moved away from the purely systemic level. Whereas balance-of-power theory is purely systemic, balance-of-threat theory incorporates both systemic factors and the leader-centric variables that were present in classical realism.[135] Because of this, Walt's balance-of-threat theory can be included in the research programme or framework called as neoclassical realism, which originates from the realist tradition and is concerned mainly with foreign policy studies. Whereas classical realism employs the *individual level* and neorealism (structural realism) the *system level* approaches, neoclassical realism utilizes a *multi-level approach*, whose research framework incorporates a combination of individual, domestic and systematic levels of analysis.

ENHANCING EXPLANATORY POWER OF THE BALANCE-OF-THREAT THEORY

This book aspires to make a contribution to the study of international relations by enhancing the explanatory power of the balance-of-threat theory. It will be done in the following five ways: first, by enhancing the implicit constructivist dimension of Walt's theory or, in other words, providing for its constructivist re-conceptualisation; second, by employing this theoretical framework to analyse inter-state relations in the post-Cold War era, in contrast to its earlier use by Walt in the Middle East during the Cold War; third, by including domestic political conditions into the analysis; fourth, by incorporating into the theoretical framework the question of the elite's future threat assessment; and, finally, by putting more emphasis on the elite cohesion and its consensus about the nature and urgency of the threat.

Threat Perceptions and Constructivism

The aspiration of the constructivist perspective to become a serious alternative to mainstream IR theory necessitates a research programme, which includes, as Hopf claims, "constructivist re-conceptualisations of balance-of-threat theory."[136] This study provides for a constructivist reinterpretation of Walt's original version of balance-of-threat theory, as it seeks to reinforce the theory's implied constructivist dimension without significantly affecting its realist component. The result is a sophisticated realist-constructivist concept that is capable of analysing "the social construction of subjectivity" — meaning the role of elite threat perceptions — in international relations.[137] Although the balance-of-threat theory was originally designed as a realist tool of analysis, *perceived intentions* as a source of threat is the point where its implicitly constructivist approach emerges.

Walt's thesis essentially constitutes both a challenge to classical realism and a revision of Waltz's theory of structural realism. The main premise underlying the balance-of-threat theory undermines, first, the key assumption of classical realism about self-centred human nature as a never changing constant in international relations; and, second, the basic principle behind structural realism that states design their foreign policies in view of the distribution of power within the insecure anarchical world of competing units.[138] Walt's theory advances an implicit counterargument that, first, the self-interest conceived by the human mind is mutable and, second, states' foreign policies are not intrinsically based on the structure, but rather it is the statesmen's subjective assumptions about the structure that shapes their states' foreign policies. Wendt embraces Walt's theory, saying that it is "the 'balance of threats', rather than the balance of power, [that] determines state action, threats being socially constructed."[139]

Although the roots of social constructivism in the study of international relations can be found as early as in the 1950s in the concepts of "security community" developed by Karl Deutsch[140] and later "imagined communities" put forward by Benedict Anderson,[141] it was the failure of both realism and liberalism to anticipate the end of the Cold War that legitimized constructivist theories and brought them into the forefront of the scholarly discourse. Generally, constructivism revolves around three main assumptions: The first one regards "anarchy" in international politics not as a brute fact, but as a social construct, something that is subject to change depending on how it is perceived. Anarchy as such does not determine any particular course of action but it can be rather anything, in Wendt's words, "what states make of it".[142] The second assumption is that interests and identities, which realists take as given, are not static and a priori given, but are rather mutable constructs created by the human mind. Although currently having a particular character, they could also have been or could be next created differently.[143] In other words, this world does not operate along some set of rules predetermined by non-human forces, but a world constructed in human minds. The third constructivist assumption says that there is a fundamental distinction between "brute facts" and "social facts" in international politics. Importantly, whereas the former remain fully independent of human action, the latter are derived from socially established practices and are, unlike the "brute facts", subject to constant change.[144]

The constructivist approach thus focuses on the conception of identities and interests and the creation of ideas and norms among individuals, especially state elites, which represent the main units of constructivist analysis. Moreover, constructivism is also concerned with the evolution of these discursive factors and with their influence on a state's behaviour. For constructivists, power is relevant insofar as it is a concept that is socially constructed, perceptions of which are derived from the way a particular group of individuals understands and responds to a set of intersubjective ideas, identities and norms.[145] The main limitation of the constructivist approach to the study of international relations is the abstract and rather vague nature of such basic terms like identity, norms and elite, which in turn provide for its loose conceptualization underscored by less, in realism much-desired, parsimony. Walt, as a realist, originally seems quite sceptical about the viability of constructivism. Since constructivist analysis can deliver only a rather inaccurate prediction of the content of ideas and the character of identity, constructivism is more likely to facilitate depicting the past conditions than anticipating future developments.[146]

Constructivism sees a social structure as comprising three elements: shared knowledge, material resources and practices.[147] Social structures are founded on a set of shared understandings, meanings, knowledge and expectations, all of which are social constructions of the past. For anthropologists and historians, social constructions of the past are of great importance because they "reflect the ways in which people are defined, apprehended and acted upon by others and [how] they define themselves."[148] Knowledge shared within a social structure is conveyed into the domain of political struggle, notably a state's foreign policy. Moreover, shared knowledge as a social construction of the past gives various meanings of one phenomenon to various social structures (understand: states and its elites). It is because, as Bond and Gilliam point out, "a world of meaning is constructed through images, or icons, that are the products of particular historical circumstances. ... They have the power to evoke the past, apprehending the present, and establishing the basis of 'imagined communities'."[149]

Constructivist perspective offers alternative understanding of some of the central themes in international relations theory.[150] In contemporary international relations where the meaning of power has taken on new dimensions, "old norms are being challenged, once clear boundaries are dissolving, and issues of identity are becoming more salient", constructivist analysis seem to be apt to meet these new growing complexities.[151] It can help to explain, for example, the strikingly different Indonesian perception of the U.S. and Chinese military capabilities. The sizeable U.S. military deployment in Southeast Asia during the 1990s involving state-of-the-art aircraft carriers appeared less threatening to Jakarta than a few second-rate warships of the rather feeble Chinese navy. This fact demonstrates that material capabilities per se can not explain why a state views less powerful and efficient armed forces as more threatening than the military capabilities of the world's "lonely superpower".[152] The constructivist perspective inherent to the balance-of-threat theory possesses the necessary explanatory power able to shed light on such "structural" puzzles.

Internal Sources of Threat Perceptions

In the following chapters, we will also see that an analysis based on balance-of-threat theory is capable of taking into account domestic conditions of the country in question. Realist paradigm assumes that there is a clear distinction between domestic and international politics and that these two realms are sharply separated.[153] For realists, a state's aggregate power is of paramount interest and its internal composition is of concern only insofar as it serves that power.[154] Also neorealists have long considered interstate relations as standing apart from the arena of domestic politics, whereby it is the distribution of power within the anarchical system of states that determines the direction of a state's foreign policy.[155] Domestic politics, ideological preferences or public opinion play only a marginal role, because pressures of the eternal "self-help"-driven inter-state competition constitute a much more pressing concern for policy-makers and statesmen.[156]

Conversely, the criticism of realism has tended to emphasize the decisive role of domestic political pressures in shaping states' foreign policy behaviour. From Plato through the era of Enlightenment, to Marx, Lenin and many of contemporary liberalists and constructivists, the imbalance in distribution of internal power was seen as the prime cause of international conflicts. Internal structure of states largely accounts for their external behaviour.[157] As liberalists point out, "minds can be changed, new leaders can come to power, values can shift, new opportunities and dangers can arise."[158] Marxists emphasize the regime's nature as the salient determinant in state's behaviour. While the wars waged by capitalist states is a manifestation of the internal class struggle, socialist states, owing to their "classless" social structure, do not wage wars.[159] Here, Beard correctly argues that "however conceived in an image of the world, foreign policy is a phase of domestic policy, an inescapable phase."[160]

The scholarship of international relations has been increasingly concerned with internal sources of foreign policy.[161] In particular, the field of diplomatic history has focused on how ideological, social and economic aspects of domestic politics shape a state's foreign relations. There have been quite a substantial number of studies published on the diplomatic history of Indonesia. However, these narrative accounts have not on the whole been used as empirical evidence placed within the framework of international relations theory.[162] Snyder makes a serious attempt to link domestic and international politics within the realist paradigm.[163] Yet, his approach has been viewed as "erroneous", for it utilizes realist perspective that underrates the impact of powerful forces within the international system on a state's behaviour.[164] Since the constructivist approach operates on the individual level, namely state elites, it could be argued that constructivist analysis of a state's foreign policy enables the examination of the policy's internal roots.

Walt's *The Origins of Alliances* is not consistent in its view on the extent to which domestic politics shapes states' foreign relations. Although the analysis of alliance formation in the Middle East discusses internal factors, such as ideology and penetration, or the establishment of extensive contacts between separate national elites, it ultimately downplays the significance of internal sources of threat. It concludes that these domestic factors are "less important than external threats" and "a minor cause of alliance formation,"[165] whereby the degree to which a state feels threatened by other states is the product only of external factors. In stark contrast to this central proposition, Walt later asserts that "... the domestic situation of the United States may be more important than anything else. External events impinge on U.S. power; internal conditions generate it."[166] He thus clearly sees domestic politics in his homeland as a catalyst for the dynamics shaping the U.S. foreign policy. It is this point that Walt implicitly denies one of the key propositions of his study.

Walt fails to explain why internal conditions are so crucial in the foreign policy making in the case of the United States and why the same does not apply to the Middle Eastern states. On the one hand, he claims that domestic situation and internal conditions generate foreign policy but, on the other, he considers only external sources of threat to be important variables affecting the direction of a state's foreign policy. Moreover, although the "internal conditions", from Walt's realist perspective, are limited mainly to "the overall health of the U.S. economy",[167] their scope is clearly susceptible to inclusion of other important aspects of American domestic situation. This ambiguity and vagueness with regard to both the scope and relevance of "internal conditions" in generating a state's foreign policy can be considered one of the main limitations of Walt's study.

This book addresses the above-outlined limitation of Walt's balance-of-threat theory by including into the analysis the consideration for the influence of "internal conditions" on Indonesian foreign policy formation. The "internal factors" capable of affecting elite threat perceptions are varied and multiple — they include in particular the nation's socio-cultural aspects, state of the political system, the role of the country's media to shape and reshape the public and elite opinion, along with psychological factors, such as historical legacy, mistrust and animosity among Southeast Asian states. In contrast to Walt's ambiguity with regards to the relevance of internal sources of foreign policy, we will see in the discussion in the following chapters that the line between external and internal threats as perceived by the Indonesian foreign policy elite is essentially blurred. The balance-of-threat theory, by virtue of its inherently constructivist nature, can thus provide a nexus between the realm of domestic politics and the world of international relations.

Elite Perceptions in a Broader Context — Long-Term Threat Assessment

The question is now whether an analysis that draws on a view or belief held by a single policy-maker and diplomat can explain the selection of policies. To what extent can a particular perception of another state or non-state actor, which may be based on more or less biased assumption or prejudice informed by a conspiracy theory, shed light on the foreign policy direction? We will demonstrate in the following chapters that a single perception against another state actor, when isolated from the elite's broader worldview, lacks the necessary explanatory power. Any particular belief or perception is relevant only when viewed in a broader context, as a part of a bigger picture. Consequently, the elite's threat assessment of a particular country needs to be seen vis-à-vis the threat assessment of other countries and non-state actors. Only a perception analysed in the context of the elite's broader worldview can generate crucial data essential to deeper understanding of the key forces driving Indonesian foreign relations.

Moreover, in order to understand the way the foreign policy elite perceives the present situation, the analysis based on the balance-of-threat needs to take into account also the elite's future threat assessment. Leifer has aptly summed up this underlying assumption in his analysis of Singaporean foreign policy. He writes that, from the Singaporean elite's perspective, "at issue has not been how to counter each and every potential and actual hegemon but whether or not such a hegemon is [in the future] likely to be a benign or a malign factor affecting Singapore's interests."[168] We will see that the future threat assessment does not necessarily affect the practical, day-to-day management of Indonesia's relations with other countries. But it is important in fuelling the security dilemma and likely to influence the elite's long-term balancing and hedging strategies vis-à-vis other state actors. The post-Cold War era has seen a fundamental strategic shift in power relations among the world's major powers. Southeast Asia itself has faced the reality of dramatic growth of China's and India's influence in regional affairs. We can possibly only guess potential future prospects of this development. However, this study suggests that we can understand present dynamics and predict more accurately future development of Indonesian foreign policy by examining the past and present Indonesian leaders' threat perceptions in context with their *future threat assessment*.

Factor of the Elite Consensus

This study on Indonesian foreign policy employs a leader-centric approach that focuses on key policy-makers' roles in shaping the country's foreign relations. This approach is sensible — as the first Indonesian President Sukarno liked to point out, "international relations are human relations."[169] Since states do not make and implement foreign policies, but governments through their leaders and elites do, the degree of *elite consensus* about a threat substantially determines which foreign policy tools will be employed to meet a particular threat. This study attempts to enhance the balance-of-threat theory's explanatory power also by putting more emphasis on the degree of elite *consensus* about the nature and urgency of the threat. This approach has become ever more important in the post-Suharto period due to Indonesia's competitive and pluralist democratic environment and the increasing salience of various non-conventional and trans-national threats.

The preceding discussion about internal sources of threat perceptions showed that, contrary to the realist premise, state behaviour may be determined less by external, systemic-level factors than by domestic-political factors.[170] It follows that the probability that a state will balance a perceived external threat is a function of the preferences and uniformity of threat perceptions of its foreign policy elite. In particular, as Schweller argues, it is "elite consensus [about the threat that] is the most necessary of necessary causes of balancing behaviour."[171] Elite consensus can be said to arise from elite cohesion, which could be defined as "the degree to which a central government's political leadership is fragmented by persistent internal divisions. Elite polarization may arise over ideological, cultural, or religious divisions; bureaucratic interests; party fractions; regional and sectoral interests; ethnic groups and class loyalties."[172]

According to Schweller, the principal issues with regards to elite consensus and state's balancing behaviour that need to be closely analysed are: first, to what degree does the foreign policy elite agree that there is an external threat?; second, do the key policy-makers agree about the nature and extent of the threat?; third, is the elite unanimous in its view of what foreign policy strategy would be most appropriate and effective to deal with and eliminate the threat?; and, finally, we also need to ask, "if there are multiple threats, do the elites agree on their rankings of external threats from most to least dangerous to the state's survival and vital interests?"[173] In this study, we will also focus on aspect of Indonesian elite's consensus to see to what extent is the Indonesian elite unanimous in its outlook or, conversely, badly divided in basic attitudes and perceptions, whereby we can assume that an existing disagreement is likely to have considerable implications for the foreign policy dynamics. In particular, we will analyse the degree to which consensus exists among the elite about the nature and urgency of the external threat.

CONCLUSION

The realist paradigm has been handicapped by the tendency among academics to fit it into one "theory of realism", to employ it to the exclusion of other perspectives and to understand this theoretical approach in rather narrow and material terms. Moreover, the attempt to achieve as much parsimony as possible has produced an evaluation of the reality that fails to capture the sheer complexity of social processes shaping a state's foreign policy. As both realism and constructivism have been in recent years established as the key theoretical competitors in Southeast Asian security studies, the region provides this study with a setting for testing the utility of a sophisticated balance-of-threat theory.

This study constitutes an attempt to explain the dynamics of Indonesia's foreign policy by employing the balance-of-threat theory. Elite (threat) perceptions both determine selection of policies and define the criteria and context in which decision-making process is executed. Analysis of perceptions may also facilitate a prediction of policy choices and, as this study seeks to demonstrate, also enable us to better understand the national security considerations and behaviour of the Indonesian foreign policy elite. The term balance-of-threat conveys two dimensions underpinning the theoretical concept. The first part, "balance", refers to its realist dimension, and the second part, "threat", signifies its constructivist component. This foreign policy study thus goes beyond the traditional, pure realism by borrowing ideas from other, competing theoretical perspectives. Indonesia's foreign policy is viewed not just as a response to the distribution of power within the anarchical structure but rather as a "social construct" generated by the process of learning and interaction of the human mind — namely, the country's leaders and policy-makers. The study employs a delicately balanced theoretical approach that combines the analysis of both "structure" and "process" as factors shaping Indonesia's foreign policy.

Notes

1   Amitav Acharya and Richard Stubbs, "Theorizing Southeast Asian Relations: An Introduction", *The Pacific Review* 19, no. 2 (June 2006): 126; some examples of these works are: David Mozingo, *Chinese Policy toward Indonesia 1949–1967* (London: Cornell University Press, 1976); Palfrey Howard Jones, *Indonesia: The Possible Dream* (Jakarta: Gunung Agung, 1980); Michael Leifer, *Indonesia's Foreign Policy* (London: Allen&Unwin, 1983); Audrey R. Kahin and George McT. Kahin, *Subversion as Foreign Policy: The Secret Eisenhower and Dulles Debacle in Indonesia* (Seattle: University of Washington Press, 1995); Paul F. Gardner, *Shared Hopes, Separate Fears: Fifty Years of U.S.-Indonesian Relations* (Oxford: Westview Press, 1997); Robert J. McMahon, *The Limits of Empire: The United States and Southeast Asia since World War II* (New York: Columbia University Press, 1999); Stig Aga Aandstad, "United States Policy towards Indonesia 1961–1965", (Ph.D. Dissertation, University of Oslo, Spring 1999).

2   Some examples include: Ralf Emmers, *Cooperative Security and the Balance of Power in ASEAN and the ARF* (London: RoutledgeCurzon, 2003); Stephen M. Walt, *The Origins of Alliances* (London: Cornell University Press, 1990).

3   A term used by Keith Shann, former Australian Ambassador to Indonesia; quoted from Karim Najjarine, "Australian Policy towards Indonesia 1965–72:

An Archival Study" (Ph.D. Dissertation, University of Western Australia, 2004).

4   Ibid.

5   A very well connected Indonesian political analyst, an insider with an access to the highest echelons of the Jakarta political establishment, asserted that in Indonesia it is very difficult to predict future tendencies in government policies. He admitted that notwithstanding his access to insider information, he is often surprised at the totally unexpected outcome of a government meeting or parliamentary committee session. Interview in Jakarta, 8 December 2004.

6   Stephen M. Walt, "International Relations: One World, Many Theories", *Foreign Policy*, No. 110 (Spring 1998), p. 29.

7   This topic was in the centre of attention also at: "Why is There No Non-Western International Relations Theory", IDSS Workshop, Singapore, 11–12 July 2005; Amitav Acharya and Barry Buzan, "Why is There No Non-Western IR Theory? An Introduction", *International Relations of the Asia-Pacific* 7, no. 3 (2007).

8   Simon Philpott, *Rethinking Indonesia: Postcolonial Theory, Authoritarianism and Identity* (New York: St. Martin's Press, 2000), pp. 64–65; David C. Kang, "Getting Asia Wrong: The Need for New Analytical Frameworks", *International Security* 27, no. 4 (Spring 2003), p. 61.

9   For a discussion on the applicability of Europe-derived IR theories in Asia, see: Kang, "Getting Asia Wrong"; Amitav Acharya, "Will Asia's Past Be Its Future?", *International Security* 28, no. 3 (Winter 2003/04).

10   J.H. Boeke, *The Evolution of the Netherlands Indies Economy* (New York: Netherlands and Netherlands Indies Council, Institute of Pacific Relations, 1946).

11   "Is the Middle Class a Harbinger of Democracy? Evidence from Southeast Asia", seminar organized by the ISEAS, Singapore, 15 December 2008.

12   Klaus Eugen Knorr, ed., *Historical Dimensions of National Security Problems* (Lawrence: University Press of Kansas, 1976), pp. 361–70; for more on this issue, see: Sharif M. Shuja, "The Historical Myopia of International Relations", *Contemporary Review* (January 2001); Takashi Inoguchi and Edward Newman, "Introduction: 'Asian Values' and Democracy in Asia", Conference Proceedings, "'Asian Values' and Democracy in Asia" Conference, Japan (28 March 1997); Stephen Hobden and John M. Hobson, eds., *Historical Sociology of International Relations* (Cambridge: Cambridge University Press, 2002).

13   Ibid., pp. 361–70.

14   Samuel P. Huntington, "The Clash of Civilizations?", *Foreign Affairs* 72, no. 3 (Summer 1993): 22.

15   Nevertheless, it is the author's presumption that similar psychological factors play an important part in interstate relations on the European continent as well; for more on this issue, see: Jihwan Hwang, "Rethinking the East Asian Balance of Power: Historical Antagonism, Internal Balancing, and the Korean-Japanese Security Relationship", *World Affairs* 166, no. 2 (Fall 2003): 85–108; Thomas J. Christensen, "China, the U.S.-Japan Alliance, and the Security Dilemma in

East Asia", *International Security* 23, no. 4 (Spring 1999); Aaron L. Friedberg, "Europe's Past, Asia's Future?", SAIS Policy Forum Series, No. 3 (October 1998).

[16] Aaron L. Friedberg, "Ripe for Rivalry: Prospects for Peace in a Multipolar Asia", *International Security* 18, no. 3 (Winter 1993/94).

[17] Friedberg, "Europe's Past, Asia's Future?".

[18] Kang, "Getting Asia Wrong", p. 61.

[19] For more ideas on this controversial issue, see John G. Ikenberry, ed., *America Unrivalled: The Future of the Balance of Power* (Ithaca: Cornell University Press, 2002).

[20] Interview with a senior Indonesian diplomat, DEPLU, Jakarta, 25 January 2005.

[21] Interview with a senior Indonesian diplomat, DEPLU, Jakarta, 28 February 2005; also discussed with a former Indonesian Minister of Foreign Affairs, Jakarta, 14 January 2005.

[22] The policy options representing liberal approaches to peace and security included: better communication and understanding among policy-makers and ordinary people from different nations, increasing economic interdependence, narrowing the gap between rich and poor nations.

[23] The policy options representing realist approaches to peace and security included: constant political effort to maintain a balance of power within Southeast Asia and between the world's biggest powers involved in the region, closer military cooperation of ASEAN states, military superiority of the United States in the region, collective security through alliances.

[24] According to Johnston, realist theory has various guises, whereby he offers its fourfold categorization: balance-of-power, balance-of-threat, power maximization, and identity realism. For a more detailed discussion, see: Alastair Iain Johnston, "Realism(s) and Chinese Security Policy in the Post-Cold War Period", in *Unipolar Politics: Realism and State Strategies after the Cold War*, edited by Ethan B. Kapstein and Michael Mastanduno (New York: Columbia University Press, 1999), pp. 261–318.

[25] Joseph S. Nye, Jr., *Bound to Lead: The Changing Nature of American Power* (New York: Basic Books, 1991), pp. 173–201.

[26] Chapter "A Realist Theory of International Politics" in: Hans J. Morgenthau, *Politics among Nations: The Struggle for Power and Peace* (New York: Alfred A. Knopf, 1985), p. 3.

[27] For more on the limitations of the balance-of-power theory, see: Richard Little, "Rethinking the Dynamics of the Balance of Power", Conference Paper, presented at the annual meeting of the International Studies Association, Honolulu (5 March 2005) <http://www.allacademic.com/meta/p69346_index.html> (accessed 14 April 2006); Hwang, "Rethinking the East Asian Balance of Power"; John A. Vasquez and Colin Elman, eds., *Realism and the Balancing of Power: A New Debate* (Upper Saddle River: Prentice Hall, 2002).

28   Morgenthau, *Politics among Nations*, p. 187.
29   Paul Kennedy, *The Rise and Fall of the Great Powers: Economic Change and Military Conflict from 1500 to 2000* (New York: Random House, 1987), pp. xv–xvi.
30   Morgenthau, *Politics among Nations*, pp. 188–89.
31   Henry Kissinger, *Diplomacy* (New York: Simon & Schuster, 1994), p. 632.
32   Jeffrey W. Legro and Andrew Moravcsik, "Is Anybody Still a Realist?", *International Security* 24, no. 2 (Fall 1999).
33   Walt, "International Relations: One World, Many Theories", p. 30.
34   Peter J. Katzenstein and Nobuo Okawara, "Japan, Asian-Pacific Security, and the Case for Analytical Eclecticism", *International Security* 26, no. 2 (Winter 2001/02): 183.
35   Charles A. Beard, *Foreign Policy for America* (New York: Alfred A. Knopf, 1940), p. 9; David Campbell, *Writing Security: United States Foreign Policy and the Politics of Identity* (Minneapolis: University of Minnesota Press, 1992).
36   It could be argued that because of their considerably different historical experience, Asian leaders were guided in the selection of policies by considerations quite different from those of their Western counterparts. More on the role of emotion in international relations, see Neta C. Crawford, "The Passion of World Politics", *International Security* 24, no. 4 (Spring 2000); Jonathan Mercer and Barry O'Neill, "Emotion and International Politics: Trust in Identity", Conference Paper, The American Political Science Association Conference, San Francisco (2001); Jonathan Mercer, "Approaching Emotion in International Politics", Conference Paper, The International Studies Association Conference, San Diego (April 1996).
37   Alan Dupont, *East Asia Imperilled: Transnational Challenges to Security* (Cambridge: Cambridge University Press, 2001), p. 4.
38   Mohammad Hatta, *Indonesian Patriot: Memoirs*, edited by C.L.M. Penders (Singapore: Gunung Agung, 1981), p. vii.
39   Michael Mastanduno, "Preserving the Unipolar Moment: Realist Theories and U.S. Grand Strategy after the Cold War", *International Security* 21, no. 4 (Spring 1997): 50.
40   Kenneth W. Waltz, *Theory of International Politics*, Reading (Boston: Addison-Wesley, 1979), pp. 71–73.
41   Hans J. Morgenthau, *Scientific Man versus Power Politics* (Chicago: The University of Chicago Press, 1967), p. 11.
42   Hobbes outlined his sober view of human nature as follows: "[...] there is no way for any man to secure himselfe, so reasonable, as Anticipation; that is, by force, or wiles, to master the persons of all men he can, so long, till he see no other power great enough to endanger him."; Thomas Hobbes, *Leviathan* (Cambridge: Cambridge University Press, 1996).
43   Morgenthau, *Politics among Nations*.

44   Chapter "International Conflict and International Anarchy", in Kenneth W. Waltz, *Man, the State, and War* (New York: Columbia University Press, 1959), pp. 159–86.

45   Waltz, *Theory of International Politics*.

46   John J. Mearsheimer, *The Tragedy of Great Power Politics* (New York: W.W. Norton, 2001), pp. 29–40.

47   Kenneth N. Waltz, "The Origins of War in Neorealist Theory", in *The Origin and Prevention of Major Wars*, edited by Robert I. Rotberg and Theodore K. Rabb (New York: Cambridge University Press, 1989), p. 40; Glenn H. Snyder, "Mearsheimer's World — Offensive Realism and the Struggle for Security", *International Security* 27, no. 1 (Summer 2002), pp. 149–73.

48   Ole R. Holsti, "Theories of International Relations and Foreign Policy: Realism and Its Challengers", in *Controversies in International Relations Theory: Realism and the Neoliberal Challenge*, edited by Charles W. Kegley, Jr. (New York: St. Martin's Press, 1995), p. 38.

49   For a detailed study of Singapore's foreign policy, see Michael Leifer, *Singapore's Foreign Policy: Coping with Vulnerability* (London: Routledge, 2000); Trish Saywell, "'Places Not Bases' Puts Singapore on the Line: Will Singapore's New Naval Base Cause Waves?", *Far Eastern Economic Review*, 17 May 2002.

50   The concept of "social distribution of knowledge" is discussed in: Peter Berger and Thomas Luckmann, *The Social Construction of Reality* (New York: Anchor Books, 1966), pp. 33–61; For more on the concept of "distribution of knowledge", see: Barry Barnes, *The Nature of Power* (Cambridge: Polity Press, 1988).

51   For more discussion on strengths and weaknesses of realist and neorealist approaches in the study of international relations, see: Richard K. Ashley, "The Poverty of Neorealism", *International Organization* 38, no. 2 (Spring 1984); Jim George, *Discourses of Global Politics: A Critical (Re)Introduction to International Relations* (Boulder: Lynne Rienner Publishers, 1994).

52   Niccolò Machiavelli, *The Prince* (New York: W.W. Norton & Co., 1992).

53   E. H. Carr, *The Twenty Years' Crisis 1919–1939* (London: Macmillan and Co., 1939), pp. 124–25.

54   Chapter "Approaches to the Study of International Politics", in K.J. Holsti, *International Politics: A Framework for Analysis* (Englewood Cliffs: Prentice-Hall, 1995), p. 6.

55   Morgenthau, *Politics among Nations*, pp. 115–84.

56   Thucydides, *The Peloponnesian War*, Book V, Chapter XVII (New York: Modern Library, 1951), p. 331.

57   R.M. Sunardi, "Australia-Indonesia Defence Cooperation: An Indonesian Perspective", in *Indonesia: Dealing with a Neighbour*, edited by Colin Brown (St. Leonards: Allen & Unwin, 1996), p. 58.

58   Joseph S. Nye, Jr., "Limits of American Power", *Political Science Quarterly* 17, no. 4 (Winter 2002/03): 549.

59   Trans-national networks involve, for example, trans-national criminal syndicates, terrorist groups, NGOs or multinational corporations.

60   Robert O. Keohane and Joseph S. Nye, Jr., "Power and Interdependence in the Information Age", *Foreign Affairs* 77, no. 5 (September/October 1998).

61   Ibid., p. 90.

62   A case in point is, for instance, the U.S.-led War on Terrorism launched after the terrorist attacks of 11 September 2001. The U.S. military campaign, which culminated with the attacks on Afghanistan and Iraq, has not proven to be very efficient. In view of the worldwide upsurge of anti-Americanism, some political observers have even considered this military campaign to some degree counterproductive; Meg Bortin, "Poll Shows U.S. Isolation: In War's Wake, Hostility and Mistrust", *International Herald Tribune*, 3 June 2003.

63   Joseph S. Nye, Jr., "Repairing America's Tattered Reputation", *Jakarta Post*, 26 January 2005.

64   For example, it is a commonly accepted idea that the United States is today's only "superpower"; it is likely that one day the U.S. will cease to be seen as a superpower, even though it may still possess the most credible military capability and most efficient economy. There may no objective reason for this change in how people conceive of status of the United States.

65   Stacy Bergstrom Haldi and Ariana Hauck, "Constructing Great Powers", Conference Paper, "Facets of Power in International Relations", Millennium Annual Conference, London School of Economics and Political Science, London, 30–31 October 2004.

66   Nye, "Limits of American Power", p. 553.

67   Hedley Bull, *The Anarchical Society: A Study of Order in World Politics* (London: The Macmillan Press, 1983), pp. 113–14.

68   Daniel Novotny, "The Onset of the American Involvement in Vietnam" (Honours Thesis, Charles University, 2002).

69   James W. Davidson et al., *Nation of Nations: A Narrative History of the American Republic* (New York: McGraw-Hill Publishing, 1990), p. 1199; Ho Chi Minh made this comment at the time when Kennedy Administration decided to commit an increasing number of the U.S. advisors and military personnel to South Vietnam.

70   Joseph Buttinger, *Vietnam: The Unforgettable Tragedy* (London: Andre Deutsch, 1977), pp. 12 and 17.

71   Davidson, et. al., *Nation of Nations*; On the mutual construction of benign images between states, see: Charles A. Kupchan et al., *Power in Transition: The Peaceful Change of International Order* (Tokyo: United Nations University Press, 2001).

72   Barnes, *The Nature of Power*, p. xi.

73   Ibid., pp. 3–4.

74   Ibid., p. xi.

75   Also discussed during the interview with a former Australian Ambassador to Indonesia, Sydney, 25 August 2004.

76   Cited from the interview with Joseph S. Nye, Jr., "Books for Breakfast Program", organized by Carnegie Council (2004), transcript available at <http://www. carnegiecouncil.org/viewMedia.php/prmTemplateID/8/prmID/4466> (accessed 12 October 2006).

77   Nicholas J. Spykman, *America's Strategy in World Politics: The United States and the Balance of Power* (New York: Harcourt, Brace and Company, 1942), p. 22.

78   Stuart N. Soroka, "Media, Public Opinion, and Foreign Policy", *Harvard International Journal of Press-Politics* 8, no. 1 (Winter 2003): 33.

79   In the early 21st century, China and India, the two rising Asian giants, have both been widely identified as potential future superpowers. Both these billion-head states are economically fast-developing, militarily potent, regionally and increasingly internationally assertive and independently-minded powers. Yet, from Washington's perspective, while China is perceived as a threatening and menacing arch-rival, India's image is that of a benign rising power characterized by an unthreatening posture. The U.S. foreign policy has approached to these two "future superpowers" accordingly. For more on this issue, see for instance: Anand Giridharadas, "India Welcomed as New Sort of Superpower", *International Herald Tribune*, 21 July 2005.

80   Some examples are: D.W. Larson, "The Role of Belief Systems and Schemas in Foreign Policy Decision-Making", *Political Psychology* 15, no. 1 (March 1994); Michael Brecher et al., "A Framework for Research on Foreign Policy Behaviour", *Journal of Conflict Resolution* 13, no. 1 (March 1969): 81–86; Judith Goldstein and Robert O. Keohane, eds., *Ideas and Foreign Policy* (Ithaca: Cornell University Press, 1993); Robert Jervis, *Misperception in International Politics* (Princeton: Princeton University Press, 1976); Alexander George, "The Causal Nexus between Cognitive Beliefs and Decision-Making Behaviour: The 'Operational Code' Belief System", in *Psychological Models in International Politics*, edited by Lawrence Falkowski (Boulder: Westview Press, 1979).

81   Steven Spiegel, *The Other Arab-Israeli Conflict: Making America's Middle East Policy from Truman to Reagan* (Chicago: University of Chicago Press, 1985), pp. 381–93.

82   Robert O. Keohane and Joseph S. Nye, Jr., "Power and Independence Revisited", *International Organization* 41, no. 4 (Autumn 1987): 728.

83   Joe Tomaka et al., "Cognitive and Physiological Antecedents of Threat and Challenge Appraisal", *Journal of Personality and Social Psychology* 73, no. 1 (January 1997).

84   One of the main assumptions of realism is the unceasing existence of insecurity (fear) as an important factor in relations between states.

85   Crawford, "The Passion of World Politics", p. 119.

86   Ibid., pp. 125–34; some other works dealing with this problem include: Richard Hermann, "The Power of Perceptions in Foreign-Policy Decision-Making: Do

      Views of the Soviet Union Determine the Policy Choices of American Leaders?",
American Journal of Political Science 30, no. 4 (December 1986): 869; Jervis,
Misperception in International Politics.

[87] Goldstein and Keohane, *Ideas and Foreign Policy*, p. 8.

[88] Barry Buzan, "The Concept of National Security for Developing Countries",
in *Leadership Perceptions and National Security: The Southeast Asian Experience*,
edited by Mohammed Ayoob and Chai-Anan Samudavanija (Singapore: Institute
of Southeast Asian Studies, 1989), p. 2.

[89] Barry Buzan, *People, States and Fear: The National Security Problem in International
Relations* (Sussex: Wheatsheaf Books, 1983).

[90] Quoted from President Sukarno's opening address to the Asian-African
Conference in Bandung in April 1955; Sukarno, "Let a New Asia and Africa
Be Born", in *Indonesian Political Thinking, 1945–1965*, edited by Herbert Feith
and Lance Castles (Ithaca: Cornell University Press, 1970), p. 457.

[91] Crawford, "The Passion of World Politics", p. 139.

[92] Soedjatmoko, "Is America Listening Enough to Asia", Conference Paper,
The United States Information Agency Cultural Affairs Conference, Penang,
13 February 1976.

[93] Gordon Robert Hein, "Soeharto's Foreign Policy: Second-Generation
Nationalism in Indonesia" (Ph.D. Dissertation, University of California, 1986),
p. 36.

[94] Quoted in June Crawford et al., *Emotion and Gender: Constructing Meaning
from Memory* (London: Sage, 1992), p. 24.

[95] George C. Bond and Angela Gilliam, eds., *Social Construction of the Past:
Representation as Power* (London: Routledge, 1994), p. 1.

[96] Dale C. Copeland, "The Constructivist Challenge to Structural Realism",
International Security 25, no. 2 (Fall 2000): 187–212.

[97] Hans J. Morgenthau, *Politics among Nations: The Struggle for Power and Peace*
(New York: Alfred A. Knopf, 1973), pp. 5–6.

[98] Jervis, *Misperception in International Politics*, pp. 3–31.

[99] Cited from: "Indonesia's Perceptions of China and U.S. Security Roles in
East Asia", seminar organized by The Habibie Centre, Jakarta (16 February
2006).

[100] Alexander Wendt, *Social Theory of International Politics* (Cambridge: Cambridge
University Press, 1999), p. 334.

[101] Robert O. Tilman, "The Enemy Beyond: External Threat Perceptions in the
ASEAN Region", Research Notes and Discussions Paper, no. 42 (Singapore:
Institute of Southeast Asian Studies, 1984), p. 2.

[102] Ibid., pp. 2–3.

[103] Ibid., p. 3.

[104] Ibid., pp. 3–5.

[105] Brecher et al., "A Framework for Research on Foreign Policy Behaviour",
pp. 81–86.

[106] James N. Rosenau, "Pre-Theories and Theories of Foreign Policy", in *Approaches to Comparative and International Politics*, edited by Barry R. Farrell (Evanston: North-Western University Press, 1966), pp. 27–92.

[107] Brecher et al., "A Framework for Research on Foreign Policy Behaviour", pp. 81–86.

[108] John Steinbruner, *The Cybernetic Theory of Decision: New Dimensions of Political Analysis* (Princeton: Princeton University Press, 1974), pp. 128–36.

[109] Susan T. Fiske and Susan E. Taylor, *Social Cognition* (Boston: Addison-Wesley, 1984), p. 162.

[110] Jervis, *Misperception in International Politics*, p. 121; see also: Richard Herrman, "The Empirical Challenge of the Cognitive Revolution: A Strategy for Drawing Inferences about Perceptions", *International Studies Quarterly*, No. 32 (1988), p. 185.

[111] Kang, "Getting Asia Wrong", p. 64.

[112] Acharya, "Will Asia's Past Be Its Future?", p. 152.

[113] David C. Kang, "Hierarchy, Balancing, and Empirical Puzzles in Asian International Relations", *International Security* 28, no. 3 (Winter 2003/04): 171.

[114] Walt, *The Origins of Alliances*.

[115] Ibid., p. 263.

[116] Ibid., p. 264.

[117] Spykman, *America's Strategy in World Politics*, pp. 65–67.

[118] Walt, *The Origins of Alliances*, pp. 277–81.

[119] Quentin Skinner, "Machiavelli", in Quentin Skinner et al., *Great Political Thinkers* (Oxford: Oxford University Press, 1992); Thucydides, *History of the Peloponnesian War* (Harmondsworth: Penguin Books, 1972).

[120] Walt, *The Origins of Alliances*, p. 262.

[121] Nye, "Limits of American Power".

[122] The phenomenon of non-traditional sources of threat to national security was also discussed at the conference "Information Revolution Impacts International Relations and Security", Centre for Security Studies, Swiss Federal Institute for Technology and Comparative Interdisciplinary Studies, Lucerne (23–25 May 2005).

[123] Walt, *The Origins of Alliances*, p. 267.

[124] Hobbes, *Leviathan*.

[125] J.W. Burton, *International Relations: A General Theory* (Cambridge: The University Press, 1967), p. 56.

[126] Bull, *The Anarchical Society*, pp. 103–04.

[127] Carr, *The Twenty Years' Crisis 1919–1939*; Morgenthau, *Politics among Nations*.

[128] Berger and Luchmann, *The Social Construction of Reality*.

[129] Walt, *The Origins of Alliances*, p. 264.

[130] Ted Hopf, "The Promise of Constructivism in International Relations Theory", *International Security* 23, no. 1 (Summer 1998); Sorpong Peou, "Realism and

Constructivism in Southeast Asian Security Studies Today: a Review Essay", *The Pacific Review* 15, no. 1 (2002); Rosemary Foot, "The Study of China's International Behaviour: International Relations Approaches", in *Explaining International Relations since 1945*, edited by Ngaire Woods (New York: Oxford University Press, 1996).

131   Hopf, "The Promise of Constructivism in International Relations Theory".
132   Goldstein and Keohane, *Ideas and Foreign Policy*.
133   Foot, "The Study of China's International Behaviour", pp. 259–74.
134   Peou, "Realism and Constructivism in Southeast Asian Security Studies Today", p. 135.
135   Mastanduno, "Preserving the Unipolar Moment".
136   Hopf, "The Promise of Constructivism in International Relations Theory".
137   Wendt, *Social Theory of International Politics*; Copeland, "The Constructivist Challenge to Structural Realism", p. 393.
138   For more on security dilemma and anarchy in international relations, see John H. Herz, "Idealist Internationalism and the Security Dilemma", *World Politics* 2, no. 2 (January 1950): 157–80; Charles L. Glaser, "The Security Dilemma Revisited", *World Politics* 50, no. 2 (October 1997): 171–201.
139   Alexander Wendt, "Anarchy is What States Make of It: the Social Construction of Power Politics", *International Organization* 46, no. 2 (Spring 1992): 396; Wendt, *Social Theory of International Politics*.
140   Karl W. Deutsch, *Nationalism and Social Communication: An Inquiry into the Foundations of Nationality* (New York: The Technology Press of the Massachusetts Institute of Technology and Wiley, 1953); Emanuel Adler and Michael Barnett, eds., *Security Communities* (Cambridge: Cambridge University Press, 1998).
141   Benedict R.O'G. Anderson, *Imagined Communities: Reflections on the Origin and Spread of Nationalism* (London: Verso, 1983); It should be noted that Anderson did not originally formulate the "imagined communities' concept as part of International Relations theory.
142   Wendt, "Anarchy is What States Make of It", p. 395; for the critique of Wendt's book *Social Theory of International Politics*, see: Steve Smith, "Wendt's World", *Review of International Studies* 26, no. 1 (2000): 151–63.
143   Steve Smith, "Reflectivist and Constructivist Approaches to International Theory", in John Baylis and Steve Smith, *The Globalization of World Politics: An Introduction to International Relations*, 2nd edition (Oxford: Oxford University Press, 2001), p. 244.
144   Chris Brown, *Understanding International Relations*, 2nd Edition (New York: Palgrave, 2001), pp. 51–56.
145   Foucault's understanding of power changed throughout his academic career. Generally, in Foucault's view, while "power" is created throughout verbal interaction — a discourse or a conversation, the extent of one's power depends on the kind of knowledge one has; Michel Foucault, *The Will to Knowledge* (London: Penguin, 1990); Michel Foucault, *Discipline and Punish: The Birth*

of the Prison (New York: Random House, 1995); Michel Foucault and Paul Rabinow, eds., *Ethics: Subjectivity and Truth* (New York: The New Press, 1998).

[146] Walt, "International Relations: One World, Many Theories", pp. 38–41.

[147] Alexander Wendt, "Constructing International Politics", in *Theories of War and Peace*, edited by Michael Brown, et al. (Cambridge: The MIT Press, 1998), p. 418.

[148] Bond and Gilliam, *Social Construction of the Past: Representation as Power*, p. 5.

[149] Ibid., pp. 16–17.

[150] Hopf, "The Promise of Constructivism in International Relations Theory".

[151] Walt, "International Relations: One World, Many Theories", p. 41.

[152] Term adopted from: Samuel P. Huntington, "The Lonely Superpower", *Foreign Affairs* (March/April 1999).

[153] John A. Vasquez, *The Power of Power Politics: A Critique* (London: Frances Pinter, 1983), p. 18; Morgenthau, *Politics among Nations*.

[154] For discussion on realism and rationalism, see Sam Roggeveen, "Towards a Liberal Theory of International Relations", *Policy*, The Centre for Independent Studies, Sydney (Autumn 2001), pp. 29–32.

[155] Waltz, *Theory of International Politics*, pp. 80–101; Stanley Hoffmann, *The State of War* (New York: Praeger, 1965), p. 26.

[156] Kenneth W. Waltz, "A Response to My Critics", in *Neorealism and Its Critics*, edited by Robert O. Keohane (New York: Columbia University Press, 1986), p. 329.

[157] For more on the role of internal structure of states in international relations, see: Waltz, *Man, the State, and War*, pp. 80–158.

[158] Robert Jervis, "Cooperation under the Security Dilemma", *World Politics* 30, no. 2 (January 1978): 168.

[159] Karl Marx and Friedrich Engels, *The Communist Manifesto* (London: Penguin, 1985).

[160] Cited from: Beard, *Foreign Policy for America*, p. 9.

[161] Jack S. Levy, "Domestic Politics and War", in *The Origin and Prevention of Major Wars*, edited by Robert I. Rotberg and Theodore K. Raab (Cambridge: Cambridge University Press, 1989), pp. 79–101; Robert Putnam, "Diplomacy and Domestic Politics: The Logic of Two-Level Games", *International Organization* 42, no. 3 (Summer 1988): 427–60.

[162] Leifer, *Indonesia's Foreign Policy;* Jones, *Indonesia: The Possible Dream.*

[163] Jack Snyder, *Myths of Empire: Domestic Politics and International Ambition* (Ithaca: Cornell University Press, 1991).

[164] Fareed Zakaria, "Realism and Domestic Politics", in *The Perils of Anarchy: Contemporary Realism and International Security*, edited by Michael Brown et al. (Cambridge: The MIT Press, 1995).

[165] Walt, *The Origins of Alliances*, pp. 266–69.

[166] Ibid., p. 284.

[167] Ibid., p. 284.
[168] Cited from: Leifer, *Singapore's Foreign Policy*, p. 99.
[169] Foreign Relations of the United States Series, FRUS, 1961–63 XXIII: 149, Embtel 2426 (Jakarta), 23 February 1961; quoted in Aandstad, "United States Policy Towards Indonesia 1961–1965".
[170] Snyder, *Myths of Empire*; Gideon Rose, "Neoclassical Realism and Theories of Foreign Policy", *World Politics* 51, no. 1 (October 1998).
[171] Randall L. Schweller, "Unanswered Threats: A Neoclassical Realist Theory of Underbalancing", *International Security* 29, no. 2 (Fall 2004): 171.
[172] Cited from: ibid., p. 180.
[173] Ibid., p. 181.

3

THE FOREIGN POLICY ELITE
AND INDONESIA'S NATIONAL
INTEREST

INTRODUCTION

In this chapter, we will focus on the concept of the *Indonesian foreign policy elite* whose perceptions are the focal point of this study. There are two terms in the Indonesian language that describe the country's elite. *Pejabat* is a broad term that refers to officials occupying all levels — the lower ranks up to the top ranks — of the government bureaucracy. The term *elit* has similar meaning as the same term in the English language — in Indonesia it is used to describe the most prominent businessmen, military leaders and policy-makers in the bureaucratic hierarchy along with the most influential journalists and intellectuals who maintain close ties with the political establishment.

The existing studies that deal with the "foreign policy elite" look particularly at the issues of elite identity, sources of diversity in the power elite, and the correlation between the elite worldview and the concept of national interests and security.[1] The following discussion will highlight the inherently ambiguous nature of the concept of Indonesia's national interests and security. We will see that the Indonesian elite encompass a variety of diverging views over what actually constitutes and how to defend Indonesia's national interests. The Indonesian elite have been subject to a diversity of ideational influences, which in turn gave rise to a plurality of disparate views and attitudes among the leadership. In contrast to the earlier Sukarno and Suharto regimes, the contemporary Indonesian foreign policy-making is determined by democratic political processes with the direct and indirect participation of a sheer variety of stakeholders who are involved in constant mixed-motive bargaining.

ELITE PERCEPTIONS AND THE CONCEPTION OF NATIONAL INTERESTS AND SECURITY

In general, "national interest" as a concept essentially refers to a goal or set of goals of foreign policy that are universal and static, yet, in the case of any particular state, the actual national interest is both specific and dynamic. It is imperative for a state's elite involved in foreign policy-making and implementation to agree on and formulate a broad end or goal — "national interest" — that will provide a long-term sense of purpose and direction to foreign policy. To this end, the formulation of national interest also involves a delicate process of balancing short-term policy objectives against long-term policy priorities which is often related to the continuous problem of balancing the imperatives of domestic politics and the long-term goals of foreign policy. In case of a possible conflict between the long-term strategic objectives underpinning a state's "national interest" and the elite's short-term immediate goals, it is the former that should guide the decision-makers in the selection of policies.

As we have pointed out in the preceding chapter, "threat" signifies the degree to which the power of a state or non-state actor is perceived by the elite as a malign factor affecting one's country's national interests and, consequently, its national security. To put it succinctly, "something" that goes against what the foreign policy elite perceives as the state's interests is a threat. As a former high-ranking Indonesian Navy official explained:

> [on] the one side, we have the concept of national interest; on the other, we have the perception of the threat, which is made by one particular state. ... This is not happening in a vacuum but in a very dynamic space, which we call international strategic environment. This influences both the [elite's conception of] national interest and the threat perceptions.[2]

Yet, it is important to note that national security and the national interest are subjective and ambiguous concepts underpinned and shaped by deep emotions and loyalties. Both of these concepts have a great variety of meanings, which are determined by perceptions or, in other words, constructions of reality and vulnerabilities in the eyes of an individual policy-maker.[3] Consequently, Buzan claims that national security "... can be used to justify a large number of policies that might either be desired by governments for almost any reason, or simply reflect changes over time in the way a state decides to deal with its problems."[4] There is thus a linkage between leadership perceptions and the management of national security. Since "national security" depends on how one perceives its substance, the concept "does not contain a single coherent strand that connects all [of its] sectors together" and, therefore, it will always remain an "ambiguous symbol".[5]

The "national interest" thus to a great degree depends on who determines its scope and content. In a developing country, such as Indonesia, in the context of the low level of education and political consciousness among the lay people and the ensuing lack of coherent, consistent and rational public opinion, foreign policy decision-making largely remains the prerogative of a relatively small elite group where the personality factor often plays a very important role. Yet, in the democratic form of politics, such as in Indonesia in the post-Suharto period, apart from being moulded by the Foreign Minister, the Cabinet and the President, the foreign policy dynamics are also influenced by various pressure groups and powerful business interests, shaped by the military establishment, tested in the light of (mostly rather passive but at times radical) public opinion, and scrutinized by the media and the political parties.[6]

Post-Suharto Era: Foreign Policy Elite and the Lack of Its Cohesion

In broad terms, the conception of Indonesia's national interests can be expressed by the question "*Apa yang Indonesia inginkan?*" — "What does Indonesia want or wish?"[7] Another definition of "national interest" could also be summed up in the question: "What is Indonesia's highest need in this period of time?"[8] As a high-ranking Indonesian navy officer emphasized, at least theoretically, "foreign policy should be flexible and calculated," whereby all of the government's policies should be designed to support and promote the nation's security and vital interests, in particular the very existence of the Republic, its integrity and sovereignty.[9] As the Navy official also affirmed, "the policy-makers should have a clear definition about national interest. [However] many countries have a difficulty to define a clear national interest."[10]

The rich data yielded by the interviews conducted in Indonesia provide strong evidence that there is a substantial disagreement among the key decision-makers about the conception of the country's national interests and what these and the international context demand. For example, one interviewee affirmed that after Suharto "we are struggling to establish what is our national interest. ... It is an on-going process — we are still discussing it."[11] To this end, Anwar also observed that "competing [Indonesian] elite views of the world and domestic priorities have led to shifts in foreign policy emphasis."[12] We will see in the following chapters that due to the existence of a variety of diverging views over "*Apa yang Indonesia inginkan?*", the elite is deeply divided over the nature and ranking of external threats according to their urgency and potential to adversely affect Indonesia's national security. This plurality of views and the ensuing lack of cohesion within the Indonesian foreign policy elite leads Lanti to conclude that "the notion of a singular Indonesian perception [is] problematic."[13]

The interviewees emphasized that there is a stark difference between the New Order regime and the post-Suharto period in how Indonesian foreign policy was formulated and implemented. During the Cold War, the Indonesian political system was "totalitarian" and it was "very easy to make political decisions" because these were "made by a limited sort of elite."[14] Hein described the predominant role of President Suharto in the decision-making process as follows:

> ... he sets the tone and the boundaries of foreign policy debate in Indonesia and controls the structures and processes of foreign policy-making through a complex system of institutional and personal linkages. Many groups provide policy input, including the Parliament, Muslim leaders, the press, the political parties, and, especially, the Armed Forces and the Foreign Ministry, but in the end it is Suharto's foreign policy. ... President Suharto himself is in charge of foreign affairs.[15]

By contrast, Indonesia has since the fall of the Suharto regime in 1998 undergone an enormous transformation of its society and political system. In the early 21st century, the country has a plural, open society comprising different competing groups that hold different views and attitudes. One respondent observed that "in Indonesia, if you have a group of leaders articulating one policy, [concurrently], you have another group of people who have a different agenda."[16] Thus, when in March 2008 President Yudhoyono — for the first time in Indonesia's history — signed a Presidential Regulation on the establishment of the position of Deputy Minister of Foreign Affairs, this step was undertaken in part because, according to a member of the DPR's Foreign Affairs Commission, "[the] President's foreign affairs policy line is not necessarily correct in the eyes of the Foreign Minister, likewise the other way round."[17]

Another interviewed leader judged that the elite represents so many diverging views owing to President Yudhoyono's lack of leadership in contrast to his much more respected predecessors, President Sukarno and Suharto.[18] A senior diplomat with a deep knowledge in foreign policy-making process in Indonesia explained:

> Of course, in the foreign policy establishment … if you interview different individuals, then you have certain attitudes. For example, if you were to interview someone with strong views, especially from the Islamic groupings, they would cite no doubt the United States as a source of threat. Australia probably would also figure high there as well.[19]

On the other hand, it has been argued that, for example, "people from DEPLU are more sophisticated" and this is why they tend to have more nuanced and balanced perceptions of external threats.[20] One respondent likened the "mixed and diverse views" of the elite to the popular Indonesian dishes called "*gado-gado*" or "*rujak*" because of the wide range of ingredients used to prepare them.[21]

FOREIGN POLICY ELITE: THE DEFINITION AND RESEARCH METHOD

This study employs a leader-centric approach, which is concerned with how key decision-makers influence the foreign policy-making process. The analysis of the nation's elite is "a dominant practice in the study of Indonesian political life"[22], which was established by earlier works done by Kahin and Feith.[23] Suryadinata pointedly argues that "the difficulty … is in determining whose perceptions should be accepted as valid. … It is reasonable to assume that the perceptions of Indonesian leaders responsible for formulating foreign policy are the crucial ones."[24] There are at least three approaches that can be employed to analyse the way in which foreign policy is formulated and the role of different decision-makers in the process: "the concentric circle approach", "the elite versus participatory policy-making approach" and "the system-analysis approach".[25]

The first approach assumes that while the most senior leaders stand at the centre of the foreign policy decision-making, the wider circles play a much less significant role as its sources. Therefore, this approach essentially disregards the role of, for example, civilians, NGOs and think-tanks, in policy formulation. The second approach is premised on the idea that foreign policy is developed by the elite, which must in turn strive to develop support for a particular policy with the public. By contrast, the third approach is based on the assumption that foreign policy-making is determined by a variety of inputs from many different actors.[26]

Feith uses the image of a set of three concentric circles in his analysis of the role of individuals in the political process in Indonesia in the lead-up to Guided Democracy. In this schema, the *inner circle* constitutes the political elite, the *middle circle* represents men of lesser political influence and, finally, the *outer circle* includes all those remaining individuals with the least influence on the political process.[27] Perhaps the most important research on the Indonesian elite's perceptions of the world to date was published by Franklin B. Weinstein.[28] For Weinstein, the foreign policy elite includes only all the most influential leaders involved in the formulation of Indonesia's foreign relations. It is because "the top elite's experiences tend to differ significantly" from those of Indonesian Government officials, policy-makers, and diplomats from the middle echelons of power.[29] Conversely, Putnam argues for the employment of an analytical framework that would take into consideration the sheer diversity of influences on foreign policy-making. Putnam suggests that

> [a] more adequate account of the domestic determinants of foreign policy and international relations must stress politics: parties, social classes, interest groups (both economic and non-economic), legislators, and even public opinion and elections, not simply executive officials and institutional arrangements.[30]

In contrast to Feith's Indonesian elite analysis, the "three concentric circle" approach could hardly be applied in this study. The explanation lies in the fact that whereas Feith's and Kahin's studies were concerned mostly with domestic political processes, this book focuses on the process of Indonesian foreign policy formation. The public tends to be more familiar with domestic political affairs than with its government's foreign policy. Citizens have generally less access to relevant and factual information on foreign affairs than domestic, which might also result in a greater scope for the manipulation of public opinion by the elite. The lay people thus tend to have a rather limited influence on the foreign policy decision-making process, leaving this "business" to "experts" who have more factual knowledge about and extensive experience in international relations. Weinstein's approach would also not be viable in the case of this study because of the distinct character of the New Order regime where foreign policy formulation was heavily dominated by the military and particularly President Suharto.

In this book, the concept of the foreign policy elite takes into account the plural and competitive democratic environment in post-Suharto Indonesia. It could be argued that this study combines "the concentric circle approach"and "the system-analysis approach". The primary focus here is on the "inner circle" and, to some degree, on the "middle circle" in Feith's analysis. The study is principally concerned with the most influential leaders and their perceptions to the exclusion of Indonesians at the middle and lower levels of governmental administration, as well as the country's two-hundred-thirty-million population. It is believed that perceptions of the middle and lower level government bureaucrats differ significantly from those of top elite echelons of power. Since the latter, the senior policy-makers exercise a much greater influence on the foreign policy-making process, their perceptions are the focal point of this research.

An analysis of elite perceptions needs to take into consideration the bureaucratic and political mechanism through which foreign policy is devised and implemented. Tilman correctly argues that

> Central to this is the question "Who makes policy?" ... the foreign affairs bureaucracy may selectively gather, filter, or subtly alter the messages it transmits to the policy-makers on top. There also will be persons who influence the policy-makers in one, several, or all areas, and these persons may be inside or outside the government.[31]

According to one respondent, "traditionally, the [Indonesian] foreign policy elite comprised of the military, foreign ministry, nationalist elite."[32] Another leader argued that the contemporary Indonesian foreign policy elite could be described as a triangle comprising business circles, military establishment and Islamic movements. These three main elements of Indonesian society are closely interconnected and exercise a profound effect on the direction of the country's foreign policy.[33]

Based on extensive discussions with the respondents about the question "Who makes foreign policy in Indonesia?", we can identify the following main elements of the elite, ranked in terms of the degree of their influence on the foreign policy:

(1) President and the Cabinet;
(2) Department of Foreign Affairs, or DEPLU (giving input to the President);
(3) other governmental institutions and Departments and the military;
(4) the Parliament, or DPR, in which interests of different political parties are represented (though not all policies need to be approved by DPR);

(5) other actors outside the government (namely the academic community, think-tanks, journalists, business community).[34]

For the purpose of this study, the target group, the Indonesian foreign policy elite (hereafter also referred to as "the elite"), is defined as a group of individuals with the utmost influence on the foreign policy-making.[35] While putting considerably more emphasis on the most influential decision-makers, the inquiry also takes into account the input from individuals outside the government. But how can we justify the inclusion into the analysis of journalists, economists, and academics who are not directly and institutionally involved in the foreign policy-making process? Firstly, as pointed out earlier, in the context of the plural political system and highly competitive democratic environment in post-Suharto Indonesia, this book defines the "foreign policy elite" in broader terms that go beyond a mere focus on the government bureaucrats. Secondly, specifically in the Indonesian case, it can be argued that there exists a close nexus between the country's respected journalists and academics and its political establishment. This relatively close connection is defined by an intriguing network of personal contacts, informal communication, and by two-way cross-fertilization of ideas and information between the country's political elite and its intellectual elite (e.g., academics and journalists). Thirdly, a significant part of the respondents have throughout their professional careers moved between different institutions both inside and outside the government. For example, one interviewed prominent journalist was also an influential diplomat and senior member of a political party. Some senior Indonesian diplomats are concurrently active in academia — they publish regularly and lecture at local universities.

ELITE HETEROGENEITY AND DIVISION: THE ROOTS

While briefly examining the historical roots of the heterogeneity among the Indonesian leadership and elite groups, this section identifies cultural and educational influences that have contributed to the ideational differences related to the modern Indonesian leaders' worldview and attitudes. In a broader sense, the origins of the contemporary Indonesian elite extend as far as primordial aristocratic families in Javanese polities and later Dutch colonial bureaucracies. Feith observed that, by the end of the 1950s, Indonesia's broader elite comprised about "200–500 persons, mainly Jakarta residents".[36] The number has certainly expanded over the last four decades, while the elite's members with direct influence in the foreign policy formation have varied significantly from one political regime to another.

The *Priyayi* Concept

Some academic literature suggests that the Indonesian elite is formed by a social class often referred to as the *priyayi*. Clifford Geertz defines *priyayi* as an appointive, salaried civil service, whose origins can be traced back to the Hindu-Javanese courts of pre-colonial times. This former Java-governing upper class and social elite was set apart from the rest of the society, in Geertz's trichotomic terms represented by the *abangan*[37] and the *santri*,[38] by its refined politeness, mastering of highly sophisticated arts, and adhering to Hindu-Buddhist mysticism.[39]

The contemporary white-collar elite, albeit it has been considerably Westernized and access to it made easier for the *wong cilik*, or "little people", has retained some of the traditions passed down through generations from the former, pre-colonial hereditary aristocracy. Although the largely secularized, often Western-educated and somewhat anti-traditional "modern" Indonesian political elite have gradually increased its prominence, the *priyayi* worldview and style of life remain "the model not only for the elite but in many ways for the entire society."[40]

For Emmerson and other scholars, Geertz's dichotomic definition of the term *priyayi* is problematic in that it combines two dimensions, status and religion. From the perspective of the Javanese themselves, beneath the *priyayi* elite social class are not *abangan* and *santri* individuals but the ordinary people. On the other hand, in terms of religious views, the *priyayi* social elite include not only individuals adhering to the Hindu-Buddhist tradition, but also those who are secular or fall into the *santri* or *abangan* religious tradition.[41] Sutherland even evokes a possible division of the governing elite into two segments she classifies as "*santri priyayi*" and "*abangan priyayi*".[42]

To obtain a complete picture, however, we also have to highlight the Islamic leadership as another group that effectively constituted a major non-*priyayi* section of the native Indonesian elite during the colonial era. Devout, self-consciously non-syncretic Muslims, also known as the *santri*, could be, according to Clifford Geertz, associated mainly with the Javanese trading element. The main attributes of the *santri* leaders, who were recruited mainly from richer peasants, traders and Islamic teachers known as *kiyayi*, were their strong connection with the world's Muslim community and arising from their great respect and substantial influence within the native Muslim population.[43] Because of their access to information and possession of the interpretative framework, the *santri* leadership was able to exert a substantial control over public opinion. It can be reasonably assumed that the roots of the Islamic element within the contemporary Indonesian elite can be related to the colonial-era *santri leadership.*

Education and the Expansion of the Native Elite

The *priyayi* social status was not entirely determined by birth into one of the upper-class aristocratic families. In fact, most of the *priyayi* did not come from the highly refined *kraton* aristocracy, but rather originated from the rural gentry. The *priyayi* status was thus also gained based on the individual's administrative position. It was during the Dutch colonial era that the local gentry and lower aristocracy of Java's earlier independent kingdoms were gradually transformed into the corps of native civil service. This *Pangreh Praja*, or the "Rulers of the Realm", as they were known, effectively functioned as subordinate agents of the Dutch colonial government, bridging the gap between the new alien masters and the common people. While progressively adopting the Western "rational" bureaucratic model and later being exposed to Western education, the elite also constituted a force that perpetuated indigenous aristocratic traditions. Over the course of some three centuries, the East Indies' native civil service evolved from disorganized and inefficient local networks into a highly organized bureaucratic system of about fifteen hundred career officials.[44]

Against the background of large-scale economic development and the Indonesian population's increasing exposure to European influences, the late 19th and early 20th century brought a change to the hitherto deep-rooted dominant position of Java's indigenous upper-class aristocratic governing elite. The challenge came from new, often non-aristocratic, native leadership groupings that emerged in the Netherlands East Indies. The main impetus for this social change arose from the Dutch colonial government's attempt to gradually adjust its attitudes and policies to the new economic, social and political realities in the archipelago. With the intensified economic development, the burgeoning new enterprises generated increased qualitative and quantitative demands on the government services. There was a heightened pressure on both the Dutch and the native civil service, firstly, to expand their numbers and, secondly, to enhance the quality of their skills, efficiency and overall performance. To meet the needs for the emerging new style of government, several educational institutions catering for the European civil service, known as the *Binnenlandsch Bestuur*, were operating in colonial Java throughout most of the 19th century. Concurrently, it became ever more obvious that the changed economic, social and political conditions necessitated the introduction of Western-style education also for native officials. Previously, only children of Europeans, also referred to as the *Indos*, and upper-class or wealthy native Indonesians were allowed to enter Dutch-language schools.

Then in the late 1870s, the *hoofdenscholen* (chiefs' schools) were constituted in Java by the turn of the century renamed as *Opleidingscholen voor Inlandsche Ambtenaren* (OSVIA, or Training School for Native Officials).[45] These educational institutions were originally designed to teach the native governmental corps general curriculum, but later also introduced more focused subjects providing them with a specialized administrative training. Between the late 19th century and the 1940s, the composition of the native elite underwent a significant transformation. Owing to several factors, particularly the increasing educational emphasis, a growing number of people from lower-class non-aristocratic backgrounds, namely ordinary civil servants, upper bourgeoisie, other well-to-do families and even some from the *santri* community, were steadily entering the hitherto upper-class aristocrat-dominated *priyayi* elite. By the turn of the century, as birth was no longer the major prerequisite for acceptance into the OSVIA, an increasing number of students in these educational institutions were drawn from the nonhereditary middle and lower ranks of the *priyayi*. The extension of Western-style education to the nonhereditary, non-aristocratic, *priyayi* and common people enabled these low and medium-class individuals to enter the native civil service corps, thus increasingly challenging the prevailing tendency to hereditary appointment of government officials. While in the past there was a strong correlation between the *priyayi* and the Javanese aristocracy, by the turn of the century the scope of the *priyayi* elite had begun to expand beyond the nobility in the highly elevated strata of the society. According to Damono, by the 1950s, lay people were trying to upgrade their social status to become *priyayi* by getting more educated, by working in the government/military establishment or by getting a *pekerjaan halus* — a "soft job" working in the office. He argues that those people who were trying to get a better education to become *priyayi* then became the so-called *"priyayi abangan"*.[46]

Aside from the access to Western education, this relative upward social mobility of the lesser *priyayi* was underpinned by two important factors. One was the trend toward direct communication between the Dutch colonial Administration and the lesser *priyayi* officials, which prompted a much closer identification of the latter with the European-led central Administration in Batavia. The second factor was an increasing awareness of the lesser officials, now well-educated and equipped with Western liberal-democratic ideas, of a social gap between themselves and their colleagues from noble or well-to-do families who, though often less capable, were traditionally entitled to keep the top ranks of the bureaucratic hierarchy. This realization produced intense resentment among the lower and middle-class *priyayi*, resulting in their strong aspiration for an administrative empowerment and elevated social status.[47] Sutherland observed that "the new tactic for dealing with over-educated *priyayi* was simply to speed their progress through the ranks."[48]

From the mid-1920s, the nationalist movement was increasingly dominated by secular politicians originating from the *priyayi* administrative background and intelligentsia, whose worldview was shaped by ideas inherent to Western liberalism or Marxism.[49] It is obvious that education served as a powerful stimulus to the national awakening and provided the nationalist movement in the East Indies with a vigorous momentum. As Wilson notes, "the value of western education became apparent to many. ... Indonesian nationalists resolved to establish private schools, not only to educate but to influence young minds as well," stressing that these were based on western foundations and traditional values.[50] For the "matter-of-fact Hatta", education of nationalist cadres was important to achieve a united Indonesia. By contrast, "the far more flamboyant Sukarno" stressed the importance of his impressive oratorical skills to be used for constant agitation and mesmerizing the masses.[51]

Education played a crucial role in facilitating the emergence of the new, often non-aristocratic, native leadership groupings in the early 20th century. The increasing number of schools enabled a growing number of Indonesians from lower classes access to Western education. Along with the now well-educated lesser *priyayi* officials, this process gave rise to yet a new element in the native society — the intelligentsia. Since birth was crucial in obtaining education, the members of intelligentsia largely originated in *priyayi* circles. They had moved out of the framework of the *Pangreh Praja* and also the traditional culture to work as professionals, notably teachers or journalists, in the embryonic middle-class institutions on the periphery of the indigenous and colonial society.[52] The native officials and intelligentsia — the old and the new *priyayi* — differed in one fundamental point: while the former supported the status quo, the latter, the victims of discrimination, were critical of the entrenched system, desiring the established elite's social acceptance. Sutherland writes that it was "this latter group, like the non-administrative *priyayi*, [that] was particularly susceptible to the appeal of democratic thought or criticism of elevated incompetents."[53]

In short, the first modern Indonesian elite were essentially established through the evolutionary process of re-stratification within the *priyayi* class, as well as between the former and the middle-to-lower strata of the society. The formation of the non-hereditary lesser *priyayi* elite, largely comprised of newly Western-educated native civil servants, professionals and intellectuals, effectively undermined the hitherto dominant position of the hereditary aristocratic ruling class. As a consequence, while the status of the lower *priyayi* was gradually rising, the standing and prestige of the upper *priyayi* was generally declining.[54]

ELITE HETEROGENEITY: THE KEY FACTORS

In the decades leading up to the proclamation of independent Indonesia, many Indonesians of non-aristocratic background, notably those who were fortunate enough to obtain Western education, were gradually absorbed into the higher echelons of the government. Clifford Geertz points out that this new elite was "not really a new elite, but rather an extension of the old."[55] After 1949, according to Robison, "political power was secured by secular elites whose power base lay initially within mass-based parties and, from 1957 onwards, increasingly within the military."[56] In the following discussion, we will point to the elite's educational background and its religious beliefs as the most important ideational influences that have contributed to the plurality of views and attitudes among the leadership.

The Elite's Educational Background

Education is an important factor contributing to elite heterogeneity. The interviewed leaders pointed to educational background as the determinant that has the potency to shape elite perceptions. It was suggested that threat perceptions among the foreign policy elite differ from those among the wider public. One respondent affirmed that "with better and higher education you tend to take a more long-term view [and you do not] short-sightedly say that a country is a threat."[57] The substantial variety of educational influences among the Indonesian foreign policy elite circles is one of the principal reasons underlying the high level of heterogeneity in elite views and attitudes.

It was suggested that the higher the academic degree the policymaker or diplomat attained, and particularly those obtained from overseas universities, the more integrated, balanced and comprehensive their worldview and the more stable and consistent their perceptions and attitudes with respect to their country's national interests and security. For example, one leader argued that, owing to a different educational background, "people from DEPLU are more sophisticated, they think in terms of comprehensive security." By contrast, "military people think in terms of the military security."[58] Moreover, since the educational emphasis and content in schools and universities tend to change with time and space, "the perceptions among the older and younger generation are different."[59]

No analysis about the role of education in influencing Indonesian elite perceptions would be complete without outlining the U.S.-sponsored effort to create a "modernizing elite" for Indonesia.[60] This is not intended to overstate the role of Western education in shaping the leaders' perceptions but rather to outline one of a number of ideational influences that have contributed to the heterogeneity of the elite and helped form its worldview. From the early 1950s, a U.S.-based private aid agency, the billion-dollar Ford Foundation, through some of the best American universities, provided funding to "remould the old Indonesian hierarchs into modern administrators [and] trained [them] work under the new indirect rule of the Americans."[61] Inspired by the thesis that "education had long been an arm of statecraft" and in an attempt to actively counter "communist aggression" in Southeast Asia, the agency enabled hundreds of prospective Indonesian politicians, economists and high-ranking military officials to study at Berkeley, MIT, Cornell, Harvard and other prestigious universities. John Howard, a long-time director in the Ford Foundation, explains that up to mid 1960s, "it was training the guys who would be leading the country when Sukarno got out."[62]

At least ten Indonesian leaders out of forty-five interviewed were educated at prestigious American universities, notably Stanford University, United States Military Academy at West Point, University of Chicago, University of California at Berkeley and others. To the author's knowledge, all of these interviewees participated in the Ford Foundation or other U.S.-funded programmes. Most of them have at some stage occupied a high position in the bureaucratic hierarchy. For example, two interviewed leaders who graduated from the University of California have respectively served as a minister in Suharto's governments and an Indonesian ambassador to the U.S.

Education, especially the expansion of the state school system, was also the most important cause behind the changes in the 1970s when the *santri*-versus-*abangan* and modernist-versus-traditionalist categories began to break down.[63] The Western-style education offered by the state schools provided those students aspiring to attain a modern life-style including an urban white-collar job with, in the Western sense, a more rational and scientifically-minded instruction. Concurrently, however, the compulsory and extensive religious instruction in all these schools, in combination with an increasing number of Islamic schools, produced a more complex and complicated Indonesian worldview. According to Liddle, this situation led to the boundary between modernism and traditionalism in Islam in Indonesia becoming increasingly blurred.[64]

The different educational backgrounds have the potency to affect the leaders' religious beliefs and, consequently, the way they perceive the outside world. This led one leader to argue that "the more educated the Muslim, the more he is realistic."[65] For example, the glaring contrast between the education of Islamic leaders on the one hand and the nationalist leaders on the other can be seen as an important cause of the Islam-nationalist discord and rivalry. As Buchori explains, the main difference stems from the fact that

> Whereas the Koran education introduced Islamic scholars solely to an Islamic orientation of life, the basically secular education of nationalist leaders provided them with a repertoire of knowledge anchored in Western culture. Thus whereas subjects like natural sciences and Western languages were alien to the Islamic leaders of that time, the nationalist leaders were ignorant about ideals of society based on Islam.[66]

The education in *madrasah* and *pesantren* is dominated by instruction in Islamic theology, which on the whole fosters dislike and suspicion of everything Western. By contrast, the nationalist leaders have largely been exposed to the curriculum that provides them with a much broader and balanced knowledge including that about Western culture and values. The different cultural orientation of these two educational systems has produced what Buchori describes as "the mental wall that divides the Islamic and nationalist communities."[67]

When explaining the role of education in fostering the religious divide within the Indonesian elite, a Muslim leader drew on his own experience:

> Although I undertook my undergraduate study in Medina, Saudi Arabia, I had the opportunity to pursue my postgraduate study at Al-Azhar University in Cairo, Egypt. This has given me the opportunity to expand my understanding of Islam and made me a broad-minded person with more balanced and nuanced views.[68]

Hence, we can for instance question the extent, to which the ostentatious anti-Americanism among the leaders of the PKS political party are caused by the fact that most of them hold a degree from Middle Eastern universities, only a few from European universities, and supposedly none of them have been educated in the United States.[69] One interviewee responded to this question in an ambiguous fashion: "It is true to some extent ... of course, not absolutely."[70] The impact of overseas education on the Muslim leaders' worldview remains an issue that needs to be comprehensively addressed by future research.

With regards to education, the data collected during the field research suggest that the diversity of elite perceptions may be accentuated by yet another distinct factor. Several respondents argued that the lack of a reading habit among the nation's elite (and the Indonesian population in general) be taken into account in any assessment of the leaders' perceptions. Since the members of the elite "do not read", it is "easy to influence" their opinions and perceptions.[71] According to another leader, generally speaking, "in Indonesia, people use 'hearsay'." Their learning approach could be summed up as "I heard that people say…"[72] It was also suggested that Indonesian leaders are "good storytellers" but the lack of reading habit contributes to the fact that they [do not] have "much reflective analysis. … [Particularly] those leaders who are 'local products', they do not have an analytical grasp."[73] As a result, Indonesian elite perceptions tend to be fickle. A high-ranking diplomat, for example, raised this issue expressing his bewilderment at the fact that "many of these people don't read … do not read whatever."[74] Describing the Indonesian elite as "wild", he also emphasized the leaders' inability to conduct a fruitful and enriching discussion because of their propensity to lead a monologue or one-way dialogue with others. The lack of reading habit results in the elite's insufficient knowledge of both Indonesian and world history. As he further explains, Indonesian leaders embody

> an aristocratic culture. They do not listen to people. … When you attend seminars, dialogues in Jakarta, it's always full. Why? Because people want to have a short-cut. [The foreign policy decision-making is] really wild guesses, really not based on solid assessment in terms of intellectual scrutiny or really willingness to discuss.[75]

Another leader agreed by pointing out that "if we organize a talk show, people do not come to discuss but by attending a seminar to learn something quickly."[76]

In contrast to the foreign policy elite, it is argued that most lay people are inclined to rely on media consumption rather than on personal experience and thorough reflective analysis for information on foreign affairs.[77] Soroka found that "interestingly, actual events themselves had no significant impact on opinion, but rather the media's interpretation of the events mattered. … threatening events by themselves matter less than how events are interpreted."[78] The research data, however, indicate that the Indonesian leader may put more emphasis on media consumption than on their own analytical grasp. Referring principally to the influence of media coverage on policy-makers' and diplomats' perceptions, Jervis propounds that their respective countries would benefit considerably if the decision makers thought through the basics more self-consciously.[79] In other words, individuals who wield power over foreign policy outcomes should be more conscious of their acts and states of mind. Rather than relying on media consumption and other auxiliary sources of information, they should rely more on their own judgements based on solid knowledge, which they have acquired through personal experience and study of relevant information. The idea that a lack of a reading habit has a substantial impact on the Indonesian elite's perceptions also needs to be tested by further research. However, the very fact that this issue was spontaneously raised by individuals with intimate experience in foreign policy decision-making indicates that it is of a great concern to them. The notion of Indonesian policy-makers and senior diplomats making decisions without sound data and relevant information means that, as a leader affirmed, "you can create all sorts of dangers in our diplomatic relations."[80]

The Elite's Religious Divide

Conflict along religious and ideological fault lines has been an innate aspect of political life in Indonesia at least since the 1920s, the early days of the nationalist movement.[81] The religious tradition plays an important role in the formulation and preservation of broad ethics and values in a particular society. As McVey puts it, "belief systems ... establish what is known and worth knowing; they set our cultural paradigms and explain the meaning of our lives."[82] We should ask here, however, to what degree do elite religious beliefs affect the Indonesian leaders' perceptions and, in the end, the selection of policies?[83]

It has been a long-term policy of consecutive Indonesian Administrations to maintain an image of a religiously homogenous and cohesive political establishment. The administrations have sought to prevent any religious divide among the country's foreign policy establishment from becoming apparent. Officially, the Muslim and non-Muslim members of the elite are deemed to share essentially the same perceptions of other countries and external security threats in general. During the research survey in Jakarta, the author suggested to several respondents a possible religious divide among the country's foreign policy elite. All of those presented with this hypothesis strongly rejected the notion of religion playing an important role in shaping the elite's perceptions of external threats. Religious divisions among the elite turned out to be one of the main challenges in data collection and evaluation. The author was faced with the dilemma of how to categorize the religious composition of the research sample so as to truthfully represent the religious make-up of the Indonesian foreign policy elite. In particular, there was a problem determining the accurate method of establishing the religious disposition or the level of religious devotedness of an individual policymaker, diplomat or journalist.

The discussion on the origins of the Indonesian elite earlier in the chapter drew attention to the dispute over Geertz's dichotomic definition of the term *priyayi*.[84] Some scholars point out that the *santri — abangan — priyayi* trichotomy is rather inaccurate and confusing for it mixes up religious traditions and social classes. As to the latter term, *priyayi* has traditionally referred to social division of Java's polities, namely to Java's governing upper class. Contrary to Geertz's argument, *priyayi* does not only include individuals adhering to the Hindu-Buddhist religio-cultural tradition. Java's social elite, both those originating in the highly refined *kraton* aristocracy and rural gentry, could effectively be followers of either *santri* or *abangan* traditions.[85] If we talk about the origins of today's Indonesian foreign policy elite, however, we should not fail to include two sources of its non-*priyayi* element. Firstly, the elite's Islamic component, which has evolved largely from the former *santri* Islamic leadership comprised of richer peasants, traders and Islamic teachers known as *kiyayi*. Secondly, the strong non-Islamic tradition that was almost non-existent among the *priyayi* ruling elite in the colonial Java, but that is relatively amply represented among the contemporary, modern Indonesian elite.

In the latter case, the non-Islamic element basically refers to those individuals who do not follow either the *santri* or *abangan* religious-cultural tradition. This section of the elite principally includes adherents of one of the branches within the Catholic or Protestant Church, or persons whose religious preferences cannot be clearly identified. The second group can be viewed as generally comprising non-conformist freethinkers or sceptics who form their own opinions about religious affairs. We can reasonably assume that the latter group has gradually emerged with the process of modernization that introduced a Western life style and modes of thinking into Indonesian cities and urban areas in general.[86] Further complicating the task of dividing the foreign policy elite in terms of the leaders' religious affiliation are the complexities of Islamic political thought. Feith and Castles identified five main streams of political thought in Indonesia between 1945 and 1965 — communism, democratic socialism, Islam, Javanese traditionalism and radical nationalism.[87] Yet, there is a large number of streams within Islamic political thought that substantially overlap with other perspectives mentioned above. There have, for example, been strong tendencies towards the blurring of the distinction between *santri* and *abangan* in the process that is also known as *santrinisation*.[88] The blurred confines between the Islamic and other perspectives mean that, for example, an Indonesian leader educated in an Islamic boarding school can also be a fervent nationalist strongly adhering to Javanese traditional values.

Similar difficulties seem to have plagued a number of scholars who have in the past examined the religious phenomena in Java. Raffles, Peacock, Geertz and others each utilized different approaches in exploring the religious practices in Java and their respective studies have tended to come to somewhat different conclusions.[89] The explanation partially lies in the fact that the religious beliefs of an individual, whether a Muslim or a non-Muslim, is basically a very private, intimate affair and hence is subject to different interpretations. As Jamhari points out,

> Javanese people consider that the spiritual quality of religiosity depends heavily on personal experience, [and that is why] the studies of religion in Java have to deal with the interpretation of the social and religious experience of people who practice the religion.[90]

And the difficulty with evaluating spiritual beliefs becomes ever more obvious if we closely look at the tortuous intellectual and spiritual journeys of some Indonesian leaders. Hanifah, for example, originally "was one of the few who stayed with the Moslem faith"[91] but later became somewhat estranged from Islam during his student years. In particular during his career as an Indonesian diplomat, he immersed himself into the wide range of Western philosophical and religious experience, only to later return to the religion of his birth, though now with an entirely different frame of mind — as a modern and liberal Muslim.[92]

Likewise, it would probably be an insurmountable task to categorize the quality of Sukarno's religious beliefs. On the one hand, he claimed to have discovered Islam at the age of fifteen, yet "it wasn't until [he] was put in jail that [he] really and truly found Islam. It was there [he] became a real believer."[93] On the other hand, nationalist leaders close to Sukarno point out that the first Indonesian President's intriguing personality was underscored by his syncretic religious beliefs. His concepts, such as *Marhaenism* or *Nasakom*,[94] epitomize Sukarno's attempt at blending religion with Marxism-Leninism and indigenous socio-political elements. "I consider Nationalism much better for Indonesia than Islam. ... I consider Digul much more important than Mecca," asserted Sukarno leaving nobody in doubts of his incorrigible syncretic religious disposition.[95] Later, in 1965,

President Sukarno issued a presidential decree providing for an official recognition of six religions, namely Islam, Protestantism, Catholicism, Buddhism, Hinduism and Confucianism.[96] According to the latest official census conducted in 2000, the majority Muslim community accounts for 88.22 per cent of the country's population. This makes Indonesia the world's most populous Muslim country. Besides the overwhelming Muslim majority, around 9 per cent label themselves as either Protestant or Catholic and the rest of the Indonesian population are adherents of Hindu, Buddhist and other faiths.[97]

The obvious question that presents itself here is whether the religious make-up of the Indonesian foreign policy elite corresponds with that of the Indonesian public. While the following discussion does not give a definite answer, it will provide some evidence to support the assumption that the moderate Muslim and non-Muslim elements within the elite have generally exerted a disproportionately high influence on the foreign policy-making process. The first elite during the Constitutional democracy in the period of 1950 to 1957 was largely educated in Western (as distinct from Islamic) schools and universities.[98] Many members of the old elite from the Dutch and Japanese colonial era later consolidated their positions in the first years of independent Indonesia. They subsequently instituted a new extensive elite political class, from which the new independent Indonesian state drew its officials and senior military officers for its embryonic armed forces. According to Said, the first elite in Indonesia was comprised of three main elements, which could be characterized as the *priyayi*, the Christians and the secularists. The top leadership of the Indonesian Armed Forces was dominated by high-ranking military officers of Christian and moderate Muslim background until the 1980s.[99] It has been observed that, in the mid-1970s,

> within the core institutions of the state, devout Muslims had been marginalized, sometimes to the point of exclusion. Javanese Muslims and Christians dominated the armed forces and the intelligence apparatus was under the sway of Ali Moertopo ... The key political think tank, Moertopo's Centre for Strategic and International Studies (CSIS), was effectively run by Chinese and Catholics. Golkar, too, preferred Christians and nominal Muslims, leaving many devout Muslim figures who had thrown in their lot with the government out in the cold.[100]

The changing religious composition of the Indonesian military leadership, which dominated the foreign policy-making during the Suharto regime, illustrates the close relationship between religion and education. It was in the early 1950s that Wahid Hashim, the father of President Wahid, began to encourage Muslims to enter government schools and enter the Indonesian military forces. Since it took the Muslims six years to complete elementary school, another six years to complete a high school and yet three to six more years to graduate from a university, it was not until around 1968 that, in Said's words, "we started seeing people in the government using neck ties, veils and praying."[101] In 1957, the Military Academy was opened and from the beginning was attended by more devout Muslims. Therefore, it was only after some two decades of Christian and Muslim *abangan* domination that in the 1970s the first Directors General of Muslim background appeared on the scene — a process called *"penghijauan"*, or *"greenization"*.[102] Then, more than twenty years after the first Muslims entered the Military Academy, "around 1981 we start seeing people of Muslim background becoming generals, in military bases mosques sprang up."[103] Said concludes that "it took the indigenous (Muslim — author's remark) army personnel forty years to reach the highest ranks."[104]

Although leaders of Muslim background at present constitute the majority of the foreign policy elite, it was argued during the series of interviews that Muslim *abangan*, non-Muslim and secular elements[105] in the elite exercise a disproportionately strong influence on the Indonesian foreign policy. One justification given for this assertion was the widespread view that the non-Muslim elite is more likely to have "a better education, more nuanced view [and thus is] more sophisticated and more upwardly mobile."[106] It was also pointed out that religion as a factor shaping elite perceptions clearly matters because, in contrast to the prevailing attitudes in the elite circles, "the Indonesian-Christian elite feel it has closer ideology to the West."[107] Moreover, according to Suryadinata, "the dominant political sub-culture, the *abangan/Pancasila* culture, was consequently reflected in Indonesia's foreign policy."[108] He also observed that the fact that *abangan* and secular nationalists are essentially dominant among the top decision-makers contributes to "the 'non-Islamic' character of Indonesia's foreign policy up to present."[109] To use Suryadinata's study of the backgrounds of Indonesia's Prime Ministers, Foreign Ministers and other most influential policy-makers, Adam Malik, Mochtar Kusumaatmadja and Ali Alatas were all "Western-educated 'secular nationalists'" and the DEPLU has for the most part been dominated by civilian career diplomats.[110]

Accepting as valid the assumption about the disproportionately high influence of the non-Muslim leaders, the author deliberately sought to include a substantially high proportion of the non-Muslim elite into the survey research sample. As Figure 3.1. shows, the non-Muslim respondents

FIGURE 3.1
The Religious Make-Up of the Interviewed Members of the Indonesian Elite

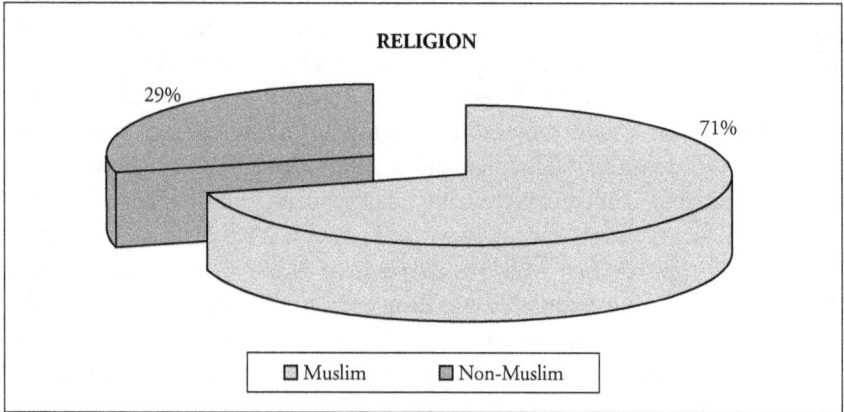

RELIGION

29%

71%

☐ Muslim   ■ Non-Muslim

Source: Author's original compilation.

accounted for about 29 per cent of the total sample. It should also be emphasized that the author originally intended to categorize the elite not just based on their nominal religious affiliation but sought also to take into account the level of the respondents' religious devotedness. The author sought to partially overcome the difficulties with establishing the degree of religious devotedness by raising this issue with several respondents and subsequently cross-checking the information obtained with other individuals deemed familiar with the former. The results of this approach, however, proved to be rather problematic. For example, while a senior diplomat with military background was characterized by his close associates and colleagues as very lax about Islam, explaining that he did not attend prayers in the mosque more than once weekly, this particular leader later spontaneously called himself a very devout Muslim. Thus, in the end, the level of religious devotedness was not taken into consideration in the quantitative analysis of the data.

"The plurality of Islam," to use the words of one respondent, "is Indonesia's advantage!"[111] Underlying this assertion is the fact that the majority Muslim elite in Indonesia is fundamentally divided. As aptly summed up by Jackson,

> As 90 per cent of Indonesians are Muslims, it might be assumed that religion would be a uniting force capable of bridging other divisions

in the society. Yet in Indonesia even religion divides, for differences between the modern and traditional orthodox Muslims, on the one hand, and the *syncretists* (or nominal Muslims), on the other, provide one of the deepest, most enduring cultural (and in some instances political) cleavages in the country.[112]

Mehden correctly observed that "Indonesia is a nation of Muslims divided in their understanding of what is entailed in being an adherent to that faith."[113] Also Samson refers to these cleavages, or the division of Indonesian society, both among the lay people and in the elite circles, along religious-cultural-political lines that range from the strongly Islamic to the nominally Islamic to non-Islamic.[114] He consequently argues that "the Islamic experience in Indonesia produced a diversity of political perceptions as it has developed over the past three centuries."[115]

THE FOREIGN POLICY ELITE:
SURVEY RESEARCH IN INDONESIA

The basic source of attitudinal data for the following analysis of the Indonesian foreign policy elite's threat perceptions was a series of in-depth interviews conducted during the author's survey research in Indonesia and partly in Singapore in the period of 2003 to 2006. Most of the interviews with the forty-five members of the Indonesian foreign policy elite, which serve as the primary source of the data used in this book, took place in Jakarta between November 2004 and March 2005.[116] The group of respondents was selected on a reputational basis by several Indonesian experts specializing in the country's foreign relations.[117]

The Questionnaire

The questionnaire,[118] along with archival study and content analysis of newspapers or magazine articles, is an indispensable tool of analysis employed in this study about Indonesia's foreign policy. Here, an attempt has been made to avoid the trap of a standardized questionnaire, which may sometime prevent a full examination of each interviewee's views by unduly narrowing the discussion. Consequently, in order to encourage a spontaneous conversation between the interviewer and the interviewees, the questionnaire contains a number of open-ended questions.

The open-ended questions have also been used to smooth a way for the respondents to reveal what is most salient in their mind. Since the focal point of this study is the phenomenon of threat perception, it is deemed crucial that the members of the Indonesian foreign policy elite reply as much as possible in their own words to demonstrate what perceptions are "on the top of their heads". The second type of item used in the survey, the closed question, which is also sometimes referred to as multiple choices, constitutes the majority of the items used in the questionnaire.

Yet, although the closed questions limit the possible reply to only several options, these options were usually not disclosed and rather a lively discussion about the topic was encouraged. The author has subsequently filled out the questionnaires (in the case of the closed questions ticked the appropriate option) based on the individual's comments on each point. If the respondent's answer was somewhat ambiguous, he or she was asked to choose from one of three or more available categories. Whenever deemed necessary by the author, they were asked to provide further explanation. The whole discussion was recorded and subsequently fully transcribed for further analysis.

The Questions

The first question was designed partially to facilitate establishment of rapport between the interviewer and interviewee. It called on the respondents to express the level of their agreement with an analogy reflecting the image of a hostile world, building on a similar survey carried out in Jakarta between 1968 and 1970.[119] This question sought to establish the extent to which the overwhelming agreement with the "Pretty Girl Analogy" in the early years of New Order has changed between then and now. The second question aimed to evaluate the realist versus idealist predisposition of the respondents.

The questions 3–10 were devised to obtain a broader picture concerning threat perceptions among the Indonesia's foreign policy elite. The respondents were asked to reveal how strong they believed in or agreed with a statement or hypothesis which suggested a particular security threat posed to Indonesia's security at present or in the coming years and decades.

Although there was a room left in the open-ended questions 3 and 10 for a possible reply suggesting non-traditional, non-military threat, the other questions stirred the interviewees' attention more toward particular state actors. As it was obvious from the earlier available studies on the Indonesian foreign policy that the country's relations with the United States and China are the source of the greatest security concern among the Jakarta political elite, questions 5–9 largely explore the elite threat perceptions towards these two powers. The questions listed in the questionnaire were principally designed to establish:

- short-term threat assessment, which generally underlines the elite's immediate policy prescriptions, and
- long-term threat assessment, which is more enduring and more important in estimating the long-term direction of a state's foreign policy.[120]

Finally, the last five questions sought to provide standard background information, such as the age of the respondent, his or her exposure to the outside world through overseas education, institutional affiliation and religion. The results generated by the questions no. 11–14 were subsequently processed and analysed against the data yielded from the preceding questions no. 3–10. By combining the data that characterize the Indonesian foreign policy elite's threat perceptions on the one side, with the respondents' background information on the other, it was possible to establish the main factors that play an important role in the formation of threat perceptions.

Interview Methodology

One of the most critical issues in a social survey research is defining the universe, the population of individuals, from which survey research samples are selected and evaluated. In the case of this study, the larger target universe was defined as "Indonesia foreign policy elite". Elite beliefs and perceptions cannot be measured directly but must be inferred from the data, in the case of this study, from available statements by relevant members of the Indonesian foreign policy elite. Holsti points to the potential problem of the representative and instrumental use of language: while the former reflects the content of an individual's belief, the latter refers to the individual's attempt to persuade or convince others.[121] To address this problem, Holsti argues that

> the analyst should rely on a number of varied sources which span time, situation, and audience to identify possible inconsistencies. For this reason, [such a study has to] examine public and private communications, speeches, and public writings found in archives and other public sources to formulate a coherent picture of the individual's beliefs.[122]

The author sought to choose a group of respondents that would provide him with a coherent picture of the Indonesian elite's beliefs. The sample, which is essentially a subset drawn from the larger population, in this case made up of all the members of the Indonesian foreign policy elite, has been determined by using *snowballing method*. Snowball sampling is generally used when the random sampling method is not viable because the nature of the universe is not known. In this case, the interviewer originally did not have precise and detailed knowledge and information about who were the most influential members of the Indonesian foreign policy elite. Consequently, he decided to establish initial contact with a relatively small group of experts who were relevant to the research topic with the intention of making contacts with the potential participants in this social survey research.[123]

The general rule was that every respondent had to be present in person during the interview. The aim was to eliminate any distortion of data, which is likely to occur if the respondent's views and opinions were conveyed through his or her colleague, aide or spokesperson. In one particular case, an Indonesian Minister of Foreign Affairs delegated one of his closest aides, a senior diplomat at DEPLU, to represent the Minister's views and opinions during the interview. This interview was conducted on two occasions in the senior diplomat's office at DEPLU but, in the final data assessment, the information collected here was not accredited to anybody else but the senior diplomat himself. Moreover, all requests by the potential respondents to be provided with the questionnaire in advance were denied. Since the main objective was to obtain information about what perceptions were salient in the respondent's mind, it was indispensable so that the interviewees responded to the question promptly and spontaneously after the author read it to them. The respondents were never told in advance or during the interview what the author hoped to find. However, in most cases, they were in the end briefed about the preliminary findings and conclusions drawn from the research, which then provided the author with an important additional feedback from the interviewees.

A social science research, both quantitative and qualitative, entails a variety of ethical issues. One of them — subjects must be able to give informed consent that they voluntarily participate in the research — was addressed by the author. Secondly, the identity of all the respondents who took part in the survey research has been and will in the future be protected.[124] Some of the respondents expressed at the beginning of the interview a concern that their name would eventually appear in this book. To address this issue, the interviewer chose to repeatedly reassure all respondents that all recorded interviews and all data collected would be kept in a safe place and the footnotes would generally mention only the respondent's institutional affiliation or his past or present position in the government bureaucracy.[125] It needs to be emphasized that in some cases where there was a risk that the respondent's identity would be disclosed through the content of his or her statement, the author decided not to reveal any information at all about the respondent — the footnote then contains only the word "interview".

The Composition of the Non-Probability Sample

For social survey research, it is crucial to define the population being studied both theoretically and operationally. The data were generated from a non-probability sample, which can be defined as "a sample that has not been selected using a random selection method." Bryman explains that "this [essentially] implies that some units in the population are more likely to be selected than others."[126] The group of respondents was selected on the basis of their reputation as politicians, decision-makers or diplomats with the utmost influence on the foreign policy-making in Indonesia. The final selection of the survey research samples was carried out based on the recommendation of an advisory panel of seven respected and prominent Indonesian international relations and politics specialists.

Each of these seven experts is widely considered both to be deeply familiar with the dynamics of the Indonesian domestic political scene and to possess an expertise in the process of the country's foreign policy-making. All but one of the experts are academics by background and three of them are practitioners in the field of foreign policy. Two members of the advisory panel are public servants working with the DEPLU, three are associated with The Habibie Centre, and three others affiliated either with the LIPI, the CSIS or The Indonesian Institute. Finally, two of the advisors are experts in the history of the Indonesian military and are linked with other smaller research institutions.

The main task of the advisory panel of Indonesian foreign policy experts was to nominate a number of potential respondents. The total size of the sample was forty-five members of the Indonesian foreign policy elite. All but nine of them were selected by the advisory panel. The exception were eight young diplomats from the DEPLU and one economist from the Department of Trade who were nominated and subsequently interviewed based on the advice and consent of their respective superiors. Although these nine individuals clearly don't (yet) belong to the group of the most influential members of the foreign policy elite, the author deemed it requisite to include a small sample of young diplomats, economists and politicians whose role in the decision-making process is likely to grow exponentially in the future.

Generally, the group of respondents was selected with the notion that it should constitute a cross section of the Indonesian foreign policy elite and be fully representative of the sheer variety of perceptions existent within this elite group. The following overview of the composition of the research sample illustrates the diversity of the respondents' professional backgrounds and their institutional affiliations:[127]

- two former presidents;
- three present or former Cabinet ministers;
- eleven prominent Indonesian diplomats, including former ambassadors (to the United States, Australia, Thailand, the Philippines and other states);
- ten leading members of the Indonesian Parliament, the DPR who were also senior officials from secular-nationalism parties GOLKAR and PDI-P, and moderate Islamic parties PPP and PAN;
- ten members of the elite with economic background, including some of the most distinguished Indonesian economists and political economists;
- five distinguished Indonesian journalists (*The Jakarta Post, Kompas, Sinar Harapan*); and
- eleven respected Indonesian scholars (affiliated with the *Universitas Gadjah Mada*, University of Indonesia, CSIS, LIPI, The Habibie Centre, The Indonesian Institute, and the Singapore-based IDSS).

Researching Elite Perceptions: Limitations

Much like virtually any academic study in the field of social sciences, also this book is not capable of covering all aspects, qualities and eventualities of the subject matter under consideration. This study's limitations ought to be even more accentuated given the fact that it concerns with the phenomenon of elite perceptions. Because of their non-material, subjective and effectively elusive character, the description and evaluation of human perceptions completely depends on the quality of the person's recollection and the accuracy of his or her narrative. First, any critique of the analytical approach, which focuses on the elite threat perceptions can raise doubts over the reliability of the elite members' accounts. We can particularly question whether the interviewees actually revealed their real perceptions?[128] Addressing the issue of finding "reality" in interview accounts, Miller and Glassner point out that "the desire of many researchers to treat interview data as more or less straightforward 'pictures' of an external reality can fail to understand how that 'reality' is being represented in words."[129]

To this end, it is also the interviewer's ethnic background and nationality that may pose a limitation in the attempt to collect data undistorted by biased and prejudice. Hence, the interviewer's nationality was emphasized at the beginning of every interview in an attempt to eliminate any methodological problem which might occur if the interviewer was directly associated with any of the main countries discussed in the questionnaire. Moreover, during the interview, the author deliberately brought up the issue of imperial aggressions in the modern history of Central and East European nations. There was a parallel drawn between the modern histories of Indonesian archipelago and the Czech Republic, both being subjected to centuries of colonial or imperial overrule. It is believed that this removed some of the hesitation on the part of the interviewees to openly express their critical thoughts and ideas about the Western countries. Unlike in the case of the United States, Australia or some of the Western European states, the Indonesians generally think of the Czech Republic in rather neutral, if not positive, terms. Thus, it is hoped that the stated nationality of the interviewer will to some degree help neutralize the potentially unfavourable disposition of the interviewees stemming from the fact that this survey is carried out under auspices of an Australia-based institution. In the context of the snowballing method utilized during the survey research, the interviewer was recommended and referred to most respondents by their colleagues, aides or friends, which in effect established a certain level of familiarity and trust towards the interviewer. This approach also significantly contributed to the minimization of bias and prejudice in the data collected.

Second, another limitation with respect to the evaluation of data stems from the inherent problem with determining the quality of the respondents' religious beliefs. We have already discussed the issue earlier in this chapter. Third, owing to some discrepancies and grammatical mistakes in the respondents' accounts in English, some minor changes to the direct quotations were done. This may raise the question of the authenticity of the quotes. However, it needs to be emphasized that all the changes to the quotation were done in a sensitive manner so that the meaning and content of the respondent's idea was not in any way distorted. In some cases, several words were added to fit the quotation into the whole context of the author's sentence. In some other cases, the inclination among some respondents to give long and extensive accounts on their perceptions necessitated the "trimming" of often-irrelevant ideas to stress only the most important aspect of their account.

Fourth, the perceptions of the Indonesian foreign policy elite might have also been influenced by other motivations and incentives that are rather impossible to discover.[130] This appears to be the case especially in countries, such as Indonesia, where the level of corruption and nepotism is high and the political elite's interests are closely intertwined and interdependent with those of the business community. Robinson and Hadiz point out that "in a world of rent-seekers and free-riders, such as those assumed to prevail in Indonesia, … the system of state power [is] the very source of these rents that sustained them and provided the cement of political relationships. …"[131] Consequently, some policies in Indonesia may well be devised and implemented for the sake of personal or family gain rather than with concern for the state interests.[132] When such conditions are prevalent, as in Indonesia, "policymaking for personal profit" as a factor shaping the elite's decisions can never be completely ruled out. However, with respect to the issues of corruption and vested interests, since it is generally difficult to gather reliable data on leaders of a regime in power, this question is only mentioned here but it will not be pursued intently in this book.

Fifth, this study does pay only a marginal attention to the situation when the threat perceptions are manipulated by the elite. Because citizens generally tend to have much less knowledge about foreign affairs than domestic affairs, there is a substantial opportunity for the elite to influence the country's public opinion by artificially generating threat perceptions. The impact of the elite-constructed messages on the public opinion is a phenomenon quite under-researched in the academic literature.[133] As the general focus of this book is on the elite's, rather than the public threat perceptions, it only briefly touches the President Sukarno's and Suharto's attempts at manipulation of the Indonesian public opinion to serve their respective regime's particular interests. Sixth, the scope of this study does not allow for a substantial elaboration on the psychological mechanisms at work in threat perceptions. The existing literature on threat perceptions is rather agnostic about the role of emotion, as well as affective and cognitive processes in generating perceptions and images about international environment. However, the author does not consider himself being academically equipped to carry out a fruitful research in the field of psychology or physiology.[134]

CONCLUSION

This chapter has illustrated that "national interest" and "national security" are inherently ambiguous concepts with a great variety of meanings which are substantially shaped by the way individual policy-makers see the world around them. The meaning of the "national interest" thus essentially depends on who determines its scope and content and, consequently, "security threat" is "something" that negatively affects this "perceived" "national interest".

In the case of Indonesia, foreign policy decision-making largely remains the prerogative of a relatively small elite group of people — in this book referred to as "foreign policy elite". In the post-Suharto period, Indonesia has had a plural, open society with also relatively diverse, heterogenous political establishment comprising different competing groups that hold different views, perceptions and attitudes. Foreign policy-making process is thus influenced by a number of actors, namely the Foreign Minister, the Cabinet, the President, political parties, various pressure groups, powerful business interests, military establishment, and, last but not the least, public opinion and the press. In this kind of environment, the Indonesian foreign policy elite is "struggling to establish what is [Indonesia's] national interest."

This chapter has also defined the "foreign policy elite" concept and discussed the historical roots of the elite heterogeneity and its internal divisions. In particular, the inquiry identified two leading factors that contribute to this heterogeneity, namely the elite educational background and religious beliefs. In the following discussion, we will see that the heterogeneity among the Indonesian foreign policy elite is a principal factor contributing to the lack of elite cohesion, which in turn affects the way the decision-makers' perceptions influence the Indonesian foreign policy outcomes.

Notes

[1]   Some of the relevant literature on the "elite" theory includes: Zhiyue Bo, *China's Elite Politics: Political Transition and Power Balancing*, Series on Contemporary China 8 (Singapore: World Scientific, 2007); David Flint, *The Twilight of the Elites* (North Melbourne: Freedom Publishing, 2003); Byong-Man Ahn, *Elites and Political Power in South Korea* (Cheltenham and Northampton: Edward Elgar Publishing, 2003); Timothy Brook and Andre Schmid, eds., *Nation Work: Asian Elites and National Identities* (Ann Arbor: University of Michigan Press, 2000); Gerald M. Easter, *Reconstructing the State: Personal Networks and Elite Identity in Soviet Russia* (Cambridge: Cambridge University Press, 2000); Richard L. Zweigenhaft and William G. Domhoff, *Diversity in the Power Elite: Have Women and Minorities Reached the Top?* (New Haven, London: Yale University Press, 1998); Eric Carlton, *The Few and the Many: A Typology of Elites* (Brookfield: Ashgate Publishing, 1996); Harold Ward Maynard, "A Comparison of Military Elite Role Perceptions in Indonesia and the Philippines" (Ph.D. dissertation, The American University, Washington, D.C., 1976); John Scott, ed., *The Sociology of Elites* (Brookfield: Edward Elgar Publishing, 1990); Samuel Eldersveld, *Political Elites in Modern Societies: Empirical Research and Democratic Theory* (Ann Arbor: University of Michigan Press, 1989).

[2]   Interview with a retired admiral of the Indonesian navy, Jakarta, 11 February 2005.

[3]   Barry Buzan, "The Concept of National Security for Developing Countries" in Mohammed Ayoob and Chai-Anan Samudavanija, eds., *Leadership Perceptions and National Security: The Southeast Asian Experience* (Singapore: Institute of Southeast Asian Studies, 1989), p. 2.

4   Ibid., p. 2.
5   Ibid., p. 15.
6   Kuik Cheng-Chwee, "The Essence of Hedging: Malaysia and Singapore's Response to a Rising China", *Contemporary Southeast Asia* 30, no. 2 (August 2008).
7   Interview with a retired admiral of the Indonesian navy, Jakarta, 11 February 2005.
8   Interview with a retired admiral of the Indonesian navy, Jakarta, 11 February 2005.
9   Ibid.
10   Ibid.
11   Interview with an Indonesian academic and expert in Indonesian military, Jakarta, 24 January 2005.
12   "Indonesian Foreign Policy: Losing Its Focus in 2000" in Dewi Fortuna Anwar, *Indonesia at Large: Collected Writings on ASEAN, Foreign Policy, Security and Democratization* (Jakarta: The Habibie Centre, 2005), p. 76.
13   Quoting Irman Lanti from: Evelyn Goh, ed., "Betwixt and Between: Southeast Asian Strategic Relations with the U.S. and China", IDSS Monograph No. 7 (Singapore: Institute of Defence and Strategic Studies, 2005), p. 29.
14   Interview with a retired Indonesian Army general, presently also affiliated with a Jakarta-based research institute, Jakarta, 3 February 2005.
15   Gordon Robert Hein, "Soeharto's Foreign Policy: Second-Generation Nationalism in Indonesia" (Ph.D. dissertation, University of California, 1986), pp. 98–105.
16   Interview with an expert on Indonesian foreign policy, Singapore, 15 May 2006.
17   D.A. Candraningrum et al., "A New Foreign Body", *Tempo*, English Edition, 7 April 2008, pp. 12–13.
18   Interview with the director of a Jakarta-based think-tank, Jakarta, 6 April 2006.
19   Interview with a senior Indonesian diplomat, a high-ranking official in DEPLU, Jakarta, 25 January 2005.
20   Interview with a former Indonesian high-ranking military officer and senior diplomat, Jakarta, 14 February 2005.
21   Interview with the director of a Jakarta-based think-tank, Jakarta, 6 April 2006.
22   Simon Philpott, *Rethinking Indonesia: Postcolonial Theory, Authoritarianism and Identity* (New York: St. Martin's Press, 2000), p. 61.
23   Some of the first analyses concerning the Indonesian elite can be found in: George McTurnan Kahin, *Nationalism and Revolution in Indonesia* (Ithaca and London: Cornell University Press, 1969); Herbert Feith, *The Decline of Constitutional Democracy in Indonesia* (Ithaca, New York: Cornell University Press, 1962).

[24] Leo Suryadinata, *Indonesia's Foreign Policy under Suharto: Aspiring to International Leadership* (Singapore: Times Academic Press, 1996), p. 5.

[25] Anak Agung Banyu Perwita, "Security Sector Reform in Indonesia: The Case of Indonesia's Defence White Paper 2003", *Journal of Security Sector Management* 2, No. 4 (December 2004): 3.

[26] Ibid., p. 3.

[27] Feith, *The Decline of Constitutional Democracy in Indonesia*, p. 108.

[28] Franklin B. Weinstein, *Indonesian Foreign Policy and the Dilemma of Dependence: From Sukarno to Soeharto* (Ithaca, New York: Cornell University Press, 1976).

[29] Ibid., p. 38; the term "top elite" refers to the individuals within the "inner circle" as used in Feith's "three concentric circles" approach.

[30] Robert Putnam, "Diplomacy and Domestic Politics: The Logic of Two-Level Games", *International Organization* 42, no. 3 (Summer 1988): 432.

[31] Robert O. Tilman, "The Enemy Beyond: External Threat Perceptions in the ASEAN Region", Research Notes and Discussions Paper No. 42 (Singapore: Institute of Southeast Asian Studies, 1984), pp. 2–3.

[32] Interview with a CSIS-based international relations expert, Jakarta, 8 February 2005.

[33] Also discussed in an interview with an Indonesian political analyst and government insider, Jakarta, 22 October 2003.

[34] Perhaps the most important insight on this issue was obtained during the interviews with two senior diplomats, Jakarta, 4 November and 7 November 2006.

[35] Harold D. Lasswell, *Politics: Who Gets What, When, How* (New York: Meridian Books, 1958), pp. 13–27.

[36] Feith, *The Decline of Constitutional Democracy in Indonesia*, p. 108.

[37] Referring to nominal Muslims, often with syncretic beliefs and preferring Islamic mysticism to the *Sharia*.

[38] Referring to devout, self-consciously non-syncretic Muslims.

[39] Clifford Geertz, *The Religion of Java* (Chicago: The University of Chicago Press, 1976).

[40] Ibid., p. 6.

[41] For more on this issue, see: Donald K. Emmerson, *Indonesia's Elite: Political Culture and Cultural Politics* (Ithaca, New York: Cornell University Press, 1976), pp. 23–24; Koentjaraningrat, "Review of The Religion of Java", *Madjalah Ilmu-Ilmu Sastra* I, no. 2 (1963): 188–91; Jamhari, "Javanese Islam: The Flow of Creed", *Studia Islamika: Indonesian Journal for Islamic Studies* 9, no. 2 (Jakarta: Center for the Study of Islam and Society, 2002); Harsja W. Bachtiar, "The Religion of Java: A Commentary", *Madjalah Ilmu-Ilmu Sastra Indonesia* 5 (1973): 85–115.

[42] Heather Sutherland, "The Priyayi", *Indonesia*, Cornell Modern Indonesia Project, 19 (1975): 64.

[43] Geertz, *The Religion of Java*, pp. 5–6.

[44]   Heather Sutherland, *The Making of a Bureaucratic Elite: The Colonial Transforma-tion of the Javanese Priyayi* (Singapore: Heinemann Educational Books, 1979), p. 1.
[45]   Ibid., p. 17.
[46]   Chapter titled "Dunia Pengetahuan Abangan dan Priayi" [The World of Knowledge of the *Abangan* and the *Priyayi*] in Sapardi Djoko Damono, *Priayi Abangan: Dunia Novel Jawa Tahun 1950-an* [*Priayi Abangan*: The World of Javanese Novel in 1950s] (Yogyakarta: Bentang, 2000), pp. 239–92.
[47]   Sutherland, *Indonesia*, pp. 72–-73.
[48]   Sutherland, *The Making of a Bureaucratic Elite*, p. 53.
[49]   Richard Robison, "Toward a Class Analysis of the Indonesian Military Bureaucratic State" in *Indonesia*, Cornell Modern Indonesia Project, No. 25 (April 1978), p. 19.
[50]   Greta O. Wilson, ed., *Regents, Reformers and Revolutionaries: Indonesian Voices of Colonial Days, Selected Historical Readings 1899–1949* (Honolulu: The University Press of Hawaii, 1978), pp. 113–14; In 1938, Mohammad Natsir proclaimed in 1938: "Education! This is the field, which now and in the near future faces an acute shortage of personnel. This is a field, which greatly needs help. Give your efforts, young men, for the education of our people, the source of all the intellect and progress of the nation." Appeared in article by Natsir, Mohammad, "Our Educational System Lacks Teachers!" in ibid., p. 114.
[51]   *Mohammad Hatta, Indonesian Patriot: Memoirs*, edited by C.L.M. Penders (Singapore, Jakarta: Gunung Agung, 1981), p. ix.
[52]   Sutherland, *The Making of a Bureaucratic Elite*, p. 56.
[53]   Ibid., pp. 57–58.
[54]   Discussed in: Robert Van Niel, *The Emergence of the Modern Indonesian Elite* (Chicago: Quadrangle Books, 1960), pp. 39–87.
[55]   Quoted in Clifford Geertz's review of the book: "The Emergence of the Modern Indonesian Elite, Robert Van Niel", *American Anthropologist*, New Series 63 no. 3 (June 1961): 604–06.
[56]   Robison, *Indonesia*, p. 19; Nurcholish Madjid explains that "secularisation does not imply the application of secularism or turning Muslim into secularists. Rather, it refers to accepting those values that really belong to the worldly domain as being profane, and to liberating the Muslim *umat* from the tendency to attach a sacred or eschatological value to them." Quoted from: "Nurcholish Madjid: Islam Yes, Islamic Parties No!" in *Indonesian Politics and Society: A Reader*, edited by David Bourchier and Vedi R. Hadiz (London, New York: RoutledgeCurzon, 2003), pp. 89–90.
[57]   Interview with a senior Indonesian career diplomat, DEPLU, Jakarta, 12 January 2005.
[58]   Interview with a former Indonesian high-ranking military officer and senior diplomat, Jakarta, 14 February 2005.

59 Interview with a leader and academic affiliated with the LIPI, Jakarta, 10 December 2004.
60 A term used in: David Ransom, "Ford Country: Building an Elite for Indonesia", in *The Trojan Horse: A Radical Look at Foreign Aid*, edited by Steve Weissman (Palo Alto, C.A.: Ramparts Press, 1975), <http://www.cia-on-campus.org/internat/indo.html> (accessed 10 November 2004).
61 Ibid., p. 2.
62 Ibid., p. 5.
63 William R. Liddle, "The Islamic Turn in Indonesia: A Political Explanation", *The Journal of Asian Studies* 55, no. 3 (August 1996): 622–23.
64 Ibid., p. 623.
65 Interview with an Indonesian academic and expert in the Indonesian military, Jakarta, 24 January 2005.
66 Mochtar Buchori, "The 'Islam-Nationalist' Divide, One Obstacle to Progress", *The Jakarta Post*, 13 June 2002.
67 Ibid.
68 Interview with an Indonesian Muslim leader, 4 September 2006.
69 Interview with an expert on Indonesian foreign policy, Singapore, 15 May 2006.
70 Interview with an Indonesian Muslim leader, 4 September 2006.
71 Interview with the director of a Jakarta-based think-tank, Jakarta, 6 April 2006.
72 Interview with an Indonesian academic and expert in Indonesian military, Jakarta, 24 January 2005.
73 Interview with an expert on Indonesian foreign policy, Singapore, 15 May 2006.
74 Interview with an Indonesian academic and former high-ranking diplomat, University of Indonesia, Jakarta, 23 February 2005.
75 Ibid.
76 Interview with an Indonesian academic and expert in Indonesian military, Jakarta, 24 January 2005.
77 Stuart N. Soroka, "Media, Public Opinion, and Foreign Policy", *Harvard International Journal of Press-Politics* 8, no. 1 (Winter 2003): 33.
78 Ibid., p. 33.
79 Robert Jervis, *Misperception in International Politics* (Princeton: Princeton University Press, 1976), pp. 410–15.
80 Interview with an Indonesian academic and former high-ranking diplomat, University of Indonesia, Jakarta, 23 February 2005.
81 Bourchier and Hadiz, *Indonesian Politics and Society: A Reader*, p. 2.
82 McVey also writes: "Religion inevitably has political significance, for it locates us in a social as well as moral universe." Ruth McVey, *Redesigning the Cosmos: Belief Systems and State Power in Indonesia*, NIAS Reports No. 14, revised edition (Copenhagen: Nordic Institute of Asian Studies, 1998), p. 4.

[83]   Hefner argues that "Muslim politics is not singular and unchanging but always in dialogue with the ideas and struggles of its age." For more on this issue, see: Robert W. Hefner, *Civil Islam: Muslims and Democratization in Indonesia* (Princeton: Princeton University Press, 2000), p. 37; Allan A. Samson, "Conceptions of Politics, Power, and Ideology in Contemporary Indonesian Islam" in *Political Power and Communication in Indonesia*, edited by Karl D. Jackson and Lucian W. Pye (Berkeley: University of California Press, 1978), p. 196; Liddle, "The Islamic Turn in Indonesia".

[84]   Geertz, *The Religion of Java.*

[85]   Koentjaraningrat, "Review of the Religion of Java", pp. 188–91.

[86]   Also discussed in an interview with an Indonesian political analyst, and government insider, Jakarta, 8 December 2004.

[87]   Herbert Feith and Lance Castles, *Indonesian Political Thinking, 1945–1965* (Ithaca and London: Cornell University Press, 1970); Bourchier and Hadiz, *Indonesian Politics and Society: A Reader*, p. 10.

[88]   Azyumardi Azra, "Islam in Southeast Asia: Between Tolerance and Radicalism", Muis Occasional Papers Series, Paper No. 5 (Singapore: Majlis Ugama Islam Singapura, Islamic Religious Council of Singapore, 2008).

[89]   Geertz, *The Religion of Java*; Thomas S. Raffles, *The History of Java* II (London: Black, Parbury, and Allen, 1817); James L. Peacock, *Muslim Puritans: Reformist Psychology in Southeast Asian Islam* (Berkeley: University of California Press, 1978).

[90]   Jamhari, "Javanese Islam: The Flow of Creed", p. 8.

[91]   Abu Hanifah, *Tales of a Revolution* (Sydney: Angus and Robertson Publishers, 1972), p. 69.

[92]   Ibid., p. ix.

[93]   Cindy Adams, *Sukarno: An Autobiography* (Hong Kong: Gunung Agung, 1965), p. 113.

[94]   This acronym and slogan drew on an earlier essay published by Sukarno in: Sukarno, "Nationalism, Islam and Marxism", *Indonesia Muda* (1926); Sukarno, *Nationalism, Islam and Marxism*, Modern Indonesian Project (Ithaca: Cornell University, 1984).

[95]   Sukarno's speech quoted in: Hanifah, *Tales of a Revolution*, p. 72.

[96]   Leo Suryadinata, Evi Nurvidya Arifin, and Aris Ananta, *Indonesia's Population: Ethnicity and Religion in a Changing Political Landscape* (Singapore: Institute of Southeast Asian Studies, 2003), p. 103.

[97]   The data are excerpted from the 2000 census conducted by the *Badan Pusat Statistik* (BPS), or the Indonesian Central Statistic Bureau. This institution carries out a nation-wide census every ten years and the last one was based on 201,241,999 survey responses; Ibid., pp. 103–06.

[98]   Soelaeman Soemardi, "Some Aspects of the Social Origins of the Indonesian Political Decision-Makers", *Transactions of the Third World Congress of Sociology* (London: International Sociological Association, 1956).

99 Drawing on a discussion with Salim Said, "The Future of Indonesian Democracy?
    — the Military, Law, Politics & Islam", open seminar, special lecture given at
    the UNSW, Sydney (30 August 2004).

100 Quoted from: Bourchier and Hadiz, *Indonesian Politics and Society: A Reader*,
    p. 139.

101 Said, "The Future of Indonesian Democracy?".

102 A term describing the process in the 1970s and 1980s when an increasing
    number of more devout Muslims were entering the ranks of the hitherto
    Christian and Muslim *abangan*-dominated Indonesian armed forces; Interview,
    Jakarta, 2005.

103 Said, "The Future of Indonesian Democracy?".

104 Ibid.; for more on the military elite, see: Indonesia Publications, ed., *The
    Indonesia Military Elite* (Lanham-Seabrook, Md.: Indonesia Publications,
    1994); Salim Said, *Legitimising Military Rule: Indonesian Armed Forces Ideology,
    1958–2000* (Jakarta: Pustaka Sinar Harapan, 2006).

105 An important section of the secular element within the elite are the so-called
    secular nationalists who include Muslim intellectuals, human rights activists or
    leading figures from various ethnic and religious minorities who seek a secular
    political system in Indonesia. For more on this issue, see: Douglas E. Ramage,
    Politics in Indonesia: Democracy, Islam and the Ideology of Tolerance (London:
    Routledge, 1995), p. 157.

106 Interview with a high-ranking diplomat and ambassador, Jakarta, 4 November
    2006.

107 Interview with a former Indonesian high-ranking military officer and senior
    diplomat, Jakarta, 14 February 2005.

108 Suryadinata, *Indonesia's Foreign Policy under Suharto*, pp. 14–15.

109 Ibid., p. 15.

110 Ibid., pp. 17 and 38; Suryadinata's research draws on the following publication:
    Mengenal Kabinet RI Selama 40 Tahun Indonesia Merdeka (Jakarta: Kreasi Jaya
    Utama, 1986).

111 Interview with an expert on Indonesian foreign policy, Singapore, 15 May
    2006.

112 Karl D. Jackson, "The Political Implications of Structure and Culture in
    Indonesia" in *Political Power and Communication in Indonesia*, edited by Karl
    D. Jackson and Lucian W. Pye, (Berkeley: University of California Press, 1978),
    p. 28; also discussed in an interview with the director of a leading Jakarta-based
    think-tank, Jakarta, 8 December 2004.

113 Quoting Fred von der Mehden in Douglas E. Ramage, *Politics in Indonesia:
    Democracy, Islam and the Ideology of Tolerance* (London: Routledge, 1995),
    p. 15.

114 Samson, "Conceptions of Politics, Power, and Ideology in Contemporary
    Indonesian Islam", p. 197; Maliki argues that during the Islamization in
    Indonesia, two simultaneous processes were taking place: first, *santrinisasi*

priyayi, during which the *priyayi* elite was becoming more spiritually aware and, second, *priyayinisasi santri,* when the *santri* elite members became more moderate in their religious beliefs. For more on this issue, see: Zainuddin Maliki, *Agama Priyayi: Makna Agama Di Tangan Elite Penguasa* [Priyayi Religion: Meanings of Religion in Elite's Hand] (Yogyakarta: Pustaka Marva, 2004), pp. 152–63.

115   Samson, "Conceptions of Politics, Power, and Ideology in Contemporary Indonesian Islam", p. 197.

116   The following studies served as a guideline for methodology and data-processing technique in this research, which involves interviews with a state's elite: Franklin B. Weinstein, "The Uses of Foreign Policy in Indonesia: An Approach to the Analysis of Foreign Policy in the Less Developed Countries", *World Politics: A Quarterly Journal of International Relations* XXIV, no. 3 (April 1972); Ole R. Holsti and James N. Rosenau, "The Structure of Foreign Policy: Attitudes among American Leaders", *Journal of Politics* 52, no. 1 (February 1990); Richard Herrmann, et al., "Images in International Relations: An Experimental Test of Cognitive Schemata", *International Studies Quarterly*, No. 41 (1997).

117   "Survey Research" in Francis C. Dane, *Research Methods* (Pacific Grove, C.A.: Brooks/Cole, 1990), pp. 119–45.

118   A copy of the questionnaire is included in the "Appendix" section at the end of this book.

119   Franklin B. Weinstein, "The Indonesian Elite's View of the World and the Foreign Policy of Development", *Indonesia, Cornell Modern Indonesia Project,* No. 12 (October 1971), pp. 97–131.

120   For discussion on short and long-term threat assessment, also see Thomas J. Christensen, "China, the U.S.-Japan Alliance, and the Security Dilemma in East Asia", *International Security* 23, no. 4 (Spring 1999).

121   Ole R. Holsti, "Foreign Policy Formation Viewed Cognitively", *Structure of Decision,* edited by Robert Axelrod (Princeton, NJ: Princeton University Press, 1976), pp. 18–55.

122   Ibid., pp. 18–55.

123   Alan Bryman, *Social Research Methods* (Oxford: Oxford University Press, 2004), pp. 98–99.

124   "Ethics in Human Research", in Gary Bouma, *The Research Process,* 3rd edition (Melbourne: Oxford University Press, 1996), p. 188.

125   Based on the policy of the UNSW, the author was obliged to pass an Ethics Committee approval prior to the fieldwork in Indonesia. The conditions of the ethics approval stipulate that the researcher has to keep all recorded interviews and all data collected in a safe place. If the researcher finds it necessary to reveal a respondent's name, he can do so only upon his or her written consent. In 2004, the Ethics Committee of the UNSW issued an ethic clearance for the author's social survey research in Indonesia. For a more thorough discussion on the issue of ethics in human research, see: ibid., pp. 188–98.

126 Bryman, *Social Research Methods*, p. 85.

127 It needs to be stressed here that, in terms of their institutional affiliation and professional background, several respondents fall into more than one category. For example, one interviewed prominent journalist was also an influential diplomat and senior member of a political party.

128 This question was raised, for example, during the author's presentation at: Daniel Novotný, "Indonesian Elite and the Power of Foreign Policy Perceptions", SISC seminar (Sydney, 29 July 2005).

129 Jody Miller and Barry Glassner, "The 'Inside' and the 'Outside': Finding Realities in Interviews", in *Qualitative Research: Theory Method and Practice*, 2nd ed., edited by David Silverman (London: SAGE Publications, 2004), pp. 125–39; this problem will be discussed in a greater detail in Chapter 3.

130 Sukma argues: "Something doesn't have to be true to be influential in a country like Indonesia. I mean people are very easily swayed by rumours, by myths and so on. And crowds can be stirred up very easily and lubricated with money." In an interview with Rizal Sukma in "Perspective: Iraq-U.S.-Indonesia", *Radio Singapore International* (Singapore, 8 February 2003).

131 Richard Robinson and Vedi R. Hadiz, *Reorganising Power in Indonesia: The Politics of Oligarchy in an Age of Markets* (London: Routledge Curzon, 2004), p. 20.

132 Robert O. Tilman, "The Enemy Beyond: External Threat Perceptions in the ASEAN Region", Research Notes and Discussions Paper No. 42 (Singapore: Institute of Southeast Asian Studies, 1984), pp. 3–5.

133 One of the exceptions is: B. Page and R. Shapiro, *The Rational Public: Fifty Years of Trends in American's Policy Preferences* (Chicago: University of Chicago Press, 1992).

134 Some of the exceptions are: Neta C. Crawford, "The Passion of World Politics", *International Security* 24, no. 4 (Spring 2000); Richard Herrman, "The Empirical Challenge of the Cognitive Revolution: A Strategy for Drawing Inferences about Perceptions", *International Studies Quarterly*, No. 32 (1988); and Richard Herrmann, James F. Voss, Tonya Y.E. Schooler, and Joseph Ciarrochi, "Images in International Relations: An Experimental Test of Cognitive Schemata", *International Studies Quarterly*, No. 41 (1997).

PART II

The Perceptions
"Antara Dua Karang"

4

ELITE PERCEPTIONS OF THE UNITED STATES

INTRODUCTION

Indonesia's attitude to the relationship with the United States in the post-Cold War period could reasonably be characterized as ambivalent and full of contradictions. Jakarta's view of America in the 1990s became more and more unfavourable. As the post-Cold War era progressed, Suharto's New Order regime was increasingly annoyed by the U.S. criticism of Jakarta's human right abuses and of its heavy-handed treatment of East Timor. The emerging distrust of America's intentions was further accentuated by the perception that Washington exploited Indonesia's weakness during the 1997 financial meltdown by making Indonesia dependent on the IMF and putting immense pressure on Jakarta to accept a multinational peacemaking force in East Timor. The United States, along with Australia and other Western powers was also alleged to be using NGOs as part of a conspiracy to separate the provinces of West Papua and Aceh from Indonesia.[1]

The U.S.-launched War on Terrorism, the wars in Afghanistan and Iraq, further exacerbated the upsurge of negative attitudes towards America as a series of anti-American demonstrations swept Indonesia in the period of 2001–05. In particular, the military campaign to overthrow the Iraqi regime gave rise to a wave of anti-Americanism that swept through Indonesia and widened the rift between the two former Cold War anti-communist allies. Some Islamic groups in Indonesia demanded that the government cut the country's diplomatic relations with the U.S. As public opinion polls indicate, Indonesian view of the United States underwent a major shift in the first five years of the new millennium. While 75 per cent of them had a favourable opinion of the U.S. in 2000, three years later, 83 per cent of the Indonesian population held an unfavourable view of that country.[2] Commenting on the poll's results, a report noted that "anti-Americanism has [not only] deepened, but it has also widened. ... People see America as a real threat. They think we [America] are going to invade them."[3] Moreover, the 2004–06 research demonstrated that 51 per cent of Indonesian leaders considered the United States, in contrast to 33 per cent Australia and 27 per cent China, as the principal malign factor affecting Indonesia's national interest and security. We should also note here that the respondents interviewed for this book claimed that the Indonesians' perception of America was the worst, and the least favourable, in the nation's history: "Never before has the U.S. image in Indonesia been so low!"[4]

Concurrently, however, despite the widespread anti-American sentiment, most senior leaders in consecutive Indonesian Administrations repeatedly emphasized that Indonesia is committed to building a strong partnership with Washington and that the continuing U.S. engagement in the region is an important aspect of Indonesia's national security and interests. The government in Jakarta ignored demands that Indonesia cut diplomatic relations with the United States and, conversely, showed a heightened interest in resuming military-to-military ties with Washington.[5] In contrast to the anti-American rallies and frequent public proclamations of Indonesian leaders against the U.S. unilateralist policies, Jakarta provided the U.S. navy with limited access to maintenance facilities in Surabaya and actively encouraged American participation in the ARF and its engagement in regional security arrangements.[6] In late 2008, there was an unprecedented wave of euphoria in Indonesia when a 47-year-old first-term senator, Barack Obama, was elected America's first African-American president. Jusuf Wanandi wrote that "many Indonesians have high hopes that a special relationship can be forged with the United States. After all, President Obama was a presidential candidate that Indonesians could relate to."[7] President Yudhoyono even proposed to establish a "strategic partnership" between Indonesia and the United States.[8]

In light of this study's key proposition that foreign relations are driven by the elite perceptions, we should then ask to what degree do the high-profile anti-American pronouncements of some leading Indonesian politicians reflect their real perceptions about the U.S.? We will demonstrate in this chapter that Indonesia's dichotomous and ambiguous approach to its relationship with the United States is to a large degree a reflection of both the elite's ambivalent attitude to the United States and its view that America is ultimately a friendly power, which is the main guarantee for peace and stability in the region. This is especially important in consideration of the fact that the elite views the U.S. as an ultimate check on the growing power and influence of China whose potential future hegemonic intentions are, as will be demonstrated in the following chapters, a source of considerable concern among the Indonesian leadership.

ELITE'S ATTITUDES TOWARDS THE UNITED STATES: HISTORICAL CONTEXT

Indonesian perceptions of the West in general vary from some very positive to those very negative ones. "Love-hate, ambivalent, distorted and the stubborn clinging on to views that are wrong" — such are the Indonesian perceptions of the West, as characterized by the country's well-known writer and feminist Julia I. Suryakusuma.[9] Although we can perhaps question the accuracy of some of the above adjectives used in her article, the survey data clearly substantiated Suryakusuma's claim that "it is the United States that Indonesia is obsessed with, both positively and negatively."[10]

In fact, out of all countries that we consider to be part of the Western civilization, the United States has been by far the most prominent in the respondents' minds, followed by China and Australia. Apart from Japan, whose Western credentials tend to be somewhat contentious, Australia was the only other Western state that figured significantly in the discussions with members of the elite. In other words, the mostly open-ended questions did not lead the interviewed leaders to pinpoint any of the European powers, or for that matter the European Union as a whole, as a serious concern for their nation's security. Dewi Fortuna Anwar, a scholar and senior official in the Habibie Administration, argues that "there was a period when Indonesia was very close to the U.S., and there was also a period when Indonesia told the U.S. to go to hell with its aid. We tell the U.S. to 'go away but come and help us'!"[11] The ambivalent, love-hate attitude has coloured the Indonesian elite perceptions of the United States from at least the early 1940s.

First Images of America

America's image among the first leaders of the independent Republic of Indonesia was generally fairly positive, though not absolutely unblemished. The United States was not seen as "a real colonialist" and especially the 1936 promise of independence for the Philippines clearly set America apart from the other colonialist powers.[12] These positive impressions of American virtues were further reinforced during WWII when the U.S. emerged as a leader of the anti-fascist alliance. In particular, the anti-colonial attitude of Franklin D. Roosevelt who came to be seen as a defender of freedom and democracy for all oppressed peoples endeared the 32nd American President and his nation to Indonesian nationalist leaders.[13]

It is hence not at all surprising that, during the Revolution of 1945–49, many leaders of the newly proclaimed independent Republic of Indonesia attached a great deal of hope and expectations on the United States. Yet, as the support coming from Washington was originally half-hearted and paltry, the elite, now governing the besieged Republic from Yogyakarta, felt disillusioned and betrayed. Two events reinforced this perception. First, a U.S. *aide-memoire* was sent to try to persuade the Republican leaders to co-operate with the Dutch. Second, Washington only recognized the Republic of Indonesia de facto and failed to exert pressure on the Dutch government to cease hostilities towards the embattled state. It was perhaps then that Indonesian leaders became increasingly doubtful as to the extent to which they could rely on unconditional and uncompromising support from the United States for the independent Indonesia in the future. One of them recalls that

> this attitude of the United States for a long time afterwards influenced the opinion of Indonesia that the United States was not after all the champion of the suppressed. ... It could be said that the United States spoiled the hope of many Indonesian leaders at that time. ... The general impression in Indonesia was then that no aid could be expected in its fight for freedom from the Western world. ... It came to be generally believed by Indonesians that the Dutch attack was backed by the United States with economic and military aid.[14]

A present Indonesian leader close to the military circles pointed out that the victorious and over-confident United States after the WWII was ready to impose its will on other nations. But in a sense, the United States behaved like any other country because "all countries are looking for *lebensraum*."[15] On balance, however, positive impressions of America in the late 1940s seem to have prevailed. Most leaders felt that Washington helped substantially the embattled Republic of Indonesia especially in 1949 by applying considerable pressure on the Dutch and thus forced them to look for a compromise with the Republic. Palar, Indonesia's first ambassador to the United Nations, argued that "had the United States and England failed to intervene, I wonder whether the Netherlands armed forces would not already have made a start with the march to Jogja."[16] The same view seems to have persisted among the elite until today, with a present senior diplomat pointing out that "the Americans and Australians supported our independence, whereas the Europeans did not." He also suggested that in the period of 1945–60s "the threat was really the colonial powers."[17]

Hence, due to its half-hearted and lukewarm support to the embattled Republic during the 1945–49 Revolution, the first Indonesian elite's impression of America could be best characterized as ambivalent. In 1948 President Sukarno shared anti-Dutch and anti-Western attitudes with the then Prime Minister Amir Sjarifuddin. A leader close to the military circles recollects that whilst initially holding pro-American attitudes, Sjarifuddin joined the Communists only after his high expectations of the United States were not fulfilled.[18] By contrast, though the Vice-President Muhammad Hatta was also displeased and disillusioned by the United States, he still sustained some confidence in the West. Hanifah writes that, at that time, Hatta "probably already saw the danger of the rising power and influence of the Communists [and, vice versa,] the Communists saw in him their most dangerous enemy."[19] We should note here that the first post-independence cabinet under the Hatta's leadership was anti-communist and hence keen to implement a pro-Western foreign policy.[20]

Downturn in Elite Perceptions of the United States

In the course of the 1950s, however, negative attitudes among the leaders involved in foreign policy decision-making gradually outweighed the goodwill the United States enjoyed by the late 1940s. Three events in the relations between Washington and Jakarta had a substantial bearing on this development: Firstly, Washington's blatant and fairly insensitive attempt to bring Indonesia into a quasi-formal alliance with the West in the early 1950s. Secondly, the United States' subversive intervention in the Outer Island rebellions directed against Jakarta in 1958. Thirdly, the U.S. official neutralism but behind-the-scenes backing of the Dutch in their attempt to deny West Irian to Indonesia.

During the first three and a half years of independence, from 1949 to 1953, Indonesian domestic politics was marked by an intense competition among various parties and interests. Consecutive Indonesian Administrations had been primarily concerned with domestic rehabilitation, especially the country's devastated economy, which necessitated toleration of Western interests. It was in this context that the image of the United States suffered a first major setback. The main reason was Washington's insufficient sensitivity to Indonesian popular sentiments and public opinion as it attempted to press the Sukiman government to sign the U.S. Mutual Security Act of October 1951. The Agreement, under which terms Indonesia committed herself to the defence of the "free world" in return for the U.S. economic aid, served as a catalyst for a strong popular sentiment to be free from the influence of Cold War rivals, whose roots could be found in the colonial experience. Sukiman's Administration was forced to bow to public sentiments and pressure and step down. The United States, for its part, lost some of its credibility and the Indonesian elite's hitherto relatively positive disposition towards Washington took a downturn.

In early 1958, the leaders' suspicion of the real U.S. intentions greatly increased owing to the American subversive policies aimed at supporting the anti-Jakarta rebellions on the islands of Sulawesi and Sumatra. It is beyond the scope of this book to elaborate on the origins and development of U.S. involvement on the side of the rebels.[21] It is, however, interesting to look at how today's Indonesian elite see a clear correlation between present U.S. policies, notably in Iraq and Afghanistan, and those five decades ago. One leader, a senior member of GOLKAR, pointed out the subversive role the CIA and its agents played in the rebellion. At one stage, a group of CIA agents was sent to train the dissidents and, allegedly, they were waiting for a long time in the depth of the rain forest but nobody showed up: "So one of them said to his colleague: 'What the fuck are we doing here?' And I think that should always [be the case] for the U.S. foreign policy that they ask themselves [if it is necessary for them to get] involved?"[22]

Only one out of the total forty-five respondents among the elite reminisced and raised the case of the United States' involvement in the Outer Island rebellions, which is in fact a very well-known and well-documented historical event. We will return to this issue in Chapter 5 when we compare the U.S. subversive role in the Outer Island rebellion with the way the contemporary Indonesian leaders perceive of and interpret China's past military incursions into the Indonesian archipelago. The fact remains that neither the Eisenhower, nor successive U.S. Administrations have ever officially acknowledged the highly embarrassing support of the anti-Sukarno and anti-Communist dissidents. Washington sought to repair the severely damaged relationship with Jakarta by offering a small amount of military aid in 1958 but it was of little avail.[23] The elite was then strongly convinced of American complicity and, as one present leader emphasized, "the suspicion against the U.S. has always been there since their involvement in the 1958 [Outer Island rebellions]."[24]

Washington's handling of the West Irian issue in the 1961–62 period served as yet another great irritant to the elite, though this did not affect their perceptions of the United States as substantially as its earlier involvement in the anti-Jakarta rebellions. Indonesian leaders had persistently argued that since West Irian had formed part of the Dutch East Indies, it should be taken from the Dutch control and incorporated into the Republic of Indonesia. Hence, ever since the 1949 agreement on Indonesia's independence Jakarta had tried to use various diplomatic means to resolve the status of the West Irian. After protracted negotiations with the Dutch had failed, to the Indonesian leaders' disappointment, Washington fell short of providing needed support for their country when it brought the dispute to the UN. One of the interviewed leaders dismissed the present burgeoning anti-American sentiments as temporary and issue-based because the United States had in the past often supported Indonesia. According to him, "it was the U.S. who put pressure on the Dutch to leave Papua".[25] In reality, however, it was only when the signs of Soviet involvement, in particular its major arms shipments to the Indonesian armed forces, caused a concern in Washington that the Kennedy Administration decided to take a more pro-Indonesia approach.

Sukarno's Idiosyncrasies and Relations with the United States

By the mid 1960s, the Indonesian leadership was effectively divided in their perceptions of the United States. To get a better understanding of the increasing anti-American sentiments in Indonesia at that time, we ought to look closely at the structure of the foreign policy elite during *Demokrasi Terpimpin*.[26] From 1959, when Guided Democracy was proclaimed by Sukarno,[27] in the period ending with his downfall in the mid-1960s, the first Indonesian President's role in the foreign policy decision-making was becoming progressively more prominent. While sitting at the helm and navigating Indonesia through the tumultuous years of the Cold War, on the domestic front, Sukarno was exercising a political balancing act between the two most powerful players and arch rivals — the radical Indonesian Communist Party, the PKI, and the conservative armed forces. In short, it was the three poles within this peculiar triangular balance of power, namely the PKI's chairman Aidit, the Indonesian Army commander General Nasution and, by far most important of all, President Sukarno, who essentially constituted the nation's foreign policy elite.

In discussing the importance of Sukarno's, and more broadly, Indonesian leaders' personal idiosyncrasies as a factor shaping dynamics of the country's foreign relations, Sukma argues that the best tool to understand

Indonesian foreign policy is the state of its domestic politics.[28] Moreover, as one interviewed leader noted, Sukarno's personal idiosyncrasies and perceptions influenced the foreign policy "more in style. But at the end, look at his policies, they were actually meant to preserve the balance in the domestic political structures between the Muslims, the Communists and the military. …"[29] Indonesia's domestic political situation admittedly played an important role in shaping Sukarno's foreign policy preferences. However, the argument that Indonesia's increasingly anti-Western foreign policy was mainly due to Sukarno's attempt to manage the balance between the PKI and the armed forces is a serious oversimplification. Here, it is exceedingly important to be aware of the fact that Sukarno's style of government was at least from 1956–57 increasingly characterized by personal rule — perhaps most symptomatic of this tendency was his famous pronouncement that he, Sukarno, was "the mouthpiece of the Indonesian people."[30] As McIntyre pointedly argues, "the decisive influence of the personal ruler makes the personality of that figure central to an understanding of the nature of the regime."[31]

First of all, we should note here that the notion of Western powers trying to dominate Indonesia had long been present in Sukarno's attitude to the West and as such preceded Indonesia's overtly anti-American foreign policy in the early 1960s. This nationalist and somewhat parochial worldview arose in the post-WWII period primarily from the perception that Indonesia as an underdeveloped country depended on the economic and hence political support of the United States and its allies. This, what Weinstein aptly described as "the universal dilemma of weakness", is an inherent and recurrent phenomenon that shapes the Indonesian elite's view of the world.[32] Sukarno's vigorous nationalism was plagued by this dilemma — how to secure external resources for economic development without compromising the country's independence. It is in this context that we need to understand the Indonesian President's apprehension of Western powers.

Sukarno's concern about the excessive influence of the West in Indonesia's domestic affairs was also reinforced by the experience of the U.S. Central Intelligence Agency's, the CIA's, involvement in the Outer-Islands rebellion in early 1958.[33] Moreover, in the period of 1963–65, the Indonesian leader, along with the Indonesian Communist Party, the PKI, grew increasingly apprehensive of the long-maturing, close ties between the U.S. and the Indonesian army. This point cast doubt on the argument that Sukarno's attitudes in the early 1960s were principally shaped by internal threats, namely the domestic political situation, rather than by perceived external threats. Sukarno's balancing act between the armed forces and the Communist Party was carried out against a background of rising tension on the domestic political front, which was further complicated and aggravated by the perceived external threat from the United States. The President's increasingly overtly hostile attitude towards the United States was channelled into his eloquent anti-imperialist rhetoric as much as into Indonesian foreign policy.[34] To balance Washington's interference in Indonesia's internal affairs and to isolate Indonesia from the exploitative world economic order, Sukarno set out to pursue a foreign policy aimed at forging closer ties with Communist nations, and in particular with China.[35]

Sukarno was certainly concerned about the balance of power between the main rival domestic political actors as he was jealously trying to safeguard his own political position. However, we should be conscious of the fact that as Sukarno exercised in the early 1960s an increasingly prominent role in the foreign policy decision-making, the collection of beliefs and assumptions peculiar to the President undoubtedly shaped his foreign policy preferences. We can well hypothesize that should Mohammad Hatta, for example, have been in the same dominant position, the course of Indonesian foreign policy would have been rather different than it was under Sukarno. The peculiar idiosyncrasies and worldview of the first Indonesian President clearly mattered. Education, for example, is regarded as one of the most potent determinants of elite worldview and attitudes. Though both were nationalists, unlike Hatta and other of his contemporaries, Sukarno did not have the experience of studying in Europe. Consequently, according to Mortimer, "[Sukarno] was never wholly captivated by the West, unlike many of his contemporaries who studied in Europe."[36]

It would thus be a serious mistake to discount the role of Sukarno's personal idiosyncrasies in shaping Indonesian foreign relations at that time. As Aandstad argues, "the two non-communists in this triangle (Sukarno and Nasution) had both been personally as well as politically alienated by the previous [U.S.] administration."[37] As for the Indonesian President, a number of different accounts suggest that Sukarno's strong grudge against President Eisenhower might have well reinforced the negative disposition in his ambivalent attitude towards the United States. This assumption is also supported by an American diplomat's memo from 1961, which suggested Sukarno's belief that the United States was "opposed to him personally" and was "plotting" against him as playing "an important part in influencing him to closer and more cordial relations with the USSR."[38] Hanifah argues that of course [Sukarno's] abnormal vanity played a big role. He cherished the memories of his arrivals in Moscow and Beijing where he was received like a Maharaja of old times, a super king or a world hero. He was [then] especially hurt when President Eisenhower kept him waiting ... Yes, he was quite bitter about the West, especially the United States.[39]

Similarly, it would also be a mistake not to take into consideration the impact of no fewer than five assassination attempts on Sukarno's emotions and his attitudes towards the United States. The first assassination attempt occurred on 30 November 1957, during his visit in his children's school in Jakarta and while Sukarno himself survived unhurt, scores of other people were either killed or seriously injured. The chief suspect was identified as the former intelligence chief Colonel Zulkifli Lubis, whose affiliation with the Western-leaning *Masyumi* political party was a widely known fact. Moreover, after Lubis fled to West Sumatra where he was offered protection by one of the dissident colonels during the anti-Jakarta Outer Islands rebellions, Sukarno's suspicion of external involvement in his assassination attempt was substantiated. The mounting evidence that the U.S. Central Intelligence Agency was backing the dissident colonels led Sukarno to strongly believe in the CIA's implication in the attempt to kill him.[40] Following other assassination attempts in November 1958, March 1960 and January 1962 Sukarno's suspicion that the United States through the CIA plotted to interfere and gain control over Indonesia's political life constituted an important factor, which informed the his perceptions of the United States.[41]

While Sukarno's peculiar anti-Western and anti-American attitudes were increasingly shaping the dynamics of Indonesian foreign policy, the remaining pro-West political parties and their leaders were gradually marginalized, either by losing popularity or being banned by the now very powerful President. Also two of the country's former top leaders, Mohammed Hatta and the Sultan of Yogyakarta, whose views did not seem to suffer from an unequivocal anti-Western bias and were rather more nuanced, had been sidelined and thus no longer were part of the foreign policy elite. For Hatta's part, his worldview could perhaps best fit into the category of an Islamic social democrat and, as such, there existed a close affinity between him and the more Western-oriented wing of Masyumi. Hatta resigned from the post of the Vice-President in 1956 following a dispute with Sukarno — he was then vehemently opposed to the President's insistence to include the PKI in the cabinet. Hatta claimed that Sukarno "was fooling himself" if he believed that the Indonesian Communists were any different from their fellow comrades in other countries.[42] Muhammad Hatta's pro-Western and anti-Communist bias meant that there was no love lost between the former and the Communist party. Not surprisingly, the PKI chairman Aidit earmarked Hatta, along with *Masyumi* and the Socialists, as "the diehards" because "their economic interest [were] being pressed more and more by the foreign monopolist and compradors [meaning the West, and particularly the United States]."[43]

With the moderate and pro-Western leaders, such as Mohammad Hatta and Sutan Syahrir, and political parties Masyumi and the Indonesian Socialist Party far from the power circles, and a perceived balance between the armed forces and PKI, Sukarno's influence on foreign policy decision-making seemed to be largely unhindered by substantial domestic political constraints and was on a steady rise. In short, Indonesia's increasing anti-American leanings in the early 1960s should be seen, in Leifer's words, in the context of "Sukarno's temperament, [idiosyncrasies] and the frenetic nature of domestic politics,"[44] including the make-up and structure of the foreign policy elite, as much as the perceived external threat generated by the U.S. interference.

"New Order" Elite and the Change in Perceptions

American-Indonesian relations improved again with the political changes after the GESTAPU "coup" in 1965. Washington welcomed the regime change in Jakarta and soon after resumed arms shipments to Indonesia and joined the Inter-Governmental Group on Indonesia (IGGI) in the rescheduling of the massive Indonesian debt. During the New Order regime, the United States was comfortable dealing with Indonesia's new "modernizing elite", namely General Suharto, the army leadership and a team of technocrats, many of whom were American-educated.[45] Some respondents emphasized that Washington did not mind and was in fact very keen to maintain friendly relations with Suharto's authoritarian regime mainly because it viewed Indonesia as a "bulwark" against the communist menace. According to an interviewed retired Indonesian Army general, "in the Cold War period, any regime that was effective would be good enough compared with a communist regime, so a military junta, military dictatorship, a military authoritarian regime was at least better than a communist regime."[46]

Likewise, the military-dominated elite's impression of the United States was more favourable than during the Sukarno regime. The New Order leadership generally viewed the United States as a friendly power. We need to see this gap in elite perceptions between Sukarno and Suharto regimes to a great extent in the context of the two Indonesian leaders' worldview and ideological predisposition. Whereas Sukarno was preoccupied with "nation and character building", Suharto's priority was economic development.[47]

Consequently, while Sukarno relished leading anti-colonial and anti-imperialist campaign of the New Emerging Forces against the Old Established Forces, whom he regarded as the main threat to his nation, Suharto's pragmatic government made up of a large number of Western-educated technocrats turned to the Old Established Forces — the Western developed countries — for much-needed economic assistance. All in all, China was at that time overwhelmingly considered as the principal threat to Indonesia, generating considerably more concerns among the Indonesian elite than the United States and the Soviet Union.

However, while the Suharto-led elite largely perceived of the United States as a friendly and benevolent power, it is more than apparent that the leaders were not completely without suspicions of Washington's intentions. As Weinstein explains, some of his respondents regarded both the United States and Soviet Union, the two Cold War rivals, as superpowers striving to relentlessly contest and dominate the world and as such posing a threat to Indonesia.[48] He also found that, during the Suharto era, "... it was certainly possible for an Indonesian leader to be highly critical of the United States, and at the same time to hope for good relations with Washington, even to be regarded as pro-American. ..."[49] Thus, Weinstein concluded that although three-quarters of the interviewed leaders believed the United States wanted Indonesia to become as strong as possible, when they referred to America, "the most frequently mentioned pejorative [word] was imperialist and interventionist."[50]

It is obvious that the New Order leadership's view of the United States and its role as a provider of economic and military assistance to Indonesia as well as a guarantor of stability in Southeast Asia was essentially ambivalent. Jusuf Wanandi, an academic whose views are generally regarded as being close to the military, stated that while the Indonesian elite "recognize the importance of the U.S. presence in the region ... the U.S. as a superpower has always created an uneasy feeling."[51] The elite's ambivalent view of the U.S. was to some extent generated by the perceived "dilemma of dependence" on America and other Western powers. As one leader noted, "during Sukarno time, what really Sukarno did was to play one against the other [meaning the West against the Soviet Union and China]."[52] However, he added that "under Suharto, we were more or less blocked to the United States because we were very much anti-Communist. So our space for manoeuvring at that time completely differs with the time with Sukarno."[53]

As shown above, the leaders interviewed by Weinstein displayed some misgiving about the United States. We can question why these elite negative perceptions and attitudes did not find an obvious expression in Suharto government's foreign policy, which in reality forged friendly relations with the United States and other Western powers. We can understand this analytical conundrum in the context of the balance-of-threat logic, which propounds that states will balance a power perceived as threatening. In other words, states will not balance a dominant power if its behaviour is perceived as non-threatening and benign.[54] The United States undoubtedly was a dominant power during the Cold War. Yet, the United States was not seen as a threat in the same sense as China (or Soviet Union) was. The Suharto leadership generally wanted to increase Indonesia's space for manoeuvring and hence Indonesia's independence vis-à-vis the main powers. The elite was well aware of Indonesia's dichotomous or almost schizophrenic need for both (dependence on) Western economic aid and, concurrently, independence from the West. We need to see the leaders' apprehension about the United States at that time in the light of this dilemma they were confronted with.[55]

While the elite perceptions of the West in general and the United States in particular were characterized by ambivalence inherent in the "dilemma of dependence", China was, according to former Suharto-era leaders, since its alleged involvement in the 1965 coup attempt considered as an "evil" and "mortal enemy".[56] Indeed, the U.S. was valued by the Suharto-led generals' group as a stabilizing force and counterweight to more serious threats, notably China, facing the region. This view was also supported by the elite's concern about Washington's growing engagement with China in the late 1970s and 1980s. There was a growing concern in Jakarta that improving Sino-U.S. relations would be at the cost of the American interest to function as a balancing force in Southeast Asia to offset potential Soviet or Chinese military adventurism.[57] Moreover, we argued in Chapter 2 that an analysis of leaders' perceptions within the balance-of-threat framework needs to include the elite consensus about what constitutes present and future security threats to the nation. Therefore, it is important here to note three facts: First, the Suharto-led group of generals completely dominated the foreign policy-making process. Second, as the general's group was cohesive, the leaders on the whole agreed that, at least until the Deng Xiaoping's *Four Modernizations* reforms in China in the early 1980s,[58] Communist China constituted a major external threat to Indonesia's national security.[59] And, finally, in this context and in the absence of a real domestic (nationalist) challenge to their policy of seeking foreign aid, the Suharto-led foreign policy elite consensually agreed upon the need for a de-facto alignment with the United States.

THE LOVE-HATE ATTITUDE TO THE UNITED STATES

The elite have always viewed the United States with mixed feelings, which comprised a peculiar blend of inspiration and distrust. This attitude mixes resentment with respect, admiration and fear, as much as jealousy with the desire to emulate. As a CSIS-based international relations expert squarely puts it: "Our relations with the U.S. are a kind of a love-and-hate from our side."[60] While the "love" aspect of the attitude means that Indonesia is seen as "part of the Western orbit", the "hate" aspect refers to the perception that the omnipresent influence of the West and particularly the United States and their ability to interfere into Indonesia's internal affairs essentially constitute a threat to the country's national security.

Indonesian elite's opinions about the United States are deeply contradictory and complicated — America's global influence, for example, is simultaneously embraced and rejected. On the one hand, America's scientific and technological achievements, music and movies are by and large admired, and the general desire for democracy and the free market model in Indonesia indicates some degree of acceptance of the U.S.-promoted ideas and principles. On the other hand, some leaders are concerned about the spread of American culture, ideas and customs. In other words, sections of the elite are opposed to what they consider as a spread of the ominous forces of "Americanism". This view is also supported by Dahana, a scholar and China expert, who also claims that "the U.S.-Indonesia relations can be described as 'love-hate relationship'".[61] In reference to the "love" aspect, he notes that

> we love American democratic political system, we love U.S. education system, and it is a fact that even among people who are against the U.S., they still send their daughters and sons to the U.S., based on the assumption that U.S. education is the best in the world. We love American pop culture and icons such as McDonalds, Pizza Hut and Coca Cola.[62]

Concurrently, however, Dahana contrasts the "love" aspect with the opposite side of the equation:

> On the other side, [we] hate American government, which is regarded as very easy in using its military muscle to invade another country in the name of fighting terrorism. In a way Chinese perception of Americans is similar to what is happening to Indonesia. Dissenters go to the U.S. for political asylum. Chinese send their sons and daughters to the U.S. for education, and yet they still recall the American aggression back in

the 19th and 20th century. China still remembers how the U.S. treated China during the containment policy. Interestingly, Chinese term for America is "beautiful country".[63]

We ought to note here that even respondents, who displayed an overall strong anti-American predisposition, admitted that "the U.S. can be both an enemy and a friend".[64] To put it differently, Washington's policies are essentially seen as a "double-edge" weapon because, as Lanti argues, they "can be both beneficial and harmful for countries in this region."[65] All in all, the idea that Indonesia has a "love-hate relationship" with the United States was embraced by most interviewed leaders.[66] However, we need to analyse the degree to which either the "love" or the "hate" aspect is more dominant. It is also important to examine the extent to which they constitute only the form rather than the substance of the elite's attitude. This will in turn enable us to juxtapose the elite's ambivalent perceptions of the United States vis-à-vis China within the balance-of-threat framework.

The "Love" Aspect of the Elite's Attitude to the United States

The "love" aspect has traditionally been centred on the U.S. image as a benevolent, benign superpower and guarantor of peace and stability in the region. This basic perception of the United States was firmly established during the Cold War era.[67] Then the U.S. military presence in Southeast Asia was seen as a security guarantee or "security umbrella"[68] that enabled ASEAN countries to concentrate on their economic development rather than on building their respective armies. Consequently, as one leader argued, "most of the ASEAN countries see that the U.S. military presence in Southeast Asia is a very friendly military power."[69] He also suggested that this U.S. security role should be maintained now and in the future:

> So I think rather than we try to beef up our military or arm race in Southeast Asia, let the U.S. become an umbrella for the security from the military perspective. So that we can use our money to develop our economy and also to develop our social affinities among the people within ASEAN.[70]

The U.S. presence not only in Southeast Asia but also in Northeast Asia is seen as a vital stabilizing element. If Washington decided, for example, to withdraw its troops from Korea and military assistance from Taiwan, it would negatively affect the balance of power and thus stability and security in the whole region.[71] As Luhulima affirms, "the United States cannot be excluded, as it is also an essential part of East Asia given its political, security and economic roles."[72] Using the Indonesian word *ramah*, meaning friendly and benevolent, when referring to the United States, a number of leaders emphasized that the so-called "superpower" "does not have any territorial design".[73] We will see in this and the following chapters that historical knowledge plays a very important part in shaping the elite perceptions about the United States and China. Historically, the United States, unlike China and Japan, is seen as not harbouring an ambition for territorial expansion.[74]

In fact, several leaders have stressed the fact that "the U.S. is helping Indonesia and the independent struggle was helped by the United States."[75] There have always been "ups and downs" in the relationship between Indonesia and the United States but the bottom line is that, apart from Australia, it was the Americans who were "the biggest supporter of the Indonesian independence."[76] History can serve as evidence that the U.S. does not want to occupy Indonesia. Rather, Washington "just wants to maintain the security in the region because [it does] not want their own interest to be in trouble."[77] And while the U.S. "self-interest" is immense, it is mostly compatible with the Indonesian interest and thus does not pose a threat to Indonesia.[78] The United States does not intend to dominate Indonesia but, instead, they "want to achieve ... basically that countries will not become enemies of the U.S."[79] In other words, American leaders essentially strive to encourage other countries to maintain friendly or at least workable relations with the United States. Therefore, the argument that the United States is trying to create an empire is seen as faulted and non-sense. The belief in a fundamentally benign nature of the U.S. power and influence led about one third of the interviewed leaders to claim explicitly that they would not mind if Indonesia were in the U.S. sphere of influence. For example, a former Indonesian President explicitly stated that "the Americans want this region is controlled by the U.S., which for me it's okay."[80]

Almost all leaders conceded that there have always been and perhaps always will be segments in the Indonesian society that look at the United States as a threat to their country. Several leaders concurrently expressed a belief that "they are in a minority".[81] The majority of Indonesian leaders do not see Washington as a hegemonic and empire-seeking superpower because they are aware of the fact that the U.S. power is effectively limited by its democracy and the "checks and balances" inherent in its political system. One leader recalled that before he left for study in the United States in the 1960s, he was like most ordinary Indonesians — he thought that America was all-mighty and its power limitless. But this perception of the United States changed during his studies at the University of California, Berkeley. The leader who characterized his generation as "I was in the same group like John Lennon and Jimmy Hendrix" recounted:

> I saw the anti-Vietnam demonstrations. At that time I realized that the American government is not that strong as it tends to think from outside. I saw it myself. … I saw how the demonstrations changed the foreign policy of America dramatically up to now. The Vietnam War remains as an issue. Not WWII, not Korean War, but certainly Vietnam is debated all the time until now and is becoming a benchmark to measure Afghanistan, to measure Iraq.[82]

In outlining the limits of American power and influence, a former President also readily referred to the Vietnam War and its long-term repercussions for the U.S. foreign policy. He was not disturbed by the U.S. military superiority and presence of its navy in the region because of its limited capacity to wage a war with other countries. The former President pointed to the past U.S. involvement in Vietnam and invasion of Iraq where the United States is presently "bogged down" — he reasoned that "Iraq without so much forest, already very difficult for the U.S. … Moreover, Indonesia with so much forest! So, I do not see the United States is a threat!"[83] We should note here the manner in which most leaders interpret historical events that in turn shape their present perceptions. They tend to construe past U.S. military actions, such as those in Vietnam and Iraq, as a valuable lesson for policy-makers in Washington. We will see later in this chapter that while the present American leadership has been seen as having learned a rather positive lesson from the relatively recent and often failed U.S. military incursions of in the region, by contrast, China's military forays in the distant past are viewed as an acrimonious legacy from which the Indonesian elite should learn a lesson.

In interpreting the "love" aspect of the leaders' attitude to the United States, we mustn't omit the importance of the elite's admiration about and inspiration by certain aspects of American political system, culture and society. It could be argued that American democracy is a source of inspiration for most Indonesian leaders. For example, Amien Rais, a politician and leader of the country's second largest Muslim organization, is well known for his open criticism of U.S. policies towards Indonesia but also in the Middle East, Iraq and Afghanistan. Yet, Rais concurrently argued that Indonesia should look for inspiration in the American political system and also adopt the direct presidential election.[84] Following Obama's win, many Indonesian leaders praised the 2008 U.S. presidential election describing it as "a showcase of politics at its most mature" and "a good political lesson" for Indonesia.[85] Other leaders point to American economic policy as an area where Indonesia should look for some inspiration. Sjahrir, a top advisor of President Yudhoyono, says that he routinely draws parallels with the former U.S. President. In his memos to the Indonesian President, Sjahrir likes to quote Bill Clinton's mantra: "It's the economy, *stupid!*"[86]

Then, there is the issue of inspiration by the American educational system and admiration for its scientific and technological prowess. As one leader who is close to Indonesia's military establishment noted, "Everybody wants to study in America ... an education obtained in the United States is a passport for a good life."[87] President Yudhoyono, for example, a graduate of the IMET programme,[88] who spent some time in the U.S. during his studies, has repeatedly called the United States his "second home".[89] Generally, in Indonesian leaders' imagination, America represents a land where "everything is possible" and a country with "the good life". One interviewed leader referred to Ahmad Sumargono, head of the radical Muslim Crescent Star Party (PBB) and author of a book titled "I Am a Fundamentalist" to emphasize that also Sumargono's son is presently studying in the United States. Another respondent, a member of the Parliament, the DPR, whose son is also presently studying and working with the United States, believes that Western and particularly U.S. education is important insofar as it dilutes anxiety and suspicions among the leaders about America's intentions towards the archipelagic nation. Several leaders even suggested that it is through the learning process at university or college in the United States that the elite's worldview "is going to converge and gradually be practically the same" as the Western worldview.[90]

To sum up, the "love" aspect in the Indonesian elite's attitude towards the United States arises from the combination of the U.S. image as a benign superpower and the leaders' inspiration by certain aspects of American political system, culture and society. Moreover, as we demonstrated in the preceding chapter, the foreign policy elite have traditionally been comprised of three main groups — military establishment, Ministry of Foreign Affairs and nationalist elite. As one leader with a deep knowledge about the foreign policy elite's attitudes argued, "they are more comfortable with the West rather than with China and even with the Soviet Union at that time. Whatever happens to U.S. policies toward Indonesia, there is always this willingness on the part of the Indonesian elite to restore and improve the relations with the U.S."[91] We can assume that from the Indonesian elite's perspective, "the U.S. influence penetrating Indonesia ... is [generally] more acceptable" than what might appear from the recent wave of anti-American sentiments.[92] This view was unequivocally endorsed by at least one third of the interviewed leaders.

THE CHANGING DYNAMICS OF THE ELITE'S ATTITUDE TO THE UNITED STATES

While the United States have essentially retained its image as a guarantor of stability and peace in Southeast Asia and beyond — the "love" aspect — this benign character has increasingly been eclipsed by unilateralist policies and aggressive actions of the United States. Yet, we will argue in the following discussion that the elite is ambivalent and deeply divided in its view of what are actually the degree, nature and implications of the "U.S. threat".

But, first, we need to contextualize the post-9/11 rise of anti-American sentiments in Indonesia within a broader post-Cold War shift in the Indonesia-U.S. relationship. During the early 1990s, U.S. foreign policy underwent a major change. In the wake of the collapse of the former Soviet-led Communist bloc and the end of the Cold War in the 1989–90 period, the foreign policy of containing the communist threat became largely irrelevant and defunct. In the early 1990s, policy-makers in Washington judged that America's interests would now be best served by spreading democracy and human rights around the world and, henceforth, "this neo-conservative incarnation of U.S. policy has been reflected in ongoing democracy promotion programmes."[93] The new American foreign policy doctrine has taken on a moral dimension.

Post-Cold War Period and the Changing Relationship with America

In the context of changed American strategic priorities, Indonesia's relation-ship with the United States throughout the 1990s became increasingly complicated. Up until the collapse of the New Order in 1998, Suharto's regime was increasingly irritated by the mounting criticism by President Clinton's Administration of the lack of democracy in Indonesia, Jakarta's human right abuses and its heavy-handed treatment of East Timor. Here, we should note the fact that Asian elites have traditionally been inclined to display sympathies to the U.S. Republican-led Administrations. Moreover, as Chanda explains, "add to that the protectionist reputation of the Democrats and the youthful President's (Clinton) exuberant denunciation of dictators "from Baghdad to Beijing," and it is easy to see why many in Asia saw Clinton's election as a recipe for trouble."[94]

Seen against the backdrop of growing U.S. pressure, perceptions of the foreign policy elite, which were then dominated by Suharto himself along with his political allies, were marked by a growing distrust of America's intentions. According to Habibie, at that time a Minister in Suharto's cabinet, the President became increasingly convinced from early 1991 that it was time for Indonesia to rebalance its relationship with the West and in particular with the United States. This was to be achieved by reducing economic and hence political dependence on the Western countries. A greater independence would benefit Indonesia because, as Habibie affirmed, "if [Western countries] want to pressure Indonesia, Pak Harto can kick them out. He himself did not say that, but I can feel it."[95] Present Indonesian leaders are generally unanimous in their view about the dramatically changed geopolitical significance of the archipelagic nation for Washington. Whereas during the Cold War years Indonesia was seen like a "pretty maiden" and as such was courted by the U.S. because of its importance as a "bulwark" against the communist menace, after 1990 America did not see any more need to cultivate its friendship with Indonesia. A former Minister of Foreign Affairs explained that

> Indonesia was seen as a force to stop Communism. That's why America was approaching us, the West was approaching us. America allowed a non-democratic, sometimes a brutal regime to be there. ... But we were a friend of the United States, especially Suharto. You can imagine that he had good credentials in the U.S. because he was so anti-Communist.[96]

According to the former Foreign Minister, with the cessation of the Cold War, Indonesia is seen less "like 'a pretty maiden'. ... Suddenly, Indonesia was seen from their point of view as, you know, we were bad. Our position ... has changed."[97]

Under Suharto's leadership, any demand for democratic reform within Indonesian society would have been fruitless in the absence of external pressures particularly from the Western states. In the context of the Cold War, Western leaders were more concerned about fighting against the communist threat than promoting democracy. As one leader affirmed, "there was no ready spectator, no ready market, and no external assistance for civil society groups in Indonesia. ... [The Indonesian NGOs] could not get the mainstream political decision makers in Washington or London or Canberra to pay attention to that."[98] As to the intensifying U.S. pressure for the Suharto's regime to democratise the country's political system, present leaders generally credit the Clinton Administration with facilitating the relatively peaceful transition towards a more democratic Indonesia. Here, we should note the difference between the Suharto government's unfavourable impressions of Clinton's Democratic Administration and the relatively positive view of Clinton's policies (particularly in comparison with the U.S. Administration of President Bush), which is largely shared by today's elite. The majority of them acknowledge that the democratic transition occurred because the internal demand had been fuelled by external pressure. Yet, whilst praising America for its role in promoting democracy in Indonesia, some leaders concurrently expressed their disillusion with the United States and other Western countries because they use the campaign for democracy as leverage to "push around" Indonesia. The United States forces Indonesia to adopt their own version of democracy, although, as one leader emphasized, "Indonesia's democracy is driven by its own cultural and societal factors."[99] In other words, the U.S. promotion of democracy in Indonesia is essentially regarded as a double-edge weapon and as such generates a great deal of ambivalent perceptions among the elite.

U.S.-Inspired "Subversion" and "Interference" in Indonesia's Internal Affairs

It needs to be stressed that, generally, Jakarta's political elite is not apprehensive of a traditional military threat to the Indonesian state. Rather, the contemporary elite is primarily concerned about non-conventional threats to their country's national security, in particular externally inspired interference and subversion. There is a belief widely shared by the nation's elite that the United States has in the post-Cold War era increasingly deployed new means of power to spread its influence and interfere in Indonesia's internal affairs. We will focus on five main perceived non-conventional threats that are high in the Indonesian elite's list of security concerns. These are in turn: the U.S. global preponderance and its unilateralism; the U.S.-launched War on Terrorism; the U.S. power stemming from its prominent norm-building position; the U.S. power over information and manipulation of international media; and NGOs operating around Indonesia functioning as Washington's agents (e.g., Trojan Horse) serving U.S. interests. The objective here is to describe the mode of thinking that lies beneath the elite's belief that the U.S. has increasingly in the post-Cold War period deployed new modern modes of power.

Initially, we need to point out the respondents' overwhelming agreement about the preponderant nature of the U.S. power and influence in the world. A senior diplomat aptly characterized this as:

> You could have all the rest of the world combined, you can not balance the United States. The U.S. is such a preponderant power in terms of its military supremacy; it is so obviously dominant that it is impossible to find a configuration of countries that can match it. It can only be matched by international norms and principles.[100]

As another respondent judged, the United States is so immensely powerful that "if the U.S. wanted the Indonesian government to extradite all citizens of Indonesia, the U.S. would achieve it."[101] Moreover, a Minister in President Yudhoyono's cabinet agreed by stating that "... the Americans are overwhelmingly superior in their defence and military budget. The total budget for one year equals more the next twenty countries put together. ... They cannot match the 385 billion dollars budget."[102] Then he argued that it is not at all surprising that "... with the overwhelming presence of the American economy, American pop-culture and American military, every country, France, Australia has this feeling that the U.S. power is too overwhelming."[103]

The survey data revealed that the leaders perceive the greatest danger for Indonesian national security as stemming from Washington's ability to interfere deep inside the country's political, economic, social and cultural sphere and hence considerably limit Indonesia's space for manoeuvring in the international arena. According to a CSIS-based international relations expert,

> [if] we define interventions in broader sense, of course, the United States is one power that is able to penetrate, to intervene, not only in terms of the military but also intervene in the sense that they can use their influence in Indonesian politics, Indonesian economy and so on. Of course, number one is the U.S.[104]

A former Minister of Foreign Affairs pointed out that "they [the U.S.] are in the position; they have the power to do so. ... The United States ... has the greatest capacity to limit not only Indonesia but [all] developing countries."[105] To that end, the perceived role of Washington in bringing down President Suharto is one of the most obvious examples of the elite's ambivalent view of the United States. With the Cold War over, Washington's pressure gradually intensified throughout the 1990s and culminated with the

U.S. Secretary of State Madeleine Albright stating that President Suharto "now ... has the opportunity for an historic act of statesmanship — one that will preserve his legacy as a man who not only led his country, but who provided for its democratic transition."[106] On the whole, Albright's statement is perceived positively by the present elite as the ultimate stimulus for Suharto to step down. Concurrently, however, in the eyes of present leaders, this reality highlights just how all pervading is the power the United States wields in contemporary international relations. Symptomatic in this regard was Suharto's "mysterious" remark that a certain foreign power had been behind his fall from office. However, when directly asked to elaborate, Suharto refused to publicly name that country.[107]

This view, which is shared by a majority of the elite, was substantiated during the Indonesian economic crisis in the late 1990s when Washington was perceived as exploiting Indonesia's weakness. The Asian financial crisis began in July 1997 when the Thai baht plummeted. The Indonesian rupiah was hit soon after. The severe depression of the Indonesian economy, which produced social tensions including rioting, looting and arson, along with the killing of students and ordinary citizens on the streets of Jakarta, marked a slow collapse of Suharto's 32-year-long authoritarian rule over the archipelagic nation. It is clearly beyond the scope of this book to discuss in detail the long-drawn-out negotiations between the United States and the International Monetary Fund (IMF), on the one side, and Suharto's government, on the other, over the IMF-led rescue plan for the embattled Indonesian economy.[108] What is exceedingly important, however, is to look at how the images of Washington's role in forcing Jakarta to accept the IMF's bailout contribute to the elite's present negative perception of the United States.

Besides recognizing Washington's pressure on President Suharto to follow the IMF-prescribed rescue plan, one particular image remains deep-entrenched in the leaders' minds. It is the almost legendary photograph of the scene in which President Suharto is affixing his signature on yet another letter of intent with the IMF, while the institution's managing director Michael Camdessus is standing over him, arms folded across his chest and with a school-master's expression in his face overseeing his "pupil" completing his complicated assignment.[109] It is exactly this image that has come for the elite to be seen as a symbol of an excessively powerful superpower dictating terms to the fragile and feeble Indonesian Government. From the point of view of many in the elite, the United States, in the disguise of a reputable international institution, such as IMF, comes officially to help Indonesia but in reality it wants to exploit the developing nation. Referring to the United States' policies towards his country, a young career diplomat pointed out that "there is no free lunch today."[110]

U.S. Economic Exploitation and Nationalism

The Indonesian elite is inclined to view U.S. policies at the time of the 1997 financial meltdown as interference in Indonesia's domestic affairs and a deliberate attempt to make their nation dependent on the IMF. With the demise of the Soviet Union, Washington's standard shifted from anti-communism to democracy. "That can be interpreted that the U.S. [was] now fed up with Suharto. He was a good boy in the past but now there is a change of values,"[111] explained a retired general and a graduate from a prestigious American university whose overseas studies were funded by a U.S.-funded programme designed to create a "modernizing elite" for Indonesia. He brought up an argument shared by many across the whole spectrum of the foreign policy elite: "Because it was not easy to create change through a political push, a theory came that it can be pushed through international economic, financial pressures through the IMF."[112] There is a widespread sense among the elite that the Western countries, in general, and the "calculating" United States, in particular, "cheat on us" by using institutions such as the IMF as a proxy to exert influence over Indonesia.[113]

We need to see these suspicions also in the context of nationalist sentiments among the Indonesian leadership. Nationalism was stipulated as one of the five principles of Pancasila and as such has long been established as an important ingredient in Indonesia's domestic politics. In real terms, it means that any perceived over-dependence on external forces, such as the United States or IMF, is likely to arouse nationalist sentiments among segments of the Indonesian population and political establishment. Consequently, nationalism needs to be considered as a factor that can affect the course of events at the level of foreign policy. However, it can be argued that nationalist sentiments, recently revealed in the form of anti-American and anti-Western expressions among both the elite and the Indonesian society at large, tend to be fickle and inconsistent.[114] Politicians' nationalist political rhetoric in the public sphere expresses form rather than substance of the government political agenda. Nationalist sentiments among the public can often be a result of manipulation by the leaders who use nationalist rhetoric to conceal their real hidden motives.

Nationalism is a recurrent phenomenon in Indonesia. In the period of 2003–06, it resurfaced again during the political debate over whether the American-owned company ExxonMobil should be given operational rights over the Cepu Block oilfield in East Java province.[115] Several prominent party leaders from the House of Representatives strongly urged the government not to grant the operational right over the Cepu Block to a foreign company. Abdillah Toha, Chairman of the National Mandate Party (PAN), for example, asserted that giving Cepu to Exxon would be like Indonesia bowing to American pressure. As to the allegations that U.S. Vice-President Dick Cheney directly asked President Yudhoyono during his visit to Washington about the Cepu contract, Abdillah argued that "in politics, questions about Presidential decisions on the management of state assets is a form of pressure."[116]

Yet, all in all, Indonesian domestic political scene was divided on that issue. It was perhaps no more obvious than in the case of the Indonesian Moslem Intellectuals Association (ICMI) and National Mandate Party (PAN), both of which represent the forces of the modern brand of Islam in Indonesia. On the one hand, the ICMI founder and former President B.J. Habibie, as well as key figures in PAN Sutrisno Bachir and Hatta Radjasa, both voiced strong support for the government's decision to grant ExxonMobil the rights to lead the Cepu operation. On the other hand, a key figure in ICMI and former Assembly Speaker Amien Rais, as well as ICMI chairwoman Marwah Daud Ibrahim, both opposed the government's decision.[117] We can see here that there were two very contradictory views on the Cepu settlement. At this point, it is particularly important to note that both originated in the same section of the Indonesian political scene, namely those representing moderate Islam. The coexistence of opposing attitudes to the same issue within the same Muslim organization and political party suggests that religion was not the main factor influencing the leaders' attitude to the issue. Moreover, given that the opposition to the government's decision to grant operational rights to the American company came from different segments of the elite, including such diverse political parties as secular-nationalist PDI-P and radical Islamic party PKS, it indicates that either nationalist sentiments or political manipulation were at play — or both.

The fact that some political parties expressed two such contradictory views on the Cepu settlement suggests that the Indonesian elite's nationalist sentiments are a fickle and vague phenomenon. We should also take into consideration that Indonesian leaders are known for manipulating and exploiting nationalist feelings for their own political or financial gain. Defence Minister Sudarsono alleged that "integrated coordination" aimed at political manipulation might have been at play during the series of simultaneous demonstrations with nationalist agenda to protest against the cabinet's decision to grant the Cepu operation to ExxonMobil.[118] The fact that the cabinet was divided over the Cepu decision and the opposition came mainly from cabinet members who are also influential businessmen, namely Aburizal Bakrie and Jusuf Kalla, suggests that not so much nationalism but rather high-level economic interest might have been at stake.[119]

We should also note the high degree of ambivalence, which is characteristic of what is generally regarded as nationalism-driven anti-American and anti-Western sentiments. This was apparent both in the case of the *crisis moneter* in 1997-8 and the Cepu settlement in 2006. The ambivalence was reflected in the perception that while the United States helped Indonesia through the IMF by facilitating the country's economic recovery, Washington concurrently wanted to exploit Indonesia's weak economic position. Amien Rais frankly acknowledged that "Indonesia's position is dilemmatic."[120] Although Washington knew Indonesia desperately needed economic assistance, the IMF repeatedly postponed sending the funds. According to Rais, "it seems like the IMF wants to interfere into our sovereignty. The U.S. was playing a game with Indonesia ... it is not without grounds if we are suspicious of the IMF's [and U.S.] real intentions behind their help to Indonesia."[121] Some four years later, in 2002, Rais conceded that "the IMF is a necessary evil" and simultaneously expressed concern about Indonesia's excessive over-reliance on the institution.[122] Similar views came also from a young career diplomat who expressed a great deal of frustration by asserting: "I hate to say that but we do not have a better option than the U.S. to turn to for financial support."[123] Amien Rais' remarks infused with a proud nationalist streak do not appear to express an outright anti-American attitude. Rather, they reflect the elite's sense of frustration inherent in the "dilemma of dependence" — how can Indonesia secure its economy's recovery from the monetary crisis without compromising national independence. Rais' words highlight the traditional elite's concern about Indonesia's ability (or perhaps disability) to maintain a position of maximum independence vis-à-vis other countries, and notably the major powers.

A former member of, to use his own words, the "Suharto crowd", who falls into the non-Muslim minority within the Indonesian elite suggested that it is mainly nationalistic leaders and politicians in Muslim parties who blame the United States and the IMF for the protracted economic difficulties facing Indonesia.[124] One part of what some Indonesian leaders consider as an "American-orchestrated conspiracy" stems from the question as to why the financial crisis in Indonesia took so long to recede and recover. Why did Indonesia have to "muddle through" the economic difficulties, when other regional countries overcame the crisis much sooner and without so many long-term effects in their societies? He argued that "the problem was the inconsistency by the administration to implement the IMF policies."[125] In other words, the protracted and severe economic crisis was a purely internal problem and by no means an external threat posed by the United States and the IMF. We should also note the correlation between this particular leader's positive impression of the United States and the relatively high degree of trust in Washington policies during the economic crisis, on the one hand, and his non-Muslim religious background, on the other. As we will demonstrate in Chapter 7, the leaders' religious affiliation constitutes an important factor that shapes their perceptions of other countries.

It could be argued that because of their ambivalent nature, nationalism-driven anti-American attitudes tend to be relatively superficial and issue-based. As Salim Said pointedly contends, "We don't want to use the term 'Western style'. Western liberalism is anathema, and capitalism is hated here, but we're [practicing] both."[126] Rizal Sukma, for example, argues that anti-American pronouncements of Indonesian leaders stem from nationalism more than xenophobia and therefore they do not "reflect an inherent and deep-seated anti-Western and anti-American attitude."[127] The research data also unequivocally indicate that economic exploitation by the United States, while causing some degree of concern, it is not generally considered as a principal and serious threat for the country and its economy. In fact, out of forty-five interviewed leaders, only one single respondent, a former President, asserted that "the most imminent threat to Indonesia is 'economic exploitation'" at the hands of the United States.[128] On the other hand, a number of leaders repudiated the notion that the United States seeks to buy valuable Indonesian assets, such as oil fields, in order to manipulate and gain control over Indonesia. When asked, the leaders explained that they do not regard the United States as a threat in economic terms if only because the American economy is, unlike the Chinese, largely complementary with the Indonesian economy.[129] According to a former Minister of Foreign Affairs, "the government at least and most of the rational people, we do not subscribe to conspiracy theories."[130]

The above analysis suggests that a gap exists between the Indonesian elite's publicly voiced nationalist sentiments aimed at eliminating the purported "U.S. economic colonialism", on the one hand, and the leaders' perceptions of the U.S. as revealed by the survey data evaluation, on the other. It could be argued that this inconsistency can be explained within the "form and substance" framework — nationalism in Indonesia, not only towards the United States but more generally, presently enters the foreign policy-making process more often in form than in substance.

Post-9/11 View from Indonesia: "U.S. Threat" and the "Bush Phenomenon"

The following analysis argues that there is a correlation between, on the one hand, the record-high level of threat assessment by the elite of the United States in the period of 2002–08 and, on the other, Washington's policies under the Bush Administration. Consequently, the present high-profile anti-American expressions can be regarded as a rather temporary phenomenon. This argument is supported by two concrete observations. First, America's threatening appearance is largely associated with the present Republican-led U.S. Administration and particularly the image of George W. Bush himself. Second, the research findings indicate that the elite is deeply divided on the degree and nature of the threat Washington's policies currently pose to Indonesia's national interests and security.

The terrorist attacks on 11 September 2001 produced in Indonesia, as much as in other countries around the world, an initial remarkable outpouring of public sympathy for America.[131] In the following three years, however, discontent and resentment towards the United States had grown both among the Indonesian society and the country's elite. Images of the America were tarnished mainly by the U.S. military attacks on Afghanistan and later Iraq. In particular, the United States-led invasion in Iraq, which began without the express approval of the United Nations Security Council, was considered as the most flagrant example of U.S. unilateralist foreign policy. This foreign policy is perceived as paying very little attention to the interests of other countries, including those with long-established friendly relations with the United States.

In the following discussion, we will see that the Indonesian elite's unfavourable perceptions of the United States can be largely ascribed to their negative impressions of U.S. President George W. Bush. A poll conducted by the Washington-based Pew Research Centre concluded that "a low regard for President Bush is more heavily correlated with an unfavourablility rating for the United States than is any other attitude or opinion tested."[132] Thus, as many as 69 per cent of Indonesians believed in 2003 that the main problem is with President Bush rather than with the United States in general. Significantly, the report also argued that "Bush's low standing emerges in country after country as the leading link to anti-Americanism."[133] In fact, when trying to describe the sources of their negative attitude towards the United States, a great majority of Indonesian leaders referred to what can be reasonably called the "Bush Phenomenon". In the elite circles, George W. Bush is commonly described with adjectives such as "arrogant, bullying, imperial, neocolonial and a new pharaoh."[134] The American President is frequently characterized as someone who "worries many people here in Indonesia"[135] and that "because of Bush ... we are very sensitive to the U.S".[136]

The respondents spontaneously raised the question whether America under the Bush's leadership still sustains its image as a benevolent superpower. Will America be using its persuasive power, or its "soft power", or will it be a harsh power to subdue the world according to what the U.S. Government thinks is "right"? Expressing the prevalent view among the elite, one leader responded to the above question by saying that "Bush worries many people here in Indonesia ... because he seems to be the second type [of American leader]. He does not use his soft power anymore ... He tells the world what he wants and he doesn't want."[137] The interviewed Indonesian policy-makers like to present pieces of evidence' to support this argument — starting with the U.S. rejection of the Kyoto Agreement and the International Criminal Court, to the President Bush's proclamation of the War on Terrorism in September 2001. Perhaps reflecting the general mode of thinking about the present U.S. Administration, the Indonesian paraphrased version of Bush's now famous statement "You're either with us or against us in the fight against terror" goes "If you are not for me, you are against me".[138]

The U.S. versus China Juxtaposition

When trying to explain their view of the United States, a number of respondents pointed out that "China seems to me to have a much more mature government than the George Bush's one."[139] This statement reflects the interesting inclination by the respondents to juxtapose their perceptions of the United States and China and their respective governments' foreign policies. We can see this attitude in the light of the prevalent sense among the elite that in the not-so-distant future Indonesia will increasingly have to "row between two reefs" — meaning navigate between two rival powers, the United States and China. One leader aptly characterized the majority's view that "[the] Indonesians are nervous. ... Never in the history of Indonesia are we in such a situation like now in which America is [so unpopular]. It is understandable if you got strong impression ... that America is seen by Indonesians now ... as a threat."[140] Then, he spontaneously contrasted America with China by pointing out that

> slowly China is perceived as a country which is modernizing itself, is
> not a threat because following Deng Xiaoping's policy developing the
> economy of China and the debacle of the Soviet Union, Communism

is not ... seen as a threat. Now, suddenly 9/11 occurred, followed by
pre-emptive doctrine of Bush. From that time on until today ... many
Indonesians [including] the elite ... are very aware ... that America is
a threat.[141]

The interviewees voiced their overwhelming preference for a multipolar
international system. In contrast to the present United States-dominated
unilateral or uni-multipolar system,[142] they believe that a multipolar
system can provide Indonesia with more security and more space for
manoeuvring in the international arena. It needs to be seen in this context
that the Indonesian elite is inclined to juxtapose Washington's and Beijing's
attitudes towards multilateralism. The leaders view much more positively
China's policies in the last decade that emphasize multilateral security and
economic cooperation as opposed to "the United States [which] has showed
that it does not pay attention to multilateralism, unlike Clinton. Bush became
more unilateral...."[143] Some respondents expressed the idea that the tendency
among leaders to compare their attitudes to the United States vis-à-vis their
attitudes to China is absolutely sensible. For example, a senior diplomat
stressed that he "can understand if people compare the U.S. with China."[144]
He referred to his own experience attending APEC meetings, in which the
United States and China are two of the most important participants. As the
diplomat explained, "the United States comes with the heavy-handed agenda,
terrorism, terrorism, terrorism, that's what they have been saying."[145] The U.S.
attitude stands in stark contrast with the Chinese approach, which includes
not only security but "China comes with 'goodies' ... they come as a more
complete package ... they also talk about ... economic development, about
free trade."[146] On the contrary, Washington has in the last two or three years
become "more uni-dimensional and uni-lateral" in the sense that its agenda
is heavily dominated by the issue of terrorism.[147]

U.S. Unilateralism as a Threat to Indonesia's Sovereignty

Generally, the elite do not view the United States as a threat to the Indonesian
state in the traditional, military terms. It is at this point that the elite
perceptions about the U.S. military threat to Indonesia stand in stark contrast
with the public perceptions. Figure 4.1 shows that more than two thirds
of lay Indonesians considered U.S. military action towards their country,
at least to a degree, as a real possibility. By contrast, rather than concerned
about the prospect of the U.S. military invading Indonesia, the survey data
highlight the relatively high degree to which the country's foreign policy elite

FIGURE 4.1
Views of a Changing World 2003;
War with Iraq Further Divides Global Publics

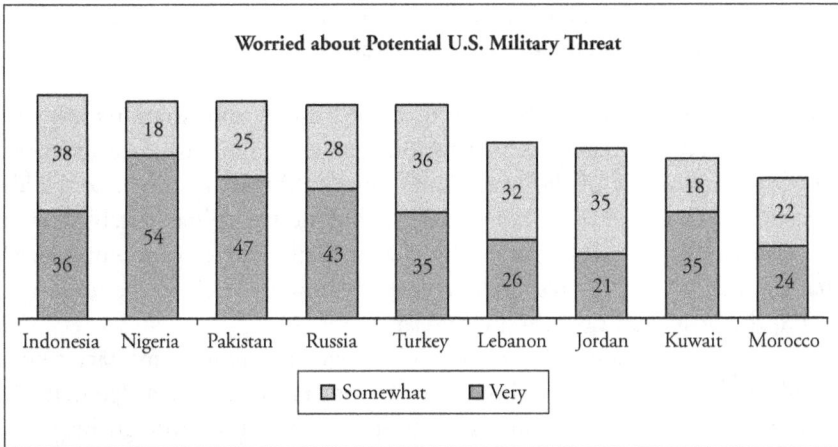

Worried about Potential U.S. Military Threat

	Indonesia	Nigeria	Pakistan	Russia	Turkey	Lebanon	Jordan	Kuwait	Morocco
Somewhat	38	18	25	28	36	32	35	18	22
Very	36	54	47	43	35	26	21	35	24

☐ Somewhat   ■ Very

Source: The Pew Research Centre, 3 June 2003.

is alarmed by the real or potential implications of the U.S. unilateral actions for the domestic political scene and wider society in Indonesia. In particular, they are concerned about President Bush's "pre-emptive strike" doctrine and the "War on Terrorism" campaign. The latter is seen, as the country's former intelligence chief Lieutenant-General Zen Maulani affirmed, as an attempt by the United States to use allegations of the existence of Islamic terrorist bases around the archipelago to gain control of Indonesia's natural resources.[148] Moreover, a senior diplomat at DEPLU expressed the opinion shared by the great majority of the elite that "the implications of the U.S. unilateral actions ... negatively affect how countries interact with each other."[149] This statement is immediately followed by a spontaneous assessment that "the U.S. unilateralism is much more dangerous than the 'China threat'."[150]

In contrast to the public perceptions, no more than five leaders out of forty-five interviewed acknowledged the possibility of a United States-launched military attack on Indonesia. This view then needs to be clearly seen in the light of the Bush Administration's military invasions in Afghanistan in 2001 and Iraq in 2003. A former high-ranking military officer explained that

> based on the precedence of the U.S. [policies in Iraq], there were strong rumours ... that if Indonesia was not able to launch strong responses

> against those terrorists, which the U.S. had intelligence that they were
> in Indonesia, then the U.S. could carry out military operations against
> Indonesia. There were strong rumours of that. And because of the
> precedence [in Iraq and Afghanistan] ... it was considered very seriously
> ... and the U.S. assured the will to carry out [the military operations
> against Indonesia], to go after those terrorists.[151]

Another leader confirmed the view that the Bush Administration's military invasions in Afghanistan generated a strong concern among the elite about the growing prominence of the "traditional military threat" to the nation. This perception was shared "not only among the Indonesian military establishment but also among the wider public."[152] Yet, it ought to be again emphasized that the majority of the respondents overwhelmingly rejected the notion of a U.S. threat in traditional military terms.

A former Indonesian President was not worried about a military threat posed by the United States, though he did not fail to acknowledge that the U.S. military is by far the world's most potent and powerful. In his view, "it is more about how to maintain our own sovereignty..."[153] He recollected that, in 2002, the Indonesian Government gave a permit to the United States to send an aircraft carrier to pass through the Java Sea. Later, however, the carrier sent M18 Hornet military aircraft into the air space of Indonesia, an act that was protested by the Jakarta government. According to another respondent, this act can also be interpreted, "as if [the United States was] threatening Indonesia."[154] Likewise, under the President Abdurrahman Wahid's leadership, Indonesia protested against what was considered as an illegal intrusion into Indonesian territory when two American war ships together with smaller vessels from the Singaporean navy trained there. Yet, according to the ex-President, the United States is much more likely to challenge Indonesia's sovereignty "culturally". This "cultural threat" challenges Indonesia's sovereignty

> by means of the American way of life, which is materialistic, [and] is so
> different from our [way of life], which is not based on materialism. ...
> It's a normal feeling of "domination" that the materialistic side of the
> West is more dominant than our traditional "culture". [But] I think that
> we will be able to balance that in the future.[155]

Another distinct case that some respondents considered as evidence of the continuing U.S. policy of interference into Indonesia's domestic political processes was the fall of the former President Abdurrahman Wahid. Generally, according to a Member of the Parliament, "the majority of the Indonesian elite know what is actually going on; how the Ambassador of the U.S. in Jakarta always influences many political figures [and] many informal leaders to influence political processes in many cases in Indonesia."[156] In this context, the United States is believed to have also been somehow implicated in the long-drawn-out process of political bickering that led to Wahid's resignation. As one leader and government insider emphasized, the Indonesian military is very pro-U.S. and "[the] military played a crucial role behind the fall of Wahid."[157] Another interviewee agreed that "America would like to repeat what they did in the past", namely supporting the army and President Suharto to eliminate U.S. enemies both inside and outside Indonesia.[158] However, according to the respondent, "that is not easy anymore because politics is changing both domestically as well as internationally."[159]

Here, we need to note that the elite's suspicions about the U.S. implication in President Wahid's fall were also fuelled by reports published by foreign media and academic institutions. Following Wahid's repeated calls in early 2000 for the establishment of an alliance among Indonesia, India and China to counter America's influence, the U.S.-based think-tank Stratfor, for example, concluded that "Washington may prefer to facilitate a transition of power [in Jakarta]."[160] The discussion will follow with an account given by one respondent whose identity will not be disclosed for obvious reasons. The leader sought to explain the way U.S. top officials were involved in the toppling of President Wahid and replacing him with Megawati Sukarnoputri who "always thought she [had] the right to be the President because she was the daughter of Sukarno."[161] The leader recounted that

> I have the witnesses, I have the proof, that Megawati, through her husband, assisted by Bob Dole, the Republican Presidential candidate, Taufik Kiemas, the husband of Mega, paid 4 million USD to Bob Dole as lobbying costs. This I know from the tax people in the United States. … So why [President] Bush was silent although he knew about the plot? Because he was respecting Bob Dole, former Presidential candidate of the same party, the Republicans.[162]

The amount of money allegedly paid to the American politician was said to be designed to lobby with relevant influential people in Washington who were asked to use various (not specified) means available to the United States to encourage the transition of power from President Wahid to the then Vice-President Megawati Sukarnoputri. When asked about further details regarding these allegations, however, the respondent refused to elaborate.[163]

Finally, some interviewed leaders tended to characterize U.S. policies towards Indonesia as a "kid's game". But in this case they refer not only to the Bush Administration but to the post-Cold War era in general. The term "kid's game", used by a senior official from DEPLU, describes the kind of game when one has to get to a pole that somebody else is holding but the pole keeps moving away. In the United States-Indonesian relationship, Washington is the pole holder and Jakarta strives in vain to reach the pole. In other words, Indonesia desperately keeps trying to fulfil every wish and requirement of Washington but then it is not enough and other new requirements come.[164] Most frequently mentioned examples are the military-to-military relations between the two countries, as well as human rights issues pertinent to East Timor, Aceh and West Papua and lately the U.S.-led War on Terrorism.

THE WAR ON TERRORISM: ELITE VERSUS PUBLIC PERCEPTIONS

We will now thoroughly analyse the elite's views of the United States in the context of the War on Terrorism. The emphasis on the U.S. anti-terrorism campaign is of a great importance here since it can be reasonably considered the principal factor that has in the 2001–06 period shaped perceptions of the United States both within the Indonesian elite and among the society at large. The War on Terrorism has been a campaign proclaimed and led by the United States with the main stated goal of ending international terrorism. Launched in response to the 11 September 2001 terrorist attacks in the United States, the War on Terrorism became a central part of U.S. President George W. Bush's foreign policy. In contrast with a traditional war that involves defined nations with their boundaries and standing armies, the main actors and strategies in the War on Terrorism encompass intelligence, diplomacy, special forces and police work.

The U.S. as "the King of Terrorists"

The following discussion presents two arguments: First, the elite is divided in its perceptions about the United States and its foreign policy dominated by the War on Terror, importantly, with the majority of the leaders sharing a rather benign view of U.S. intentions.[165] Second, there has been a substantial gap in perceptions on this issue between the elite and the lay people in Indonesia.

The U.S. military campaigns in Afghanistan and especially in Iraq gave rise to a strong wave of anti-American sentiment among the Indonesian

FIGURE 4.2
Views of a Changing World, June 2003; The Pew Global Attitudes Project

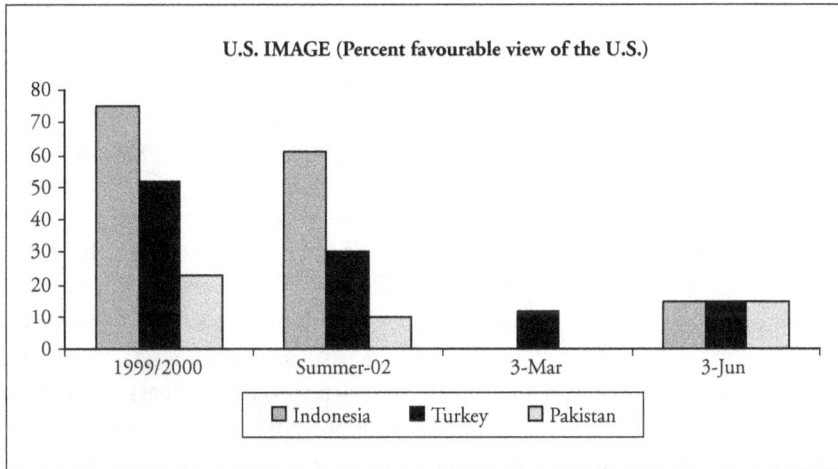

Source: The Pew Research Centre.

population. As Figure 4.2 illustrates, the percentage of Indonesians who held a favourable view of the United States declined sharply from 75 per cent in the year 2000 to merely 15 per cent in 2003. First, "the U.S. is seen in Indonesia as a *'penindas'*, meaning 'neo-colonialist'",[166] mainly owing to the suspicions that Washington was exploiting the War on Terrorism for its own hegemonic ambitions, namely gaining control of the ever more valuable natural resources in Iraq. Second, the U.S. was also widely seen as stigmatising Islam. The common perception among the general public was that the United States was anti-Islam in nature and that, in the context of the post Cold War strategic environment, Washington had replaced communism with Islam as the principal threat to America. This basic distrust towards the U.S. Government and in particular President Bush among the Indonesian population augmented the position and gave credibility to the cause of the vocal radical Islamic groups. Tellis pointedly argues that

> what Osama bin Laden appears to have done successfully is to make an appealing argument that Washington's support of unjust, despotic, and corrupt Muslim states, its war against Muslim countries like Afghanistan and Iraq, and its favouritism toward Israel, actually represents evidence that the United States is at war with Islam itself and, consequently

leaves the weaker Muslim community with no alternative to armed resistance. As long as millions of Muslims believe this claim, many passive sympathizers will elect for active terrorism, and the war on terrorism will not be won.[167]

Anti-American sentiment among the Indonesian population was also fuelled by some high-level public pronouncements of the country's top leaders. Referring to the widespread sense among the public that the terrorist organization Jemaah Islamiya (JI) does not really exist, but rather has been constructed by the CIA and Zionist conspirators to gain control over Indonesia, former President Wahid affirmed that "none of the news that terrorists are here is convincing to me."[168] The country's former intelligence chief Lieutenant-General Maulani alleged that Washington uses the War on Terror as a pretext to gain control over Indonesia's abundant natural resources. And since "the world's largest oil producers are in the Islamic world ... [the U.S. is] applying a preventive strategy, to prevent Islamic countries, including Indonesia, from becoming advanced countries."[169] In another widely publicized public pronouncement, Vice-President Hamzah Haz from the Muslim-based United Development Party (PPP) asserted that "one proof that the U.S. is the real terrorist is that it attacks any country at random without approval of the United Nations." This is why, as Haz declared, America is not only a terrorist but is even *"rajanya teroris"* — *"the king of terrorists"*.[170]

It is easy to gain the impression from these high-profile hard-line statements that the elite's attitudes to the U.S. largely correspond with those of the wider public. For example, according to Smith, "... while many Indonesian officials view the U.S. military presence in the Asia/Pacific as benign, deep-seated suspicion about U.S. intentions still exists with regard to the Muslim world."[171] However, the research data clearly revealed a much more nuanced and balanced elite perceptions about the United States in the context of the anti-terrorism campaign and its repercussions for Indonesia. Illustrative of that is Foreign Minister Hassan Wirayuda's categorical dismissal of the "U.S. as a king of terrorists" rhetoric. While Wirayuda asserted that "the statement was reflecting Vice-President Hamzah Haz's personal opinion," he simultaneously emphasized that "the Indonesian government values the United States' leading role in the global coalition in combating terrorism."[172]

In fact, the research data indicate that only a minority of Indonesian leaders share similar hard-line and bellicose attitudes towards the United States in the context of the War on Terrorism. There are certainly a number of important issues, which have caused some degree of irritation among the elite. Some respondents were concerned that Indonesia had been subject to pressures to act strongly against Muslim groups considered by Washington as being perpetrators of terrorist acts. Here, a Member of Parliament for the PAN party says his main concern is that "America is always trying to influence Indonesian policy related to militant Islam."[173] As a former Minister of Foreign Affairs emphasized, "we do not know what they want from us ... there is a certain irritation on both sides ... on our side because we are wrongly perceived as hesitant [in dealing with terrorist suspects]."[174] Washington's excessive diplomatic and political pressure on Indonesia was also interpreted by one leader as "a pretext, it is only a reason to expand ... to find way to accommodate their [the U.S.] expansionist appetite."[175] He then quickly emphasized that while most of the Indonesian public see the United States as the biggest threat now, because of its anti-terrorism policy, "I still consider [the U.S. policy] more of a pretext rather than a real threat."[176]

Some respondents also interpreted the United States-led War on Terrorism as being a part of the broader U.S. drive to spread American values. A senior diplomat referred to his own experience during his recent visit in North Korea where he could see clearly what the United States did globally and in the Asian region in particular. It was in North Korea where he clearly realized that the main objective of the Americans is to spread their own values including democratisation and human rights. He affirmed that "the war on terror, what I saw in North Korea, of course, is the means of the United States to spread their own values. For Indonesia ... there is some bigger agenda."[177] For another career diplomat, "the War on Terrorism has been used by the U.S. to project their power overseas."[178] Many leaders also questioned the moral dimension of America's actions in Afghanistan and Iraq — here a prominent Muslim leader and politician emphatically concluded:

> Realistically speaking, both Bush and Bin Laden have the same fundamentalist character: "either with us, or against us." It is this kind of character and mindset that has dragged the world into the situation of enmity and hate. Both are the true enemy of civilized human beings. Bush has abused democracy and human rights slogans to invade on other nations; Bin Laden has hijacked God to destroy the edifice of human civilization.[179]

However, the majority of the interviewed leaders still consider the U.S. anti-terrorism campaign not as a direct threat to Indonesian national security but rather as an offence to the sensitivities and national pride of the Indonesian people. The most mentioned example here was the controversial case of the terrorist suspect Hambali, also known as Riduan Isamuddin, who was arrested by Thai authorities and subsequently handed over to the CIA. Washington later rejected a number of requests by Jakarta for Hambali to be handed over to Indonesian authorities for interrogation. While terrorism is largely seen as an issue where Indonesia's and America's interests converge, the leaders feel humiliated because the U.S. authorities repeatedly refused to extradite Hambali — an Indonesian citizen — back to Indonesia.[180] A similar irritant for the elite was the perceived U.S. interference in the trial of Muslim cleric Abu Bakar Baashir, the alleged spiritual leader of the militant *Jemaah Islamiyah* organization. Washington exploits the War on Terrorism, for example, "when the U.S. government tries to seduce Megawati to send Abu Bakar Bashir to the U.S. as a prisoner."[181] As a noted scholar with LIPI asserted, "I myself, you know, I am a Muslim, I am against Islamic radicalism but as an Indonesian citizen I will reject any idea whether he is a terrorist to be sent to the U.S. Why? Because this is our national pride and also our national sovereignty to defend our citizens."[182]

Perception Gap and the Role of Personal Experience

It could be argued that there is a perception gap within the Indonesian foreign policy elite with regard to the War on Terrorism, with the leaders of Islamic parties holding the most critical and austere anti-American views. According to an Indonesian CSIS-based academic, "yes, it's quite understandable … from the ideological point of view. They [sizable segments of the Muslim elite] are always sensitive and suspicious towards the U.S."[183] However, it is apparent that even within one Muslim party can be found two quite diverging perceptions of the United States with regard to the War on Terrorism. This was particularly apparent in the case of two senior members of Indonesia's second largest Muslim organization *Muhammadiyah* — one is a member of parliament for the PAN political party and the other is an influential politician and a noted Muslim scholar. Whereas the former acknowledged the seriousness of the terrorist issue in Indonesia, though criticizing the U.S. approach in tackling the problem,[184] the latter leader rebuffed the notion of the global threat of terrorism by asking "Who is Osama bin Laden?" And he had a quick answer: "The U.S. created him" because it suits America, whose aim is to dominate the world.[185]

It could be argued that there is also a perception gap of the United States with regard to the War on Terrorism between the elite and the lay people in Indonesia. It was apparent from Figures 4.1 and 4.2 that the United States-launched War on Terrorism generated a dramatic upsurge in anti-American sentiments in Indonesian society. The Indonesian public generally saw the U.S. anti-terrorism policy as anti-Islam and bent on stigmatizing the Islamic religion, while largely disregarding the terrorist threat. A scholar with a deep knowledge of non-traditional security issues agreed that "the point here is there is a gap in perception between the Indonesian political elite and the society."[186] At the grassroots level, for a great majority of lay people in Indonesia, terrorism and Islamic extremism were not high on their list of concerns. As one respondent affirmed, "When you talk to ordinary people, terrorism is number five or number six in their list of priorities."[187] By contrast, the interviews with Indonesian leaders have shown that most of the elite understands very well the threat stemming from international terrorism and consider this issue a point where Indonesia's and America's interests largely converge.

Whilst admitting that Washington might exploit the War on Terrorism to influence Indonesia's internal affairs, in the words of one interviewed leader, "it does not necessarily mean negative or positive."[188] It was particularly leaders coming from a non-Muslim and moderate Muslim background who explicitly supported the U.S. anti-terrorism policies towards Indonesia. Generally, they considered the War on Terrorism not to be only in the United States interest but primarily in Indonesia's own interest.[189] It is very reasonable to assume that Indonesia is harboring terrorists and thus the United States is understandably and justifiably concerned about Indonesia's willingness and ability to eliminate and eradicate this threat.[190] To this end, a noted economist and academic who comes from a non-Muslim background asserted:

> In fact, I wish Bush were even more explicit about that. Bush said we are not fighting against Islam and Islamic countries, we are fighting against terrorism. But I don't think it is honest enough. I would say, yes, I am not fighting against Islam but with Islam. Because Al Qaeda and other fundamentalist groups were against the United States in the name of Islam. ... So, if the U.S. should attack Al Qaeda, because [its members are] Muslims [who fight in the name of] Islam.[191]

We should also note here that in several cases the respondents' high level of trust towards the U.S. intentions with respect to its anti-terrorism policy was owing to the leaders' more or less direct personal experience with terrorism. As we emphasized in preceding chapters, historical knowledge and personal experience is bound to significantly shape the elite perceptions. For example, one interviewed leader was intimately confronted with international terrorism while he was serving as a high-ranking diplomat at the Indonesian Embassy in Thailand. In March 1981, a domestic Garuda

GA 206 flight was hijacked by a group of armed man belonging to the Islamic organization *Komando Jihad*. The Indonesian airliner later landed in Bangkok and after protracted negotiations between the hijackers and the Indonesian authorities the aircraft was stormed by special commandos killing four of the five hijackers and freeing all fifty-five hostages aboard. Four years later, he had yet another first-hand experience with terrorism — this time during the bombing of the Borobudur Buddhist temple in Central Java, which was also carried out by a group of Islamic extremists.[192] This personal experience lead the leader to trust Washington in its pursuit of "preventive action" when it pressures Jakarta to deal with the threat of terrorism. After all, he asserts that terrorism was not invented by the Americans — "terrorism is not a creation of the Americans, [War on Terrorism] is the reaction [to terrorism]."[193]

An Indonesian expert in international relations with close ties with the DEPLU provides another example of how a personal experience with terrorism, though a much less direct one, can shape one's attitude to terrorism and hence his perception of the United States and its policies. First, during his recent trip to Pakistan, he visited several *madrasah* where he met a number of Indonesian students. He explained that he found that "some Indonesian students ... were kept in the dark. ... Nobody can control it. Even the Indonesian Embassy does not have access to [the Indonesian students] in the religious schools in Pakistan."[194] Second, while pointing to Indonesia as being "one of safe havens ... for those who are involved in terrorism," he referred to the following event:

> I have a personal experience when an Afghan man knocked on my door at 3 a.m. and then I asked him where do you come from? "From Afghanistan." "What are you doing here?" "Because I am collecting money for charity activities here." It was in Jakarta in my house. He just knocked on my door. They come door by door. It is just one case. I just imagine now, the point is that if they come into Indonesia without permission [illegally], the Indonesian government does not have any control over their activities. That's the point.[195]

This personal experience was important for the leader insofar as it made him realize just how weak was Indonesia's capacity and effectiveness to control its vast and sprawling territory. As a result, Indonesia unwittingly exported instability and hence became a danger for other countries. It is in this context that Indonesians should understand the heightened interest of the major powers in ensuring that Indonesia does not serve as a breeding ground and haven for Islamic terrorists. He then concluded by emphasizing "that's why I do not believe in the conspiracy theory that the major powers, like the

U.S., even Japan and Australia, actually want to break Indonesia up. I do not believe that."[196]

It was precisely the awareness of Indonesia's ineptitude to efficiently deal with the terrorist issue that led a majority of respondents to acknowledge Indonesia's own part in the problem. In other words, Indonesia itself is to blame because the country is to a great extent a source of the terrorist problem. Several interviewed leaders also stressed the fact that terrorism is in fact a problem both externally and internally. As a Minister in President Yudhoyono's cabinet noted, "externally, [we have] to deal with the terrorist groups in Southeast Asia. But it's also a domestic [problem] because ... the Islamic groups ... come within each country. That's why it is an external as well as an internal threat."[197] This combination of external and internal dimension of security with regards to the terrorist issue has created lots of ambivalence in the elite's threat perceptions. We can reasonably assume that particularly those respondents with academic background who, in the author's view, are capable of a more thorough, complete and complex analysis of Indonesia's security position, recognize that terrorism is by nature a "multi-dimensional, multi-layered and multi-sourced" source of threat."[198] Consequently, almost all respondents who have attained a higher academic degree considered the notion that the United States-led War on Terrorism posed a threat to Indonesia's national security and interests as unfounded and a serious oversimplification.

Thus, an academic and government insider affirmed that the United States-led War on Terrorism actually puts lots of constraints on Indonesia's position in world affairs. However, he emphasized that "it is not that the limitation is imposed from outside but more originates from inside and the external factors only make things more complicated for us domestically."[199] For another respondent, it is Indonesia's own mistake and weakness that it has not been able to implement a very clear policy on terrorism, which would not be contrary to the interests of the United States and other countries.[200] According to a research analyst affiliated with LIPI,

> in my opinion of course the U.S. as a superpower has an interest in Indonesia, [but] it depends on the Indonesian people whether we use U.S. aid for the benefit of [all] the Indonesian people or [only] for the benefit of certain people in Indonesia, certain people from the military, police or the terrorist themselves.[201]

It was also emphasized that "if you look at the American threat perception, it is very clear for them that the threat of terrorism is number one."[202]

Consequently, what Washington wants to achieve is for countries to eliminate and eradicate the presence of terrorist networks (within their territories), which has the potential to pose a threat to the U.S. national security. This is why many in the Indonesian elite circles view the argument that the United States is trying to create an empire by means of its anti-terrorism campaign as faulted and highly speculative.[203]

High-Profile Anti-Americanism: Form versus Substance

In the light of these nuanced, balanced and complex elite perceptions, how can we explain the high-profile anti-American pronouncements by Indonesian leaders? Here, two interrelated explanations will be presented. First, we need to see this dichotomy in the context of the Islamization of Indonesian society and culture during at least the last three decades.[204] In particular, the radical Islamic discourse, which was steadily growing in the post-Suharto era, has with the re-establishment of a more open and democratic political system moved from the periphery to the centre stage.[205] According to an Indonesian ex-President, we can find the origins of anti-American sentiments in Indonesian society in Suharto's "Islamic policy" that was initiated after 1989. He argued that

> [Suharto] gave so much interest to develop Islamic institutions, including the Indonesian Association of Muslim Intellectuals. Because of this then, of course, he has to find something else to be against and since the Communism began to fade away as a threat to us that he substituted it with the United States.[206]

It was in the aftermath of the 9/11 terrorist attacks in the United States and especially following the U.S. military interventions in Afghanistan and Iraq that the process of Islamization of Indonesian politics became ever more pronounced and the high-profile anti-American pronouncements increasingly a part of Indonesian political landscape. The second war in Iraq coincided with the pre-election political campaign in Indonesia, during which notable leaders from Islamic parties sought to score political points by frequently referring to the sensitive issue of the anti-terrorism campaign. As a result, strident anti-American and anti-Western sentiments were turned into an important political bargaining tool and as such they became an inherent part of the official political discourse in Indonesia.[207] Faced with political and societal pressures of this kind, the leaders (namely those with serious political ambitions) would think twice to publicly reveal attitudes to the United States and the War on Terrorism that ran against mainstream public sentiments. According to Siti Musdah Mulia, a progressive Muslim feminist and chief researcher at Indonesia's Ministry of Religious Affairs, the recent U.S. actions in Iraq and elsewhere have created a situation in which "the moderates are finding it more difficult to discuss issues like human rights and democracy when photos of Americans torturing Iraqis keep appearing."[208]

Second, the Islamic parties emerged from the 2004 elections slightly empowered as the Islamic share of the vote increased from 15 to 20 per cent.[209] Against the backdrop of the increasingly vocal hard-line Islamic rhetoric and surging anti-American sentiments, it is not at all surprising that even moderate or secular Indonesian leaders were not willing to "go against the grain" and express public support for United States-led anti-terrorism campaign. We ought to note here that the pressure of the Islamic political parties in combination with public opinion constituted a massive constraint in particular on the President Megawati Sukarnoputri who was, as a woman and a nominal syncretic Muslim, particularly open to attack from Muslims on the ground that she lacked Islamic credentials.[210] Smith argues that "the primary concern over the Iraq intervention is what it means for state sovereignty and the way in which U.S. global actions will play out with the wider *masses* in Indonesia, whose power, when exercised, still causes considerable angst for Jakarta's political elite."[211] Moreover, already some ten years ago, Liddle observed that "both *abangan and secularists*, whose numbers have probably grown as a result of economic modernization and the creation of consumer society, have had good reason to keep their beliefs to themselves."[212] The reason for the contemporary elite's "considerable angst" about the potential power of Indonesian *masses* is quite simple — the leaders are concerned that their own political future would be jeopardized if they were seen as U.S. puppets.[213] This view was also confirmed by a respondent with close links to DEPLU. Referring to the general two-facedness of the elite, he argued that many leaders would display anti-American attitudes for the public and, with their political career in mind, cover their real concerns "by saying, oh, this is not terrorists and this is just a security disturbance or whatever you call it." In reality, however, "they did not admit it [publicly] but they actually realize the danger [of terrorism]."[214]

OTHER NON-TRADITIONAL SOURCES OF THREAT

The U.S. is seen as having increasingly deployed new means of power in the post-Cold War era designed to spread its influence and interfere in Indonesia's internal affairs. Generally, it is possible to identify three areas of what the respondents referred to as dangerous non-conventional sources of threat:

- the U.S. power stemming from its prominent norm-building position,
- the U.S. power over information and manipulation of international media,
- NGOs operating around Indonesia functioning as Washington's agents serving U.S. interests.

The U.S.' Norm-Building Position as a Double-Edge Weapon

The U.S. power stemming from America's prominent norm-building position is essentially seen as a double-edge weapon in Washington's hands. Similarly, as we have seen in the previously discussed cases of the War on Terrorism and IMF-funded economic assistance, both of them were regarded by the elite as being both beneficial and harmful for Indonesia. Generally, Indonesian leaders consider international rules and norms as Western products. They are "articulated and promoted by the major powers, such as the European Union and the United States, but not yet Japan."[215] This norm-building position is perceived as giving particularly the United States the power to force other weaker countries, including Indonesia, to adopt new regulations to conform with the new internationally acceptable norms and regulations.

The pervasive sense of vulnerability, which stems from Indonesia's difficulties in conforming to these "Western" international norms, also feeds the elite perceptions of the United States as a security concern for Indonesia. For example, the release of the annual U.S. State Department Human Rights Report in 2004 that sharply criticized Indonesia served as a powerful irritant for the country's elite. As a response, Marty Natalegawa, a senior Indonesian diplomat, declared that "the U.S. as Indonesia has consistently stated, and especially since the horrific disclosures on Abu Ghraib, does not have the moral authority to assume the role of judge and jury on matters of human rights."[216] Not many leaders believe that Indonesia would in the foreseeable future "be able to overcome these constraints."[217]

Owing to its prominent norm-building position, as a former high-ranking Army officer and senior Golkar party member asserted, "the United States has the ability to create conflict."[218] For example, Washington is perceived as exerting a heavy influence on the United Nation's agenda. Some of the world's most pressing issues, namely arms control, drug trafficking, human trafficking, terrorism and piracy, presently constitute a significant problem for

Indonesia. Apart from terrorism, piracy has been highlighted as potentially another issue that could be added to the agenda of the UN, which would in turn allow the international community to interfere in Indonesia's internal affairs. Since Japan, Singapore, Australia, but mainly Great Britain and the United States "have a big say [in the UN], piracy could be used as a leverage on Indonesia."[219] As outlined earlier, many respondents displayed a peculiar tendency to point to United States as meddling into Indonesia's internal affairs, while simultaneously stressing the benign nature of America's intentions. In this particular case, one respondent emphasized that if Washington sought to bring the issue of piracy on to the UN agenda, it did not mean that the U.S. should be seen as a threat for Indonesia. He concluded that "Indonesians are themselves to blame [for Washington's interference], because the playmaker is the U.S. ... and Indonesians need a foreign power like the U.S. to lead it."[220]

The U.S.' Power over Information

The elite's suspicion that Washington uses its power over information for manipulation of international media to exert influence over Indonesia can be to some extent placed within the context of the "Media-Imperialism" debate.[221] Generally, media imperialism can be defined as a process, "whereby the ownership, structure, distribution or content of the media in any one country are singly or together subject to substantial pressures from the media interests of any other country or countries without proportionate reciprocation of influence by the country so affected."[222] The Media-Imperialism concept originally arose in the 1970s from the growing concerns about Western domination of the international media. The research data did not reveal much concern about Western media and governments' capability to influence the distribution or content of the Indonesian media. We should note here that the prevalent view among the elite is that the Indonesian media is sufficiently independent and not very much influenced and manipulated by foreign influences.

Rather, the research data highlighted a considerable measure of disquiet among the elite about the distinct danger to Indonesia stemming from misrepresentation or misperception of Indonesian "realities" by foreign governments and media. This misrepresentation or misperception is principally seen as a creation of Western, and particularly American, government and media, which are ascribed an immense power owing to their capacity to shape or deliberately and calculatingly manipulate others' image and perception about Indonesia.[223] As a former President affirmed, you get some distortion about Indonesia in the world. Because every minute you see in the CNN and in the CNBC television bomb in Iraq, Palestine and so on. And the people think look these are all Muslims so that means Indonesia must be like that. ... They only show the radicalism and these radicals do not represent the Indonesian nation. This distortion through the media that is the real threat. And this threat is even bigger than the military threat from any country in the world.[224]

In a broader sense, this case illustrates the increasing importance of *information* as one of the key sources of a state's soft power and a vital variable shaping interstate relations. It is the set of information available that generates an image or a perception. The quantity of information available in the international media and the World Wide Web is boundless and immeasurable. But more important than the quantity is the quality of information. A piece of information does not just exist but it is created by somebody who has a reason and incentive to create it. It follows that information can have a direct impact on an individual's, a company's or a state's credibility. As Keohane and Nye note, "... credibility is the crucial resource, and asymmetrical credibility is a key source of power."[225] Yet, in the light of an array of studies that focus on various non-traditional security concerns, this topic remains rather under-explored.

During the interviews, some leaders described their main concern as "information threat" or "threat from misperception".[226] As an ex-President asserted, "this is the real threat. It is not a military threat, it is not an economic threat, it is the information threat."[227] In particular, the respondents expressed their apprehension about the danger to Indonesia arising from the perceived lack of *asymmetrical credibility*. The latter term refers to a state possessing a more favourable image and reputation vis-à-vis other countries, whereby, as argued earlier, asymmetrical credibility is a key source of power. The research data showed the high degree to which the leaders are concerned about their country's image and reputation because they view these attributes as an important source of Indonesia's power, influence and standing in the international arena. Generally, the "information threat" or "threat from misperception" is such a situation, in which Indonesia and the "Indonesian realities" are misunderstood, misconceived or misperceived by foreign countries, their people, businesses and governments. The Indonesian foreign policy elite correctly believes that, presently, the image of any country is exceedingly important in the light of an increasingly globalized world characterized by the free-flowing capital and free-roaming tourists, all of these being underpinned and regulated by the immense power of the global media and information technology. The interviewed leaders frequently emphasized that Indonesia is at present perceived worldwide, regardless of whether rightly or unjustly, as a country that doesn't really arouse much foreign investors' confidence, as a safe haven for terrorists, and an unstable place where tourist hotels are frequently blown up. As the interviews conducted in Indonesia attest, all these factors inform the country's elite's national security considerations.

The foremost example here would be the controversial issue of travel warnings issued by the United States and other Western governments that are designed to forbid or discourage their citizens from travelling to Indonesia. When in May 1998 European, American and Japanese governments instructed their citizens to leave Indonesia and to refrain from visiting that country, some interviewees expressed their suspicion that the travel warnings were manipulated to weaken the Republic of Indonesia. This suspicion was fuelled by the realization that the Western governments did not differentiate between the situation in Java and the situation in Bali where no riots or social unrest occurred.[228] On a number of occasions, Indonesian politicians criticized Western countries, arguing that the travel warnings for their citizens who wanted to visit Indonesia were not necessary and that they were causing economic hardship especially for people in Bali.[229] While some interviewees conceded that Western governments "have the right to" issue those travel warnings, they generally regard it as one of the means used by the United States and other Western countries to interfere in Indonesia's internal affairs.[230] The case of repeated travel bans barring the noted American terrorism expert Sidney Jones from visiting Indonesia illustrates the elite's concern about the information threat. Explaining why Jones was for the second time not allowed to enter Indonesia, the country's Home Affairs Minister Hamid Awaluddin allegedly argued that Jones was considered capable of considerably influencing public opinion around the world on the problem of terrorism in Indonesia and thus constituted a security threat for Indonesia.[231]

We can see that the current negative image of Indonesia, also frequently referred to as a "misperception" by the country's elite, is considered a major security concern in Jakarta. Obviously, the reason is its impact on the Indonesian economy. The unfavourable perception of Indonesia by contrast with other states decreases the inflow of foreign direct investment (FDI). This situation has an adverse effect on the Indonesian economy, making the country as a whole more vulnerable and all sorts of external threats more imminent.[232] A former President directly linked the currently negative image of Indonesia with the decreasing amount of FDI flowing into the country and the ensuing implications for its national security. Referring to the information about Indonesia available in international media, the ex-President pointed out that the "misperception" is "done I do not know on purpose or engineered by somebody or whatever but it has a negative impact on Indonesian economic growth and development. And economic growth and development is very important for the increase of the quality of life of the people."[233]

The negative image of Indonesia could either have an adverse affect on the country's economy or, in the worst scenario, potentially lead to a miscalculated and irrational reaction, including a military strike, by a foreign power toward Indonesia.[234] It is the latter situation that constituted perhaps both the main limitation and challenge to the principle of nuclear deterrence between the United States and the Soviet Union during the hot years of the Cold War. If one side were to believe that its adversary was preparing for a military strike, the ensuing pre-emptive action would have been a path to a global disaster. In this context, some of the interviewed leaders voiced their disquiet about the possibility of growing and escalating mutual distrust between Indonesia and other countries. Julia I. Suryakusuma pointedly argues that

> your definition of yourself is provided not only by you and by other people's definition or perception of you, but also by your definition of other people. It is a dialectical relationship. If the West has a certain perception of Indonesia — that it is a Muslim country, that it has dangerous fundamentalist groups (a notion that CNN helps to propagate when it only depicts the riots and violent acts) and even that it harbours terrorists, this also has an effect on Indonesian perceptions of the West, which would naturally tend to be negative. … Once a perception exists, it is only too easy for it to solidify into a stereotype…[235]

More specifically, the leaders' concern about U.S. power over information was clearly demonstrated following the publication in July 2004 of declassified U.S. documents that dealt with the highly sensitive issue of Indonesia's takeover of West Papua thirty-seven years ago. The western half of the island of New Guinea stood in the centre of a major dispute between Indonesia and Holland throughout the 1950s. After all diplomatic negotiations failed, Sukarno set out to achieve the nationalist goal of incorporating West Papua into the archipelago by utilizing a coercive diplomacy. The 1962 Agreement, which was mediated by the United States, provided for an initial transfer of the territory to the United Nations authority and stipulated that the ultimate transfer to Indonesia would take place a year later. Based on another point in the agreement, Indonesia was to carry out the "act of free choice" with the advice and assistance of the UN by 1969 to determine whether or not the local population of around 2 millions wished to remain subject to the Indonesian authority. The general view is that the exercise, which took place in July and August 1969, was stage-management by Suharto's government. The publication of the declassified U.S. documents in July 2004 highlighted the Indonesian foreign policy elite's apprehension about a security threat stemming from what it perceives as the unassailable American power over media and information. Although the documents were published by a private research group, the National Security Archive, based in Washington, this act was perceived by many in Jakarta as a deliberate effort by the U.S. Administration to meddle in Indonesia's internal affairs. Adding to these suspicions was the fact that the document release coincided with current presidential election campaign in Indonesia.

It is a view widely shared by the Indonesian leaders that the United States has in the post-Cold War era increasingly reached to indirect means, such as the IMF, its influence over global media and information flows or, as one interviewed policy-maker put it, other such "soft things [to] interfere into other countries' domestic affairs".[236] From the Indonesian point of view, the released information about events more than thirty decades ago were very sensitive because they raised questions about the legitimacy of the "act of free choice" and the subsequent takeover of the disputed territory. Thus, a number of policy-makers voiced their apprehension about possible U.S. intentions. A legislator on the Parliament's International Relations and Military Affairs Committee contemplated "what is the motive and what's going on behind the scenes? Why now, suddenly, does the U.S. government raise this issue with us?"[237] There was a view that the sensitive documents were released with the aim to use them as leverage in future dealings with Indonesia. Some leaders reminisced about the Australian-led intervention in East Timor and wondered whether "a certain group within the U.S. government has the intention to support separatists [OPM, or Organisasi Papua Merdeka] in West Papua. This is a threat to the unity of the Republic of Indonesia."[238] Reacting to the news that twenty U.S. senators called for the United Nations to inquire into the situation in West Papua, Imron Cotan, Indonesian ambassador to Australia, sternly warned that "we will not in any way or shape let the senators of any particular country to rewrite our history."[239]

NGOs as Washington's Agents

The third non-conventional security concern of the elite is directed towards Non-Governmental Organizations (NGOs) operating around Indonesia, which are sometimes seen as Washington's agents (eg. Trojan Horse, Third Column) that serve the U.S. interests. Some leaders are inclined to suspect that foreign governments have established NGOs as part of a conspiracy aimed at interfering in the country's internal affairs or even to separate provinces of West Papua and Aceh from Indonesia. Referring to the activities of some NGOs operating throughout the archipelago, a high-ranking military officer, for example, alleged that "we are facing modern warfare, which does not use military power in its initial stages. It is much cheaper, yet more effective than traditional warfare."[240] The notion that foreign powers, and especially the United States, use new non-conventional ways to "conquer Indonesi" is not to be found only in the policy-makers' rhetoric. Also Indonesia's Defence White Paper in 2003, for example, defined the government's perception of threats to Indonesia as being overwhelmingly of non-conventional nature. The Paper explicitly outlined the changing nature of threats that Indonesia is presently facing.[241]

Significantly, a recent study published by the military academy in Bandung argues that Indonesia faces a phenomenon that can be called "Modern War" or "Modern Warfare". According to a source close to the Indonesian military establishment who is also familiar with the publication, "what they mean with the modern warfare is the war is not conventional like before, they don't use weapons but they use intelligence."[242] Furthermore, the respondent also asserted that "there is a belief particularly in the army circles that the United States also used the NGO people so they said there is about 6,000 U.S. intelligence [agents] in Indonesia right now and most of them are actually Indonesian citizens, particularly those working for the NGOs."[243] It is also in this context that we can see, for example, the repeated expulsion of Sidney Jones, a noted American terrorism expert, from Indonesia. As noted earlier, Jones was barred from entering Indonesia for a second time in 2005 reportedly after a review by several Indonesian authorities. The decision to expel Jones was allegedly based on input from several state agencies, including the intelligence services, the National Police and the Ministry of Foreign Affairs.[244] One day after Sidney Jones was barred from entering Indonesia and was accused of being a threat to the country, President Yudhoyono ordered the lifting of the travel ban for Ms. Jones because "the reason for the ban [was] no longer relevant."[245] This case again illustrates the substantial degree to which the

Indonesian elite is polarized and divided in its threat perceptions and attitudes.

ANTI-AMERICANISM AS ISSUE-BASED OCCURRENCE

The author's own impressions and observations from the discussions with Indonesian leaders together with the results from several public opinion polls suggest that, generally, Indonesian attitudes towards the United States can be characterized as fickle and inconsistent. The dramatically changing perceptions in the society at large about the United States-led War on Terrorism indicate that Indonesian sentiments are unstable and in constant flux. While "never before [had] the U.S. image in Indonesia been so low" as in the wake of America-led intervention in Afghanistan and Iraq,[246] Indonesians' negative perceptions of the United States took a significant upturn throughout the 2004–05 period. As we found earlier in this chapter, the percentage of Indonesians who held a favourable view of the United States dropped considerably from 61 per cent in 2002 to mere 15 per cent a year later. This was by far the most dramatic slump among all 20 countries where the survey was conducted.[247] Conspicuously, during the 2005–06 period, the survey conducted by The Pew Research Centre in Indonesia revealed a similarly dramatic increase in favourable views of the United States as well as support for the United States-led War on Terrorism among the Indonesian population. What is particularly remarkable here is the fact that this upward tendency in Indonesians' attitudes towards the United States goes against the general trend among most of other countries where the survey took place.

Figure 4.3 shows that while in 2005 the support for the War on Terrorism among populations in Western countries was generally waning and the opposition to the American anti-terrorism policies in most of Muslim world continued to be widespread, Indonesia was a "striking exception" to this pattern. With only 23 per cent of Indonesians supporting the U.S.-led War on Terrorism in 2003, this number had soared up to 50 per cent in 2005.[248] Similarly, we can see in Figure 4.4 that this shift in opinion coincided with a substantial improvement in the perception of the American President George W. Bush among the Indonesian population. While in 2003 as many as 69 per cent of Indonesians judged that the low regard for President Bush rather than the United States in general was the source of anti-American sentiments, two years later only 43 per cent of Indonesians ascribed their negative opinion of the United States to Bush personally.[249] In other words,

FIGURE 4.3
Support for the U.S.-Led War on Terrorism;
The Pew Global Attitudes Project

Waning Support for U.S.-led War on Terror				
	2002	**2003**	**2004**	**2005**
	Percemt favour			
U.S.	89	—	81	76
Netherlands	—	—	—	71
Poland	81	—	—	61
Russia	73	51	73	55
G.B.	69	63	63	51
France	70	60	50	51
Germany	70	60	55	50
Canada	68	68	—	45
Spain	—	63	—	26
Indonesia	**31**	**23**	—	**50**
Lebanon	38	30	—	31
Pakistan	20	16	16	22
Turkey	30	22	37	17
Jordan	13	2	12	12
India	65	—	—	52

Source: The Pew Research Centre, June 2005.

the earlier discussed "Bush Phenomenon", or the profound impact of Bush's low standing on Indonesians' perceptions of the U.S., became much less prominent in 2005.

One question naturally arises at this point: What factors caused such a dramatic improvement in the average Indonesian citizen's perceptions of the United States and the War on Terrorism? Here, we can identify two important events that had a substantial impact. One was the string of terrorist acts in Indonesia, namely the Bali bombings in 2002 and 2005, as well as the Marriott Hotel and the Australian Embassy bombings, which left a deep imprint on the average Indonesian's psyche. The other one was the instructional training video footage recorded in terrorist training camps that were shown on the Indonesian television. Coupled with the fact that mostly Indonesians died in the hands of the terrorist perpetrators, in the eyes of the average Indonesian, the terrorist attacks to some extent justified

FIGURE 4.4
Sources of Anti-American Sentiment; The Pew Global Attitudes Project

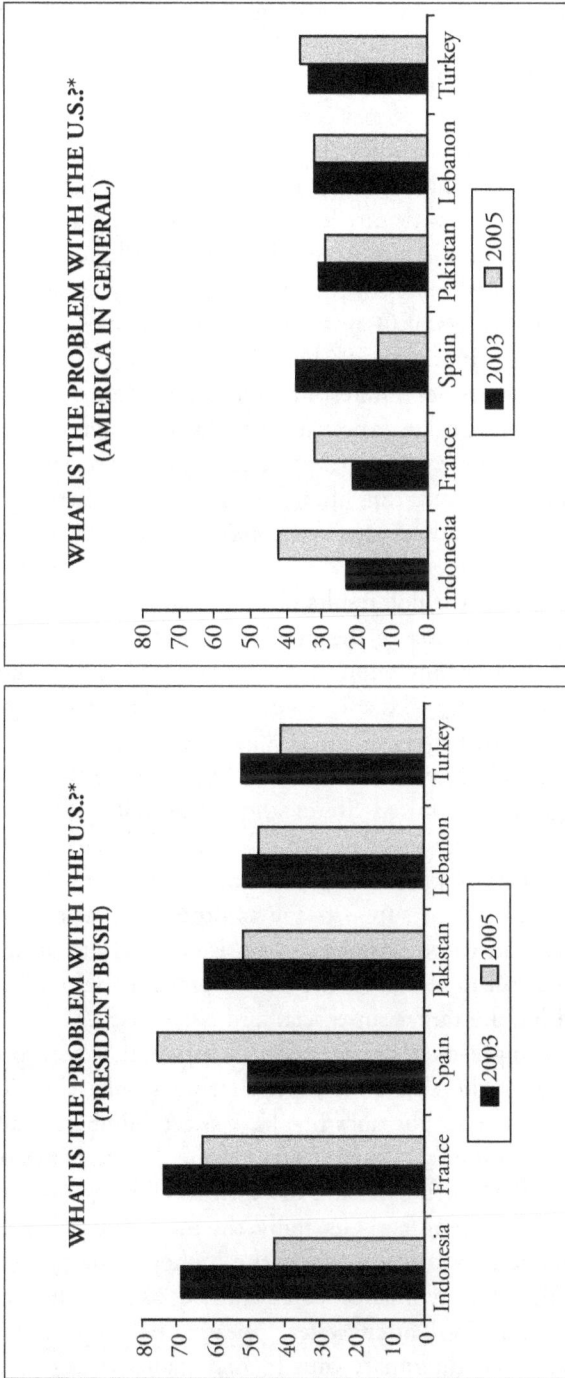

WHAT IS THE PROBLEM WITH THE U.S.?*
(PRESIDENT BUSH)

WHAT IS THE PROBLEM WITH THE U.S.?*
(AMERICA IN GENERAL)

Source: The Pew Research Centre, June 2005.

the United States-led anti-terrorism campaign. Importantly, as the Figure 4.5 shows, the improving view of the United States and its anti-terrorism policies coincided with a significant drop in confidence in Osama Bin Laden — cut by more than a half, from 58 per cent in 2003 down to 23 per cent in 2005.

The other event was the well-publicized, massive U.S. relief effort in the wake of the devastating tsunami and the earthquake that hit the eastern parts of Indonesia. Based on Figures 4.5 and 4.6, while it is apparent that the U.S. humanitarian efforts in the Aceh province contributed to more favourable views of the United States in Indonesia, this seems to be the case especially among the supporters of Osama Bin Laden. Moreover, as Figure 4.7 shows, the percentage of Indonesians who believe that the United States takes into account other countries' interest had more than doubled between 2003 and 2005 — Indonesia again experienced by far the highest increase among all the surveyed countries. One respondent expressed a belief that "there is a sense of mutual appreciation after the tsunami and earthquake in Aceh. ... Aceh has changed Indonesians' [outlook] ... that there is a world out there that's compassionate enough."[250]

A close look at the poll results suggests that the upsurge of anti-American sentiments in Indonesia in the 2001–04 period might have been nothing but a short-lived phenomenon in a country that has never been known as a place noted for deep-rooted anti-Americanism — both among the Indonesian public at large and at the elite level. What is especially conspicuous about the results shown in Figures 4.1 to 4.7 is the considerable shift in the Indonesian perceptions of the United States and its policies — in both directions — within a relatively short period of time. The sheer scale of the shift is particularly obvious when compared with other countries — both Muslim and non-Muslim. This supports the assumption that the attitudes among Indonesians tend to be unstable, inconsistent and in constant flux. It also indicates that, all in all, anti-American feelings in Indonesia are not deeply entrenched but are rather superficial and issue-based.

This finding evokes the question as to whether perceptions about the United States at the elite level experienced a similar shift in the 2004–05 period. While the author does not have exact numbers available regarding the change in Indonesian leaders' view of the United States before and after its tsunami relief effort, extensive discussions with respondents on this issue indicate one important fact. Generally, the more senior was the respondent's position in the administration and the higher academic degree she or he had attained, the more nuanced, stable and consistent their perceptions and attitudes towards the United States appear to be. In particular, more senior policy-makers and diplomats with higher academic degrees obtained from

FIGURE 4.5
Dramatic Drop in Support for Global Terrorists among Indonesians
since Tsunami

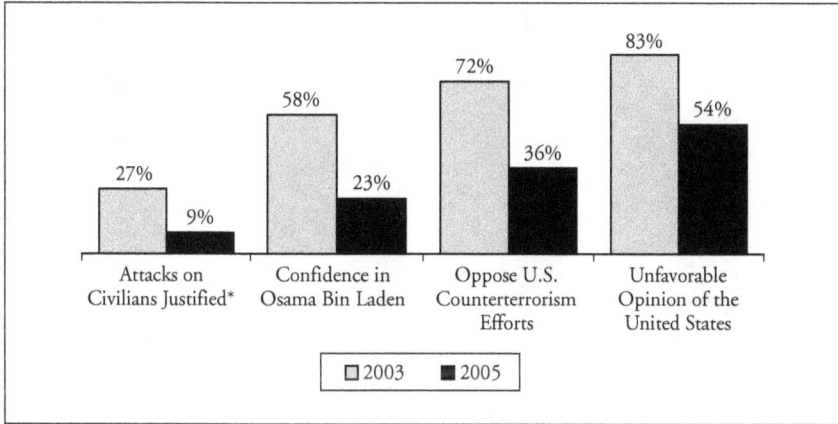

* Comparison year is 2002
Source: The Pew Research Centre, 2005.

FIGURE 4.6
Tsunami Relief Boosts U.S. Image;
The Pew Global Attitudes Project

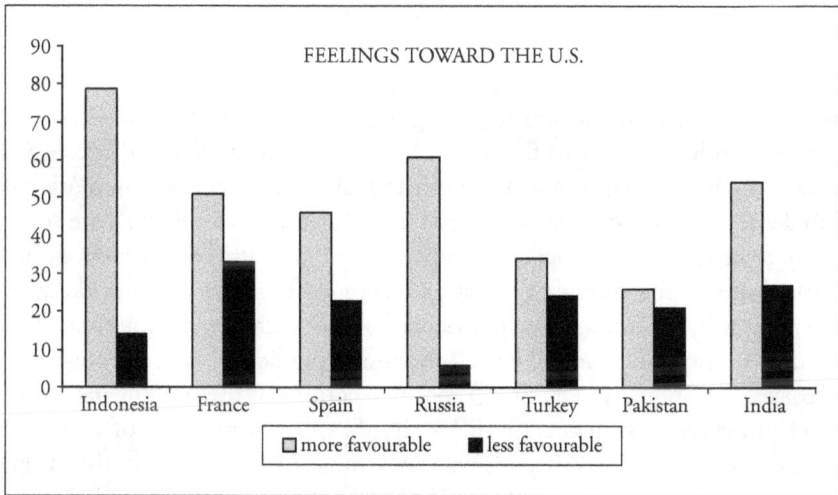

Source: The Pew Research Centre, July 2005.

FIGURE 4.7
Does U.S. Foreign Policy Consider Others' Interest?;
The Pew Global Attitudes Project

Does U.S. Foreign Policy Consider Others' Interest?			
	2003 %	2004 %	2005 %	03–05 change
United States	73	70	67	–6
Canada	28	—	19	–9
Great Britain	44	36	32	–12
France	14	14	18	+4
Germany	32	29	38	+6
Spain	22	—	19	–3
Netherlands	—	—	20	n/a
Russia	22	20	21	–1
Poland	—	—	13	n/a
Turkey	9	14	14	+5
Pakistan	23	18	39	+16
Indonesia	25	—	59	+34
Lebanon	18	—	35	+17
Jordan	19	16	17	–2
India	—	—	63	n/a
China	—	—	53	n/a

Source: The Pew Research Center, July 2005.

overseas universities who have been exposed to the dealings of international relations have more balanced, integrated and comprehensive views of external world. Conversely, the respondents with lower academic degree from local, provincial institutions and with less direct exposure to international intellectual discourse on issues pertinent to international relations are more likely to have fickle and inconsistent perceptions and attitudes corresponding with those of the public. The latter respondents are also more likely to have inwardly oriented view, to articulate rather extreme opinions and they tend to be swayed, much like the Indonesian public, by various conspiracy theories. We argued in Chapter 3 that perceptions of the middle and lower level government bureaucrats differ significantly from those of top elite echelons of power. To this end, we can assume that it is mainly the latter, the senior policy-makers — those with relatively more consistent, balanced and comprehensive perspective of the outside world — whose views and perceptions exert a much greater influence on the foreign policy-making process and policy implementation.

On the whole, the elite is, much like the public at large, polarized in its view of the U.S. humanitarian assistance in Aceh. While the leaders share some of the common people's suspicions and ambivalence about Washington's real motivations, most of them displayed largely positive view on that issue. One interviewed leader articulated the rather ambivalent, "love-hate" attitude to the United States by saying that [while] "in the case of Aceh, we are grateful [to the U.S.] ... but we also remember [that] at one time, they wanted to break up the Republic of Indonesia."[251] Concurrently, a number of respondents explicitly refused the notion that there are some hidden intentions behind America's tsunami relief effort. At least three interviewed Indonesian leaders emphasized that they had actually encouraged Bush's Administration, either during their trips to the United States or through the U.S. Embassy in Jakarta, to work to improve America's image by helping the tsunami-hit Aceh.[252]

Finally, it is obvious that the Indonesian elite has viewed quite positively the 2008 election of Barack Obama as the new U.S. President. In fact, while some leaders pointed to Obama's long journey to the presidency as an inspiring phenomenon that aspiring Indonesian politicians should learn from, others emphasized Obama's relationship with Indonesia because he used to live and went to school in Jakarta. Tacitly contrasting Obama with his predecessor, Mahfudz Siddiq, a senior member of the Muslim PKS party argued that "I'm sure someone with a multicultural background such as Obama would view terrorism from a more balanced perspective. Indonesia would expect that he see terrorism not only from its aspect of violence, but also the aspect of the economic disparity in this era of globalization."[253] In this "new world international order branded by U.S. President Obama," as Wimar Witoelar, a political commentator and former presidential spokesperson, claimed that "no doubt Barack Obama deserves the Nobel Peace Prize [and] his success is Indonesia's success."[254] According to a political analysis published in *Kompas*, despite negative sentiments against America during George W. Bush Presidency, especially in the context of the War on Terrorism and the Iraq occupation, these feelings are only a short-term deviation from a traditionally much more benign attitude towards the United States.[255] As one respondent asserted: "What the United States have done or now doing in Aceh, that to me is the real United States — compassionate, helpful, efficient, generous."[256] We can reasonably assume that it is this statement that quite accurately characterizes the prevailing and more enduring sentiment about the United States among the Indonesian foreign policy elite.

CONCLUSION

We have found that the elite's attitude towards the United States has traditionally been ambivalent and full of mixed feelings. The text highlighted the "love" aspect of the attitude and showed that the "hate" aspect has recently overshadowed the "love" aspect, as the U.S. "benignity" has increasingly been eroded by what is viewed as America's overtly assertive and unilateralist policies. Yet, we have also seen that the high level of threat perceptions towards the United States during Bush's presidency was rather a temporary phenomenon. They need to be mainly seen in the context of what the respondents consider as insensitive and arrogant policies and attitudes of the George W. Bush Administration.

Barack Obama's election as the first African-American president in 2008 was greeted with considerable enthusiasm in Indonesia. Obama's refreshing candour and efforts to re-invigorate the alliances that the Bush Administration had disrupted have generated considerable optimism in Jakarta in the potential and prospects for continual and substantial improvement in Indonesia-U.S. relations. The Secretary of State Hillary Clinton's visit to Indonesia on her first overseas trip was hailed as America's attempt to "reach out" to the Muslim world. Reinforcing this positive perception of "Obama's America" was also the U.S. formal accession to ASEAN's Treaty of Amity and Cooperation in July 2009 with Hillary Clinton's commenting on this "historical" act that "the United States is back in Southeast Asia". Overall, there is a general sense among the Indonesian foreign policy elite that, in terms of their long-term goals and strategic objectives, Indonesia under President Yudhoyono and the United States under President Obama's leadership are despite occasional lapses moving in much the same direction. While not without potentially considerable challenges lying ahead, on balance, the relationship between Jakarta and Washington is likely to continue its upward trajectory, potentially yielding significant benefits for both countries.

By and large, the anti-American sentiments in Indonesia tend to be superficial and issue-based and as such they enter the foreign policy decision-making more in form than in substance. It can be concluded that, first, the "hate" aspect of the elite perceptions of the United States appears to be rather shallow and transient in nature; and, second, whilst being essentially ambivalent and even currently hostile towards America, the elite is fundamentally committed to constant restoration and improvement of its relations with Washington.

Notes

1   These issues are discussed in greater depth later in this chapter.

2   Data based on a poll of more than 15,000 people in twenty countries conducted in May 2003 by the non-partisan Pew Research Centre, the United States; the poll's results published in Meg Bortin, "Polls Show U.S. Isolation: In War's Wake, Hostility and Mistrust", *International Herald Tribune*, 3 June 2003.

3   Ibid.

4   Interview with a journalist and chief editor of a Jakarta-based national newspaper, Jakarta, 15 February 2005.

5   "RI Ties with U.S. in Nation's Interest: Ministers", *Jakarta Post*, 11 October 2001.

6   Interview with a CSIS-based international relations expert, Jakarta, 8 February 2005.

7   Jusuf Wanandi, "Obama and Indonesia-US Relations", *East Asia Forum*, 24 January 2009 <http://www.eastasiaforum.org/2009/01/24/obama-and-indonesia-us-relations/> (accessed 10 October 2009).

8   "SBY Bertemu Obama di KTT APEC" [SBY to Meet Obama during APEC Summit], *Jawa Pos*, 17 November 2009.

9   Article "A Marriage of Inconvenience: Indonesian Perceptions of the West", in Julia I. Suryakusuma, *Sex, Power and Nation: An Anthology of Writings 1979–2003* (Jakarta: Metafor Publishing, 2004), p. 53.

10 Ibid., p. 65.

11 Comments by Dewi Fortuna Anwar, "Indonesia's Perceptions of China and U.S. Security Roles in East Asia", seminar organized by The Habibie Centre, Jakarta (16 February 2006).

12 Franklin B. Weinstein, *Indonesian Foreign Policy and the Dilemma of Dependence: from Sukarno to Soeharto* (Ithaca, New York: Cornell University Press, 1976), p. 66.

13 Not only in Indonesia, but ordinary people and elites in other Asian countries saw a sign of hope in the anti-colonial proclamations of F.D. Roosevelt and looked to the United States for support. The Vietnamese leader Ho Chi Minh, for instance, supposedly sent several letters to F.D. Roosevelt and his successor Harry Truman, pleading for support against the French army striving to reconquer its former colony.

14 Abu Hanifah, *Tales of a Revolution* (Sydney: Angus and Robertson Publishers, 1972), pp. 259–61.

15 Interview with an Indonesian academic and expert in the Indonesian military, Jakarta, 24 January 2005.

16 L.N. Palar, "A Brief For Indonesia's Independence", in *Regents, Reformers and Revolutionaries: Indonesian Voices of Colonial Days, Selected Historical Readings 1899–1949*, edited by Greta O. Wilson (Honolulu: The University Press of

Hawaii, 1978), p. 181; Jogya, or Yogyakarta, is a city in the central Java that served as the Republic's capital from November 1945 until December 1949.

17   Interview with a senior Indonesian diplomat, DEPLU, Jakarta, 12 January 2005.

18   Interview with an Indonesian leader, scholar and senior diplomat close to the military circles, Jakarta, 7 April 2006.

19   Hanifah, *Tales of a Revolution*, p. 273.

20   Rizal Sukma, *Indonesia and China: The Politics of a Troubled Relationship* (London: Routledge, 1999), p. 20.

21   Kenneth Conboy and James Morrison, *Feet to Fire: CIA Covert Operations in Indonesia, 1957–1958* (Annapolis: Naval Institute Press, 1999); Soo Chun Lu, "United States Relations with Indonesia, 1953–1961" (Ph.D. dissertation, Ohio University, 1997).

22   Interview with an Indonesian politician, diplomat and journalist, Jakarta, 4 February 2005.

23   "Chapter 1: January 1961-Winter 1962: Out from Inheritance", in Stig Aga Aandstad, "United States Policy Towards Indonesia 1961–1965" (Ph.D. dissertation, University of Oslo, 1999); drawing on the section titled "Re-evaluating Indonesian Policies: West Irian and Strategic Importance".

24   Interview with an Indonesian politician, diplomat and journalist, Jakarta, 4 February 2005.

25   Interview with an Indonesian expert in international relations, CSIS, Jakarta, 21 February 2005.

26   J.D. Legge, *Sukarno: A Political Biography* (New York: Praeger, 1972).

27   Herbert Feith, *The Decline of Constitutional Democracy in Indonesia* (Ithaca, New York: Cornell University Press, 1962).

28   Sukma, *Indonesia and China: The Politics of a Troubled Relationship*.

29   Interview with a CSIS-based international relations expert, Jakarta, 8 February 2005.

30   Feith, *The Decline of Constitutional Democracy in Indonesia*, p. 24.

31   Angus McIntyre, *The Indonesian Presidency: The Shift from Personal toward Constitutional Rule* (Lanham: Rowman & Littlefield Publishers, 2005), p. 31.

32   Weinstein, *Indonesian Foreign Policy and the Dilemma of Dependence*.

33   Audrey R. Kahin and George McT. Kahin, *Subversion as Foreign Policy: The Secret Eisenhower and Dulles Debacle in Indonesia* (Seattle and London: University of Washington Press, 1995).

34   "Let us build anti-imperialist economies, genuinely national economies that stand on their own feet, mutually assisting each other, and not relying upon the so-called aid of the imperialists!"; Quoted from: Sukarno, "Storming the Last Bulwarks of Imperialism", *Indonesian Political Thinking, 1945–1965*, edited by Herbert Feith and Lance Castles (Ithaca and London: Cornel University Press, 1970), p. 469.

[35] Peter Christian Hauswedell, "Sukarno: Radical or Conservative? Indonesian Politics, 1964–65", *Indonesia*, 15 (April 1973).

[36] Rex Mortimer, *Indonesian Communism under Sukarno: Ideology and Politics, 1959–1965* (London: Cornell University Press, 1974), pp. 80–81.

[37] Aandstad, "United States Policy towards Indonesia 1961–1965"; drawing on the section titled "Re-evaluating Indonesian Policies: West Irian and Strategic Importance".

[38] Ibid., "Foreign Relations of the United States Series, FRUS, Kennedy Administration Volumes, 1961–63 XXIII: 147, Memo, Rusk to Kennedy, February 14, 1961", section "The Sukarno Visit: All Personal".

[39] Hanifah, *Tales of a Revolution*, p. 286; about Sukarno's strong grudge against President Eisenhower, see: John M. Allison, *Ambassador from the Prairie: Or Allison in Wonderland* (Boston: Houghton Mifflin, 1973); Cindy Adams, *Sukarno: An Autobiography* (Hong Kong: Gunung Agung, 1965).

[40] McIntyre, *The Indonesian Presidency: The Shift from Personal toward Constitutional Rule*, p. 45.

[41] Ibid., pp. 44–47.

[42] Mohammad Hatta, *Indonesian Patriot: Memoirs*, edited by C.L.M. Penders (Singapore, Jakarta, Gunung Agung, 1981), p. x.

[43] D.N. Aidit, *Problems of the Indonesian Revolution* (Bandung: Demos, 1963), pp. 279–438.

[44] Michael Leifer, *Indonesia's Foreign Policy* (London, Boston: Allen&Unwin, 1983), p. 59.

[45] The issue of the educational influences, including the role of the elite's education in the United States, was discussed in Chapter III.

[46] Interview with a retired Indonesian Army general, presently also affiliated with a Jakarta-based research institute, Jakarta, 3 February 2005.

[47] Interview with an Indonesian journalist affiliated with *Kompas*, Jakarta, 16 February 2005.

[48] Weinstein, *Indonesian Foreign Policy and the Dilemma of Dependence*, pp. 114–15.

[49] Ibid., p. 78.

[50] Ibid., p. 79.

[51] Jusuf Wanandi, "Indonesia: Domestic Politics and Foreign Policy", a paper presented at the Third U.S.-ASEAN Conference, "ASEAN in the Regional and International Context", Chiang Mai, Thailand (7–11 January 1985).

[52] Interview with an Indonesian academic and expert in the Indonesian military, Jakarta, 24 January 2005.

[53] Ibid.

[54] Michael Mastanduno, "Preserving the Unipolar Moment", *International Security* 21, no. 4 (Spring 1997): 54; Coral Bell, "American Ascendancy and the Pretence of Concert", *The National Interest* (Fall 1999), p. 55.

[55] Weinstein, *Indonesian Foreign Policy and the Dilemma of Dependence*.

[56] Interviews with a former senior minister in Suharto's Government and a former Indonesian Army general during the New Order regime, Jakarta, 14 January 2005 and 14 February 2005.

[57] Jusuf Wanandi and Hadi Soesastro, "Indonesian Security and Threat Perception'", a paper presented at the Pacific Forum Symposium, "National Threat Perceptions in East Asia/Pacific", Waikola, Hawaii (6–8 February 1982); Sheldon W. Simon, "ASEAN Strategic Situation in the 1980s", *Pacific Affairs* 60, no. 1 (1987): 78–79.

[58] The main objectives of Deng's reforms were four-fold: agriculture, industry, science and technology and the military. By successfully achieving these aims was to transform China into a modern, industrial nation; the issue of Indonesian foreign policy elite perceptions of "China threat" will be discussed in the following chapter.

[59] Interview with an Indonesian academic and expert in the Indonesian military, Jakarta, 24 January 2005; Chapter V discusses in detail the changing New Order elite perceptions of China in the 1980s.

[60] Interview with a CSIS-based international relations expert, Jakarta, 8 February 2005.

[61] Speech by A. Dahana, "Indonesia's Perceptions of China and U.S. Security Roles in East Asia", seminar, The Habibie Centre, Jakarta (16 February 2006).

[62] Ibid.

[63] Ibid.

[64] Interview with a young Muslim leader, an expert in a well-known Jakarta-based think-tank, Jakarta, 25 February 2005.

[65] Irman G. Lanti, "Indonesia", in *Betwixt and Between: Southeast Asian Strategic Relations with the U.S. and China*, edited by Evelyn Goh, IDSS Monograph No. 7 (Singapore: Institute of Defence and Strategic Studies, 2005), p. 30.

[66] Interview with an Indonesian journalist affiliated with *Kompas*, Jakarta, 16 February 2005; interviews with other leaders, Jakarta, 6–7 April 2006.

[67] Dahana, *Indonesia's Perceptions of China and U.S. Security Roles in East Asia*.

[68] Term used in: Lanti, "Indonesia", p. 30.

[69] Interview with an Indonesian scholar and IR expert affiliated with LIPI, Jakarta, 24 February 2005.

[70] Ibid.

[71] Interview with an Indonesian politician and leader of a Muslim organization, Yogyakarta, 2 March 2005.

[72] C.P.F. Luhulima, "Time to Institutionalise East Asia Cooperation" *Jakarta Post*, 18 February 2005, p. 6.

[73] Interview with an Indonesian scholar and IR expert affiliated with LIPI, Jakarta, 24 February 2005.

[74] Interview with an Indonesian expert in international relations, CSIS, Jakarta, 21 February 2005.

[75] Interview with a former Indonesian President, Jakarta, 1 March 2005.

76 Interview with an Indonesian expert in international relations, CSIS, Jakarta, 21 February 2005.
77 Interview with an Indonesian scholar and IR expert affiliated with LIPI, Jakarta, 24 February 2005.
78 Interview with a former Indonesian President, Jakarta, 10 January 2005.
79 Interview with a senior Indonesian diplomat, Jakarta, 8 February 2005.
80 Interview with a former Indonesian President, Jakarta, 1 March 2005.
81 Interview with a senior diplomat, Jakarta, 12 January 2005.
82 Interview with an Indonesian leader, diplomat and scholar, Jakarta, 23 February 2005.
83 Interview with a former Indonesian President, Jakarta, 10 January 2005.
84 Rizal Sukma, *Islam in Indonesian Foreign Policy* (London, New York, RoutledgeCurzon, 2003), pp. 88–90.
85 Dian Kuswandini, "U.S. Election Gives RI Politicians Lessons in Grace: Analysts", *Jakarta Post*, 7 November 2008.
86 George Wehrfritz and Joe Cochrane, "The Biggest Sleeper: Indonesia, Asia's Overlooked Giant, is Stable at Last. But Now the Hard Work Begins", *Newsweek International*, 6 March 2006.
87 Interview with an Indonesian leader, scholar and senior diplomat close to the military circles, Jakarta, 7 April 2006.
88 IMET is the U.S.-funded International Military Education and Training assistance programme that enables foreign military officers to study in the United States.
89 "Shock Therapy to Defeat Terrorism", *Times Online*, 8 November 2004; posted on the official web site of the Embassy of the Republic of Indonesia in Ottawa, Canada, <http://www.indonesia-ottawa.org/information/details.php?type=news_copy&id=229> (accessed 11 June 2005).
90 Interview with a senior official of the PDI-P political party and senior member of the Indonesian Parliament (DPR), Jakarta, 23 February 2005; interview with a former senior official of the Suharto government, Singapore, 17 April 2006.
91 Interview with a CSIS-based international relations expert, Jakarta, 8 February 2005.
92 Interview with an Indonesian expert in international relations, CSIS, Jakarta, 21 February 2005.
93 For more on this issue, see: Steve Smith, "U.S. Democracy Promotion: Critical Questions", in *American Democracy Promotion: Impulses, Strategies and Impacts*, edited by Michael Cox, G. John Ikenberry, and Takashi Inoguchi (Oxford: Oxford University Press, 2000), pp. 63–84.
94 Nayan Chanda, "A View from Asia (II)", *Foreign Policy* (Winter 1997/1998), p. 66; A 1996 poll of Asia's business executives showed that while the Republican Presidents Bush and Reagan had the highest percentage of admirers, 45.5 and 24.6%, respectively, the Democratic Presidents Clinton and Carter were viewed

positively by 20.9 and 9% of respondents, respectively. Based on data published by the *Far Eastern Economic Review* (hereafter cited as FEER), April 1996.

[95] Interview with B.J. Habibie in *Forum*, Jakarta, 10 March 1997.

[96] Interview with a former Indonesian Minister of Foreign Affairs, Jakarta, 14 January 2005.

[97] Ibid.

[98] Interview with an Indonesian leader and academic affiliated with LIPI, Jakarta, 14 February 2005.

[99] Interview with a former admiral of the Indonesian Navy, Jakarta, 24 February 2005.

[100] Interview with a senior Indonesian diplomat, a high-ranking official in DEPLU, Jakarta, 25 January 2005.

[101] Interview with a former admiral of the Indonesian Navy, Jakarta, 24 February 2005.

[102] Interview with a minister in President Yudhoyono's cabinet, Jakarta, 28 February 2005.

[103] Ibid.

[104] Interview with an Indonesian expert in international relations, CSIS, Jakarta, 21 February 2005.

[105] Interview with a former Indonesian Minister of Foreign Affairs, Jakarta, 14 January 2005.

[106] Madeleine Albright's speech of 20 May 1998, quoted in: John Bresnan, "The United States, the IMF, and the Indonesian Financial Crisis", in *The Politics of Post-Suharto Indonesia*, edited by Adam Schwarz and Jonathan Paris (New York: Council on Foreign Relations Press, 1999), p. 100.

[107] "Foreign Power Made Me Quit, Says Suharto", *Straits Times*, 28 January 1999, p. 23.

[108] For a more thorough discussion about the 1998 economic and political turmoil in Indonesia and the fall of Suharto, see: *The Fall of Soeharto*, edited by Geoff Forrester and R.J. May (Bathurst: Crawford House Publishing, 1998).

[109] Noam Chomsky, "Indonesia, Master Card in Washington's Hand", *Indonesia* (October 1998), pp. 1–4.

[110] Interview with a young Indonesian career diplomat, formerly posted in a Central European country, DEPLU, Jakarta, 2 February 2005.

[111] Interview with a retired Indonesian Army general, presently also affiliated with a Jakarta-based research institute, Jakarta, 3 February 2005.

[112] Ibid.

[113] Interview with an Indonesian Army general and a member of GOLKAR, Jakarta, 15 February 2005.

[114] On Indonesian elite's nationalist sentiments particularly toward Singapore, see: Endy M. Bayuni, "Indonesia: Big Nation Led by Small Minds", *Jakarta Post*, 18 February 2007.

[115] John McBeth, "Over a Barrel in Oil Search", *FEER*, 16 September 2004.

116 Tomi Y. Aryanto et. al., "The Ever-Active and Far-Reaching U.S. Lobby", *Tempo*, 28 March–3 April 2006, pp. 15–16.
117 "Habibie Bawa ICMI ke SBY", *Jawapos*, 23 March 2006; "SBY Tidak Ngeper, Tapi Popularitasnya Turun: Di Balik Sodokan Amien Rais Ke Freeport & Exxon", *Rakyat Merdeka*, 20 March 2006.
118 John McBeth, "Papuan Anger Focuses on World's Richest Mine", *Asia Times Online*, 23 March 2006, <http://www.atimes.com/atimes/Southeast_Asia/HC23Ae01.html> (accessed 25 March 2006).
119 Interview with an Indonesian academic and former cabinet minister, Singapore, 17 April 2006.
120 "Amien Rais: Ada Gajala IMF Permainkan Kita" [Amien Rais: There are Indications that IMF Plays a Game with Us], *Republika*, 18 June 1998, p. 1.
121 Ibid.
122 Shefali Rekhi, "IMF? We Don't Need It, Says Amien", *Straits Times*, 21 November 2002.
123 Interview with a young career diplomat, DEPLU, Jakarta, 25 February 2005.
124 Interview with an Indonesian academic and former cabinet minister, Singapore, 15 April 2005.
125 Ibid.
126 Quoting Salim Said in an interview; Wehrfritz and Cochrane, "The Biggest Sleeper: Indonesia, Asia's Overlooked Giant".
127 Rizal Sukma, "Indonesia and the Problem of Remembering and Forgetting", in *Memory and History in East and Southeast Asia: Issues of Identity in International Relations*, edited by Gerrit W. Gong (Washington, D.C.: The CSIS Press, 2001), p. 123.
128 Interview with a former Indonesian President, Jakarta, 10 January 2005.
129 Also discussed in an interview with Indonesian academic and director of an influential think-tank, Jakarta, 6 April 2006; the issue of Chinese "economic threat" will be dealt with in the following chapter.
130 Interview with a former Indonesian Minister of Foreign Affairs, Jakarta, 14 January 2005.
131 Evelyn Goh, "Hegemonic Constraints: The Implications of 11 September for American Power", *Australian Journal of International Affairs* 57, no. 1 (April 2003).
132 "U.S. Image Up Slightly, But Still Negative: American Character Gets Mixed Reviews", *The Pew Global Attitudes Project*, The Pew Research Centre (24 June 2005).
133 Ibid.
134 Suzanne Charlé, "Losing Friends in Indonesia", *The Nation*, 29 December 2003, p. 4.
135 Interview with a former Indonesian Minister of Foreign Affairs, Jakarta, 14 January 2005.

[136] Interview with an Indonesian expert in international relations, CSIS, Jakarta, 21 February 2005.

[137] Interview with a former Indonesian Minister of Foreign Affairs, Jakarta, 14 January 2005.

[138] The paraphrase of the Bush's speech was used during the interviews by a number of Indonesian leaders.

[139] Interview with an Indonesian academic and former cabinet minister, Singapore, 15 April 2005.

[140] Interview with an academic with close contacts to the Indonesian military, Jakarta, 24 January 2005.

[141] Ibid.

[142] "Uni-multipolar" is a term used in: Samuel P. Huntington, "The Lonely Superpower", *Foreign Affairs* (March/April 1999).

[143] Interview with an Indonesian leader and academic affiliated with the LIPI, Jakarta, 14 February 2005.

[144] Interview with a senior Indonesian diplomat, a high-ranking official in DEPLU, Jakarta, 25 January 2005.

[145] Ibid.

[146] Ibid.

[147] Ibid.

[148] "U.S. Using Terror Claims to Control Indonesia", *Straits Times*, 27 May 2002.

[149] Interview with a senior diplomat, Jakarta, 12 January 2005.

[150] Ibid.

[151] Interview with a retired, former high-ranking officer in the Indonesian armed forces, Jakarta, 3 February 2005.

[152] Interview with a leader and academic affiliated with the LIPI, Jakarta, 10 December 2004.

[153] Interview with a former Indonesian President, Jakarta, 10 January 2005.

[154] Interview with a young Muslim leader, an expert in a well-known Jakarta-based think-tank, Jakarta, 25 February 2005.

[155] Interview with a former Indonesian President, Jakarta, 10 January 2005.

[156] Interview with a member of DPR, Indonesian Parliament, for the National Mandate Party (PAN), Jakarta, 7 February 2005.

[157] Interview with the director of a leading Jakarta-based think-tank, Jakarta, 22 October 2003.

[158] Interview with an Indonesian academic and expert in the Indonesian military, Jakarta, 24 January 2005.

[159] Ibid; on the domestic front, one example of changing politics mentioned during the discussion is the diminished political role of the army.

[160] "U.S. Wary of Indonesia's Ties with China", *Stratfor*, Global Intelligence Update (April 2000).

[161] Interview, Jakarta, 2005.

[162] Interview, Jakarta, 2005.

[163] Interview, Jakarta, 2005.

[164] Interview with a senior Indonesian diplomat, Jakarta, 12 January 2005.

[165] Also discussed during an interview with a senior official of the PDI-P political party and senior member of the Indonesian Parliament (DPR), Jakarta, 23 February 2005; the respondent argued that both the elite and the wider Indonesian population is divided in their views on the U.S.' policies towards Indonesia in the context of the War on Terrorism.

[166] Interview with a senior official of the PDI-P political party and senior member of the Indonesian Parliament (DPR), Jakarta, 23 February 2005.

[167] *Strategic Asia 2004–05: Confronting Terrorism in the Pursuit of Power*, edited by Ashley J. Tellis and Michael Wills (Seattle: National Bureau of Research, 2004), p. 15.

[168] "Bali Bomber Ali Imron Gets Life Term", *Straits Times*, 19 September 2003.

[169] "U.S. Using Terror Claims to Control Indonesia", *Straits Times*, 27 May 2002.

[170] This is the original version of Hamzah Haz's statement: "Bukti Amerika Serikat biangnya terorisme, begitu mudahnya menyerang negara lain dengan membabi buta, tanpa persetujuan Perserikatan Bangsa Bangsa (PBB). Ini bukan hanya teroris tetapi 'rajanya teroris'"; "Hamzah Haz: AS 'Rajanya Teroris'" [Hamzah Haz: The U.S. is the King of Terrorists], *Kompas*, 29 March 2003.

[171] Anthony L. Smith, "A Glass Half Full: Indonesia-U.S. Relations in the Age of Terror", *Contemporary Southeast Asia* 25, no. 3 (December 2003).

[172] This issue was discussed with Tim Sebastian in "Hardtalk", *BBC TV*, 22 September 2003.

[173] Interview with a member of DPR, Indonesian Parliament, for the National Mandate Party (PAN), Jakarta, 7 February 2005.

[174] Interview with a former Indonesian Minister of Foreign Affairs, Jakarta, 14 January 2005.

[175] Interview with an Indonesian academic and expert in the Indonesian military, Jakarta, 24 January 2005.

[176] Ibid.

[177] Interview with a senior Indonesian diplomat, a high-ranking official in DEPLU, Jakarta, 25 January 2005.

[178] Interview with a young career diplomat, DEPLU, Jakarta, 25 February 2005.

[179] Ahmad Syafii Maarif, "Reactualising Humanistic Values in Contemporary Muslim Society", public speech at The Grassroots' Club, Singapore, 24 October 2008, p. 4.

[180] Interviews with a senior Indonesian diplomat, DEPLU, Jakarta, 12 January 2005 and a journalist and chief editor of a Jakarta-based national newspaper, Jakarta, 15 February 2005.

[181] Interviews with an Indonesian scholar and IR expert affiliated with LIPI, Jakarta, 24 February 2005 and an Indonesian academic and expert in the Indonesian military, Jakarta, 24 January 2005.

[182] Interview with an Indonesian scholar and IR expert affiliated with LIPI, Jakarta, 24 February 2005.

[183] Interview with an Indonesian expert in international relations, CSIS, Jakarta, 21 February 2005.

[184] Interview with a member of DPR, Indonesian Parliament, for the National Mandate Party (PAN), Jakarta, 7 February 2005.

[185] Interview with a senior member of *Muhammadiyah Muslim* organization, 23 February 2005.

[186] Interview with an Indonesian expert in international relations, CSIS, Jakarta, 21 February 2005.

[187] Ibid. As we will see later in the chapter, this basic attitude among the Indonesian society at large started to change somewhat throughout the year 2005.

[188] Interview with an Indonesian expert in international relations, CSIS, Jakarta, 21 February 2005.

[189] Interview with a senior official of the PDI-P political party and senior member of the Indonesian Parliament (DPR), Jakarta, 23 February 2005.

[190] Interview with a senior Indonesian diplomat, Jakarta, 8 February 2005.

[191] Interview with an Indonesian economist and academic, Jakarta, 3 February 2005.

[192] Interview with a former Indonesian high-ranking military officer and senior diplomat, Jakarta, 14 February 2005.

[193] Ibid.

[194] Interview with an Indonesian expert in international relations, CSIS, Jakarta, 21 February 2005.

[195] Ibid.

[196] Ibid.

[197] Interview with a minister in President Yudhoyono's cabinet, Jakarta, 28 February 2005; The minister elaborated by saying that, internally, the Islamic groups generally have two aims — they seek social justice and ultimately want to overthrow the local corrupt governments.

[198] Interview with a senior Indonesian diplomat, a high-ranking official in DEPLU, Jakarta, 25 January 2005.

[199] Interview with a CSIS-based international relations expert, Jakarta, 8 February 2005.

[200] Interview with a retired Indonesian Army general, presently also affiliated with a Jakarta-based research institute, Jakarta, 3 February 2005.

[201] Interview with an Indonesian scholar and IR expert affiliated with LIPI, Jakarta, 24 February 2005.

[202] Interview with a CSIS-based international relations expert, Jakarta, 8 February 2005.

203 Ibid.

204 Bachtiar Effendy, "Islam and the State: The Transformation of Islamic Political Ideas and Practices in Indonesia" (Ph.D. dissertation, The Ohio State University, 1994); Julia Day Howell, "Sufism and the Indonesian Islamic Revival", *The Journal of Asian Studies* 60, no. 3 (August 2001): 701–29; Anies Rasyid Baswedan, "Political Islam in Indonesia: Present and Future Trajectory", *Asian Survey* 44, no. 5 (September/October 2004).

205 According to the Islamic tradition, Islam and politics are inseparably intertwined — Ayatollah Khomeini once remarked that "Islam is politics or it is nothing"; Bernard Lewis, *The Crisis of Islam: Holy War and Unholy Terror* (New York: Random House Publishing Group, 2003).

206 Interview with a former Indonesian President, Jakarta, 10 January 2005.

207 Bilveer Singh, "The Challenge of Militant Islam and Terrorism in Indonesia", *Australian Journal of International Affairs* 58, no. 1 (March 2004).

208 Bill Powell, "Struggle for the Soul of Islam", *Time Asia*, 13 September 2004, p. 41.

209 C.S. Kuppuswamy, "Indonesia: Elections 2004", South Asia Analysis Group, <http://www.saag.org/papers10/paper981.html> (accessed 24 January 2005).

210 Lee Kim Chew, "Militant Islam Poses Stern Test for Mega", *Straits Times*, 13 May 2002.

211 Smith, "A Glass Half Full: Indonesia-U.S. Relations in the Age of Terror", p. 462.

212 William R. Liddle, "The Islamic Turn in Indonesia: A Political Explanation", *The Journal of Asian Studies* 55, no. 3 (August 1996): 624; terms "abangan" and "secularists" emphasized by the author of this book.

213 Charlé, "Losing Friends in Indonesia", p. 4.

214 Interview with an Indonesian expert in international relations, CSIS, Jakarta, 21 February 2005.

215 Interview with an Indonesian leader and academic affiliated with LIPI, Jakarta, 14 February 2005.

216 Marty Natalegawa, "U.S. Has No Moral Authority to Preach Human Rights", *Jakarta Post*, 22 May 2004.

217 Interview with an Indonesian leader and academic affiliated with LIPI, Jakarta, 14 February 2005.

218 Interview with an Indonesian Army general and a member of GOLKAR, Jakarta, 15 February 2005.

219 Interview with the chief editor of an influential Jakarta-based newspaper, 28 January 2005.

220 Ibid.

221 Also discussed at "Media and Identity in Asia" Conference, Curtin University of Technology, Miri, Sarawak, Malaysia (15–16 February 2006).

222 Oliver Boyd-Barrett, "Media Imperialism: Towards an International Framework for the Analysis of Media Systems", in *Mass Communication and Society*, edited by James Curran et al., (London: Edward Arnold, 1977), p. 117.

223 For more on this issue, see: Daniel Novotny, "Indonesia's Elite: Media as a Source of Threat in the Information Era", in "Media and Identity in Asia" Conference, Curtin University of Technology, Miri, Sarawak, Malaysia (15–16 February 2006).

224 Interview with a former Indonesian President, Jakarta, 1 March 2005.

225 Robert O. Keohane and Joseph S. Nye Jr., "Power and Interdependence in the Information Age", *Foreign Affairs* 77, no. 5 (September/October 1998).

226 For more on this issue, see: Daniel Novotny, "The Threat from Misperception", *Postscript* II, no. 6, a journal published by The Habibie Centre, Jakarta (June 2005).

227 Interview with a former Indonesian President, Jakarta, 1 March 2005.

228 Richard Mathews, "The Impact of the May Crisis in Bali, West Nusa Tenggara, East Nusa Tenggara and East Timor" in Forrester and May, *The Fall of Soeharto*, pp. 84–86.

229 "Mega to Skip Bali Commemoration", *Jakarta Post*, 7 October 2003.

230 Interview with a young Muslim leader, an expert in a well-known Jakarta-based think-tank, Jakarta, 25 February 2005.

231 "Indonesian President Orders Lifting of Ban on U.S. Terror Expert", *Jakarta Post*, 29 November 2005.

232 For more on this topic, see also the section discussing Indonesian elite perceptions of China in Chapter V.

233 Interview with a former Indonesian President, Jakarta, 1 February 2005.

234 For more on this topic, see also the section discussing Indonesian elite perceptions of Australia in Chapter VI.

235 Suryakusuma, *Sex, Power and Nation: An Anthology of Writings 1979–2003*.

236 Excerpted from an interview with a young, female Indonesian diplomat, DEPLU, 25 February 2005.

237 Alan Sipress, "Declassified U.S. Papers Spark Indonesian Rebuke", *Washington Post*, 18 July 2004.

238 Ibid.

239 "U.S. 'Concern' over West Papua", *The Australian*, 14 July 2004.

240 "Foreigners Scheming to Break Up RI: TNI", *Jakarta Post*, 6 January 2004.

241 Department of Defence of the Republic of Indonesia, "Mempertahankan Tanah Air Memasuki Abad 21" [Defending the Land and Water at the Start of the 21st Century], Indonesia's Defence White Paper (2003).

242 Interview with an Indonesian scholar and IR expert affiliated with LIPI, Jakarta, 24 February 2005.

243 Ibid.

244 Tony Hotland, "Govt Deems Jones a Threat to Domestic Security", *Jakarta Post*, 29 November 2005.

245 "Indonesian President Orders Lifting of Ban on U.S. Terror Expert", *Jakarta Post*, 29 November 2005.

246   Interview with a journalist and chief editor of a Jakarta-based national newspaper, Jakarta, 15 February 2005.

247   "Views of a Changing World, June 2003", *The Pew Global Attitudes Project*, The Pew Research Centre (June 2003).

248   "U.S. Image Up Slightly, But Still Negative: American Character Gets Mixed Reviews", *The Pew Global Attitudes Project*, The Pew Research Centre (24 June 2005).

249   Ibid.

250   Interview with an Indonesian politician, diplomat and journalist, Jakarta, 4 February 2005.

251   Ibid.

252   Interview with a journalist and chief editor of a Jakarta-based national newspaper, Jakarta, 15 February 2005.

253   Kuswandini, "U.S. election gives RI politicians lessons in grace: Analysts".

254   Wimar Witoelar, "Nobel Prize for Obama shows Indonesia the way forward", *Jakarta Post*, 13 October 2009.

255   "Pemilu 2004: ASEAN Harus Tetap 'Corner Stone'" [Elections 2004: ASEAN Has to Remain as a "Corner Stone"], *Kompas*, 1 April 2004 <http//www.csis.or.id> (accessed 4 April 2004).

256   Interview with an Indonesian politician, diplomat and journalist, Jakarta, 4 February 2005.

5

ELITE PERCEPTIONS OF CHINA

INTRODUCTION

In this chapter, we will look closely at the current Indonesian foreign policy elite's perceptions of China. As we have seen in the preceding chapter, the elite have a deeply ambivalent, love-hate attitude towards the United States. In the light of the Indonesian leadership's concern about U.S. predominance and notably the George W. Bush Administration's assertive and unilateralist policies, the following discussion shows that the rise of China is welcomed insofar as it provides Indonesia with a greater space for manoeuvring vis-à-vis the United States and other major powers. Yet, in contrast with the United States that is ultimately viewed as *ramah*, a friendly power and the main guarantee for peace and stability in the region, this chapter highlights the Indonesian elite's deep-rooted sentiments held towards China, and its perceptions of the former "Middle Kingdom" that have been shaped by the long history of mutual interaction as well as China's geographic proximity.

The increasingly close economic, political and cultural ties between Indonesia and China stand in contrast to Jakarta's rather problematic and volatile relationship with Washington after 2002. We can question here whether the marked upswing in the Indonesia-China bilateral relations can be interpreted as a departure from the New Order's cautious approach to the long-standing "China threat" phenomenon. While pointing to some positive effects of China's rise for Indonesia, the leaders are simultaneously very much concerned about the prospect of facing a giant with hegemonic intentions at Indonesia's doorstep. Here, this chapter draws on the preceding one, and within the framework of balance-of-threat theory, it provides a comparative account of the elite perceptions of China and the United States in the context of the *"mendayung antara dua karang"* thesis.

POST-SUHARTO PERIOD: CHANGE AND CONTINUITY OF THE "CHINA THREAT" PERCEPTION

The preceding chapter drew attention to the recent rise of anti-American sentiments among Indonesia's population and growing suspicion about Washington's global actions among the country's elite. In contrast to Jakarta's rather volatile and problematic relationship with Washington, especially from 2002 onwards, Indonesia's relations with China have displayed an overall upward tendency. Generally, the relationship between Indonesia and China has, from the late 1980s, evolved from hostility to tentative rapprochement to the present rapid expansion of mutual cultural, economic and political ties.

As we have pointed out, President Sukarno was highly suspicious about the intentions of the Western powers, namely the United States. Nonetheless, it would be a mistake to assume that the Indonesian leadership and Sukarno himself at that time fully trusted China. Based on the available resources, the opposite was the case. Despite the close alliance that developed between Indonesia and China in the wake of the policy of *konfrontasi*, Beijing was still viewed in Jakarta with suspicion. The negative perceptions of China need to be seen in the light of the Chinese funds channelled to the PKI, which generated fear among the army leaders and Muslim groups of Chinese subversion and communist revolution.[1] These qualms in Jakarta were reinforced by Indonesia's growing dependence on China coupled with an expanding isolation from alternative sources of economic and diplomatic support. Such concerns were almost never expressed by the Indonesian leaders in public. In private, however, the Army commander General Yani, for example, asserted in 1965 that the principal threat posed to Indonesia came from China in the north. Sukarno, in response, pointed out that in fact Indonesia faced threats from all sides, meaning China was among them.[2] In a private conversation with John Fitzgerald Kennedy, after agreeing with the U.S. President's warning against the communist threat to Indonesia's independence, Sukarno argued that "a country could never be independent as long as its economic assets were controlled from abroad."[3] Even Sukarno himself was not completely free from suspicion of China even though he regarded it as his country's main ally. Weinstein writes:

[Sukarno] seems to have made no effort, at least in private, to deny that China was a threat. A variety of foreign policy elite members, some of whom had known Sukarno well, told the author in 1969 and 1970 of their conviction that Sukarno had merely been "using" the Chinese, whom he never really trusted.[4]

In the early 1970s, Weinstein found that two thirds of the Indonesian foreign policy elite saw China as a serious threat to Indonesia.[5] Later, in 1994 and again in 1998, Beijing's expressions of "concern" about the bloody anti-Chinese riots in Medan and Jakarta reinforced the elite's suspicions about China's long-term intentions with regards to Indonesia's ethnic Chinese.[6] The series of declarations from Beijing condemning the violent acts and repeated appeals to the Indonesian government to investigate and punish those responsible were perceived in Jakarta as an unacceptable Chinese interference in Indonesia's internal affairs and a dangerous precedent for future relations between the two countries. In 1996, a large-scale Indonesian military exercise around Natuna islands in the South China Sea was widely considered as a reaction to Jakarta's growing apprehension about China's policy of creeping assertiveness, namely its territorial claims in the region.[7]

In the light of these for Jakarta deeply disturbing developments, Indonesia for the first time since independence sought the formalization of its security relations with an external power, Australia. The Agreement on Maintaining Security signed between the two neighbours in 1995 was by some experts considered as "Jakarta's [response to] long-standing suspicions of China's intentions in the region."[8] And while in 1996, as one former high-ranking military officer emphasized, "the military was very much concerned about [the defence of] the Natunas" against a potential Chinese military incursion,[9] in 1999, in a reversal to Jakarta's previous official policy towards China, Indonesia's newly elected President Abdurrahman Wahid proposed the establishment of a new alliance involving Indonesia, China and India.[10] In marked contrast to President Suharto's view of China, President Wahid reiterated that his administration's foreign policy priority was the improvement and strengthening of relations with Beijing. The reaction from a wide spectrum of the Indonesian political elite largely acclaimed and welcomed the new foreign policy agenda of moving Indonesia closer to China.[11] In support of Wahid's agenda, for example, the speaker of the Indonesian Parliament, Amien Rais, stressed that because "political hegemony has been used [against Indonesia] by superpower countries in international community ... we need Asian strength from countries like China."[12]

Sino-Indonesian diplomatic relations were restored in August 1990 after a 23-year hiatus. This act was preceded by significant changes inside China and in Beijing's foreign policy.[13] In 1979, China's newly empowered party boss, Deng Xiaoping, had urged that the Communist regime pursue economic development and modernization. The communist ideology as a factor in China's foreign relations has since been largely discarded. The country's economy has grown since 1979 at an average annual rate of 9 per cent. The 25-year-long uninterrupted economic growth has been gradually translated into China's augmented power projection capabilities and expanded economic and political influence.[14] In the post-Cold War era, Indonesian foreign relations have begun to give rise to new security concerns among the country's foreign policy elite.

Since the re-establishment of relations in 1990, Jakarta has increasingly implemented a policy of engaging China. This involves forging a web of economic, political, diplomatic and cultural ties with Beijing. This trend has become more pronounced after the fall of President Suharto in 1998. The "China threat" is now conspicuously missing from contemporary official Indonesian political discourse.[15] On the security front, China has been engaged in the ASEAN Regional Forum (ARF) since its first meeting in 1994. Indonesia has also actively participated in ASEAN-China Free Trade Agreement negotiations and endorsed the idea vigorously promoted by China to create an East Asian Community. One of the milestones of the growing Sino-Indonesian cooperation was the "strategic partnership" agreement between the two countries that was signed on the sidelines of the Asian-African Summit in Bandung in April 2005.[16] In the light of these recent developments in Indonesia, China's ascendancy and expanding influence has been characterized as so "sophisticated and well executed as to be 'a thing of beauty'".[17] Apparently, the Indonesian wider public also view China's ascendency largely positively. According to a 2005 poll conducted by the U.S.-based Pew Research Centre, 79 per cent of Indonesians favour another country or group of countries becoming as powerful as the United States (see Figure 5.1); 60 per cent welcomed the idea of a strong China that could rival the U.S. military strength; 70 per cent believed China's growing economy is a good thing for Indonesia (see Figure 5.2).

In his 1976 study, Weinstein concluded that two-thirds of his respondents saw China as a serious threat and more than half of them pointed to China as the principal threat to Indonesia. All in all, China was at that time seen as being a greater threat than other countries, including the United States and the Soviet Union.[18] By contrast, the data yielded by this research project have showed that the United States and Australia are presently seen as

FIGURE 5.1
Better If Another Rivalled U.S. Military Power?;
The Pew Global Attitudes Project

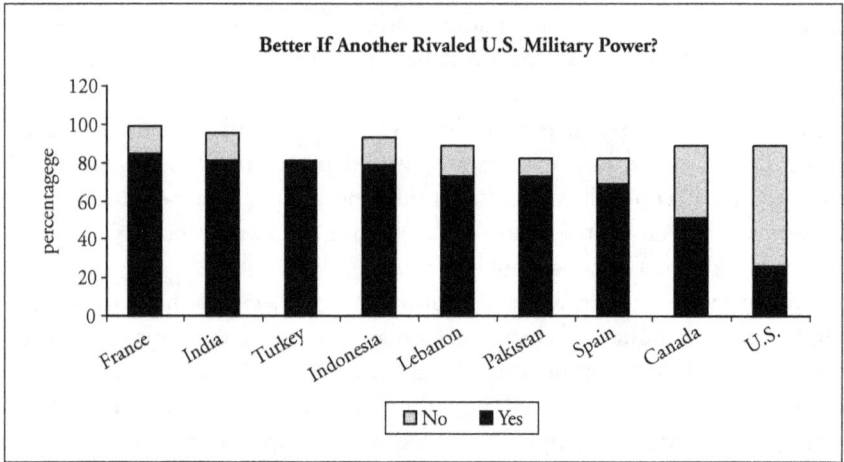

Better If Another Rivaled U.S. Military Power?

Source: The Pew Research Centre, June 2005.

FIGURE 5.2
Views of China;
The Pew Global Attitudes Project

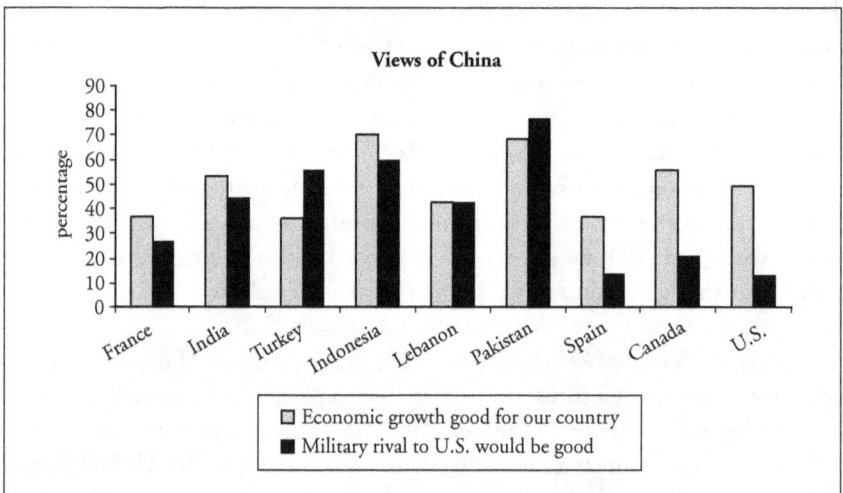

Views of China

Source: The Pew Research Centre, June 2005.

posing greater security risks to the archipelagic nation. While 27 per cent of Indonesian leaders now consider China, 51 per cent of them named the United States and 33 per cent Australia, as currently the principal malign factor negatively affecting Indonesia's national interests and security. On the surface, it seems that the relatively smooth process of China's growing clout in Southeast Asia has not caused much alarm in Indonesia. We can question whether the Indonesian Government's policy of engaging China after the fall of Suharto can be interpreted as a fundamental change in the Indonesian elite's traditional perception of China as an expansionist power.

The traditional realist international relations theory predicts that a rising power challenging the immediate status quo in the interstate system will prompt other smaller states to display a balancing behaviour to maintain the perceived power equilibrium. It seems that the Indonesian foreign policy elite's decision-making process has not followed this basic premise of the Western-designed realist theory. Instead of balancing Beijing's growing clout in the region, Indonesia has increasingly engaged China. This situation leads some scholars to suggest that Asian countries have generally chosen to *bandwagon* China and thus apparently embrace Asia's past hierarchical "Middle Kingdom"-centred tributary system.[19] The current attitude of the elite to the rise of China seems to indicate that "now history is returning to its "natural state" of Chinese pre-eminence."[20] The ancient Chinese hegemony over Southeast Asia appears to be reasserting itself. From a long historical perspective, in Ott's words, "the 300-year colonial period can be seen as an interregnum, and the 1949–1978 period of establishing a Communist state and activism in Cold War East-West conflict an aberration."[21] Also Stuart-Fox expresses the view that Southeast Asian states are in the future likely to respond to a more powerful, confident and assertive China as they did in the past. Rather than striving to maintain a perceived balance of power, they will "ensure their security by enrolling as good tributaries in the Chinese order."[22]

Some respondents pointed out that "China is a challenger"[23] and Indonesia has to try "to address that challenge."[24] Can we assume that the "China threat" notion disappeared with the fall of President Suharto and the demise of the New Order regime? In the following discussion, we will see that although the present Indonesian leaders tend to describe China as a "challenge" rather than a "threat" (as during the New Order regime), the substance of their security concerns vis-à-vis China has not undergone a significant change. In the author's view, the way the leaders generally chose to describe their attitude to the question of China's rise, using the word "challenge", suggests that the elite merely no longer considers the "China threat" term as a politically expedient expression of its concerns. Rather, the elite's perceptions of China continue to be shaped by deep-rooted sentiments and stereotypes about the country and its people's mentality within a larger framework of the elite's "realpolitic" view of Indonesia's geopolitical position. While Stuart-Fox endorses the "Asia's Past Will Be Its Future" argument,[25] he points to the persistent nature of the traditional Indonesian concern about the hegemonic and expansionist intentions of the "Middle Kingdom": "Given its deep-rooted suspicions of China, its large population and its Islamic heritage, Indonesia still stands as probably the principal opponent to increased Chinese influence in Southeast Asia."[26] And, as Rizal Sukma succinctly contended, "… China remains a major security concern for Southeast Asian states."[27]

THE MISSING "LOVE" ASPECT IN THE ELITE'S ATTITUDE TO CHINA

When comparing the Indonesian elite's view of the United States with that of China, we will observe that while the Indonesian leaders' attitude towards the West and particularly the United States can be described as "love-hate", their perceptions of China also tend to be ambivalent but conspicuously lack the "love" aspect. The author admits to having been surprised at the fact that the interviewed leaders were basically unable to express, either spontaneously or when later explicitly asked about it, the "love" aspect of their attitude towards China. Since the respondents' description of China was essentially devoid of any positive characterization, the author usually raised a question, such as: "Can you mention something that you feel inspired by, that you like or admire about China?" Some of them were obviously taken aback when this question was raised, and usually a long interval of silence followed. By contrast, even those respondents who are widely known as staunch critics of the United States and its policies readily found a number of aspects of American culture and society, which they admire. When trying to find the clue behind this lack of "love" aspect in the elite's view of China, several respondents used one word to describe their sentiments held towards that country — "pragmatic". As one said, "[our] attitude to China is very pragmatic."[28] But is the "love" aspect of the attitude towards China missing completely? According to a young Indonesian academic, "I … think that the "love" word is not the right lexicon here. I mean [that] it does not exist. Indonesia-China relations are purely based on a pragmatic consideration, as China is a potential major power, potential market, potential competitor…"[29]

Several leaders also emphasized what they consider as a general lack of knowledge and information about China available in Indonesia. For example, one respondent asserted that "China is a challenge, it is not like or dislike, something that invites curiosity ... there might be many things you can learn from China but I do not know what ... I can put the U.S. and Britain into the same box ... [But] China belongs to a separate box...."[30] Referring to the limited information available about China especially during the New Order regime, an influential executive officer with serious political ambitions recalls: "... we all thought that a Chinese fishing boat will come sending the troops. ... We were worried that lots of Chinese, because the country is so poor, they want to emigrate here. And we will get more Chinese living in Indonesia."[31] For the elite, China is definitely an interesting and challenging phenomenon that generates anxiety but concurrently remains something of a mystery.

THE ELITE IMAGES BEHIND THE "CHINA THREAT"

There are four main factors that can help explain this attitude towards China. Apart from the above-mentioned lack of knowledge about China, these are deep-rooted stereotypes and prejudices about China substantially reinforced by the manipulation of the New Order regime, the traditionally secretive and reticent communist regime in Beijing (in contrast to Western countries) and the resultant lack of affinity between the Indonesians and the Chinese. The origins of the deep-rooted perceptions about China as a threat to Indonesia are imbedded in several images of China and the Chinese, which are largely shared by the country's elite. We can also see these images as four main stereotypes or prejudices that can be summed up as follows:

- China is gigantic
- China is arrogant
- China is aggressive and expansionist
- China is Indonesia's geopolitical rival.

Whether or not these elite images about China describe the reality is not really important. What matters is whether the members of the Indonesian foreign policy elite believe in the images.[32] A number of respondents endorsed one of the main assumptions behind this study — a former admiral of the Indonesian navy succinctly summed up the assumption as: "The fact is not important; [what is] important is the image."[33] It can be discerned from the leaders' pronouncements about China that the above outlined four images constitute an integral part of the Indonesian elite's worldview. This can be seen in the relatively high degree of frequency of the adverb "always" in the leaders' references to China. To mention a few examples, Jusuf Wanandi from the Jakarta-based CSIS asserted that "China will *always* be seen as posing a threat to Southeast Asia, in view of her size and past experiences in which China considered Southeast Asia as within her sphere of influence."[34] Or, as Ali Moertopo observed, China "will *always* raise great concerns in Southeast Asia because of its history..."[35] And, in the words of one respondent, "historically, China is *always* a rival civilization."[36] (author's emphasis) This point again invites a comparison with the Indonesian elite's perceptions of the United States. Whereas the leaders' attitude towards China generally indicates a strong, innate belief in the permanent and immutable nature of China's qualities, the respondents rarely use the adverb "always" when referring to the United States. This may further support the argument that the elite's sentiments towards the United States are rather transient and short-lived and not as deep-rooted as in the case of China.

First Image — "China is Gigantic"

The geographic proximity between a smaller state and a great power results in a dependency relationship, whereby the latter exerts an influence over the former much more than vice versa. For the smaller and weaker states living in China's shadow, this situation generates the sense in Southeast Asia of being excessively influenced by the larger entity. It is then not at all surprising that one of the most frequent nouns used by the respondents when they referred to China was a "giant". For example, one interviewed leader noted that "China will be bigger ... there is going to be a big *giant*."[37] In the view of the majority of respondents, however, China has never really ceased to be a "giant". Traditionally, China has been a "hungry *giant*" because of its inherently expansionist national character.[38] For some respondents, "the *giant* is still sleeping now."[39] Yet, one of the country's most prominent Muslim leaders countered that "China is not a sleeping *giant*, China is an awakening *giant*!"[40] Similarly, another respondent warned that "China is like a sleeping *dragon*. Once you wake this *dragon*..."[41] (author's emphasis).

For most of the elite, the notion of the erstwhile "Middle Kingdom" looms large on the horizon. The series of interviews has clearly demonstrated that the recent process of deepening Indonesia's ties with China "does not mean that the fear of China has completely finished."[42] In the words of a former high-ranking government official, "that fear will *always* be there simply because of the asymmetrical relationship. Smaller countries will *always* be worried about the bigger countries."[43] The particular combination of China's size and proximity keeps alive and reinforces the traditional Indonesian elite's sensitivity towards that country and perpetuates the "China threat" perception. (author's emphasis)

Second Image — "China is Arrogant"

The Indonesian elite's view of China has also been shaped by the image of China as an arrogant power. This image largely draws on the deep-rooted impression of Imperial China, which regarded itself as "the centre of the world". Generally, the traditional Chinese view of the world revolved around the belief that China stood at the centre of the universe. While the core area inhabited by the Chinese was seen as the "Middle Kingdom", all the people living in the surrounded territories were considered as less culturally advanced, or "barbarian", for their perceived lack of civilization. The Chinese Emperor, or the Son of Heaven, did not rule only the realm of the "Middle Kingdom" but he was a universal ruler and, as such, stood symbolically at the centre of the world. The Chinese worldview was intrinsically Sino-centric.[44] As Stuart-Fox points out, "the Chinese were acutely aware of the difference between themselves and non-Chinese 'barbarians', and of their own cultural superiority, no matter what desirable products the barbarians might possess."[45]

This self-perception informed China's intercourse with non-Chinese peoples in the *Nanyang*, or Southern Ocean, the name the Chinese used when they referred collectively to the Southeast Asian region. The peoples of Southeast Asia were considered as inferior in every respect to the Chinese. Although Chinese superiority had primarily cultural dimensions, it also had a dimension of racial superiority to the extent that, as Stuart-Fox points out, "the non-Chinese were likened to animals and stood well below Chinese in the socio-cultural hierarchy."[46] The manifestation of this hierarchical relationship was what is known as the "tribute system", whereby the degree of China's superiority and control over the political entity was determined in terms of the frequency and amount of tribute presented to the Chinese emperor.

The content evaluation of the interview transcripts indicates the persisting belief among most Indonesian leaders that the current Chinese worldview continues to be influenced by the self-perception of China as "the centre of the world". It is important to consider the Suharto's government decision in 1972 to cease using the term "Tiongkok", which means the "Middle Kingdom", and replace it with the term "Cina".[47] The former term was frequently used by the Chinese community in the Dutch East Indies and, from the perspective of the indigenous Indonesians, it expressed the inherent arrogance of the

Chinese sense of cultural and racial superiority. The government's resolution to replace "Tiongkok" with the term "Cina" or "orang Cina" in reference to China and the Chinese people can be seen as a deliberate effort of the elite to uproot the deep entrenched Indonesian perception of the China as being a superior civilization.[48] While one young career diplomat noted that "China still shows the 'Middle Kingdom' thinking,"[49] his more senior colleague agreed that "culturally, China has more thinking like a Middle Kingdom" and warned that "we have to be more realistic!"[50]

Third Image — "China is Aggressive and Expansionist"

The notion of "China threat" needs to be seen in the context of the elite's persistent image of China as a traditionally expansionist power.[51] China has traditionally included the region of Southeast Asia in its security environment and, thus, in its security considerations. In the words of the Sinologist C.P. Fitzgerald, "Chinese influence, Chinese culture and Chinese power have always moved southwards since the first age of which we have reliable historical evidence."[52] To protect themselves against the inferior peoples living beyond the borders of the "Middle Kingdom", the Chinese erected the Great Wall in the north and northwest and launched military conquests in the southeast. To get a better understanding about the elite's impression of China as an aggressive and expansionist power, later in this chapter, we will also draw attention to the leaders' familiarity with historical episodes from as far as 13th century about China's naval expedition to Java. Referring to the Indonesian Government's anxiety about present Chinese claims in the South-China Sea, Juwono Sudarsono observed that

> China has strong traditional notions that the South China Sea [and Southeast Asia generally] is its sphere of influence. The fact that China maintains its claim based on the ancient notions of cultural primacy rather than modern day concepts of state sovereignty makes the issue even more perplexing.[53]

The survey research in Indonesia shed some light on the current foreign policy elite's attitude towards China in the context of the present growth of its power and influence. In one of the questions the respondents were asked to say how strongly they agreed with the following statement: *"China has traditionally been expansionist rather than defensive in its foreign policy goals and this is why Indonesia has to always be very cautious in its dealings with this East Asian power."* As Figure 5.3 illustrates, based on the answers to this question,

FIGURE 5.3
Need for Caution in Dealings with China?

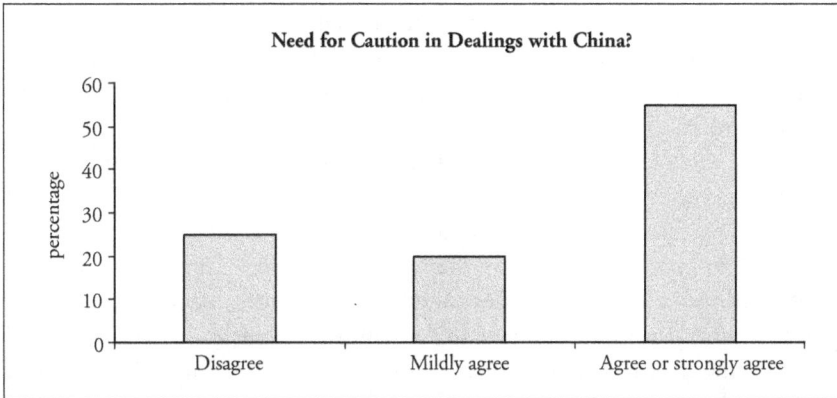

Source: Survey research conducted by the author in 2004–05.

about three fourths of interviewed leaders were convinced that "China still shows a certain level of expansionist motives."[54] While only 25 per cent of respondents explicitly disagreed with the above statement, 20 per cent mildly agreed and 55 per cent of them agreed or strongly agreed with the validity of the statement.

China is generally viewed as a traditionally assertive power that relentlessly pursues its interests. One leader expressed the prevalent scepticism among the foreign policy elite about China's innate character: "If you think about expansionism, you think of China — they are very aggressive."[55] Another respondent cautioned that, historically, "all Chinese emperors were able to build strong military ... sailing to Java in the past."[56] This elite perception was also reflected in the well-publicized characterization of China by Dewi Fortuna Anwar, a senior official in the President B.J. Habibie's Administration: "China respects strength... If [the Chinese] see you as being weak, they'll eat you alive."[57] China is "so offensive" and it still wants to exert its dominance over its neighbours.[58] As a senior diplomat observed,

> this is why China does not want Korea to be united ... if [Korea] is united, it will be [very powerful in terms of its] military, economy and politically ... this is an evidence that China wants to have only weaker states on its borders [China] has hegemonic ambitions [and] is waiting until it has the power to handle a united Korea.[59]

To this end, Hadi Soesastro of CSIS suggested during a seminar held in Jakarta whether it would be better, in the end, to have China acting as the benevolent hegemon.[60]

No less than two-thirds of the interviewed leaders believe that China's present influence in Indonesia does not have a physical dimension. "Southeast Asia does not regard China as expansionist in the physical sense. It is a more cultural expansion."[61] Typical were these statements by senior diplomats: China is "expansionist in influence, [though] not physically"[62] and "China has learned how to influence Indonesia … through culture and economy."[63] Some leaders stressed that the cultural threat comes primarily through Confucianism, whereby they cautioned that "Confucianism is not a good influence … we should be aware of the Chinese influence."[64] Whilst generally admitting the existence of the cultural threat from China, several respondents questioned its scope: "I do not see what the cultural threat would be. Because we have adopted lots of the Chinese culture. Look at our food."[65] It was also emphasized that expansionist tendencies are an attribute of all major powers. As a former admiral of the Indonesian navy reasoned, "China is expansionist but many countries are also; [for example] lately Japan has been expansionist."[66]

Fourth Image — "China as Indonesia's Geopolitical Rival"

The fourth image stems from the elite's perception that China is essentially Indonesia's geopolitical rival.[67] To obtain a better understanding about this negative impression of China, we need to first draw attention to the elite's sense of standing and entitlement within the Southeast Asian region. Generally, the sense of entitlement originates in the Indonesian leaders' belief that the archipelagic nation is *primus inter pares* among all regional countries — according to Michael Leifer, it is based in particular on "an extensive geographic scale, a strategic location, a large population as well as on a national revolutionary tradition."[68]

The elite's sense of Indonesia's standing and entitlement within Southeast Asia is historically determined as it draws on their strong belief in the archipelago's pre-colonial importance. The inspiration from what is perceived as the nation's great and glorious past has shaped Indonesian leaders' worldview. For example, President Sukarno often recalled in conversation with visiting dignitaries the 14th century Hindu-Javanese kingdom of Majapahit.[69] Also an official publication released by the Indonesian Department of Information in 1960 emphasizes the nation's grand history:

With this, we hope to contribute something to a better understanding
abroad of our people and of their national character, culture and ideals.
The knowledge of our glorious past has always given us Indonesians a
real inspiration, and has stimulated our common efforts to build up …
the Republic of Indonesia.[70]

And further reinforcing the belief in Indonesia's leadership credentials
within Southeast Asia is the leaders' awareness that Indonesia is, apart
from Vietnam, the only nation in the region to have attained its
independence through revolution. Both Sukarno and Ho Chi Minh
proclaimed independence of Indonesia and Vietnam, respectively, within
several days of each other in August 1945. Though being vigorously
anti-communist, the armed forces leadership during the Suharto period
believed that there was a special affinity between Indonesia and Vietnam
based on the perceived common struggle for independence. McMichael
observed that

[while] armed forces leadership, and in particular its commander
General Moerdani, have high regard for Vietnam's military prowess and
revolutionary credentials, Foreign Minister Mochtar shares the view that
Indonesia and Vietnam enjoy a special relationship based on a common
experience of national revolution.[71]

The ascendancy of China since the late 1970s resulted in an increased
projection of its influence in Southeast Asia. This process has given rise to
the adverse perspective of China among the Indonesian leadership based
on the view that Beijing's policies towards the region infringe into what
is regarded as a territory where Jakarta exercises a special prerogative. As
one interviewed leader posited, "the natural competitors of ours are our
neighbours, [namely] China."[72] Moreover, in the light of the three-decade-
long steadfast high growth of China's GDP, the *krisis moneter* of 1997–98,
which hit especially the Indonesian economy so hard, only deepened the
elite's sense of national vulnerability vis-à-vis China. As a Minister in the
President Yudhoyono's Administration pointed out, "our sense of regional
entitlement in Southeast Asia will have to face this notion of competition
between China and Japan in Southeast Asia. About resources, about
market, and also militarily."[73] In the context of the elite's sense of regional
entitlement, from the perspective of the current Indonesian leadership,
"China is a challenger. Historically, China is *always* a rival civilization."[74]
(author's emphasis)

THE "CHINA THREAT" PHENOMENON IN A HISTORICAL CONTEXT

The deep-rooted stereotypes and prejudices about China can also be seen in its two dimensions: the historical-traditional dimension, namely the way historical events shape present elite perceptions about China, and the internal-societal dimension, namely the aspect of the deep-rooted stereotypes and prejudices about the ethnic Chinese Indonesians.[75] We will first analyse the historical-traditional dimension of the Indonesian foreign policy elite's attitude towards China. In understanding the contemporary elite's view of China's ascendency, we have to go well beyond the traditional realist variables, such as the country's population, its economic output or military expenditures; in the case of China, emotive factors, notably traditional enmity and national pride, need to be taken into the consideration.

One of the most revealing facts highlighted in the interviews is the degree to which the sentiments held towards China are deep-rooted. The Indonesian elite's attitude towards China is shaped by historical knowledge that reaches at least as far back as the 13th century. A member of the Indonesian parliament assuredly asserted in the mid 1980s that "if history teaches us anything it is that China is Indonesia's number one enemy."[76] While the Indonesian leaders interviewed for this study generally did not express such strong negative views about China, their perceptions of that country continue to be to a large degree the product of centuries-long encounters between the people from around the archipelago, on the one hand, and what was earlier known as the Middle Kingdom, on the other. Gong is right in arguing that "… remembering and forgetting issues and structures helps define perception.…"[77] Referring, among others, to traditional enmities and antagonism in Southeast Asia, he asserts that "indeed, potential strategic realignment in East Asia is structured by relationships often expressed *in historical terms*. Among them [is] Chinese nationalism — issues of Chinese nationalism involve complex Chinese feelings of superiority and inferiority."[78] (author's emphasis).

Attitudes to the "Chinese Envoy's Cut Ear" Phenomenon

The earliest known contact between these two entities is presumed to have occurred in the 3rd century B.C. during visits by Chinese traders to various kingdoms that in the past occupied the current territory of the Republic of Indonesia.[79] However, the most entrenched image, which until today shapes the Indonesian elite's attitude towards China, draws on a historical event that occurred much later. In the 13th century, China's Yuan dynasty under its second emperor Kublai Khan sought to extend its territory and influence into Southeast Asia. Facilitating this expansion was the formidable Chinese navy built during the former Song dynasty. The Indonesian kingdom of Singhasari was one of the political entities to be incorporated into Yuan's sphere of influence. Yet King Singhasari is said to have refused to bow to Chinese demands and instead humiliated Kublai Khan by cutting off his envoy's ear. When a Chinese naval expedition later arrived off the coast of Java to retaliate and punish King Singhasari for this bold act of defiance, Javanese military forces repelled and defeated it.[80]

It is this particular story that can be reasonably regarded as the essence, the fundamental element of the Indonesian perception of China. The prominent place of this event in the historical knowledge among the Indonesians is more understandable in the light of the fact that this historical episode is part of standard curriculum at junior high schools around Indonesia. A prominent politician pointed out that

> the ear of the Admiral was cut off to humiliate. Now if you go to the schools in Eastern Java, that's being taught as a part of history. Whether it's totally correct or not, it's beside the point. The point is that, psychologically, the Javanese children are being taught that we could handle the Chinese.[81]

This story constitutes a basic element in the Indonesian elite's attitude towards China. In fact, at least ten out of forty-five interviewed leaders spontaneously brought up this episode. This is significant in that the structured questionnaire included mostly open-ended questions, whereby none mentioned or specifically asked about this issue. The interviewed leaders generally recount the historical episode in the same fashion: When China was a "superpower", during the rule of Kublai Khan, the "Middle Kingdom" attempted to subjugate Indonesia. After the Chinese envoy's ear was humiliatingly "chopped off", Kublai Khan's troops returned only to be defeated by the brave Indonesian forces.[82] The respondents are unanimous on the point that this story constitutes an important lesson for Indonesia, and that Indonesians should always be mindful of China's past actions. As one respondent asserted, "the psychology is there and now we talk about the modern state, foreign policy, strategic thinking. ... You talk to perceptive Indonesians [and] the story of China is not over...."[83] In other words, the elite agree that China has been around for centuries and Indonesia needs to reconcile with the reality that China is going to stay.

A disagreement exists, however, on how this historical event should be interpreted. On the one hand, several respondents confidently argued that since Indonesians dared to "chop off" the Kublai Khan's envoy's ear, it shows that "psychologically, we have never felt … an underdog of China."[84] The Indonesians do not need to be concerned about another Chinese military invasion because, owing to this historical episode, "China will consider that this will happen [to them] again."[85] Consequently, the Indonesian people do not have a substantial reason to be worried about China.[86] On the other hand, a clear majority of the interviewed leaders cautioned that "history repeats itself", whereby the Chinese invasion of Java in the 13th century is no exception to this rule.[87] While it is highly unlikely that a Chinese military intervention in Indonesia will occur in the foreseeable future, some respondents emphasized that China has returned and is presently conquering the archipelago by means of economic and political influence.[88] Referring to the seven-centuries-old event in the relations between the Indonesian archipelago and China, one respondent asserted that "history is very important" in predicting how China will treat Indonesia in the future.[89] Another interviewed leader noted that Indonesia has to tread carefully in its relations with China (and Japan): "Of course, because of the historical perspective, the historical experience, with the Chinese, with the Japanese. For example, China, during the Kublai Khan, the Japanese during the 20th century…."[90] We can thus see here the degree to which the Indonesian leaders' sentiments towards China are substantially reinforced by one particular historical event.[91]

A number of respondents displayed a tendency to juxtapose Indonesia's historical experience with China and the United States. The elite's attitude towards the United States stands in sharp contrast to its view of China. The respondents overwhelmingly agreed that if history is to provide any clue about the future dynamics in interstate relations, then the United States, unlike China and Japan, "do not have a territorial expansion ambition."[92] The data indicate that the elite's sensitivities towards the United States are not as deep-rooted and also not as complex as those felt towards China. This becomes more apparent if we look at the two well-known cases of American and Chinese military interventions in the archipelago. In the centre of attention here are the United States' involvement in the Outer Island rebellions, as discussed in Chapter 4, and the Chinese naval expedition to Java. The first one was indirect and subversive, the second one constituted a direct military assault. Whereas the American intervention occurred in a not-so-distant past, some fifty years ago, the Chinese attack on Java took place about seven centuries ago, reportedly around 1298. What is quite striking is the difference between how these two well-known historical events are recollected by the country's elite. While only one leader out of forty-five interviewed reminisced about the relatively recent American intervention in the Outer Island rebellions, at least ten of them spontaneously brought up the centuries-old story of how the brave Javanese people humiliated the Chinese.

A comparison of the elite's assumptions about what clues these two historical events give about possible future behaviour of the United States and China, respectively, is also telling. In the light of the numerous U.S. military involvements in the Southeast Asian region over the last half a century, the interviewed leaders showed a peculiar tendency not to raise these issues and link them to America's current actions. They were largely oblivious of or tended to downplay the significance of past U.S. interventions not only in the late 1950s in Indonesia but also in Vietnam, Cambodia, Laos and elsewhere around the region. On a number of occasions, they voiced the assumption that Washington has learned from its past mistakes.[93] By contrast, the respondents clearly consider China's past actions as a warning sign, as a clue that indicates a possible consequence of China's present ascendancy. When trying to explain this difference in how Indonesia's past encounters with the United States and China shape the present elite's perceptions about the two countries, one leader concluded that "while the U.S. is a threat "in a broader sense", China is a "more traditional" threat.[94] According to a retired high-ranking Army officer, the Indonesian elite tends to view contemporary China through the prism of "our past experience and tradition of Chinese foreign policy, although [China's] actual actions and policies would be based in contemporary context. ... [Still] Indonesia should be realistic."[95]

NEW ORDER, SUHARTO, AND "CHINA THREAT"

The contemporary Indonesian foreign policy elite's view of China and its rise cannot be understood without considering the development of post-independence Sino-Indonesian relations. Rizal Sukma argues that the Suharto's government freezing of diplomatic ties with China for a hiatus of twenty-three years is best understood in terms of the efforts made by the authoritarian military-based regime to sustain its political legitimacy.[96] Sukma also observed that "the question of perceptions — both public and elite — served as the most important context within which Indonesia's policy towards [China] was formulated and carried out."[97] We will now point to the present Indonesian elite's assumption that the "China threat" was to some extent real and to some extent artificially created by the Suharto government. In the following discussion, we will argue that Indonesia's attitude towards China during the New Order was shaped by a combination of the elite's real security concerns about the "China threat" and its attempt to use the "China card" to shore up its legitimacy.

The watershed event in the evolution of Sino-Indonesian relations was the 30 September 1965 abortive coup for which responsibility was attributed to the Indonesian Communist Party, the PKI, that allegedly received support from Beijing and from the overseas Chinese community in Indonesia. The coup led to the fall of President Sukarno and establishment of the military-dominated New Order regime under the leadership of Major-General Suharto. According to Mackie and MacIntyre, President Suharto was, much like his predecessor during the Guided Democracy period, *primus inter pares* among the elite in the early years of the New Order regime.[98] Beginning in the early 1980s, with the concentration of power in his hands, they argue that

> Suharto has ... imposed the stamp of his personality and political style upon the New Order so strongly (as did his predecessor, Sukarno, upon the "Guided Democracy" years, 1959–65) that we simply cannot disregard the personal factor in any analysis of the political, social or structural dynamics of the regime.[99]

Consequently, as in Sukarno's case, Suharto's personal perceptions were also central to understanding of the development of Indonesian foreign policy during the New Order years.

From 1965, Indonesian foreign policy embarked on a starkly divergent course. In contrast to Sukarno's flamboyant foreign policies, Suharto's *Orde Baru* regime, faced with a marked deterioration in Indonesia's economic position, reoriented Indonesian foreign relations to the objective of economic development. The New Order regime's cautious and suspicious approach to relations with China, epitomized by the "China threat" rhetoric, stood in contrast to President Sukarno's proposal to establish the "Jakarta-Beijing Axis". The army-dominated New Order elite made clear that it considered communism in general, and Communist China in particular, as the main threat to Indonesia's national security. The army leaders, including Suharto himself, had developed a strong anti-communist mindset from the early days of the republic. Here, Elson offers an insightful view:

> Like many of his officer fellows, Suharto was developing a strong antipathy to communism. Notwithstanding his initial appreciation of the meaning and purport of the 1948 Madiun affair, he had taken with relish to the task of clearing Communists and their sympathisers from his Central Java sectors. ... At a more practical level, he probably saw

the extraordinary success of the PKI in the regional elections of 1957 as a direct challenge to his own authority and power.[100]

Another formative experience that possibly never lost its hold on Suharto's general outlook was the killing of six generals during the 1965 abortive coup. Suharto personally supervised the proceedings during which the generals' remains were recovered from a deep well on the southern outskirts of Jakarta. According to Elson's account, "The grim proceedings were a traumatic experience, which, Suharto claims, brought tears to his eyes, as the bodies of six generals … were brought to the surface."[101] Commenting on the traumatic experience, Suharto himself recollected:

> I will never forget this, truly I will never forget this. Who could forget something as barbaric as this? Since witnessing with my own eyes what had been discovered at *Lubang Buaya*, my primary duty was to crush the PKI, to smash their resistance everywhere, in the capital, in the regions, and in their mountain hide-outs.[102]

These accounts indicate that Suharto's belligerent stance vis-à-vis China may be in part understood in terms of his personal aversion to communist ideology as embodied in the PKI and its subversive activities.[103]

However, we also need to acknowledge that the regime's legitimacy was based on its ability to restore and maintain social order and on pursuing the policy of economic development to bring the country to prosperity. Suharto's government repeatedly asserted that the greatest threat to national stability and economic development stemmed from communist subversion at the hands of the remnants of the PKI, the Indonesian ethnic Chinese and Communist China.[104] By posing as the guardian of the state against communist threats, it is argued, the army sought to buttress its position as the only and indispensable defence against the "China threat".[105] It remains a disputed question as to what extent Suharto and other New Order leaders were genuinely concerned about the "China threat" and to what degree the relations with Beijing were kept "frozen" for more than two decades with domestic politics in mind. In fact, the security situation in Indonesia markedly improved and stabilized after 1968 following a series of successful military operations against the PKI strongholds especially in East Java. By 1971, Greg Fealy concludes, "the communist movement no longer represented a serious threat to Indonesian security."[106] Yet, although the intensity of the danger posed by China further decreased throughout the 1970s, as Beijing substituted its Maoist revolutionary foreign policy for one stressing economic modernization, Jakarta's official (as opposed to other regional states) attitude towards the communist state did not change and the Sino-Indonesian diplomatic relations remained "frozen" until August 1990.

The Elite's View: The "China Threat" both Real and Contrived

We will now look closely at what actually the present Indonesian foreign policy elite thinks in retrospect about the validity of the Suharto government's claim that Communist China posed the biggest security threat to Indonesia. The starting point was the following question: "*How strongly do you feel about the previous Suharto's government often reiterated claim that during the New Order regime communist China posed the biggest (external) threat to Indonesia?*" As Figure 5.4 demonstrates, while about one third of the respondents strongly believed in the real existence of the "China threat", 24 per cent slightly believed in it and 42 per cent of interviewees asserted that they didn't believe in the validity of this New Order claim. In other words, about 58 per cent of all interviewed members of the foreign policy elite felt that China posed a danger to Indonesia during the New Order era at least to some extent. The data have shown that those respondents who fall into the "strongly believe" category generally did not at all question

FIGURE 5.4
Did "China Threat" Exist during the New Order?

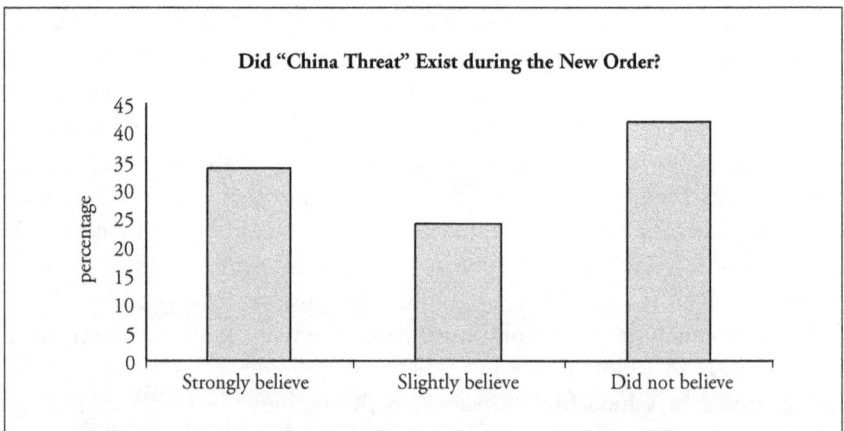

Source: Survey research conducted by the author in 2004–05.

the validity and soundness of the "China threat" theory; most interviewees categorized as "slightly believe" justified their view by arguing that while the validity of the "China threat" was undeniable, the scope and magnitude of the threat was exaggerated by the Suharto's Administration; and, finally, the "don't believe" group almost universally rejected the "China threat" theory affirming that it was artificially created and deliberately overstated by the New Order regime.

First, the leaders in the group that strongly believes in the real existence of the Chinese menace talked of their utter disappointment and disillusionment when they learned about Beijing's subversive activities directed against the Republic. The strong belief in the existence of a security threat from China was, according to a former high-ranking Army officer, "...the continuation of a perception that originated in the Cold War era. ... The history of overseas Chinese and betrayal by the PKI created some ... warnings, which formed our thinking and ideas of a threat from China."[107] "During those times, threats from China were imaginable," concluded the retired Army general.[108] A former Foreign Minister recollected:

> We were very close to China ever since China proclaimed the People's Republic of China. And became more and more close during Sukarno to the effect that we were its closest ally. ... When 1965 came ... we found that China was behind [the coup]. The disillusion was so great; the disappointment was so great towards China, who we have always considered as a friend, suddenly becoming our mortal enemy ... that for years we did not want to have anything to do with China.[109]

The "strongly believe" group is largely comprised of former high-ranking military officers and other individuals who previously constituted part of the military-dominated New Order elite. One of them, a former Army officer asserted that "after Chou En Lai's visit Sukarno said that Indonesia should develop a 'fifth force' [and] China would send arms to the 'fifth force'! China sent *Chung* rifles. China was willing to send weapons! The Chinese weapons were also used to kidnap and kill the seven generals."[110] He then sought to emphasize that the Indonesian Communists were "supported by Beijing, not Moscow."[111] Another influential New Order-era leader explained the roots of the strong anti-Chinese sentiments among the elite:

> It was a psychological consequence of the abortive coup of the Communist Party and the strong suspicion that China was behind it ... There were a number of Indonesian delegations in Beijing to celebrate the October 1 anniversary. And Chou En-Lai told the delegation there

was a change in Jakarta and he did not know that Nasution escaped. ...
What happened 40 years ago it was really drastic ... the entire general
staff was kidnapped and murdered ... those who were the peoples'
heroes....[112]

Two leaders judged that Suharto and his government were somehow misled
into believing that China's communist ideology posed a threat to Indonesia's
national security. A former Indonesian President claimed: "It was based on
the wrong assumption that communism was a threat while we know that
communism is not a threat and [it was believed] only by the New Order
administration."[113] While stressing that there was no serious, direct threat
posed by China to Indonesia for most of the New Order period, one leader,
however, pointed out that what is important is that "the threat was real
in the minds of those people who made the policies."[114] When asked why
Suharto and the military-dominated elite referred primarily to the ideological
threat from China rather than the Soviet Union and other communist
countries, the interviewed leaders almost universally pointed to the "allergy
towards Chineseness", or the inherent Chinese mentality, as well as the
distinct features of the Chinese form of communist ideology. As a Minister
in President Yudhoyono's Cabinet explained, "the PKI was moving more
towards the Chinese line than towards the Soviet line. Because they thought
it was more relevant to agrarian conditions in Asia. The Soviet experience
was more European."[115] The general agreement among the interviewees in
the "strongly agree" category was that "China and communist ideology are
[Indonesian] military's eternal enemies."[116] This view was also supported by
a former President who asserted: "Suharto built his view on China, on the
existence of the communist ideology. The military people *always* think that
communism is a threat. So, since communism is a threat, they perceive China
as a threat."[117] (author's emphasis)

While not denying the existence of the "China threat", some respondents,
however, emphasized that they at some stage began to have doubts about
how serious the danger really was. A former high-ranking military officer
contended that "China was in 1965 considered an evil enemy but later
[there were having] doubts whether China was a real threat. [There were]
doubts among intellectuals, some generals studying overseas got to read
different versions of the 1965 coup [and thus] doubts came to the military
circles."[118] For most of them, the period when doubts first came to their mind
coincided with the early years of economic reforms in China under Deng
Xiaoping when the Chinese regime ceased to be "ideologically aggressive
[and] did not endanger us."[119] Despite the Suharto's government's continuous

"China threat" rhetoric, it was in the early 1980s that the New Order elite's perceptions started to change. In the words of an international relations expert, "when China ceased to be so indoctrinated by Mao's ideology, when China changed, the perception [by other countries] towards China also changed."[120]

For some, China ceased to be a threat for Indonesia only with the coming of Gorbachev's *perestroika*, the breakdown of the Iron Curtain in Europe in 1989 and the collapse of the Soviet Union in the early 1990s. To this end, one interviewed leader observed:

> Slowly China [was] perceived as a country which [was] modernizing itself, [was] not a threat because [of the] Deng Xiaoping policy of developing the economy of China and the debacle of Soviet Union. ... The debacle of the Berlin wall was a sign that communism has no future any more.[121]

A former President shared the same view that "China threat [existed] until the collapse of the communist system."[122] According to another respondent,

> actually, since 1990s the perceptions have changed, because we saw in the early 1990s that China very clearly put priority on the economic development. At that time, the so-called communist ideology and communist states fell everywhere. But to some extent I can see that some elements within the Indonesian society still see China as a threat.[123]

As a former Minister in Suharto's government pointed out, it was President Suharto's growing confidence in Indonesia's stability and vigour, and particularly in the country's economic development, that prompted him to "allow ... to probe the possibility of 'defreezing' of [China-Indonesia relationship]."[124] In the words of an influential journalist, "in the 1985–88 period, Suharto thought that Indonesia's economy was strong enough [and this is why] then China was no longer a threat."[125] As another member of the foreign policy elite explained, Suharto decided to "defreeze" Indonesia's relations with China "... because at that time [the New Order elite] was confident that we can take care of our country. Economically and ideologically, we came to the conclusion that the communists were already finished."[126]

Second, while most interviewees in the "slightly believe" category did not deny the validity of the "China threat" theory, they questioned the real scope and magnitude of the danger. They overwhelmingly believe that the degree of the menace was exaggerated by the Suharto government. A former Foreign Minister contradicted himself by initially contending that

I can never recall us clearly stating, publicly, especially our President, saying that China is our biggest threat. Yes, [there were] no diplomatic relations, [we were] angry at China, suspicious of China. The China threat was real because of the secretive support China gave to the PKI. ... [But] when we said the threat is from the North, we don't mean China alone. We meant the four countries (China, the Soviet Union, Japan, and the United States) interacting with themselves. And their interaction could become a threat to us.

Yet, the former Foreign Minister then candidly admitted: "But, of course, in the course of time maybe it has become bigger, it was made bigger by the government that wanted to show them as the villains. ... The common public [were] not quite aware to what extent the Chinese were a real danger...."[127]

Several interviewees also argued that China was a real danger for Indonesia's national security in the 1960s and to some extent in the 1970s but in the 1980s it was used as a tool by the Suharto's regime to keep the country's population in line. In the 1960s and 1970s, as one leader points out, "if we say that [the threat] was real, there are some elements of truth. ... Because at that time China still officially declared that [it was] going to export the ideology. They [did] not drop it."[128] Later in the 1980s, however, it was getting more difficult for the New Order regime to convince the Indonesian population about the danger of communist ideology. Using an Indonesian expression, according to a LIPI-based academic, "communism *tidak laku*, communism could [no longer] be marketed, sold to Indonesians."[129] A member of the Indonesian Parliament and a senior leader of *Muhammadiyah* concluded that [while] at the beginning it was real, in the 1960s, in the 1980s, it was not a real threat but Suharto used it."[130] Another senior member of *Muhammadiyah* shared a similar view: "After Mao died, China stopped being a threat."[131]

And, finally, the "don't believe" group almost universally rejected the "China threat" theory affirming that it was artificially created — in the words of one leader — "planted, engineered, orchestrated" by the New Order regime to sustain its legitimacy.[132] For one leader, during the New Order period, the "China threat" was "more exaggerated. China had lots of internal problems."[133] "China did not have the capacity [to pose a threat to Indonesia]," claims another respondent adding that "China was only a scapegoat."[134] As one government insider argued, "It's very clear. There is a need for the New Order regime at that time to exaggerate the threat because the communist threat served as a foundation for state and regime legitimacy at that time, even though the actual threat was not that high." Furthermore, he also pointed out that

> China tried to influence domestic politics in Indonesia but from 1967 and especially from 1971 up to the restoration of diplomatic ties I do believe ... that it has become a tool of the New Order in order to strengthen its legitimacy because the legitimacy of the New Order as the saviour of the nation from the communist threat actually rests on the threat perception of China.[135]

Several interviewed leaders admitted that they were directly involved in the New Order government's "propaganda" about the danger posed by China. One interviewee who worked in "Suharto's structures" said that he was involved in "creating the 'China threat' notion": "I was in the activities. It was planted, it was propaganda, threat from the North, threat of communism."[136] Referring to the alleged elaborate sting operation conceived by former intelligence chief Moertopo, he recollected that

> To make a reason to re-elect Suharto, *Komando Jihad* was set up [and] in the early 1970s we were embarrassing *Pancasila*, talking to the former *Darul Islam* and telling them that [they will counter] the communist threat [that] was coming from the north. Before every election, the China and communist threat was stirred up.[137]

Some interviewees expressed the view that this propaganda significantly affected the perception of China both among the Indonesian public as well as at the elite level. Today's negative perceptions of China are to some extent the result of Suharto's manipulation and, as one respondent opined, "had Sukarno and the PKI prevailed, the picture of China would be different now."[138] Thus, the repercussion of the Suharto's regime "brainwashing" is that, it is argued, the Indonesian view of China is to some degree distorted. A senior career diplomat concluded:

> In the past, the Suharto regime did "brainwashing", claiming that China was our enemy. The weakness of this approach is that [today] we do not know much about China. Indonesia should be cautious about China but if the relations are managed properly, then Indonesia can also benefit from the relations.[139]

The preceding analysis leads to three important conclusions: First, we have seen that the contemporary Indonesian leadership encompasses a variety of differing views and perspectives about the validity of the "China threat" during the New Order period. It shows that threat perceptions are purely subjective and depend on the individual's personal life experience and worldview. Second, the extent to which China is considered as a malign factor negatively affecting Indonesia's national security largely depends on the leaders' sense of weakness and vulnerability or, conversely, their sense of strength and confidence in Indonesia's social and political stability and, most importantly, the country's economic standing. As we will find later in this chapter, the perceived *economic threat* from and the lack of *asymmetrical credibility* vis-à-vis China significantly shape the elite's attitude towards that country. Third, most respondents believe that the security threat China posed to Indonesia actually diminished with the introduction of Deng Xiaoping's economic reforms and the collapse of the Soviet Union. Yet, we will find in the following Indonesian leadership's prudent assessment of present and future security risks generated by the rise of China that the "China threat" notion tends to be deep-rooted — it goes well beyond Suharto's regime's policy, which only made this Indonesian elite's pervasive attitude towards China ever more pronounced.

THE ETHNIC CHINESE AS A "TROJAN HORSE" INSIDE INDONESIA

The Indonesian foreign policy elite's distinct attitude towards China can be also understood in terms of its internal-societal dimension. The internal-societal dimension revolves around the deep-rooted stereotypes and prejudices about the ethnic Chinese Indonesians among Indonesia's *pribumi*, or indigenous Indonesians. In other words, the elite perception of China cannot be fully understood without mentioning the Indonesian leaders' traditionally negative sentiments towards the ethnic Chinese Indonesians.

Generally, there are a number of different deep-entrenched unfavourable images underpinning Indonesian sentiments about the ethnic Chinese but they are all characterized by one common aspect — "otherness". The ethnic Chinese are considered as inherently different: they are the "other" and, as such, they stand apart from the majority of the *pribumi* Indonesians. In the words of Ariel Heryanto, the ethnic Chinese in Indonesia are "one of the four main 'Others' ... the other being the 'West', 'Communism', and 'Fundamentalist Islam'".[140] As with the latter three constructs, also the notion of the ethnic Chinese as the "other" has evolved over time, being shaped by centuries of encounters between the people from around the archipelago and the Chinese immigrants. Generally, we can identify three main dimensions of the ethnic Chinese' "otherness": racial-nationalist, cultural-religious, and socio-economic.

Three Dimensions of the Ethnic Chinese' "Otherness"

First, the racial-nationalist dimension of their "otherness" has its roots in the persistent Indonesian perception that the ethnic Chinese physically originate from and are mentally connected with a geographically different location, China. There is a general tendency among the Indonesians to see the ethnic Chinese Indonesians as a separate *bangsa*, meaning race — they are the *bangsa Cina* — whose allegiance goes always to their homeland, China. We can find the origins of this deep-rooted Indonesian perception primarily during the Dutch colonial era in the privileged position of the ethnic Chinese community. The Dutch law provided for a three-fold division of the society in the Dutch East Indies — below the Dutch colonial elite were the Chinese classified as "Foreign Orientals", while the lowest stratum of the society was reserved for the native Indonesians, called "Inlanders".[141] The Chinese who possessed the necessary entrepreneurial skills played the role of "middlemen" between the Dutch colonial Administration and the native Indonesian population. Moreover, reinforcing the "otherness" of the Chinese in Indonesia was the official policy of racial segregation implemented by the Dutch authorities. During the colonial period, especially in 19th century Java, the Chinese community was forced to live in special ghettoes, thus further deepening the divide between themselves and the *pribumi* Indonesians. According to Skinner, the consequence of the Dutch policy of systematic ethnic segregation was the fact that "there were no Chinese to speak of residing in Javanese villages prior to the second decade of the 20th century."[142]

As Ali Moertopo bluntly stated in 1981, China "will always raise great concerns in Southeast Asia [also] because of … its connection with subversion and infiltration of local communist parties [and] the presence of the overseas Chinese who are not yet fully assimilated."[143] Arief Budiman observed that during the *reformasi* era when the official policy of discrimination against the ethnic Chinese Indonesians had been formally abolished, the latter would like to demonstrate to the *pribumi* that "they can be both good Chinese and good Indonesian citizens who love their motherland."[144] Yet, some three decades later after Ali Moertopo's statement and notwithstanding the "change of course" during the *reformasi* era, the negative perception among the country's leadership evidently still persists. The prevalent view among the interviewed members of the Indonesian foreign policy elite is that the Chinese "always remember their *tanah asli*", or their mother land, "have strong culture [and] always speak their language."[145] The ethnic Chinese are seen as having a strong and lasting allegiance to their homeland, China. One interviewed leader, for example, pointedly used the expression familiar to most Indonesians: "Once Chinese, always Chinese."[146] Indeed, the Indonesian phrase "*sekali Cina, tetap Cina*" reflects the enduring perception that the Chinese mentality does not change with the time.

To this end, several leaders also articulated the view that "no affinity [exists] between the Indonesians and the Chinese."[147] As an international relations expert emphasized, "cultural affinity is more important then ideology or political regime."[148] The lack of "cultural affinity" derives from the fact that the Chinese are more ethnically exclusive than most Americans and Europeans. Consequently, "unlike Americans, Chinese don't embrace foreigners — [one] can not become Chinese."[149] According to a former Minister of Foreign Affairs, it is natural that, "[Indonesian] people are inclined towards the West" and not so much to China.[150] Several leaders argued that unlike the United States, "China is no inspiration" for Indonesia or that "we need China but it does not give us any benefit [apart from the economics]."[151]

Second, the cultural-religious dimension points to the perceived deep cultural and religious divide between the ethnic Chinese minority and the indigenous Indonesians. Religious differences play a crucial role in generating a sense of cultural incompatibility and the ensuing social gap between the two groups. The belief system among the peoples of maritime Southeast Asia was for centuries dominated by Hinduism and Buddhism. Since Muslim (including possibly Chinese-Muslim) merchants and missionaries introduced Islam to the Indonesian archipelago in the 15th century, it has gradually established itself as the predominant religion in the region. Along with Islam came a different worldview that has fundamentally reshaped the relations between the henceforth predominantly Muslim Indonesian archipelago and China. Mozingo writes that

> with the spread of Islam throughout the islands in the 15th century, the formerly tranquil relations between Indonesians and Chinese began to deteriorate. Islam introduced not only a religious creed sharply antagonistic to Chinese beliefs and customs, but also a rival Moslem merchant class anxious to displace the Chinese traders.[152]

Here, Stuart-Fox concluded that "the space this opened between China and the Malays/Indonesians and overseas Chinese has hardly been bridged to this day...."[153]

In his comparative account of the different levels of the ethnic Chinese assimilation in the societies in Thailand and Java, Skinner argues that religion is "one of the most important variables of all" in explaining why they assimilate in some countries more than others.[154] While the differences in religious beliefs continue to influence the Muslim majority's perception of the ethnic Chinese community to this day, we need to admit that the degree and scope of this influence today is debatable. However, it is reasonable to assume that religious differences breed cultural divisiveness. To this end, it is evident that the Indonesian elite's attitude towards the ethnic Chinese is coloured by the belief in the existence of negative qualities of the ethnic Chinese Indonesians. There is a sense, for example, that the ethnic Chinese overall cultural disposition, namely their character and behavioural attitudes, is considerably different from the cultural disposition of the *pribumi*. The former are seen as first and foremost concerned about their economic prosperity and well-being — Abu Hanifah writes:

> The pragmatic Chinese were always a puzzle to everybody and they were known to change position to save their hides. ... They always sided with the regime that was just in power ... they were incorrigible opportunists. ... Their philosophy seems to be that life is the most important thing. Dying is a sad story opening up the great unknown. So one should make as much as possible out of life whatever the cost.[155]

Thirdly, the socio-economic dimension of the ethnic Chinese' "otherness" stems from the deep economic and social division between the Chinese community and the majority of indigenous Indonesians. From the perspective of the *pribumi* Indonesians, today's strong influence of the ethnic-Chinese companies and conglomerates in all sectors of the Indonesian economy can to a certain degree be attributed to their privileged position during the Dutch colonial era. David Mozingo observed that, in the 17th century,

> the Dutch discovered that the Chinese could perform several key economic roles in the colony: as middlemen collecting agricultural produce for export; as retail merchants; and as licensed operators of salt, opium, and other revenue-producing monopolies. Because it helped implement the Dutch plan of exploitation, Chinese economic dominance in the villages and towns was encouraged.[156]

The older generation in Indonesia would probably still recollect the overseas Chinese as hated tax collectors and cruel overseers on plantations. While a prevalent public perception in Indonesia assumes that the Chinese Indonesians dominate 70 per cent of Indonesia's economy, according to Bertrand, this assumption exists "despite absence of clear evidence."[157]

As a prominent politician publicly asserted during the 1956 All-Indonesian National Importers Congress, even after the revolution, the Indonesians "will still be oppressed by the Chinese. ... We must face this danger together..."[158] Moreover, much like in the Dutch colonial era, also later during the New Order regime, the ethnic Chinese were widely seen as opportunistically benefiting from their close connections with the Suharto family.[159] A. Dahana, a leading Indonesian expert on China, observed that "There is a strong belief among the public that collusion between Chinese businessmen and the Indonesian bureaucracy is rampant. This belief is fuelled by a strong suspicion that at high levels, there is collusion between elite members of the bureaucracy and the Chinese [big businessmen]."[160]

Based on mid-1990s estimates, the resources of the fifty million overseas Chinese living in Southeast Asia were estimated at nearly US$2 trillion and their annual income was approximately US$0,5 trillion, thus roughly equal to the GDP of mainland China. It was also assumed that the ethnic Chinese were in control of about 90 per cent of the Indonesian economy.[161] As A. Dahana points out, the problem does not stem so much from "the existence of a economic gap between the poor and the rich [but rather] because the Chinese are always identified with the rich, any grudge or dissatisfaction towards the government is always attributed to the Chinese."[162] Their privileged economic position goes hand in hand with the perception that the ethnic Chinese community constitutes a sort of separate social class superior to that of the majority of pribumi Indonesians. In this context, we can talk of the phenomenon that is best described as "social jealousy". One respondent aptly defined "social jealousy" as "the [Indonesian] mindset that the Indonesians are disadvantaged vis-à-vis the Chinese."[163] He argued that "if they [the Indonesians] can not get over that, they can not get beyond practical needs with China."[164] In other words, as long as the deep economic and social division between the Chinese community and the majority of indigenous Indonesians persists, the "social jealousy" factor needs to be taken into consideration in explaining the Indonesian elite's distinct attitude towards China.

The Ethnic Chinese: Chinese Nationalism as a Threat to Indonesia

Following the fall of President Suharto, the *reformasi* era has been marked by a shift in the Indonesian Government's treatment of the ethnic Chinese.

The official policy of discrimination has been replaced by an attempt to give the ethnic Chinese community wider opportunities in civil society. As Amien Rais pledged in his speech during the 1999 presidential campaign, "we have to treat all different ethnic and racial groups on an equal footing. ... The best way to solve the [ethnic Chinese] problem is to stop calling our Chinese brothers and sisters *Warga Negara Keturunan*, and treat them the same as other ethnic groups."[165] Yet, although the "fifth column" or "Trojan horse" rhetoric regarding the ethnic Chinese has basically disappeared from the public discourse in Indonesia, the series of interviews conducted with the country's leaders suggests persistent doubts about the ethnic Chinese' loyalty to the Indonesian nation.

Part of the "China threat" thesis is based on the premise that the growing cultural and economic ties between China and the overseas Chinese communities in Southeast Asia may be exploited by Beijing that can use them as a strategic leverage against the regional states.[166] In particular, the Indonesian elite's view is characterized by a sense of disquietude that growing nationalism in mainland China will cause it to attempt to use the ethnic Chinese community as a potent foreign policy instrument to exert dominance over Indonesia. When asked about the possibility of resuming diplomatic ties with Beijing, President Suharto asserted in 1973 that this will happen only if China "really demonstrates a friendly attitude towards us, is not hostile to us, and ceases to render assistance and facilities to the former PKI leaders who are positively involved in the rebellion."[167]

Weinstein found during his research project in Indonesia a general scepticism about the loyalty of the ethnic Chinese to Jakarta. His respondents described the local Chinese as "a corps of agents", "a cancer in our system" or "our enemy, that is to say, loyal to China, until proven otherwise."[168] A major study on the ethnic Chinese in Indonesia pointed to the persistent elite perception of the ethnic Chinese as agents for Chinese hegemony. It suggested that the ethnic Chinese in Indonesia serve as an important foreign policy instrument in Beijing's hands.[169] This became obvious, for instance, in the cautions reaction to the 1984 proposal to establish direct trade links with China. Suryadinata observed that the elite was divided on the issue:

> [One] group ... argues that the "overseas Chinese" are now under control and no longer pose a major problem. ... On the contrary, the [other] group thinks that the presence of [China's] diplomats could be a security risk. The [latter] group still remembers the 1965 coup, which is believed to have been supported, if not engineered, by Beijing. There is still a lingering suspicion of ethnic Chinese although the majority are now Indonesian nationals.[170]

The nationalist newspaper *Merdeka* that belonged to the second group warned that "Peking may use it as an approach to encourage relations in the field of foreign policy. If this is done, then the aim of the direct trade link will bring about a political consequence, which Indonesia may find hard to accept."[171]

In 1990, certain Muslim groups expressed their concern that the restoration of Indonesia's diplomatic relations with China would only strengthen the dominant economic position of the ethnic Chinese capitalists. The increasing economic and social gap between the ethnic Chinese and *pribumi* Indonesians would only add fuel to the flames — the ensuing aggravation of the resentment and hatred towards the ethnic Chinese would make the latter's assimilation more difficult.[172] Referring to these perceptions among indigenous Indonesians, Arief Budiman writes that with the more liberal and permissive environment, which was further enhanced by the 1999 election of Abdurrahman Wahid as Indonesian President, "some *pribumi* started to whisper, 'If we keep letting the Chinese advance, they will become arrogant and think they can control this country.'" As a consequence, Budiman observed that "some Chinese sensed this change of feeling among the *pribumi* [and] they felt that if the euphoria continued unchecked, it might rekindle latent anti-Chinese feeling."[173]

Several leaders interviewed for this book worried about the growing cultural awareness of the ethnic Chinese, pointing, for example, to the government's decision to approve the Chinese New Year, or IMLEK, as a national holiday. They argued that "the Chinese community in Indonesia should be integrated" and warned that the ethnic Chinese are "still only half Indonesian."[174] The elite is alarmed by the prospect of seeing the Indonesian ethnic Chinese' allegiance shifting towards China as it rises in power and prestige. A section of the Indonesian leadership believes that, based on the historical experience, the "opportunist" wealthy ethnic Chinese would be inclined to identify themselves increasingly with China. They are concerned about two possible future developments: In the first, the ethnic Chinese conglomerates would channel large amounts of financial resources to mainland China. In the second, Beijing would use the ethnic Chinese community's economic clout in Indonesia to influence and manipulate domestic Indonesian politics. In either case, it is believed that the consequences for Indonesia's national security would be potentially dire.

The notion of the ethnic Chinese-owned conglomerates moving their capital and wealth to China has been an issue in Indonesia at least since the 1970s. During the New Order regime, official government institutions questioned the commitment of the ethnic Chinese' companies to Indonesia, pointing to their perceived reluctance to contribute their financial resources to the broader economic growth in the country. The Lippo Group, for example, was criticized because it was, since 1990, stealthily moving its capital out of Indonesia not only into China and Hong Kong but also to Australia and the United States.[175] According to the data available, in 1991, the ethnic Chinese-owned Dharmala conglomerate received as much as 35 per cent of its earnings overseas and, by 1994, the Liem group also generated 35 per cent of its revenues from overseas operations.[176] The strong view that the capital outflow from Indonesia to China continues because, as one respondent asserted, "China is still mainland for the [ethnic] Chinese community", seems to persist among sections of the foreign policy elite.[177]

In the author's view, the main difference with the New Order regime is that the Indonesian leaders are now more reluctant to express their real attitudes towards the ethnic Chinese because anti-Chinese rhetoric is at present considered as socially unacceptable. Yet, the old sentiments clearly persist. The long-term distrust with regard to the ethnic Chinese community did not only lead several respondents to argue that "the government should remind the ethnic Chinese to be loyal to Indonesia and not to invest so much money in mainland China."[178] It is also manifested in the elite's concern about new Chinese immigrants. One interviewed leader explained why they are seen as a security problem:

> Because every year there has been a number of the Chinese not only women to become prostitutes in the Jakarta area but also they come to Indonesia and it is very easy for them to change their name, passport to become Indonesian citizens. And because of the corrupt officials at the airport it is quite easy for them to become Indonesian citizens. So I think it will also be a dangerous social relationship between native Indonesians and the newcomers from China.[179]

Ultimately, the Indonesian foreign policy elite is uneasy about the possibility that, in the future, the ethnic Chinese community will become a powerful vanguard in China's quest for hegemony in the region. Referring to this concern, a former Indonesian ambassador to Japan warned in an unprecedented interview with a leading Japanese newspaper of a "Chinese economic intervention in the region". He argued that such an intervention would exploit the presence of ethnic Chinese communities in Indonesia and other Southeast Asian countries, which would in turn enable Beijing to establish Chinese-sponsored "puppet governments."[180]

The Immutable Nature of "Chineseness"?

Weinstein's major survey of Indonesian leaders' perceptions made an important and groundbreaking contribution to the understanding of the Indonesian elite's attitude to China. The New Order regime used the notion of the communist threat posed to the Indonesian society by the Mao's regime in China as one of the means to support its legitimacy. Weinstein found that the leaders' apprehension about China actually did not arise so much from the Maoist ideology or China's communist infiltration, but rather from the leaders' unfavourable view of the Chinese national character. The Chinese national character and the perceived character of the ethnic Chinese Indonesians are generally seen all but identical. As Weinstein observed, the widespread notion among the Indonesian elite is that "all Chinese are inherently aggressive."[181] He writes here that "[it] is hard to overemphasize the importance of the overseas Chinese in the foreign policy elite's perception of the Chinese threat. When asked what they thought about China, the foreign policy elite members frequently responded with comments on the Indonesian Chinese."[182] Weinstein concluded in his study on the Indonesian foreign policy elite's perceptions that

> in the first place, China's aggressiveness was generally attributed more to the country's *Chineseness* than to its communism. Of 51 leaders who explained why they considered China aggressive, only 29 per cent cited communism as the principal motivation, while 43 per cent pointed to the "Chinese factor" and 27 per cent accorded equal weight to communism and *Chineseness*.[183]

Weinstein's important finding that the elite was concerned about the China threat more in terms of Chinese nationalism and the innate Chinese character than its communist and Maoist ideology indicates one crucial fact: Regardless of the nature of the Chinese regime and its ideology, the Indonesian foreign policy elite's basic perception of China as an expansionist power can be considered as a constant that is unlikely to undergo a significant change in the near future.[184] The author's research found that while the scope and depth of the anti-Chinese sentiments among the foreign policy elite has diminished, the leaders' inclination to link their largely unfavourable perceptions of the ethnic Chinese and the notion of *Chineseness* to their view of China clearly persists. In his 1976 study, Weinstein reported that "[the] Indonesian leaders vied with one another to demonstrate the depth of their hatred for the Chinese, and they usually did so by telling of their antipathy toward the Chinese in Indonesia, thus revealing the extent to which China and the local Chinese merged in their thinking."[185]

It needs to be emphasized that none of the interviewed leaders sought to "parade" their anti-Chinese belligerence. In the words of one interviewee, there is "no [more] phobia about the China threat" in the elite's perception of that country.[186] However, although the most overt and pronounced anti-Chinese expressions were conspicuously missing in the Indonesian leaders' rhetoric, the tendency to mention their view of the perceived inherently negative Chinese character when discussing China has not much abated. More than 50 per cent of the respondents made a spontaneous reference to the ethnic Chinese and *Chineseness* while discussing their view of China. As a Cabinet Minister pointed out, the notion of *Chineseness*, which is largely based on the perceptions of the ethnic Chinese Indonesians, is one of the main sources of the Indonesian elite's wariness about the "China threat".[187] One respondent put it clearly: "… I would also refer to the pre-independence period when there was a strong sentiment between pribumi and ethnic Chinese — well, until now, it's still strong in some areas — the issue is always the same: wealth! People tend to see China and ethnic Chinese as another two sides of one coin."[188] When asked what they thought about China, the respondents made frequent references to the ethnic Chinese Indonesians. Explaining the linkage between China and the ethnic Chinese Indonesians, one respondent asserted:

> … to some extent I can see that some elements within the Indonesian society still see China as a threat. But it has nothing to do with the mainland China. But simply because the relationship, the interaction, between the Chinese and the Indonesian native people is complicated by the economic factors and other issues…."[189]

In some cases, when the leaders clearly referred to the perceived "Chinese character", it was obvious that they tried to do it in an implied manner. For example, while explaining Jakarta's response to its territorial dispute with China over the 272-island Natuna archipelago in the South-China Sea, a former Minister of Foreign Affairs recalled: "We had some difficulties with the Chinese about the waters around Natuna Islands … the Chinese drew a line following their coastline and down to Southeast Asia and very close to the Natuna Islands. And we tried to ask them 'what is this line?'" Here, tacitly referring to the perceived *Chineseness*, the former Foreign Minister remarked: "And they said, eeeh, eeeh, that is a traditional line, and you know how the Chinese are. They don't want to tell us!"[190] Referring to what is seen as a precedent of China's expansionist policies in the past, it was argued that "China will [again] move towards this kind of scenario. There is a sign."[191] When asked what the sign was, a number of interviewees pointed out that "the Chinese are economically powerful in Indonesia."[192] It is through the ethnic Chinese community that "China already controls Indonesia's economy — to a certain extent."[193] On several occasions, when the author questioned the rationale of the elite's belief that China is intrinsically expansionist by nature, several leaders pointed to the "disloyalty of the ethnic Chinese." They were concerned that "the Indonesian ethnic Chinese could be used by Mainland China" as a means to expand its influence to Indonesia.[194]

Only a handful of interviewees disputed the prevailing notion of China's expansionist and militarist past. They pointed out that "China says it has never fought wars with the states in the region. [In fact] the U.S. has been more militant."[195] While a young career diplomat argued that "China has never been expansionist,"[196] a senior member of the PDI-P party asserted that "I have never believed in China's subversion. ... Historically, China has never been an aggressor."[197] A former President concluded:

> Indonesia has never been colonized by the Chinese. Never. But the Indonesian archipelago was colonized by the Europeans, the Dutch and the Portuguese. ... Even Islam in Indonesia was introduced by the Chinese. ... And lots of Indonesian culture is very much influenced by the Chinese culture. In all history there was never the moment that we were colonized by the Chinese. We don't have the same feeling as Czechoslovakia or the Polish and Russia and Germany.[198]

Of the total of forty-five leaders, only five interviewees explicitly repudiated the notion of *Chineseness* or, in other words, the concept of China as an inherently aggressive and expansionist power. Based on the discussion above, it is possible to agree with Sarah Turner, who argues that "the history of antagonism towards the ethnic Chinese in Indonesia will not be forgotten...."[199] We can also accept as valid Rizal Sukma's contention that "the course of Indonesia-China relations in the future will be influenced by Indonesia's persistent perceptions of the ethnic Chinese minority."[200] Also because of the Indonesian leaders' deep-rooted notion of *Chineseness* and their largely unfavourable view of the ethnic Chinese, and since the latter's and China's character are essentially seen as identical, it is then understandable that the negatives outweigh the positives in the elite's perceptions of that country.

THE ELITE'S AMBIVALENCE ABOUT CHINA'S RISE

Since the early 1980s, China has sustained one of the world's highest rates of economic growth. Beijing has steadily increased its military expenditures and expanded its influence as a key player on the regional "chessboard".[201] China's economic and political ascendancy has been an important development affecting Southeast Asia after the end of the Cold War. Beijing's growing ties with Southeast Asia have presented Indonesia and other regional states with complex opportunities and challenges. It is now almost conventional wisdom that China's rise is and will be a source of both positive as well as negative implications, both having a military-economic security dimension. We will now assess the Indonesian foreign policy elite's perceptions of China's rise. While Indonesia's bilateral relationship with China has steadily improved, according to Irman Lanti, "the rise of China generates mixed reactions among Indonesians."[202] Whilst pointing to certain positive effects of China's growing projection of power and influence in Southeast Asia, the majority of the elite talks openly about their concern about the uncertainties regarding China's future behaviour on the international stage. As one leader emphatically cautioned, "we still do not know what [China's] policy will be in the next twenty or fifty years after they are already successful in developing their economy."[203] One respondent aptly summed up the prevalent mood among the foreign policy elite: "You feel uneasy about the rise of China."[204]

The author's research has demonstrated the relatively high degree to which the elite is apprehensive about the future implications of China's ascendancy for Indonesia's national security. Drawing on the structured questionnaire, the respondents were presented with the following statement and question: "*Beijing has lately pursued what seems to be a liberal foreign policy accompanied by the rhetoric of multilateralism and international cooperation. How likely is it that once China becomes an economically and militarily strong power, Beijing will impose its will on its weaker neighbours?*" As Figure 5.5 shows, based on the answers to this question, about 11 per cent of interviewed leaders were convinced that this future scenario is "very likely", 27 per cent of them believed that it is "likely", 40 per cent thought that it is "possible" that such a future eventuality will happen and, finally, 22 per cent rejected the notion of China's hegemonic intentions as "unlikely". All in all, we can see here that more than three quarters, or 78 per cent, of the interviewees admitted that they were — at least to some degree — concerned about the future implications of China's ascendancy for Indonesia. Next, we will examine in turn the aspects of the rise of China that the Indonesian leaders

FIGURE 5.5
China in the Future Goes Hegemonic?

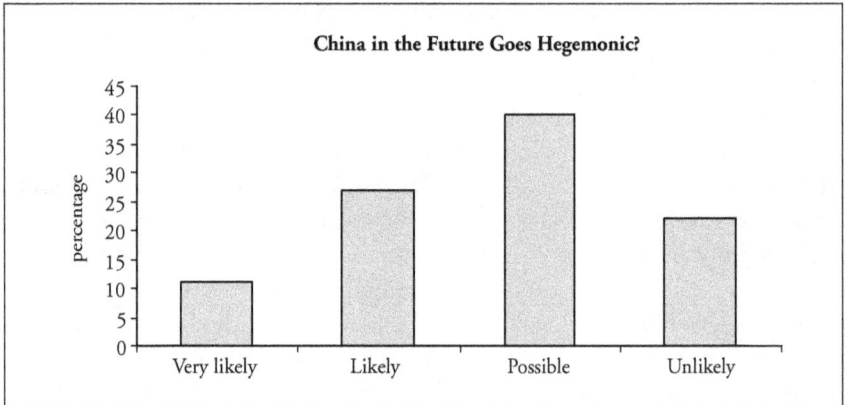

Source: Survey research conducted by the author in 2004–05.

view with alarm and then what the elite regards as a positive side of this process.

China as an "Economic Threat"

Perhaps the most potent reason why in 1990 Suharto's regime finally made the long-delayed decision to "de-freeze" Indonesia's diplomatic relationships with China was the growing desire of the Indonesian elite to benefit from the rapid economic growth of China. A former Foreign Minister explained:

> Big change came, of course, when the ... Cold War ended. ... a new world constellation emerged. ... China was both a threat and an opportunity for us. ... A threat because it was so *big* ... it was *the biggest* country in the world, it is there, it is our neighbour, it is getting richer and it will most probably [arm itself and become very powerful]. [But] it is also an opportunity because it has a huge market. China instilled in us both a fear and also an incentive. And [Indonesia] has been trying to ... make it more an incentive than a fear.[205]

Another leader emphasized that during the Cold War era "Everybody tried to isolate, contain China because it did not have anything to offer to the world. But at the moment China opened up and focused much more on the economy and the rest of the world has become much more interested in China."[206]

Some respondents pointed out that "China has become from a threat to Indonesia to a potential economic partner"[207] while conceding that "[although] China is still our competitor but now China is not only a threat but also an opportunity."[208] Some others now refer to China as "a challenge and an opportunity,"[209] "a partner, very promising country,"[210] or "more an opportunity than a threat."[211] "China is also an opportunity," especially because of "its need for natural resources."[212] An article in a popular Indonesian magazine discussing Indonesia's dilemmatic situation concerning China was aptly titled "*Antara Madu dan Racun*" — "Between Honey and Poison".[213] "*Antara Madu dan Racun*" is the name of a popular Indonesian song, as much as it is a commonly used maxim; it refers to a dilemmatic situation, in which one has to symbolically make a "risky" choice from two closed fists, whereby one of them is hiding sweet "honey" and the other one deadly "poison".

With the economic ties between Indonesia and China expanding, the perception of the "China threat" gradually took on a new dimension.[214] The main concern in Jakarta is not the "China threat" in the Cold War guise of another Soviet Union competing with the United States in the military domain. Whereas in the early and mid 1990s, China was still viewed as a threat mainly because of its military actions in the South China Sea and large-scale arms purchases, from the mid and late 1990s, the Indonesian elite's concern has increasingly shifted to the booming Chinese economy.[215] Beijing is now ruled by the "Coca-Cola Communist Party", remarked a senior leader of the Muslim organization *Muhammadiyah*, referring to the now economy-driven, instead of the erstwhile ideology-driven, policies of the Chinese regime.[216] As Arya B. Gaduh, a researcher with the CSIS in Jakarta, contends, the anxiety among the elite has increasingly been about China's international competitiveness and economic dominance that it can use in the political and diplomatic domain to achieve its objectives.[217]

Throughout the 1990s, these concerns were regularly echoed from the highest places. It was during his first visit to China in November 1990 that President Suharto expressed his amazement and bewilderment at the pace and extent of China's economic development and his apprehension about its implications for Southeast Asia. Later, in August 1996, President Suharto made a rare move by commenting publicly on his view of China as being, at least in economic terms, a threat to Asia. He emphasized that he was particularly "concerned that [China] may dominate the global market with its economic power which is capable of producing low-priced goods."[218] Robert Lowry concluded in his 1996 study of Indonesia's Armed Forces that, viewed from the Army's corporate perspective, "China continues to be seen as the greatest potential direct threat to Indonesian sovereignty."[219]

These misgivings were reinforced during and following the 1997 monetary crisis in Southeast Asia because of the elite's acute awareness about the lacklustre performance of the Indonesian economy, especially in comparison with other countries in Southeast and Northeast Asia. In the early 21st century, China's bilateral economic deals with Burma, Cambodia and Thailand generated fears in the region of economic dependence on China that could gradually lead to political dominance.[220] Sensing similar concerns among the elites in the regional capital cities, China has sought to present its growing economic power as having a positive and benign influence on other countries. Beijing has repeatedly reassured Indonesia and its regional neighbours that its economic ties with Southeast Asia will benefit both sides, with its Prime Minister going so far as describing China as "a friendly elephant", which poses no threat to Southeast Asia.[221] Faced with such a complex situation, what is the Indonesian foreign policy elite's perception of the increasing projection of China's economic influence in the region?

According to the data, more than 50 per cent of interviewed leaders expressed their concern about what they commonly refer to as the "economic threat" from China. In other words, four out of five respondents who explicitly stated that they regarded China as a security threat to Indonesia believed that this danger stems mainly from the country's "economic threat". It was obvious from the interviews that the elite's view on this matter is characterized by ambivalence. While the leaders wanted Indonesia to tap into China's economic development and expected that the country should benefit from the relations, they simultaneously regard China as a dangerous economic competitor and worried that Indonesia's bilateral engagement with Beijing would allow the latter to expand its economic dominance and political influence.[222] Generally, the elite concedes that Indonesia simply does not have a choice but to accept the reality of China becoming a major power Indonesia has to deal with. According to one leader,

> [in] the old days, Indonesia tried to manage the relations by insulating itself from China; [there were] no trade, no diplomatic, or any other relations with China. But after it became very clear that whether we like it or not, China is becoming a major power, we now do not have a choice. ... In this way, [Indonesia should] take the advantage China has to offer....[223]

Whilst pointing out that an economically developed and prosperous China offers economic opportunity to Indonesia, another respondent expressed a widespread view by saying that "we are still afraid that, for example, if China is successful in their economic development maybe it will affect the Indonesian economy."²²⁴ He then added that "[it] has already started from ten years ago. The Chinese products not only come to Indonesia and replace a large number of products, for example garments and foot ware in Indonesia, but it also affects our exports to Australia and also to other countries."²²⁵

The overwhelming impression of China among the interviewees was that "China can produce everything [and thus] its capacity and capability are both a threat for the region."²²⁶ One leader complained that "during Suharto, Indonesia was an exporter of plywood and garment, [but] today, Indonesia imports even plywood from China."²²⁷ Hence, it is not surprising that Indonesia — facing pressures from local producers — listed nearly 400 categories of sensitive and highly sensitive goods to be excluded from the ACFTA (ASEAN-China Free Trade Agreement). When compared with other ASEAN neighbours, Indonesia's economy has more sectors that compete with China — these include agriculture (rice, sugar, soybeans, corn), electronics, automobiles, textile and chemical industries.²²⁸ The fear of China's "economic threat" is so intense among some interviewed members of the foreign policy elite that they openly warned that, in the words of a young career diplomat, already now "China [is] controlling the Indonesian economy."²²⁹ His more senior colleague then emphatically emphasized: "I have warned people in DEPLU and former President Gus Dur about China."²³⁰ Several respondents suggested that their personal experience has significantly influenced their rather unfavourable outlook towards China. For example, one leader recollected:

> I have visited China several times and I could see that they can produce everything and also they can feed themselves without other countries' assistance. With this capacity, we can imagine [the consequences for Indonesia] if they are spreading their economic power with their cheap products.

He then concluded that "Indonesia cannot compete with China — Indonesia is flooded with cheap Chinese products, poor quality but poor people do not need high quality products. China is an economic threat ... they have their own potential."²³¹

A senior official from the Indonesian Department of Trade and Industry who is one of the representatives negotiating a Free Trade Agreement (FTA) between ASEAN and China asserted:

> When I attend a FTA negotiation meeting with China, their approach is very rigid and tough. When China is strong, they will interfere with

Indonesia and ASEAN. During negotiations, China sometimes pushes too hard on the ASEAN states. In every FTA meeting with China, Indonesia is especially careful with China.[232]

His colleague shared this view when he cautioned that "we have to be careful how to design the FTA agreement with China."[233] Also another leader who is familiar with the ASEAN-China FTA negotiations contended that "China is very offensive," pointing to the source of his information — his friend Mari Pangestu who is presently serving as the country's Minister of Trade. When Mari Pangestu lived in Shanghai, the respondent recalled, "several times she said [to me] that Indonesia still has the opportunity to make a deal, benefit from the trade with China."[234] A young career diplomat based his unfavourable view of China's growing economic muscles on his recent study trip to Australia: "China is a threat for every country. [It is an] economic threat even for Australia with shops where everything made-in-China costs two bucks."[235]

When analysing the roots of the widespread perception of the "economic threat" China poses to Indonesia, the Indonesian leadership's worldview is characterized by scepticism and a pervasive sense of weakness and vulnerability. From the point of view of the elite, the fundamental reason for the "economic threat" posed by China is quite clear: The rapid growth of the Chinese economy, by contrast with the lacklustre performance of the Indonesian economy, will gradually be translated into a dependency relationship between the two countries. In other words, the weaker economy in Indonesia will make the whole country more vulnerable vis-à-vis the rising Chinese economic powerhouse. At this point, we can touch on the "Pretty Maiden Analogy" that was originally used to characterize the Indonesian elite's distinct worldview in the context of the Cold War bipolar conflict. It was shown that, in the 1970s, Indonesian leaders referred to the "Pretty Maiden Analogy" to describe Indonesia's position in what they considered to be an exploitative and hostile world. In such a world, other countries sought to take advantage of the "pretty maiden" Indonesia that was ascribed a great economic and geopolitical importance.[236] In this research, the respondents were presented with a following question: "*In the past Indonesia was seen by many 'like a pretty maiden who [was] constantly being approached by men who [wanted] to take advantage of her.' How strongly do you agree that Indonesia is today in this position?*" As Figure 5.6 shows, more than three-fourths of all interviewed leaders agree at least to some degree that Indonesia is subject to a wide array of hostile forces trying to exploit the country's weakness. Importantly, in contrast to Weinstein's study, the

FIGURE 5.6
The "Pretty Maiden" Analogy, Based on the Research Data Evaluation

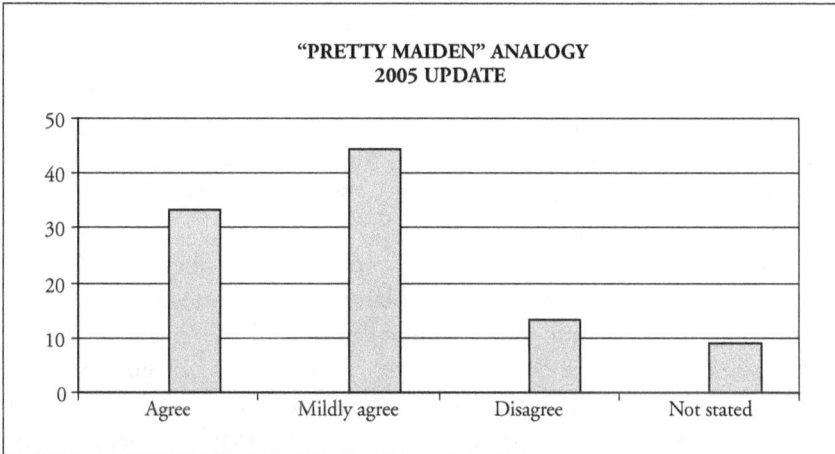

Source: Author's original compilations.

contemporary elite largely understands the "Pretty Maiden Analogy" as an expression of Indonesia's "lack of prettiness" or, in other words, the sense of weakness and vulnerability vis-à-vis the outside world. Referring to the "Pretty Maiden Analogy", the prevalent sense among the respondents was that "China is prettier than Indonesia."[237] As a well-known Muslim politician observed, "China but also Thailand and Malaysia and other countries have achieved their prosperity better. "Beautiful girl" [Indonesia] has lots of rivals."[238]

We can see the elite's tendency to compare Indonesia with other countries — "now some new countries are more promising, like China and Vietnam"[239] — in the light of their acute awareness that "economic competitiveness is crucial now."[240] As one leader asserted, "Indonesia is not as competitive as China, which is more efficient. ... These are real challenges for Indonesia. This is more real than any military challenges."[241] A former member of President Suharto's Cabinet warned that "[the] capital was in the last few years moving from Indonesia to China and Vietnam. Indonesia was more competitive before 1997. The productivity of the Chinese and, for example, Vietnam is much higher than in Indonesia. This is becoming a threat."[242] The leaders' scepticism about Indonesia's ability to compete was a commonplace during the interviews. This discussion points to the increasing complexities in what factors are deemed to be paramount in safeguarding a state's national security. It is apparent that the state of Indonesian economy features very prominently in the elite's overall national security considerations. According to the data, over 80 per cent of the interviewed respondents expressed their belief that Indonesia's domestic problems, including those related to the economic sphere, constitute a bigger threat to the island nation's security than any type of external threat.[243] Notwithstanding this awareness, one group of leaders are either confident that "China needs us because we are a big market"[244] or they use the language of self-pity — a former President complained that "the Indonesians suffer from prejudice. ... Prejudice and suspicion are an obstacle [for Indonesia]."[245]

Another group of leaders openly criticized what they described as an inherent Indonesian mentality of blaming all Indonesian failures on external forces. As one respondent pointedly emphasized, "before we blame other nations, we have to blame ourselves. ... Indonesia can not be proud of itself."[246] Another interviewed leader contended that "we [should] not consider China as a threat but as an economic potential."[247] Then, a high-level diplomat argued that the Indonesian elite should address the problem of China rather than just complain about "the economic threat":

> It is precisely to address the rising attractiveness of China as a market, as a place for investment, as a place to do business with. That ASEAN is now coming together as an ASEAN Economic Community, a block of 550 million-head market, [it is] precisely to deal with the Chinese challenge. Because China is becoming [economically] more and more attractive. But we have to solve, to address that challenge ... We cannot stop the unstoppable, trying to make China unattractive, we cannot do that. But what is in our control is to make us attractive.[248]

Aptly summing up the whole discussion about the current economic dimension of the "China threat", a retired Army general laconically concluded that "[We] must also benefit from China's growth ... if we did not do it, we would be stupid."[249]

The Uncertainty about the Growing Chinese Military Might

Indonesia's Defence White Paper 2003 titled "*Mempertahankan Tanah Air Memasuki Abad 21*" [Defending the Homeland at the Start of the 21st Century] outlined the Indonesian Government's perception of threats to the country. Although this important official document states that "the current strategic environment renders the threat of invasion or military aggression low",[250] some official pronouncements of Indonesian public figures as well as the data collected indicate the existence of a more nuanced view among the foreign policy elite. This became particularly obvious, for example, when Washington's lifting of the United States-imposed restrictions on military sales and cooperation with Indonesia in June 2006 was by some experts considered as prompted by economic and security concerns. According to Suzie Sudarman, the director of the Centre for American Studies at the University of Indonesia, "increasing the country's defensive capabilities was important, especially in the face of China's military modernization, which could pose a threat to countries in the region."[251]

The majority of the interviewed leaders emphasized that the Indonesian foreign policy elite has primarily been concerned about the "socio-political threat from China [and] never really conventional military threat."[252] As a high-ranking diplomat asserted, "... even at the lowest point of Indonesia's relations with China, for instance, ... we never perceived China, then it was in the 1970s, as a threat in the conventional sense; it was more threat in terms of ideology."[253] Also the Indonesian armed forces during the New Order regime did not perceive the "China threat" in conventional military terms. The country's defence establishment was rather concerned about Beijing's attempts to exploit Indonesia's weakness, namely its lack of political and social cohesion.[254] "The fear of China was primarily domestic in Indonesia. There was not fear of China invading Indonesia."[255] As one interviewee explained, "[it] was very much ideological, not about the military. Because China was not capable at that time of doing military operations, invading Southeast Asia, for example."[256]

Notwithstanding the fear of "economic threat" posed by China, the more traditional concern about the possible use of force by Beijing has not by any means completely dissipated. The data indicate that sections of the foreign policy elite believe in the continuing utility of the use of force in international relations. It has shown that 38 per cent of respondents consider the "balance of power" and also 38 per cent of them "closer military cooperation of ASEAN states" as two of the most efficient approaches to peace and security in Southeast Asia. To this end, there is a widespread belief among the Indonesian leadership that the rapidly growing Chinese economy will be translated into an enhanced military power which may in turn lead Beijing to pursue aggressive expansionism in the region. Illustrative of these concerns in the elite's outlook was the statement published in the 1995 Indonesian Defence White Paper that warned against China's economic growth, which "together with her advancing technology will at some time lift [China] to become the pre-eminent country

in the region, both economically and militarily."[257] The publication of
this document coincided with the increased apprehension in Jakarta over
Beijing's disputed claims in the South-China Sea during the 1995–96
period.

   It is clearly beyond the scope of this study to analyse in depth the conflict
in the South China Sea territory that involves a number of overlapping
claims raised by China and several Southeast Asian states. With regard
to the Natuna Islands, a chain of 300 islands and atolls, in 1993, Beijing
raised the eyebrows of policy-makers in Jakarta by the publication of a
controversial map, which laid claims to part of the territorial waters of the
Natunas. Jakarta initiated a series of bilateral discussions with Beijing over the
Chinese maps that extended the demarcation of China's territory to include
the Indonesia-owned major natural gas field about 180 kilometres northeast
of the Natuna Islands.[258] A former Foreign Minister recalled: "We had
some difficulties with the Chinese about the waters around Natuna Islands
[when] the Chinese drew a line following their coastline and down to
Southeast Asia and very close to the Natuna Islands. And we tried to ask
them 'what is this line?'"[259] However, as Indonesia's former chief diplomat
points out, China's position on the Natuna gas field remained ambiguous
and unclear:

> We said, look, even if the Spratley Islands are yours, which is still
> disputed, according to the Law of the Sea, you cannot draw a line
> that far. Because most of those islands are uninhabited. And
> uninhabited islands, you can not draw 200 miles. You can only draw
> 12 miles. So, please, what is this line because it comes too close
> to us? They said you don't have to worry. We have nothing with
> Indonesia; we have never claimed any part of Indonesia. We had to be
> satisfied with that. But, at that point, we were a bit worried about the
> Natunas.[260]

This development coincided, in 1995, with the conclusion of the Indonesia-
Australia military defence agreement, which essentially meant a departure
from Jakarta's *bebas-aktif* foreign policy of avoiding alignment with external
powers. In September 1996, Indonesia conducted in the waters around the
Natuna and Riau Islands its most massive joint exercise in years.[261] The
interviews with present and former senior military officers indicate that
China's rhetoric and actions in the mid-1990s increased the long-standing
suspicion among the Indonesian armed forces of China's long-term intentions
in the region. Explaining the reasons for holding the large-scale exercise in
1996, a former Army general asserted:

Yes, because [the Chinese demarcation line was] nearing the borders of the Indonesian national territory. The military was very much concerned about [the defence of] the Natunas. ... Anything that relates to the national borders, then the military would become sensitive, but outside that that would be seen as lying in the domain of the Ministry of Foreign Affairs.[262]

Allen S. Whiting conducted a series of interviews with political elites in several Southeast Asian capital cities between December 1995 and January 1996 and he described his experience from Indonesia as follows:

In Jakarta, civilian and military officials alike referred to the distant time when "suzerainty" sanctioned Peking vesting Javanese kings with legitimacy. More widely, the 15th century naval expeditions of Cheng Ho received negative attention in Singapore, Kuala Lumpur, and Hanoi. These Ming dynasty fleets were explicitly cited as possible precedent for future attempts at domination when the Chinese navy acquires an aircraft carrier and the associated power projection capability.[263]

The invocation of these historical episodes does not necessarily mean that the Indonesian elite anticipates China is likely to embark on aggressive expansionism by military means in the near future. There is awareness that, for the immediate future, without the blue-water navy, China is lacking the capacity to project its military influence far from its shores. Yet, the elite is concerned about Beijing's prospective polices in the South-China Sea and particularly the situation in which Beijing decides to resolve the long-term dispute around Indonesia's Natuna Islands by military means. This sense of uncertainty is reinforced by the earlier outlined sense of vulnerability vis-à-vis China especially in the light of the latter's large-scale arms acquisitions. The Indonesian leaders' threat perception regarding the Natuna Islands is shaped by the acute awareness that, as one respondent aptly put it, "if the Chinese want, they can take [the Natunas] and the Indonesian elite knows it!"[264]

As several respondents asserted, the elite's continuing anxiety about the future prospect of China's foreign policies towards Indonesia is not only in terms of the "economic threat", but "it is [still] traditional [as well]."[265] The lack of transparency in China's military build-up, as well as the lack of clarity about Beijing's military budget and its expanding major weapons acquisitions, keeps the elite's sense of foreboding about future Sino-Indonesian relations alive. Referring to the linkage between China's economic growth and its arms purchases, one interviewed leader argued that the elite's concern "[is] also related to the economy. For example, if [China's] GDP increases in the next twenty years whether they will build up their armed forces and whether there will be a competition, I mean negative competition between China and [other states] related to security."[266] According to Hadi Soesastro, China's attitude towards Japan, including its refusal to support Tokyo becoming a permanent member of the UN Security Council, and the lack of transparency in developing China's military capabilities, create instability in Asian security and demonstrate China's inclination to dominate the region.[267] The concern is not necessarily that China will opt for the use of force but it is more about the uncertainty as to how far Beijing will go to pursue its interests and the ways this will affect the dynamics of interstate relations in the region. As one leader squarely put it, "... nobody is so sure that the military power China has acquired will not be used in order to put pressure on regional countries in order to pursue their national interest."[268] This development can lead to such a dangerous situation, as a young career diplomat cautioned, when "China has the [military] capacity to push the U.S. to choose China over Taiwan."[269] Ultimately, in the words of an international relations expert, "China now puts more emphasis as well on the development of its Southern Fleet in the South China Sea. [It is] not directly threatening Indonesia but it changes the strategic configuration within Southeast Asia."[270]

The Positive Side of China's Rise

Generally, there are three reasons as to why the Indonesian foreign policy elite consider China's growing power and influence as an opportunity — a process that has a positive impact on international relations in Asia. First, it is the view that Beijing can provide a counterweight to the U.S. unilateralist policies. Second, it eases Indonesia's perceived dependency on the United States and the West in general. Third, China's participation in regional security arrangements provides an assurance that it will follow the rules and principles set by the Southeast Asian countries associated with the ASEAN grouping.

First, the Indonesian leaders welcome the rise of China because they believe that this process will make it possible to re-establish something that could be called a "healthy balance" among the world's major power. In particular, the interviewed leaders directly linked the benefits of China's ascendancy to what some describe as malevolent unilateralist tendencies in the U.S. hegemonic position. Expressing the prevalent attitude among the elite, one respondent suggested that "it would be better for us if we did not have such a powerful single superpower."[271] As a senior diplomat put it, "the U.S. unilateralism is much more dangerous than the 'China threat'."[272] "I do not believe in unilateralism," claimed one respondent, referring to Washington's policies especially in the period of 2001–05, and immediately pointed out that this is where "the rise of China is good [because it] creates more balance."[273] Another respondent boasted that "I supported the nuclearization of China [in the UN] because I do not want the U.S. to be a world policeman like that."[274] Overall, there was an almost universal agreement among the interviewed leaders that, as an aide close to the President put it, "[because] China gives less pressure these days unlike the U.S., China has become a natural friend." The presidential aide also pointedly asserted: "The more the West, especially the U.S., pressures Jakarta, the more is China happy."[275]

The idea of an imaginary "balance" between the United States and China was frequently mentioned during the series of interviews. We can see this idea in the context of the common belief among the elite that in the future the archipelagic nation will increasingly have to *"mendayung antara dua karang"* or "row between two reefs" — meaning the United States and China.[276] As a Minister in the President Yudhoyono's Cabinet observed,

> [we] feel, first, that China is now entitled to play a stronger role in East Asia. Second, that it naturally must compete [economically and culturally] with Japan. It has [now] become much more balanced from a heavily dominated American cover ... Overall, I think it helps us balancing between the United States, China, Japan and also India.[277]

The idea of a more powerful China fits into the Indonesian foreign policy elite's concept of an ideal balance of power in Asia and globally. It is argued that not only the rise of China but "if [also] the EU becomes very important to balance the U.S., India will grow and become a more important country, then we [Indonesian leaders] can play one against the other."[278]

Second, the rise of China is welcome by the elite because it is seen as capable of reducing Indonesia's perceived economic and political dependency on the United States and the West in general. "If the U.S. pressures Indonesia, we must find other options, other alternatives," said a high-level official from the Indonesian Foreign Ministry and, as much as most of the other respondents, refers primarily to the controversial issue of the U.S. arms embargo against Indonesia.[279] As another member of the foreign policy elite contended, "[so] many embargoes have been imposed on Indonesia and [thus]

Indonesia was forced to seek alternatives also. Indonesia [had to] diversify its supply of arms."[280] The U.S. arms embargo was imposed against Indonesia in 1992 following clashes between the Indonesian army and protesters in East Timor in which more than 200 demonstrators were killed. Later, in 1999, the embargo was tightened in the wake of the 1999 crisis in East Timor when militia groups with the support of elements within Indonesian security forces killed hundreds of civilians during the UN-sponsored independence ballot. Perhaps the most insightful discussion on the matter of diversification of Indonesia's arms supplies was with a leader who is known for his close ties with the Indonesian military establishment. According to him, "[for] many years, because of our closeness to the U.S., most of our military equipment was coming from the U.S. So it is not so easy to change it because if you buy a weapon, you buy a weapon system...." On the matter of easing this dependency on the United States, he asserted that "[if] America keeps us to the corner, then we [will] start buying somewhere else. ... China is very active in Indonesia today, offering us military equipment with [no restrictions] on it, no requirements to constrain us." Finally, he concluded that

> [there] are two problems with that. We have to ... change our [whole] weapon system. [And] we do not have the money to buy it. [But] if America is still pressuring us [in the future], we are willing to buy definitely military equipment from China, the EU and East European countries. ... And China is waiting. They are lobbying in Jakarta, I know them personally. ... But Indonesian elite still expects that our relations with America could be improved in the near future. Otherwise, if we are cornered completely, we will not have a choice and we will start diversifying.[281]

Third, China's active participation in regional security arrangements is seen as providing an assurance that Beijing will follow the rules and principles set by the regional ASEAN grouping. When discussing this matter, the interviewed leaders often mentioned that their positive impression of China derives to a great extent from the fact that Beijing is one of the signatories of the Zone of Peace, Freedom and Neutrality (ZOPFAN) declaration and the Treaty of Amity and Cooperation (TAC). While ZOPFAN calls upon the signatories to recognize and respect the fact that Southeast Asia is a region free from any form of interference by outside powers, the TAC commits all parties to settling disputes and differences by peaceful means and renouncing the use of force.[282] As one respondent noted, "[we] were quite encouraged when China signed the TAC because the basic principle there is the non-use of force [which may help] to prevent China from going to negative scenario of being a major power that will use its military power in order to dictate and impose its will...."[283]

It needs to be emphasized that the leaders are again inclined to juxtapose the attitude of Beijing with Washington's attitude to the regional security arrangements in Southeast Asia. One respondent contended that

> [the] United States [under President George W. Bush] has showed that it does not pay attention to multilateralism, unlike Clinton. Bush became more unilateral, more concerned about the Middle East and Northeast Asia. He did not pay attention to Southeast Asia. ... China, on the other hand, played this benign power. So China filled in the vacuum that the U.S. left.[284]

The respondents emphasized the fact that, in contrast to the United States, China signed in recent years the ZOPFAN and TAC. The fact that Beijing signed both the Declaration and the Treaty signifies in the eyes of some leaders that "we should not be disturbed by the rise of China [as] we [now] have many ways to handle it through ASEAN and ARF."[285] The rationale behind this mode of thinking is simple: China is a signatory of the TAC and thus Beijing will think twice about embarking on military adventurism in Southeast Asia because it would breach the agreement. One leader argued that Beijing has decided to participate because of "the smartness of Chinese leadership, namely Zhu Rongji. China has a benevolent dictator."[286]

The majority of the elite is hopeful that the most efficient and perhaps also only solution to the dilemma with regards to the rise of China is to get Beijing "onboard", "to make China a part of the regional architecture."[287] The rules and principles set by ASEAN are believed to be capable of preventing a potential conflict between Southeast Asian countries, on the one hand, and China, as well as Japan and the United States, on the other, from turning into an actual conflict. As a former Minister of Foreign Affairs argued,

> [between] these three (China, U.S. and Japan), there must be an agreed set of guidelines, of principles, of relationships. That is contained in the ZOPFAN [and] the Treaty of Amity and Cooperation. ... Some of the major powers have signed [them]. ... There must be an arrangement whereby this relationship between Southeast and Northeast Asia can be guided by mutually acceptable guidelines [and] principles of interaction.[288]

A high-level diplomat, who is closely involved in the ASEAN+3 process, shared the same view. He said that by means of community building, as embodied in the ASEAN, ASEAN+3, ARF, TAC and EAC, "[we] are not trying to have exclusionary policies against China. ... Rather, we take them in, absorb them and make sure that they interact in and with the region under certain norms which we had set, so it is not something that they had set." The senior diplomat then concluded that "[our] interest is basically to make sure that China is engaged in and with the region in a positive manner."[289]

The Vexing Uncertainty about China's Rise

While Jakarta's official policy has been to engage China, the above discussion has highlighted the large degree to which the Indonesian elite's view of China's rising might is essentially ambivalent. The leaders' attitude towards China is informed by the simultaneous existence of two conflicting views — one sees China as a threat and the other as an opportunity. A comparison with India is telling: while India's economic and political clout is also growing, its rise has not evoked significant misgivings among the Indonesian leadership. As we will find in the following chapter, in contrast with China, the elite generally views India's ascendancy as a overwhelmingly positive and welcome process. In fact, no less than two-thirds of all respondents described their view of China as ambivalent — "China is still between the opportunity and a threat."[290] As Indonesia's foremost expert on China stressed, "the emergence of China as the second power to the U.S. now makes this mixed feeling stronger. On the one hand, they [the elite] are very attracted to China's power, which can be used for [a more] assertive foreign policy. But on the other hand, the feeling of suspicion still lingers on."[291] Several respondents expressed the view that while the "China threat" notion still colours the elite's attitude towards that country, the scope and nature of the threat is less clear than before. Said one interviewed leader: "I believe that for many Indonesians the perception of the threat of China will remain ... ill-defined. Because it is *so big*, economically it is so booming...."[292]

The fact that the perceived threat China poses to Indonesia is at present rather indistinct and ill-defined can be explained in terms of an existing dilemma. A senior diplomat described this dilemma as follows:

> We are not ... sure what kind of China is more of a problem. A strong China or a weak China? ... The fact that we have China, the

largest country in the world in terms of population, in our midst,
is a reality, something that we have to come to terms with. I do not
think we necessarily have to see China as a threat. In fact, China that
is now progressing and prospering and benefiting from the system
is becoming increasingly a status quo power. It has every interest to
maintain the system as we have now ... On the contrary, China that
is failing, China that is regressing, that is not economically advancing,
not prospering, that would be that type of China that would be likely
to pose a threat.[293]

The senior diplomat also pointed out that the contemporary relations between
Indonesia and China are "as good as they have ever been."[294] The view that
Sino-Indonesian relations have improved considerably since the early 1990s
was embraced by the majority of all respondents. As a well-known scholar
observed, "[since] the diplomatic opening between Indonesia and China,
our cooperation has been better and better. Not only scientific. For example,
LIPI itself has project cooperation with China and then trade and military-
to-military relationships are getting better."[295]

Yet, the vexing question of whether an increasingly powerful China will
continue to demonstrate restraint gives rise to the widespread view among
the elite expressed in the statement that "we always have to be on guard."[296]
A CSIS-based academic described the situation this way:

China has changed from a threat in the 70s and 80s into kind of
challenge. Number one because we are not sure actually whether a
more powerful China will continue to be a positive factor for regional
security. So nobody is actually sure that the peaceful rise of China will
definitely benefit the whole region.[297]

With regards to the elite's doubts and scepticism, the respondent also
explained:

So this uncertainty, how China will transform itself, after they
reach a more advanced economy and military status, is a source of
challenge that Indonesia together with other ASEAN countries have
to deal with, have to manage. This uncertainty actually makes it
really difficult to define China as a threat. We prefer to see China
as both partner and competitor; both challenge and opportunity are
there.[298]

The elite is acutely aware that "because of this rise of China you do not
know actually where China is going...."[299] As Dewi Fortuna Anwar asked:

"Will China play the role like they played in the 15th century and act as the Middle kingdom in the East Asia region?"[300] Pointing to the Indonesian elite's qualms about the Chinese "exclusive" version of the East Asian Community (EAC) concept that would exclude from participation India, Australia and New Zealand, an international relations expert asserted: "I have spoken with many people in the Foreign Ministry about the EAC and they said: 'This is a China's scheme.' ... China is really a big thing we have to deal with in the future."[301] A former high-ranking military officer spoke for most of the elite when he declared that

> [there] is a possibility that with the process that China opens up its economy and gains a sort of more liberal regional outlook, they start to enjoy this position [or] maybe [also] they come to second thoughts. ... Maybe that they can abandon [their present policy] that can be seen as a contrast to their past militarist assertive policies and [will be] willing to launch again an offensive foreign policy. That could be a possibility, which we cannot [underestimate].[302]

Here, the former Foreign Minister was quick to emphasize: "But we do not close our eyes that China can be both an opportunity as well as a threat. It depends on our policies, on how they will be."[303]

CONCLUSION

We have found in this chapter that the Indonesian foreign policy elite consider China as an ambiguous threat that is, however, increasingly displaying its positive side. The discussion highlighted the leaders' ambivalent feelings about China's rapid economic growth, its steadily increasing military expenditures and the dilemma of how to face the ensuing complex opportunities and challenges. The elite views China as a threat and, concurrently, as an (economic) opportunity. In particular, with respect to China's "economic threat" and the uncertainty about China's growing military might, the elite believes that China's rise has both positive and negative implications for Indonesia. On the other hand, the increasing projection of China's power and influence is welcome by the elite insofar as it helps Jakarta to eliminate some pressures generated by the perceived assertive and unilateralist policies of the United States.

Yet, the leaders' perceptions of China continue to be shaped by a deep-rooted concern about China's expansionist tendencies. In the discussion about the historical-traditional dimension of the elite's perception of China, we have pointed to the elite's historical knowledge about the former

"Middle Kingdom" that reaches as far back as the 13th century as an aspect that is feeding the deeply entrenched nature of the Indonesian leaders' sentiments held towards China. Moreover, the Indonesian leaders' perception of China cannot be fully understood without taking into consideration deep-rooted stereotypes and prejudices held towards the ethnic Chinese Indonesians. While the elite's attitude towards the United States can be described as "love-hate", the elite's perceptions of China are also ambivalent but conspicuously lack the "love" aspect. The Indonesian leaders' current attitude towards China can be best described as purely "pragmatic". To that end, the elite's deep-rooted sentiments held towards China and the resultant suspicions and uneasiness about Beijing's perceived expansionist intentions will in the future move the Indonesian leaders to implement foreign policies designed to keep China at arm's length and its power in check.[304]

Notes

1   Martin Stuart-Fox, *A Short History of China and Southeast Asia: Tribute, Trade and Influence* (Crows Nest: Allen & Unwin, 2003), pp. 178–79.

2   Franklin B. Weinstein, "The Indonesian Elite's View of the World and the Foreign Policy of Development", *Indonesia*, Cornell Modern Indonesia Project, No. 12 (October 1971), p. 97.

3   U.S. Department of State, "FRUS 1961–63 XXIII: Memo of Conversation, President Kennedy, Rusk, Jones, Steeves, Rostow (U.S.), President Sukarno, Leimena, Zain (Indo)" (24 April 1961).

4   Franklin B. Weinstein, *Indonesian Foreign Policy and the Dilemma of Dependence: From Sukarno to Soeharto* (Ithaca, New York: Cornell University Press, 1976), pp. 297–98; also discussed in: Weinstein, "The Indonesian Elite's View of the World and the Foreign Policy of Development", p. 97.

5   Weinstein, "The Indonesian Elite's View of the World and the Foreign Policy of Development", pp. 92–93.

6   Rizal Sukma, "Recent Developments in Sino-Indonesian Relations: An Indonesian View", *Contemporary Southeast Asia* 16, no. 1 (June 1994): 40–41; "China Speaks out on Indonesian Riots", *BBC News*, 16 November 1998.

7   Richardson, "Indonesia Plans War Games to Caution China".

8   Ian James Storey, "Indonesia's China Policy in the New Order and Beyond: Problems and Prospects", *Contemporary Southeast Asia* 22, no. 1 (April 2000): 162.

9   Interview with a retired Indonesian Army general, presently also affiliated with a Jakarta-based research institute, Jakarta, 3 February 2005.

10   President Wahid reportedly said that such an alliance would help rectify the "lopsided" power of the West. For a more detailed assessment, see "China/India/

Indonesia Alliance?", *Stratfor*, Global Intelligence Update (14 October 1999); "U.S. Wary of Indonesia's Ties with China", *Stratfor*, Global Intelligence Update (12 April 2004).

11   Abubakar E. Hara, "Arah Politik Luar Negeri Gus Dur" [The Direction of Gus Dur's Foreign Policy], *Republika*, 4 November 1999.

12   "Gus Dur's Foreign Policy to Go East, Says Amien", *Straits Times*, 2 November 1999.

13   Denny Roy, "The Foreign Policy of Great-Power China", *Contemporary Southeast Asia* 19, no. 2 (September 1997).

14   Richard J. Newman, "The Rise of a New Power" *U.S. News and World Report* (20 June 2005), pp. 40–42.

15   Hadi Soesastro, "Hakikat 'Kemitraan Strategis' Indonesia dan China" [The Essence of "Strategic Alliance" between Indonesia and China], *Kompas*, 1 August 2005.

16   "Spirit Bangkit", *Media Indonesia*, 27 April 2005.

17   "China-Indonesia Relations and Implications for the United States", a conference organized by USINDO, The George Washington University, Washington, D.C. (7 November 2003).

18   Weinstein, *Indonesian Foreign Policy and the Dilemma of Dependence*, p. 93.

19   David C. Kang, "Getting Asia Wrong: The Need for New Analytical Frameworks", *International Security* 27, no. 4 (Spring 2003).

20   Marvin Ott, "A Historic Geopolitical Relationship Reasserts Itself", a paper presented at the conference "China-Indonesia Relations and Implications for the United States", USINDO Report, The George Washington University, Washington, D.C. (7 November 2003).

21   Ibid.

22   Martin Stuart-Fox, "Southeast Asia and China: The Role of History and Culture in Shaping Future Relations", *Contemporary Southeast Asia* 26, no. 1 (April 2004): 133.

23   Interview with an expert on Indonesian foreign policy, Singapore, 15 May 2006.

24   Interview with a senior Indonesian diplomat, a high-ranking official in DEPLU, Jakarta, 28 February 2005.

25   For more on this issue, see: Kang, "Getting Asia Wrong"; Amitav Acharya, "Will Asia's Past Be Its Future?", *International Security* 28, no. 3 (Winter 2003/04).

26   Stuart-Fox, "Southeast Asia and China", p. 135.

27   Rizal Sukma, "U.S.-Southeast Asia Relations after the Crisis: The Security Dimension", background paper prepared for "The Asia Foundation's Workshop on America's Role in Asia", Bangkok, (22–24 March 2000).

28   Interview with an expert on Indonesian foreign policy, Singapore, 15 May 2006.

29   Interview with a young Indonesian scholar, Singapore, 8 June 2006.

30   Ibid.

31   Interview with an Indonesian executive officer who is working for an U.S.-based major private financial institution, Jakarta, 2 February 2005.

32   The theory of "The Peaceful Rise of China" coined by a prominent Chinese intellectual Zheng Bijian often had the opposite effect of what Zheng had hoped. Rather than feeling reassured, the slogan that included the positive adjective *peaceful* made international observers more nervous, not less. An article that deals with this "intractable paradox" concluded that "because China wasn't trusted, talking about a 'peaceful rise' had the effect of further eroding trust in China. It was like trying to convince people they were, in fact, about to experience a peaceful earthquake. [...] [Thus] China's greatest strategic threat [may well be] its national image."; For a more detailed discussion, see: Joshua Cooper Ramo, "An Image Emergency", *Newsweek*, 25 September 2006, pp. 28–29.

33   Interview with a retired admiral of the Indonesian navy, Jakarta, 11 February 2005.

34   Quoted in Aileen S.P. Baviera, "China's Relations with Southeast Asia: Political Security and Economic Interests," PASCN Discussion Paper, No. 99-17 (1999).

35   Cited in: Dewi Fortuna Anwar, "Indonesia's Relations with China and Japan: Images, Perceptions and Realities", *Contemporary Southeast Asia* 12, no. 3 (December 1990): 235.

36   Interview with an expert on Indonesian foreign policy, Singapore, 15 May 2006.

37   Interview with an Indonesian journalist affiliated with *Kompas*, Jakarta, 16 February 2005.

38   Weinstein, *Indonesian Foreign Policy and the Dilemma of Dependence*, p. 120.

39   Interview with a young Indonesian career diplomat, DEPLU, Jakarta, 25 February 2005.

40   Interview with an Indonesian politician and leader of a Muslim organization, Yogyakarta, 2 March 2005.

41   Interview with a senior Indonesian diplomat, a high-ranking official in DEPLU, Jakarta, 25 January 2005.

42   Interview with an Indonesian leader and academic affiliated with LIPI, Jakarta, 14 February 2005.

43   Interview with an Indonesian leader and academic affiliated with LIPI, Jakarta, 14 February 2005.

44   For a more detailed discussion, see: C.P. Fitzgerald, *The Southern Expansion of the Chinese People: The Southern Fields and Southern Ocean* (Canberra: Australian National University Press, 1972).

45   Stuart-Fox, *A Short History of China and Southeast Asia*, p. 23.

46   Ibid., p. 18.

47   Leo Suryadinata, *Dilema Minoritas Tionghoa* [Dilemma of the Chinese Minority] (Singapore: Heinemann Educational Books, 1982).

48   Charles A. Coppel and Leo Suryadinata, "The Use of the Terms 'Tjina' and 'Tionghoa' in Indonesia", in Leo Suryadinata, *The Chinese Minority in Indonesia: Seven Papers* (Singapore: Chopmen Enterprise, 1978).
49   Interview with a young Indonesian career diplomat, DEPLU, Jakarta, 25 February 2005.
50   Interview with a senior Indonesian career diplomat, DEPLU, Jakarta, 12 January 2005.
51   "China Looks to the South Pacific", *Stratfor*, Stratfor Global Intelligence Update (21 May 2001).
52   Fitzgerald, *The Southern Expansion of the Chinese People*, p. xiii.
53   Juwono Sudarsono, "The Implications of China's Growth", in *Surviving Globalisation: Indonesia and the World* (Jakarta: *The Jakarta Post*, 1996), p. 95.
54   Interview with a young Indonesian career diplomat, DEPLU, Jakarta, 25 February 2005.
55   Interview with the chief editor of an influential Jakarta-based newspaper, 28 January 2005.
56   Interview with an Indonesian Army general and member of GOLKAR, Jakarta, 15 February 2005.
57   Michael Richardson, "Indonesia Plans War Games to Caution China", *International Herald Tribune*, 16 August 1996.
58   Interview with an Indonesian journalist affiliated with *Kompas*, Jakarta, 16 February 2005).
59   Interview with a senior Indonesian diplomat, a high-ranking official in DEPLU, Jakarta, 25 January 2005.
60   For the full transcript of the discussion, see: "China and the Idea of an East Asian Community", a seminar organized by the CSIS, Jakarta, 18 January 2005 <http://www.csis.or.id/tool_print.asp?type=events&mode=past&id=51> (accessed 20 January 2005).
61   Interview with an Indonesian leader and academic affiliated with LIPI, Jakarta, 14 February 2005.
62   Interview with a senior Indonesian diplomat, DEPLU, Jakarta, 12 January 2005.
63   Interview with a senior Indonesian diplomat, Jakarta, 8 February 2005 and a former Indonesian high-ranking military officer and senior diplomat, Jakarta, 14 February 2005.
64   Interview with a former Indonesian high-ranking military officer and senior diplomat, Jakarta, 14 February 2005.
65   Interview with an Indonesian leader and academic affiliated with LIPI, Jakarta, 14 February 2005.
66   Interview with a former admiral of the Indonesian Navy, Jakarta, 24 February 2005.
67   What is the relation between image and perception? It can be assumed that while image is supplied by perception, an image has concurrently the potential to change a perception.

68 Michael Leifer, "Indonesia's Encounters with China and the Dilemmas of Engagement", in *Engaging China: The Management of an Emerging Power*, edited by Alistair Iain Johnston and Robert S. Ross (London: Routledge, 1999), p. 87; Stuart-Fox, "Southeast Asia and China", p. 135; see also Paige Johnson Tan, "Navigating a Turbulent Ocean: Indonesia's Worldview and Foreign Policy", *Asian Perspective* 31, no. 3 (2007).

69 M. Yamin, "Unity of Our Country and Our People", in *Indonesian Political Thinking, 1945–1965*, edited by Herb Feith and Lance Castles (Ithaca, New York: Cornell University Press, 1970), pp. 466–72; Harold Crouch, *Army and Politics in Indonesia* (Ithaca, New York: Cornell University Press, 1978), p. 44.

70 *A Chronology of Indonesian History*, Departemen Penerangan [Department of Information], Jakarta (1960), p. 17.

71 Heath McMichael, "Indonesian Foreign Policy: Towards a More Assertive Style", Australia-Asia Papers No. 40 (Nathan: Griffith University, February 1987), p. 5.

72 Interview with a senior official of the PDI-P political party and senior member of the Indonesian Parliament (DPR), Jakarta, 23 February 2005.

73 Interview with a Minister in President Yudhoyono's cabinet, Jakarta, 28 February 2005.

74 Interview with an expert on Indonesian foreign policy, Singapore, 15 May 2006.

75 Rizal Sukma, "Indonesia's Perceptions of China: The Domestic Bases of Persistent Ambiguity" in *The China Threat: Perceptions, Myths and Reality*, edited by Herbert Yee and Ian Storey (London: RoutledgeCourzon, 2002), pp. 188–91.

76 Quoted from an interview in: Chapter "China: Ally or Adversary?", in Robert O. Tilman, *Southeast Asia and the Enemy Beyond: ASEAN Perceptions of External Threats* (Boulder: Westview Press, 1987), p. 84.

77 Gerrit W. Gong, *Memory and History in East and Southeast Asia: Issues of Identity in International Relations* (Washington, D.C.: The CSIS Press, 2001), p. 28.

78 Ibid., pp. 30–31.

79 For a more detailed discussion about the early contact between the Indonesian archipelago and China, see: Nicholas Tarling, ed., *The Cambridge History of Southeast Asia*, Volume I, Part I (Cambridge: The Press Syndicate of the University of Cambridge, 1999); Stuart-Fox, *A Short History of China and Southeast Asia*, pp. 23–25; Fitzgerald, *The Southern Expansion of the Chinese People*, pp. 1–18.

80 For a more detailed account of this historical event, see: Satyawati Suleiman, *Concise Ancient History of Indonesia* (Jakarta: The Archaeological Foundation, 1974).

81 Interview with an Indonesian politician, diplomat and journalist, Jakarta, 4 February 2005.

82 Interview with a journalist and chief editor of a Jakarta-based national newspaper, Jakarta, 15 February 2005.

83   Interview with an Indonesian politician, diplomat and journalist, Jakarta, 4 February 2005.

84   Interview with an Indonesian journalist, a foreign relations commentator, Jakarta, 21 February 2005.

85   Interview with a young Indonesian career diplomat, DEPLU, Jakarta, 28 February 2005.

86   Interview with a young Indonesian career diplomat, DEPLU, Jakarta, 25 February 2005.

87   Interview with an Indonesian politician and leader of a Muslim organization, Yogyakarta, 2 March 2005.

88   Interview with a young Indonesian career diplomat, DEPLU, Jakarta, 28 February 2005.

89   Interview with an Indonesian expert in international relations, CSIS, Jakarta, 21 February 2005.

90   Interview with an Indonesian scholar and IR expert affiliated with LIPI, Jakarta, 24 February 2005.

91   This issue was also discussed in some detail during the interview with an Indonesian academic and expert in the Indonesian military, Jakarta, 24 January 2005.

92   Interview with an Indonesian expert in international relations, CSIS, Jakarta, 21 February 2005.

93   Interview with an Indonesian leader, diplomat and scholar, Jakarta, 23 February 2005.

94   Interview with an Indonesian expert in international relations, CSIS, Jakarta, 21 February 2005.

95   Interview with a retired Indonesian Army general, presently also affiliated with a Jakarta-based research institute, Jakarta, 3 February 2005.

96   Rizal Sukma, *Indonesia and China: The Politics of a Troubled Relationship* (London: Routledge, 1999).

97   Sukma, "Indonesia's Perceptions of China", p. 138.

98   Jamie Mackie and Andrew MacIntyre, "Politics", in *Indonesia's New Order: The Dynamics of Socio-Economic Transformation*, edited by Hal Hill (St. Leonards: Allen and Unwin, 1994), pp. 4–12.

99   Ibid., pp. 3–5, 46.

100   R.E. Elson, *Suharto: A Political Biography* (Cambridge: Cambridge University Press, 2001), p. 70.

101   Ibid., p. 109.

102   Ibid., p. 109.

103   Crouch, *Army and Politics in Indonesia*; Adrian Vickers, *A History of Modern Indonesia* (Cambridge: Cambridge University Press, 2005), pp. 156–60.

104   Greg Fealy analyses the case of the release of about 700,000 Indonesia's *tapols*, or political prisoners. He argues that Suharto's regime kept deferring the release of the political prisoners owing to, first, the "deep-seated communist-phobia

within the Indonesian government and the armed forces" and, second, the regime's policy of using the *tapols* to promote the perception of communist peril to legitimize the more repressive aspects of Suharto's government; Greg Fealy, "The Release of Indonesia's Political Prisoners: Domestic versus Foreign Policy, 1975–1979", Working Paper 94 (Clayton: Centre of Southeast Asian Studies, Monash University, 1994), pp. 11, 12.

105 Justus M. Van der Kroef, "National Security, Defence Strategy and Foreign Policy Perceptions in Indonesia", *Orbis* 20, no. 2 (Summer 1976),: 461–96; Sukma, *Indonesia and China: The Politics of a Troubled Relationship.*

106 Fealy, "The Release of Indonesia's Political Prisoners", p. 10.

107 Interview with a retired Indonesian Army general, presently also affiliated with a Jakarta-based research institute, Jakarta, 3 February 2005.

108 Ibid.

109 Interview with a former Indonesian Minister of Foreign Affairs, Jakarta, 14 January 2005.

110 Interview with a former Indonesian high-ranking military officer and senior diplomat, Jakarta, 14 February 2005.

111 Ibid.

112 Interview with an Indonesian politician, diplomat and journalist, Jakarta, 4 February 2005.

113 Interview with a former Indonesian President, Jakarta, 10 January 2005.

114 Interview with an Indonesian leader and academic affiliated with LIPI, Jakarta, 14 February 2005.

115 Interview with a Minister in President Yudhoyono's cabinet, Jakarta, 28 February 2005.

116 Interview with the director of a leading and respected Jakarta-based think-tank, Jakarta, 22 October 2003.

117 Interview with a former Indonesian President, Jakarta, 10 January 2005.

118 Interview with a former Indonesian high-ranking military officer and senior diplomat, Jakarta, 14 February 2005.

119 Interview with an Indonesian academic and expert in the Indonesian military, Jakarta, 24 January 2005.

120 Interview with an Indonesian leader and academic affiliated with LIPI, Jakarta, 14 February 2005.

121 Interview with an Indonesian academic and expert in the Indonesian military, Jakarta, 24 January 2005.

122 Interview with a former Indonesian President, Jakarta, 1 March 2005.

123 Interview with an Indonesian expert in international relations, CSIS, Jakarta, 21 February 2005.

124 Interview, Jakarta, 2005

125 Interview with an Indonesian journalist affiliated with *Kompas*, Jakarta, 16 February 2005; also discussed during an interview with a former admiral of the Indonesian Navy, Jakarta, 24 February 2005.

[126] Interview with an Indonesian academic and expert in the Indonesian military, Jakarta, 24 January 2005.

[127] Interview with a former Indonesian Minister of Foreign Affairs, Jakarta, 14 January 2005.

[128] Interview with an Indonesian expert in international relations, CSIS, Jakarta, 21 February 2005.

[129] Interview with an Indonesian scholar and IR expert affiliated with LIPI, Jakarta, 24 February 2005.

[130] Interview with a member of DPR, Indonesian Parliament, for the National Mandate Party (PAN), Jakarta, 7 February 2005.

[131] Interview with a senior member of *Muhammadiyah* Muslim organization, 23 February 2005.

[132] Interview with the chief editor of an influential Jakarta-based newspaper, 28 January 2005.

[133] Interview with an Indonesian academic and former cabinet minister, Singapore, 15 April 2005.

[134] Interview with an Indonesian scholar and IR expert affiliated with LIPI, Jakarta, 24 February 2005.

[135] Interview with a CSIS-based international relations expert, Jakarta, 8 February 2005.

[136] Interview with the chief editor of an influential Jakarta-based newspaper, 28 January 2005.

[137] Ibid.

[138] Interview with an expert on Indonesian foreign policy, Singapore, 15 May 2006.

[139] Interview with a senior Indonesian diplomat, a high-ranking official in DEPLU, Jakarta, 25 January 2005.

[140] Ariel Heryanto, "Ethnic Identities and Erasure: Chinese Indonesians in Public Culture", in *Southeast Asian Identities: Culture and the Politics of Representation in Indonesia, Malaysia, Singapore, and Thailand*, edited by Joel S. Kahn (New York: St. Martins' Press, 1998), p. 97.

[141] William G. Skinner, "Change and Persistence in Chinese Culture Overseas", *Journal of the South Seas Society* 16 (1960): 91.

[142] Ibid., p. 94.

[143] Cited in: Anwar, "Indonesia's Relations with China and Japan", p. 235.

[144] Arief Budiman, "Portrait of the Chinese in Post-Suharto Indonesia", in *Chinese Indonesians: Remembering, Distorting, Forgetting*, edited by Tim Lindsey and Helen Pausacker (Singapore: Institute of Southeast Asian Studies, 2005), p. 100.

[145] Interview with a young Indonesian career diplomat, DEPLU, Jakarta, 25 February 2005.

[146] Interview with a journalist and chief editor of a Jakarta-based national newspaper, Jakarta, 15 February 2005.

[147] Interview with an expert on Indonesian foreign policy, Singapore, 15 May 2006.

148 Interview with an academic and international relations expert, 1 February 2005.

149 Interview with George Yeo, Singapore's Minister of Trade and Industry; published in Michael R.J. Vatikiotis, "Catching the Dragon's Tail: China and Southeast Asia in the 21st Century", *Contemporary Southeast Asia* 25, no. 1 (April 2003): 75.

150 Interview with a former Indonesian Minister of Foreign Affairs, Jakarta, 14 January 2005.

151 Interview with the director of a leading and respected Jakarta-based think-tank, Jakarta, 6 April 2006.

152 David Mozingo, *Chinese Policy toward Indonesia 1949–1967* (London: Cornell University Press, 1976), p. 34.

153 Stuart-Fox, *A Short History of China and Southeast Asia*, p. 71; Mozingo argues that apart from the rise of Islam, there were other two factors that generated serious frictions between the two societies — Imperial China's decline under the impact of the West and the Dutch conquest of Indonesia. He then also concludes that "these historically based frictions have lasted and have aggravated the Sino-Indonesian relationship until present day." For more detailed discussion, see: ibid., p. 34.

154 Skinner, "Change and Persistence in Chinese Culture Overseas", p. 96. Whilst describing Theravada Buddhism, the predominant religion in Thailand, as "tolerant and permissive", Skinner points out the "relatively intolerant and exclusivist" nature of Islam, the predominant religion in Java. We might risk some degree of simplification by likening the religious beliefs in Java before the arrival of Islam to the situation in 19th and 20th century Thailand. However, it is reasonable to assume that, in contrast to the current situation in Indonesia, both the personal and institutionalized system of beliefs and worship in Hindu-Buddhist kingdoms in 14th century Java made the acculturation to the Javanese culture much easier.

155 Abu Hanifah, *Tales of a Revolution* (Sydney: Angus and Robertson Publishers, 1972), pp. 207–08 and 253.

156 Mozingo, *Chinese Policy toward Indonesia 1949–1967*, p. 35.

157 Jacques Bertrand, *Nationalism and Ethnic Conflict in Indonesia* (Cambridge: Press Syndicate of the University of Cambridge, 2004), p. 66.

158 Assaat, "The Chinese Grip on Our Economy" in Feith and Castles, *Indonesian Political Thinking, 1945–1965*, pp. 343–46.

159 Freedman argues that "ultimately, the tension between Sino-Indonesian and pribumi stems from two sets of perceptions: that the 'Chinese' are suspect as citizens, and that they have gained disproportionately from economic development and favouritism from Suharto." For more on this issue, see: Amy L. Freedman, *Political Participation and Ethnic Minorities: Chinese Overseas in Malaysia, Indonesia, and the United States* (New York: Routledge, 2000), p. 117.

160   A. Dahana, "The Ethnic Chinese in Indonesia: Issues of Identity", in *Ethnic Chinese as Southeast Asians*, edited by Leo Suryadinata (Singapore: Institute of Southeast Asian Studies, 1997), p. 70.

161   "Meet the Real Masters of East Asia's Economies. Hint: They Ain't Japanese", *International Economy* 10, no. 6 (November/December 1996): 1.

162   A. Dahana, "The Ethnic Chinese in Indonesia: Issues of Identity", p. 70.

163   Interview with an expert on Indonesian foreign policy, Singapore, 15 May 2006.

164   Ibid.

165   The term *Warga Negara Keturunan* means non-indigenous citizens in the official Indonesian vocabulary; Paul Jacob, "Pledge to Give Wider Opportunities to Chinese", *Straits Times*, 27 January 1999.

166   David S.G. Goodman, "Are Asia's 'Ethnic Chinese' a Regional-Security Threat?", *Survival* 39, no. 4 (Winter 1997/98): 140–55.

167   Cited in: Harvey Stockwin, "Suharto Meets the Auditors", *Far Eastern Economic Review*, 19 March 1973, p. 11.

168   Weinstein, *Indonesian Foreign Policy and the Dilemma of Dependence*, p. 121.

169   Leo Suryadinata, *Pribumi Indonesians, the Chinese Minority, and China: A Study of Perceptions and Policies*, 2nd edition (Singapore: Heinemann Asia, 1986); also discussed in Lauren Carter, "The Ethnic Chinese Variable in Domestic and Foreign Policies in Malaysia and Indonesia" (M.A. thesis, Simon Fraser University, 1995).

170   Suryadinata, *Pribumi Indonesians, the Chinese Minority, and China*, p. 208.

171   Ibid., p. 206.

172   Sukma, "Recent Developments in Sino-Indonesian Relations", p. 35.

173   Budiman, "Portrait of the Chinese in Post-Suharto Indonesia", p. 100.

174   Interview with an Indonesian journalist affiliated with *Kompas*, Jakarta, 16 February 2005.

175   Rajeswary Ampalavanar Brown, "Irrational Exuberance: The Fatal Conceit of Chinese Financial Capitalism in Contemporary Indonesia", in *Diaspora Entrepreneurial Networks: Four Centuries of History*, edited by Ina Baghdiantz McCabe, Gelina Harlaftis, and Ioanna Pepelasis Minoglou (Oxford, New York: Berg, 2005), p. 329.

176   *Tempo*, 28 September 1991, p. 86; *Asian Wall Street Journal*, 25–26 February 1994, pp. 1, 8.

177   Interview with an Indonesian journalist affiliated with *Kompas*, Jakarta, 16 February 2005.

178   Ibid.

179   Interview with an Indonesian scholar and IR expert affiliated with LIPI, Jakarta, 24 February 2005.

180   Saydiman Suryohadiprojo, "How to Deal with China and Taiwan", *Asahi Shimbun*, Tokyo, 23 September 1996.

181   Weinstein, *Indonesian Foreign Policy and the Dilemma of Dependence*, p. 118.

182   Ibid., p. 120.
183   Ibid., p. 118.
184   Ibid., pp. 118–21.
185   Ibid., p. 121.
186   Interview with an academic and international relations expert, 1 February 2005.
187   Interview with a Minister in President Yudhoyono's cabinet, Jakarta, 28 February 2005.
188   Interview with a young Indonesian scholar, Singapore, 8 June 2006.
189   Interview with an Indonesian expert in international relations, CSIS, Jakarta, 21 February 2005.
190   Interview with a former Indonesian Minister of Foreign Affairs, Jakarta, 14 January 2005.
191   Interview with a young Indonesian career diplomat, DEPLU, Jakarta, 25 February 2005.
192   Interview with a young Muslim leader, an expert in a well-known and respected Jakarta-based think-tank, Jakarta, 25 February 2005.
193   Interview with a young Indonesian career diplomat, DEPLU, Jakarta, 25 February 2005.
194   Interview with an academic and international relations expert, 1 February 2005.
195   Interview with an Indonesian academic and former cabinet minister, Singapore, 15 April 2005.
196   Interview with a young Indonesian career diplomat, DEPLU, Jakarta, 2 February 2005.
197   Interview with a senior official of PDI-P, Jakarta, 22 February 2005.
198   Interview with a former Indonesian President, Jakarta, 1 March 2005.
199   Sarah Turner, "Speaking Out: Chinese Indonesians after Suharto", *Asian Ethnicity* 4, no. 3 (October 2003): 352.
200   Sukma, "Indonesia's Perceptions of China", p. 196.
201   There has been a wide array of studies published in recent years that deal with the phenomenon of China's rise. For more detailed discussion on the issue, see: Michael E. Brown et al., eds., *The Rise of China* (Cambridge: The MIT Press, 2000); Robert G. Sutter, *China's Rise in Asia: Promises and Perils* (Lanham, Oxford: Rowman & Littlefield Publishing Group, 2005); S.G. Goodman and Gerald Segal, eds., *China Rising: Nationalism and Interdependence* (London, New York: Routledge, 1997); "China to Boost Military Spending", *BBC News*, 4 March 2005; Fareed Zakaria, "Does the Future Belong to China?", *Newsweek*, 9 May 2005; Jiang Wenran, "The 'China Threat' Revisited", *Straits Times*, 10 March 2005.
202   Irman G. Lanti, "Indonesia", in *Betwixt and Between: Southeast Asian Strategic Relations with the U.S. and China*, edited by Evelyn Goh, IDSS Monograph No. 7 (Singapore: Institute of Defence and Strategic Studies, 2005), p. 31.

203 Interview with an Indonesian scholar and IR expert affiliated with LIPI, Jakarta, 24 February 2005.
204 Interview with a journalist and chief editor of a Jakarta-based national newspaper, Jakarta, 15 February 2005.
205 Interview with a former Indonesian Minister of Foreign Affairs, Jakarta, 14 January 2005.
206 Interview with an Indonesian leader and academic affiliated with LIPI, Jakarta, 14 February 2005.
207 Interview with a former Indonesian President, Jakarta, 1 March 2005.
208 Interview with a senior official from the Indonesian Department of Trade, Jakarta, 27 January 2005.
209 Interview with a journalist and chief editor of a Jakarta-based national newspaper, Jakarta, 15 February 2005.
210 Interview with a young Muslim leader, an expert in a well-known and respected Jakarta-based think-tank, Jakarta, 25 February 2005.
211 Interview with a senior Indonesian career diplomat, DEPLU, Jakarta, 12 January 2005.
212 Interview with an Indonesian academic and former cabinet minister, Singapore, 15 April 2005; For more on China's quest for energy, see: David Lague, "The Quest for Energy to Grow" in *Far Eastern Economic Review*, 20 June 2002.
213 "Poros Baru Jakarta-Peking: Antara Madu dan Racun" [New Axis Jakarta-Beijing: Between Honey and Poison], *Gatra*, Jakarta, vol. XII, no. 51, 8 November 2006.
214 During a seminar held in Jakarta, senior Indonesian diplomat Hashim Djalal contended that China's economy in 2015 will be the biggest of the world and asked how Southeast Asian states should look at China then; For the full transcript of the discussion, see: "China and the Idea of an East Asian Community", seminar, CSIS, Jakarta, 18 January 2005, <http://www.csis.or.id/tool_print.asp?type=events&mode=past&id=51> (accessed 30 January 2005).
215 Interview with an Indonesian journalist, a foreign relations commentator, Jakarta, 21 February 2005 and with a senior Indonesian diplomat, a high-ranking official in DEPLU, Jakarta, 25 January 2005.
216 Interview with a senior member of *Muhammadiyah* Muslim organization, 23 February 2005.
217 Arya B. Gaduh, "The Competitive Threat of Nations Just a Pseudo-Fear Among Countries", *Jakarta Post*, 5 January 2004.
218 The interview originally appeared in the Japanese publication *Nihon Kezai Shimbun*, later reprinted by *Agence France Presse*, 14 August 1996.
219 Robert Lowry, *The Armed Forces of Indonesia* (Sydney: Allen & Unwin, 1996), p. 4.
220 Michael Vatikiotis, "A Too-Friendly Embrace", *Far Eastern Economic Review*, 17 June 2004.
221 Ibid.

[222] For more on the development of Indonesia-China economic interaction, see: Sadanand Dhume and Susan V. Lawrence, "Buying Fast Into Southeast Asia" in *Far Eastern Economic Review*, 28 March 2002.

[223] Interview with an Indonesian leader and academic affiliated with LIPI, Jakarta, 14 February 2005.

[224] Interview with an Indonesian scholar and IR expert affiliated with LIPI, Jakarta, 24 February 2005.

[225] Ibid.

[226] Interview with a senior Indonesian diplomat, a high-ranking official in DEPLU, Jakarta, 25 January 2005.

[227] Interview with an Indonesian journalist affiliated with *Kompas*, Jakarta, 16 February 2005.

[228] Etel Solingen, "From 'Threat' to 'Opportunity'? ASEAN, China, and Triangulation", in *China, the United States, and Southeast Asia: Contending Perspectives on Politics, Security, and Economics*, edited by Evelyn Goh and Sheldon W. Simon (New York: Routledge, 2008), p. 25.

[229] Interview with a young Indonesian career diplomat, DEPLU, Jakarta, 25 February 2005.

[230] Interview with a senior Indonesian diplomat, Jakarta, 8 February 2005.

[231] Interview with a senior Indonesian diplomat, a high-ranking official in DEPLU, Jakarta, 25 January 2005.

[232] Interview with a senior official from the Indonesian Department of Trade, Jakarta, 27 January 2005.

[233] Interview with a senior official from the Indonesian Department of Trade, Jakarta, 2 February 2005.

[234] Interview with an Indonesian journalist affiliated with *Kompas*, Jakarta, 16 February 2005.

[235] Interview with a young Indonesian career diplomat, DEPLU, Jakarta, 25 February 2005.

[236] Weinstein, *Indonesian Foreign Policy and the Dilemma of Dependence*.

[237] Interview with a senior Indonesian diplomat, a high-ranking official in DEPLU, Jakarta, 25 January 2005.

[238] Interview with an Indonesian scholar and politician, Yogyakarta, 3 March 2005.

[239] Interview with a senior official from the Indonesian Department of Trade, Jakarta, 27 January 2005.

[240] Interview with a minister in President Yudhoyono's cabinet, Jakarta, 28 February 2005.

[241] Interview with an Indonesian leader and academic affiliated with LIPI, Jakarta, 14 February 2005.

[242] Interview with an Indonesian academic and former cabinet minister, Singapore, 15 April 2005.

[243] See Figure 6.1. in Chapter 6.

244 Interview with a senior official from the Indonesian Department of Trade, Jakarta, 2 February 2005.

245 Interview with a former Indonesian President, Jakarta, 1 March 2005.

246 Interview with an Indonesian scholar and politician, Yogyakarta, 3 March 2005.

247 Interview with a senior Indonesian career diplomat, DEPLU, Jakarta, 12 January 2005.

248 Interview with a senior Indonesian diplomat, a high-ranking official in DEPLU, Jakarta, 28 February 2005.

249 Interview with a former Indonesian high-ranking military officer and senior diplomat, Jakarta, 14 February 2005.

250 Department of Defence of the Republic of Indonesia, "Mempertahankan Tanah Air Memasuki Abad 21" [Defending the Land and Water at the Start of the 21st Century], Indonesia's Defence White Paper (Jakarta, 2003), p. 36.

251 Abdul Khalik and Kurniawan Hari, "TNI Told End of U.S. Bans No Reason for Complacency", *Jakarta Post*, 7 July 2006.

252 Interview with a leader and academic affiliated with the LIPI, Jakarta, 10 December 2004.

253 Interview with a senior Indonesian diplomat, a high-ranking official in DEPLU, Jakarta, 25 January 2005.

254 Dewi Fortuna Anwar, "Indonesia: Domestic Priorities Define National Security", in *Asian Security Practice: Material and Ideational Influences*, edited by Muthiah Alagappa (Stanford: Stanford University Press, 1998), pp. 477–512.

255 Interview with an Indonesian leader and academic affiliated with LIPI, Jakarta, 14 February 2005.

256 Interview with an Indonesian expert in international relations, CSIS, Jakarta, 21 February 2005.

257 Indonesian Ministry of Defence and Security, "The Policy of the State Defence and Security of the Republic of Indonesia", The Defence White Paper (Jakarta, 17 August 1995), pp. 4–5.

258 M. Richardson, "China's Expansionist Claims Unsettle Its Asian Neighbours; But ASEAN Wants to Engage Not Contain China", *International Herald Tribune*, 25 November 1996.

259 Interview with a former Indonesian Minister of Foreign Affairs, Jakarta, 14 January 2005.

260 Ibid.

261 Alan Dupont, "Indonesian Defence Strategy and Security: Time for a Rethink?", *Contemporary Southeast Asia* 18, no. 3 (December 1996): 288–90.

262 Interview with a retired Indonesian Army general, presently also affiliated with a Jakarta-based research institute, Jakarta, 3 February 2005.

263 Allen S. Whiting, "ASEAN Eyes China: the Security Dimension", *Asian Survey* XXXVII, no. 4 (April 1997): 302.

264 Interview with an expert on Indonesian foreign policy, Singapore, 15 May 2006.

265 Interview with an Indonesian expert in international relations, CSIS, Jakarta, 21 February 2005.
266 Interview with an Indonesian scholar and IR expert affiliated with LIPI, Jakarta, 24 February 2005.
267 Soesastro, "Hakikat 'Kemitraan Strategis' Indonesia dan China".
268 Interview with a CSIS-based international relations expert, Jakarta, 8 February 2005.
269 Interview with a young Indonesian career diplomat, DEPLU, Jakarta, 25 February 2005.
270 Interview with an Indonesian expert in international relations, CSIS, Jakarta, 21 February 2005.
271 Interview with an Indonesian academic and expert in the Indonesian military, Jakarta, 24 January 2005.
272 Interview with a senior Indonesian career diplomat, DEPLU, Jakarta, 12 January 2005.
273 Interview with a journalist and chief editor of a Jakarta-based national newspaper, Jakarta, 15 February 2005.
274 Interview with an Indonesian economist and academic, Jakarta, 3 February 2005.
275 Interview with an aide to the Indonesian President, Jakarta, 24 October 2003.
276 Muhammad Hatta, *Mendayung antara Dua Karang* [Rowing between Two Reefs] (Jakarta: NV Bulan Bintang, 1988).
277 Interview with a minister in President Yudhoyono's cabinet, Jakarta, 28 February 2005.
278 Interview with an Indonesian academic and expert in the Indonesian military, Jakarta, 24 January 2005.
279 Interview with a senior Indonesian diplomat, a high-ranking official in DEPLU, Jakarta, 25 January 2005.
280 Interview with an Indonesian leader and academic affiliated with LIPI, Jakarta, 14 February 2005.
281 Interview with an Indonesian academic and expert in the Indonesian military, Jakarta, 24 January 2005.
282 Source: ASEAN Official Website <http://www.aseansec.org/1217.htm> (accessed 11 April 2006).
283 Interview with a CSIS-based international relations expert, Jakarta, 8 February 2005.
284 Interview with an Indonesian leader and academic affiliated with LIPI, Jakarta, 14 February 2005.
285 Interview with a former admiral of the Indonesian Navy, Jakarta, 24 February 2005.
286 Interview with an Indonesian academic and former cabinet minister, Singapore, 15 April 2005.

[287] Interview with a senior Indonesian diplomat, a high-ranking official in DEPLU, Jakarta, 25 January 2005.

[288] Interview with a former Indonesian Minister of Foreign Affairs, Jakarta, 14 January 2005.

[289] Interview with a senior Indonesian diplomat, a high-ranking official in DEPLU, Jakarta, 28 February 2005.

[290] Interview with an Indonesian scholar and IR expert affiliated with LIPI, Jakarta, 24 February 2005.

[291] Interview with an Indonesian scholar and foremost expert on China, Jakarta, 3 July 2006.

[292] Interview with an Indonesian economist and academic, Jakarta, 3 February 2005.

[293] Interview with a senior Indonesian diplomat, a high-ranking official in DEPLU, Jakarta, 25 January and 28 February 2005.

[294] Interview with a senior Indonesian diplomat, a high-ranking official in DEPLU, Jakarta, 25 January 2005.

[295] Interview with an Indonesian scholar and IR expert affiliated with LIPI, Jakarta, 24 February 2005.

[296] Interview with a senior Indonesian diplomat, a high-ranking official in DEPLU, Jakarta, 25 January 2005.

[297] Interview with a CSIS-based international relations expert, Jakarta, 8 February 2005.

[298] Ibid.

[299] Ibid.

[300] Cited from: "Indonesia's Perceptions of China and U.S. Security Roles in East Asia", seminar organized by The Habibie Centre, Jakarta (16 February 2006).

[301] Interview with an Indonesian expert in international relations, CSIS, Jakarta, 21 February 2005.

[302] Interview with a retired Indonesian Army general, presently also affiliated with a Jakarta-based research institute, Jakarta, 3 February 2005.

[303] Interview with a former Indonesian Minister of Foreign Affairs, Jakarta, 14 January 2005.

[304] Similar conclusion was presented also by Pan Yi-Ning: "Indonesia's Perceptions of China and U.S. Security Roles in East Asia", seminar organized by The Habibie Centre, Jakarta (16 February 2006).

PART III

Elite Consensus and Policy Outcomes

6

THE BIGGER PICTURE
Elite Perceptions of Other Powers

INTRODUCTION

This chapter is concerned with the Indonesian elite's perceptions of other important regional and extraterritorial state actors, namely Australia, Japan, India and the ASEAN countries. The preceding two chapters both analysed separately, and also juxtaposed, the elite perceptions of the United States and China in the context of the *"mendayung antara dua karang"* thesis — this signifies the Indonesian elite's belief that, in the future, the island nation will increasingly have to "row between two reefs". In other words, much like in the bipolar Cold War era, Indonesia will have to manoeuvre between two rival superpowers — the United States and China, both of whom have proven to be of the highest concern to the interviewed members of the Indonesian foreign policy elite.

However, we will argue in this chapter that, when compared with the Cold War era, the elite is more confident in Indonesia's ability to successfully "navigate" between the "two reefs". The confidence arises from the leaders' belief that the future state and nature of international relations will allow Indonesia to decrease its perceived excessive political and economic dependence on the West in general and the United States in particular. Because, as a former President asserted,

> as to the United States, we depend heavily on it, on imports, on international trade, on everything including the United Nations, which is so much influenced by the United States. ... [But] we don't want to

be dependent too much on the Europeans and the United States. ... You want to lessen your own costs by creating more competition.[1]

As we have found, the current process of China's ascendancy is welcome in Jakarta insofar as it helps Indonesia to eliminate negative implications of the perceived assertive and unilateralist policies of the United States. Yet, the discussion on China also highlighted the elite's continuing deep-rooted suspicions and uneasiness about Beijing's perceived expansionist aspirations. These perceptions, it was argued, will in the future induce the Indonesian leaders to implement a hedging strategy to eliminate any potential threat by China to their country's national interests and security. According to the data from the 2004–06 survey, an important aspect of the *hedging* strategy is the concept of an *inclusive* foreign policy — the idea behind the concept is that Indonesia should establish and maintain at least workable relations with as many states as possible. As several leaders pointed out, "that is why ASEAN and Indonesia are trying through an *inclusive* policy to bring [Australia, New Zealand and India] into the East Asian cooperative scheme."[2]

The technique behind the *inclusive* policy concept is based on the assumption that with more state actors having a stake in regional security, the different positions, interests and resultant pressures on Indonesia from these states will offset and neutralize each other. This is not to say that the idea behind the inclusive foreign policy is new in Indonesia — in 1953, Mohammad Hatta argued that "for economic reasons, also, Indonesia must have relationships with diverse countries."[3] When the question was raised during the interviews whether the inclusive policy signifies that Indonesian policy-makers and diplomats consider every country as a "friend" of Indonesia, one leader aptly expressed an idea widely shared by the respondents: "... actually we do not choose enemy or friends; we want to make everyone as a friend. That's expression of a non-allied position. We don't define our foreign relations from who is an enemy but we define who are our friends."[4] However, it was mostly immediately emphasized: "But the degree of friendship is different!"[5]

According to one interviewed leader, the *inclusive* foreign policy will give Indonesia "the only bargaining power for us to deal with [the big powers]", emphasizing that this approach will enable the country to "[manage] all of these complex relationships for the Indonesian benefit."[6] As a result, it is believed that the security threats to Indonesia will be reduced and eliminated. We can perhaps find a precedent for this foreign policy approach during the Sukarno era when, as one interviewee argued that "what really Sukarno did was to play one against the other. ... Under Suharto, we were more or less blocked to the United States ... so our space for manoeuvring at that time completely differs with the time with Sukarno."[7]

From the Indonesian elite's perspective, Jakarta's relations with Washington and Beijing are and will be more and more important in the future. The leaders' primary concern is how Indonesia handles these two competing major powers in the region and the way it manages its security environment. Both the United States and China are perceived to be the two major external factors with the greatest potential to adversely affect Indonesia's national interest and security. However, the data collected indicate a prevalent belief among the elite that, in the post-Cold War era international relations, Indonesia has to play "a completely different set of games."[8] Indonesia's space for manoeuvring is no longer limited either to the United States or to China. Referring to the changing broader context of the "row between two reefs" thesis, one leader pointedly argued: "Now we have so many 'rocks' (or 'reefs')!" [9]

Under present conditions, what Huntington in his influential article calls "a strange hybrid, a *uni-multipolar* system with one superpower and several major powers",[10] the Indonesian elite wants their country to use its relations with other less powerful states as a leverage to eliminate the negative effects of the Sino-American competition. According to Djisman Simandjuntak from the Jakarta-based CSIS, "the optimal situation now seemed to include a wider diversity of economic partners for Southeast Asia, including, Europe, China, the United States, Australia, and New Zealand as well as Japan."[11] As argued in the following chapter of this study, the respondents overwhelmingly agreed that the U.S. military presence in the region constitutes an important element in the elite's long-term national security strategy. However, several leaders also pointed out that "it has its downside as well." As one respondent explained,

> ... the U.S. is now the only superpower and so the U.S. does not have to think about other factors before it executes certain policies. ... If the Soviet Union still existed, it would not be easy for the U.S. to invade Iraq. ... For smaller countries and middle power a *multi-polar* structure is more desirable because it will put limitations on the major powers.[12]

In the following discussion, we will analyse in turn Indonesian elite perceptions of Australia, Japan, India and ASEAN countries. Here, special emphasis is laid on the leaders' attitude towards these countries in the context of their previously discussed perceptions of the U.S. and China. In other words, we will characterize the position and role of Australia, Japan, India and ASEAN countries in the elite's attempt to implement an *inclusive* foreign policy and its effort to handle Indonesia's relations with the two competing major powers. Several important major state actors are missing from the analysis, namely South Korea, Russia, and the European Union. However, as we pointed out earlier, the structured questionnaire used during the interviews contained a number of open-ended questions that played an important part in the overall survey research strategy as they prompted the members of the Indonesian foreign policy elite to reply as much as possible in their own words and thus reveal what perceptions were salient in their mind. Consequently, the fact that only Australia, Japan, India and ASEAN countries are included in the following analysis signifies that during the interviews the respondents focused principally on these state actors.

AUSTRALIA

The case of Australia illustrates how significantly elite threat perceptions can change over a period of little more than three decades. Perhaps the most striking fact about Indonesia's southern neighbour is that Weinstein's study on Indonesian foreign policy elite's perceptions of the major powers from 1976 did not include a separate section on Australia. In fact, one would find scarcely a reference to Indonesia's largest neighbour in his book. This fact needs to be emphasized because the place of Australia in the elite's threat assessment in the 1970s is in a sharp contrast with the situation today.

In contrast to Weinstein's findings in the early 1970s that basically paid no attention to Indonesia's southern neighbour, Australia has proven to be one of the highest concerns among the present Indonesian leadership. Based on the data evaluation, the country's foreign policy elite ranked Australia as presently the second most serious state-based threat to Indonesia. In other words, 33 per cent of the interviewed leaders consider Australia (in contrast to 51 per cent of them naming the U.S. and 27 per cent China) as currently the principal state-based malign factor negatively affecting Indonesia's national interests and security.

From a Benign to a Threatening Impression

Indonesia's relations with Australia have developed since the end of World War II (WWII) and during these six decades they have experienced high and low tides. Still, it could be safely argued that most Indonesians, both in the society at large and at the elite level, had, as Andrew MacIntyre aptly put it, "either little impression of Australia or a gently benign impression of Australia as a small rich country and generally friendly neighbour."[13] By contrast, a 2004 survey among aspirants for diplomatic careers with the Indonesian

Department of Foreign Affairs revealed that about 95 per cent of the 6,000 candidates held anti-Australian sentiments.[14] Yet, at least one third of the interviewed leaders also claimed that "one of the most important goals of Indonesian foreign policy is the relationship with Australia."[15]

In his memoirs, the diplomat Abu Hanifah credits Australia along with India for putting the Indonesian question to the United Nations in July 1947. The Australian resolution proposed an immediate cessation of hostilities and submission of the dispute between the Dutch and the Republic to a third party for arbitration.[16] Several interviewed leaders have also highlighted the fact that "the Americans and Australians supported our independence, whereas the Europeans did not."[17] One pointed out that Australia "[was] really one of the biggest supporters of Indonesian independence."[18] A former Minister of Foreign Affairs agreed that, initially, the Australians were good friends of the Indonesians as they sided with the young Republic against the Dutch, boycotted Dutch ships and supported Indonesia in the Security Council of the UN. The ex-minister simultaneously emphasized that after Sukarno launched the campaign to liberate West Irian, Canberra sided with the Dutch; later during the Vietnam War the Australians sided with the United States and there was a great degree of estrangement between Indonesia and Australia as the latter thought that Jakarta was going leftist.[19]

Defence has been a substantial element of the relationship between Indonesia and Australia. This security cooperation culminated in the security agreement between Indonesia and Australia signed in December 1995. One of the chief reasons behind this security agreement was the Suharto government's effort to adopt a more assertive stance against China and its irredentist claims in the South China Sea in general and in the waters around Indonesia's Natuna Islands in particular. This "assertive engagement" with Australia, which was by some interpreted as an abandonment of Indonesia's traditional non-aligned stance, was designed to demonstrate Jakarta's determination to protect its national interests.[20] Sunardi explains that the Suharto government's decision to maintain increasingly close security cooperation with Canberra needs to be seen in the light of "Russian disengagement and the contraction of the U.S. commitment to the region."[21] In this context, there was a growing apprehension among the Indonesian elite about what Sunardi characterizes as

> ... a strong tendency for China to project its power southwards. The Spratly Islands' incidents and the new Chinese law on territorial boundaries have posed new concerns to its neighbours. To Southeast Asian countries, the Japanese behaviour during World War II has always

been traumatic; they may also remember only too well the Chinese southward power projection in the past.[22]

East Timor as a "Turning Point"

It could be reasonably argued that Australian military involvement in East Timor in 1999 was the watershed event that brought about a substantial change in the Indonesian foreign policy elite's perceptions of its southern neighbour. Indonesians, both among the lay people and the elite, started to take a darker view of Australia. Ever since the Indonesian army occupied the former Portuguese colony in 1975, hundreds of thousands of Timorese died as Jakarta unsuccessfully tried to suppress the independence movement in the territory. For more than two decades, Australia was one a very few countries that had provided tacit support for Indonesia's acquisition and occupation of East Timor. Canberra's official policy on East Timor did not change following the Dili massacre in November 1991 that attracted widespread international condemnation.

Canberra's changing attitude and, particularly, its pressure on Jakarta in 1999 to accept a multinational peacemaking force in East Timor, generated a growing distrust of Australia. As a result of what was overwhelmingly viewed as a stark and unanticipated reversal of Canberra's past policies on the East Timor issue, the Indonesian leaders were increasingly concerned about Canberra's real intentions and began to consider Australia as a potentially dangerous neighbour. As a senior diplomat asserted, from the Indonesian elite's perspective, it was "incomprehensible why Australia after thirty years 'betrayed' Indonesia with East Timor."[23] The feeling of acrimony and suspicion among the Indonesian top leadership was revealed, for example, during the Australian Prime Minister John Howard's official visit to Jakarta in February 2002. Akbar Tanjung, Speaker of the House of Representatives, and Amien Rais, Speaker of the People's Consultative Assembly, both refused to hold official, one-on-one meetings with the Australian Prime Minister in order to express the level of distrust that was present in their view of the country.[24] In the words of another senior diplomat, "perceptions of threat [towards Australia] were high during and after the East Timor crisis."[25]

The survey data evaluation established that this negative perception of Australia is a reflection of three particular images that are overwhelmingly shared by the Indonesian leaders: first, Australia is the main ally or "deputy sheriff" of the U.S. in the region; second, Australia has (territorial) designs on West Papua; and, third, Australians consider Indonesia as a major security threat to their country.

First Image: Australia as a "Deputy Sheriff"

In September 1999, Australian Prime Minister John Howard endorsed the Bush Administration's "pre-emption doctrine" and proclaimed what has since been dubbed as "Howard Doctrine".[26] It was declared that Australia would assume a more active role in Asian security matters, including possible interventions in the region, and it would pursue this new policy as — to use the metaphor coined by Australia's Asian neighbours — a the U.S. "deputy sheriff".[27] Howard's strategic doctrine of pre-emption, combined with lingering resentment over Australia's military involvement in East Timor, as well as later in Afghanistan and Iraq alongside the United States, constitutes a major source of concern for the Indonesian elite. As to Australia's close alliance with the United States, Anthony L. Smith concludes that this connection "… has proven to be a liability in normalizing Australia-Indonesia relations; many Indonesians see the United States as having negative designs on their country for which Australia is a willing partner."[28] Some leaders interpreted Howard's words as that their country was the intended target. Thus, a respondent who is known for her close links with the top army leadership asserted: "The military sees Australia as its primary threat at the moment."[29]

One leader argued that "Australia is the biggest problem for Indonesia [because] it is perceived as very close to the U.S."[30] A former high-ranking army officer aptly expressed the prevalent view among the elite by saying that Australia is now acting as a "regional sheriff" whereby it has been "appointed [to this position] to safeguard the U.S. interests in the region."[31] Here, another respondent, a senior official of the PDI-P Party, suggested that Australia's actual role is to "organize the U.S. affairs in the South Pacific and Japan's in East Asia."[32] One leader contended that the elite's suspicion towards Australia is because it forms, along with the United States, Japan and Singapore, one of the so-called "four anchors" that "encircle" Indonesia.[33] Indonesian policy-makers are puzzled as to how to interpret the close economic, political and military cooperation between these four countries, with every initiative by Washington being supported by Canberra, Tokyo and Singapore.

Another major irritant is Canberra's close cooperation with Washington in the War on Terrorism. As one respondent asserted, "the U.S. War on Terror actually put lots of constraints on Indonesia's position in world affairs because there is a series of problems of terrorism in the country that affect our relations not just with the U.S. but also other countries like Australia." It is not only the anti-terrorism campaign but also the suspicions about Australian designs on West Papua that led a senior officer of the GOLKAR Party to allege that America and Australia use modern technology and means to "test Indonesia's capability to defend itself."[34] The elite is generally inclined to ascribe to both Australia and the United States similar characteristic features. Describing the "U.S. foreign policy [that] is imperialistic," a senior official of the *Muhammadiyah* emphasized that, during his recent visit to Canberra, he personally reminded Prime Minister John Howard that "Australia should not behave like America or Great Britain."[35]

Second Image: Australian Territorial Design on West Papua

The second impression of Australia among the interviewed leaders is that Indonesia's southern neighbour is the primary threat to the country's national cohesion, particularly in relation to the troubled eastern-most province of West Papua (formerly known as Irian Jaya).[36] Thus, in 2002, Speaker of the House of Representatives Soetardjo Soerjogoeritno claimed that the House received reports accusing Australia of helping to fund NGOs, including pro-separatist groups, in Aceh, East Timor and West Papua provinces.[37] Then in 2006, commenting on Jakarta's protest over the Australian Department of Immigration's decision to grant temporary visas to forty-two refugees from West Papua, the Coordinating Minister for Political, Legal and Security Affairs, Widodo Adi Sutjipto, argued that Canberra's act "confirms suspicions that there are elements in Australia which are aiding the separatist movement in Papua."[38] Defence Minister Juwono Sudarsono stressed that a number of senior members of the Free Papua Movement (OPM) have long set up their residence in Australia. The Minister also accused some international NGOs of manipulating the case as a part of their relentless campaign to achieve West Papuan independence.[39]

The author admits to having been struck that these and similar views were frequently expressed during the interviews even with the most senior and influential Indonesian leaders, some of whom were graduates from Australian universities. It is obvious that Australia's attitude during the East Timor crisis of 1999 considerably reinforced the leaders' apprehension of Canberra's designs in the eastern part of Indonesia. One respondent who holds a doctoral degree from an Australian university stated that "... from the political point of view, particularly from the experience of what happened in East Timor during 1999 to 2001, I think some people in the government are quite afraid that Australia also will campaign for the independence of Papua."[40]

Further adding to these qualms was Australian Prime Minister Howard's announcement in December 2004 that his government would take steps to strengthen Australia's maritime security in the light of the terrorist-related threats to maritime assets around the world. In particular, the proclaimed establishment of a 1,000 nautical mile Maritime Identification Zone around Australia, which effectively overlapped with Indonesian waters, raised concerns in Jakarta. The proposed 1,000 nautical mile Maritime Identification Zone covers huge territorial waters of Indonesia including the Java, Makassar and Maluku Seas. One report in Indonesian media warned that

> ... under a new security initiative, [Australia] would simply send its forces over to the adjacent neighbourhood and deal with the threat pre-emptively, with or without the consent of the adjacent neighbourhood, in this case, Indonesia. ... That such an initiative should cause unease with Australia's two main neighbours (Indonesia and New Zealand) is probably not surprising.[41]

Pointing out that "Australia's 1,000-nautical-mile-initiative is seen with suspicion" in Indonesia, one interviewed leader asserted that Howard's announcement of the Maritime Identification Zone was for the Indonesian elite "like a thunderstorm during clear day light." It strengthened the conviction of some policy-makers and diplomats that "it must be directed against us."[42] Stressing that "this is the opinion of many Indonesian scholars and policy-makers", a senior diplomat who is also an expert on maritime law and security summed up the questions that plague the elite as: "What is going on? Why does Australia have so much interest in this Eastern part of Indonesia? Does it have some designs? In the long run, in the next twenty years, what will Australia do with the eastern part of Indonesia?"[43]

The Indonesian leaders feel especially ambivalent about the connection between the government in Canberra and the NGOs and the manner and extent to which these two entities influence Australia's policy on various issues pertinent to West Papua. Referring to the so-called "Howard Doctrine" and the 1,000-mile-initiative, a former Foreign Minister argued:

> ... apart from the government in Australia, there are very, very many NGOs in Australia and some misguided intellectuals who on the basis of human rights and justice want to be involved in certain issues in Indonesia and continue to send people there ... not [necessarily with the intention] to occupy it but to make it difficult for us.[44]

Similarly, another respondent, an expert on the West Papuan separatist movement, asserted that

[even] though the Australian government always says that we want to see Indonesia as one country but sometimes the Australian NGOs … have projects in Papua … because of their ideological background and political activities, sometimes it is quite difficult for the Australian NGOs to be non-political agents, not to have political agenda. If you read in the internet during 2001 and 2003, I think, there was a discussion in Australia that one Australian NGO spread propaganda about Papuan independence.[45]

It is noteworthy that unlike in West Papua, Australia's involvement in other parts of the archipelago through its NGOs as well as businesses did not give rise to security concerns of a similar magnitude. As one interviewee pointed out, "[if] you talk to the people in the Foreign Affairs Department or maybe Indonesian Intelligence, they will have the opinion that the Papua [problem] is much more difficult to settle compared to Aceh."[46] Apart from the obvious geographic proximity and the history of Canberra's involvement in Papua New Guinea, which shares a border with Indonesia's West Papua province, the Indonesian elite's apprehension of Australia has also a religious context. At least three leaders observed that both the majority of the East Timorese and the West Papuans share the same religion with the Australians, whereby the common religious background is seen here as a major liability:

> From some people's perspective, they see Papua as more dangerous because, from the religious perspective in Australia, they try to have the Papuans because they are Christian. And also because of the geographic proximity between Papua province and Papua New Guinea and also the Torres Straits islands. So I think this is why some people in Indonesia still see that it is possible that Australia still has another agenda on Papua after East Timor.[47]

In expressing their view of Canberra's foreign policies towards Indonesia during the John Howard Administration, some Indonesian leaders left diplomatic niceties aside. With regard to the 1,000-mile Maritime Identification Zone, the Minister of Defence, Juwono Sudarsono, for example, cautioned that Indonesia would deploy its naval forces to repel Australian warships that entered the archipelago's territorial waters.[48] When asked about how the Indonesian Government would respond in the future if Australia's perceived interference in the eastern part of the archipelago continues, a former Indonesian ambassador to Australia emphatically (and apparently half-jokingly) asserted: "Indonesians in 1298 cut off the ear of a Chinese Admiral. [Now] we can do it to the Australians."[49]

Third Image: Threat from Misperception

The data collected during the series of in-depth interviews have also revealed a considerable measure of disquiet about another distinct kind of security concern. The generally fairly open informal discussions with the members of the Indonesian foreign policy elite indicate the large degree to which they are concerned about the serious threat to Indonesia stemming from misperceptions.[50] This refers to the situation in which Indonesia and the "Indonesian realities" are, what they call, misunderstood, misconceived or misperceived by foreign countries, their people, businesses and governments. The Jakarta foreign policy elite believe that, presently, the image of any country is exceedingly important in the light of an increasingly globalized world characterized by free-flowing capital and free-roaming tourists, all underpinned by the immense power of the global media and information technology. Most respondents also judged that Indonesia is at present perceived, regardless of whether rightly or unjustly, worldwide as a country that doesn't really arouse much foreign investor confidence, as a safe haven for terrorists, and as an unstable place where tourist hotels are frequently blown up. All these factors have, as the interviews attest, a direct impact on the Jakarta elite's national security considerations.[51]

The negative image of Indonesia could either have an adverse affect on the country's economy or, in the worst scenario, potentially lead to a miscalculated and irrational reaction, including a military strike, by a foreign power on Indonesia. It is the latter situation that constituted perhaps both the main shortcoming and challenge to the principle of nuclear deterrence between the United States and the Soviet Union during the hot years of the Cold War. If one side were to believe that its adversary was preparing for a military strike, the ensuing pre-emptive action would have been a path to a global disaster. Currently, sections of population in some countries believe that Indonesia constitutes a threat to their national security. According to Professor McAllister from the ANU in Canberra, "to the extent that the [Australian] public identifies a security threat to Australia, there is a greater consensus than ever before (that) that threat comes from one country: Indonesia..."[52] From the Indonesian perspective, confirming the Australian phobia about the threat from Indonesia was the earlier discussed warning of the Australian Prime Minister John Howard that Canberra could potentially launch pre-emptive strikes in the region if it believed there were terrorist threats.[53] During the interviews, several politicians and diplomats expressed apprehension at a possible overreaction or irrational reaction on the part of its southern neighbour.[54]

Simon Philpott has argued that fear and anxiety among both the Canberra political establishment and Australian society at large constitute an integral element of Australia's relations with Indonesia. Philpott also argues that "[the] images and metaphors used to describe Indonesian society and assumptions about 'our' and 'their' national character reflect an enduringly negative view of Indonesia."[55] The interviews with Indonesian leaders indicated their awareness of what is widely considered as Australia's innately negative attitude towards Indonesia. One respondent concluded that "... Australia from the military perspective is not a threat to Indonesia. [But] Australia is still thinking Indonesia is still a threat to Australia."[56]

This situation is seen in Jakarta as a recipe for a potentially fatal misunderstanding between the two countries. As a former Foreign Minister asserted, "[we] do not view Australia as a threat, but somehow Australians, and this Australian government (Howard's government), sometimes thinks Indonesia is a threat." To illustrate, he recounted a story that he called a "joke". Once he participated in a seminar between Indonesia and Australia about security issues and threat perceptions. Both sides quickly agreed that the threat came from the North. "When we talked threat from the North, we talked about China," said the former Minister of Foreign Affairs and concluded that it was much later that he found out that "when [the Australians] talked about threats from the North, they meant Indonesia."[57] Several respondents judged this situation as quite serious. "When Daniel (the author) says I am his threat, then I will [naturally] think that Daniel is my threat as well," says a young diplomat explaining the widespread view among the Jakarta elite. "It is a natural reaction!"[58]

The Role of the Leaders' Personal Experience in Australia

As demonstrated in the earlier discussions on the U.S. and China, respondents' personal experiences can significantly influence their views of and attitude towards a particular country. Thus, at least one fourth of the interviewed leaders, most of them being career diplomats, explicitly suggested that their experience as undergraduate or postgraduate students enrolled in an Australia-based university has shaped or reshaped their perceptions of that country. Since the 1950s, the number of Indonesian students in Australia has been increasing from year to year.[59] According to unofficial information obtained from DEPLU, every year a group of mostly young Indonesian career diplomats attends one to two years of study at an Australian university. In 2000, for example, between twenty and thirty individuals (also called Batch 2000) out of the total sixty-two diplomats who graduated from the Junior

Diplomatic Course passed the special entrance test and were sent to study in Australia. Apparently, their living expenses and the tuition fees were covered by the Australian Government.[60]

Despite the fact that the studies were paid for by the Australian government, it is worth noting that, on balance, the participants' impression of that country and its people was rather unfavourable. For example, one respondent recalled being surprised at how little the Australian people knew about their largest neighbour and how much their view of Indonesia was distorted. He recollected that

> ... sometimes my mates in the student apartment had very funny questions. For example, my friend in the flat asked me whether Indonesia is like Fiji. That's why I was very angry sometimes with that kind of question and I said you know ... I think that Jakarta is quite better compared to Sydney and Canberra. ... You know some areas of Indonesia are quite modern.[61]

One career diplomat admitted that his view of Australia and its people somewhat improved as a result of his experience in that country. Before he went to study in Australia, his view of that country was largely negative based on the overall impression gained from watching Australian television programmes. Realizing that "the Australians were rude on TV and spoke more frankly [than Indonesians]", the young diplomat originally thought that "the Australians were aggressive and mean."[62] However, after some time living in a major Australian city he found, as he put it, that "[if] the Australians are so outspoken, it does not mean that they are evil or aggressive."[63] Yet, he stressed that he was startled by the general outlook of the Australian people who considered Indonesia as a major security threat to their country. This is why, as he concluded, it is a "natural reaction" if the Indonesians are worried about Australia and its policy of pre-emptive strike.[64]

Another young career diplomat who studied in Australia for two years admitted having been taken aback at the extent to which the media, politicians and ordinary people in Australia portrayed Indonesia as a threat to their country. Although he had had a largely unfavourable impression of Indonesia's southern neighbour before he first visited the country, he said that his studies in Australia "perhaps reinforced this opinion."[65] To be sure, the young diplomat conceded that "the Australians are very nice" but instantly added that "...even they have problems with the Aborigines [and also] the Australia's 'Defence White Book' represents a pretty aggressive point of view."[66]Another diplomat who often participates in diplomatic negotiations on various issues with his Australian counterparts concluded: "Lots of Indonesians think: 'Australia is heavy-handed; it does not like us'!"[67]

Indonesian Elite's Sense of Vulnerability

When analysing the roots of the Indonesian foreign policy elite's prevalent security concerns about Australia, it can be argued that the leaders' sense of weakness and vulnerability vis-à-vis that country is an important factor that generates and reinforces the perceptions of threat. As demonstrated earlier, the assessment of the degree to which the present leadership embraces the "Pretty Maiden Analogy" established that the elite's worldview continues to regard the outside world as exploitative and hostile. Thus, much like with the earlier discussed cases of the United States and China, Australia is also considered a malign factor negatively affecting Indonesia's national security insofar as it constantly seeks to take advantage of Indonesia.

Australia is generally considered as one of the countries with the biggest capacity to exert a substantial influence on the domestic configuration within Indonesia. An international relations expert with close ties to DEPLU asserted that "… still very much basically Australia is perceived as a power that has the capacity to intervene in the Indonesian territory. And one of the examples is basically the Maritime Identification Zone when Australia extends the security zone in their maritime territory 1,000 nautical miles".[68] "It is easy to take advantage of Indonesia because of its internal problems," argued another interviewed leader pointing to the "frequent travel warnings by Australia." Although Canberra has the right to issue those travel warnings, in her view, since this act hurts Indonesia's already fragile economy, the government's warnings are tantamount to "interference into Indonesia's domestic affairs."[69]

As to the elite's sense of vulnerability, the overwhelming consensus among the Indonesian leaders is that the external threats originate for the most part in Indonesia's own internal socio-political and economic problems. These, in turn, produce the overall scepticism and lack of confidence among the elite in Indonesia's strength and capacity to deal with external security threats. As one leader noted, "of course, there is a perception, it is about political interaction, economic sensitivities — of Singapore, Australia — but the main security concern is still very much internal problems.[70] As Figure 6.1 shows, the respondents overwhelmingly — some 73 per cent of them — regard threats to Indonesia's national security that are internal in origin as more serious and dangerous than external threats.

FIGURE 6.1
Degree of Urgency: External versus Internal Threats, based on the Research Data Evaluation.

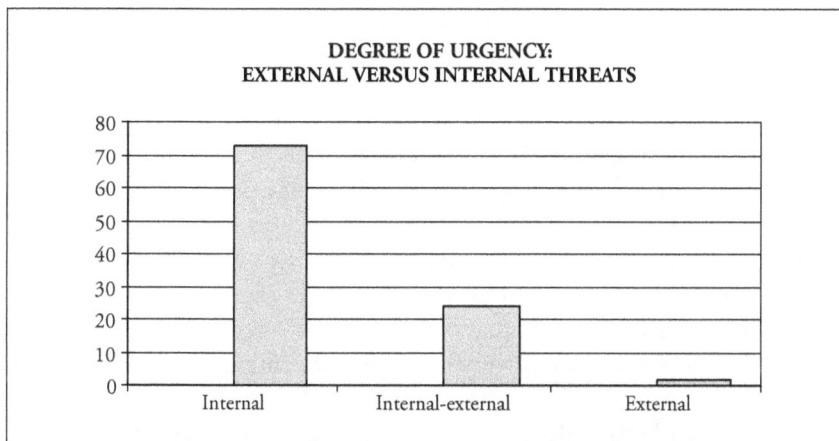

DEGREE OF URGENCY:
EXTERNAL VERSUS INTERNAL THREATS

```
80
70
60
50
40
30
20
10
 0
      Internal        Internal-external        External
```

Source: Survey research conducted by the author in 2004–05.

Illustrative of the sense of vulnerability was the reaction in the Indonesian media to the warning of Juwono Sudarsono, the country's Defence Minister, that Indonesia would deploy its naval forces to deter Australian warships that entered the archipelago's waters. The Minister's words were criticized as empty in light of the poor state of the warships in the Indonesian Navy that are not capable of patrolling Indonesia's territorial waters let alone repelling foreign vessels. Endy M. Bayuni pointedly concluded in her commentary: "If we had the force that Juwono talks about in the first place, perhaps Australia would not have such a low opinion of our naval capability in protecting such a vast expanse of water, and Canberra would not have to come up with such an initiative."[71]

It is not only the poor state of Indonesian military equipment that generates concerns. Several leaders suggested that the Indonesian government's flawed and misguided policy on the West Papuan problem actually makes it easier for Australia and other countries, both governments and NGOs, to intervene in Indonesia's internal affairs. More generally, from the Indonesian elite's perspective, the case of both West Papua and East Timor also demonstrated the considerable power of non-governmental organizations that, when united behind a particular cause, can force a government to change its policies.[72] Here, one leader argued:

> But in my opinion this depends on the internal policy of the Indonesian government itself. If the special autonomy status in Papua is implemented and if the people in Papua are happy to become Indonesian citizens it is highly unlikely that foreign countries will intervene either through so-called humanitarian intervention.[73]

Conspicuously, during the interviews, no more than eight respondents explicitly expressed their trust in Australia, its government and people. Those who did so condemned the elite's views of Australia as a threat to Indonesia as being the result of either nationalistic feelings or conspiracy theories. For example, a former President described as ridiculous President Megawati Sukarnoputri's assertion that Australia was a threat to Indonesia because "it would like to occupy parts of Indonesia for benefits of 'imperialism'", adding that "I said in many occasions that this kind of narrow-minded nationalistic feelings should be thrown out. Australia, the U.S. and China and others are our friends."[74]

This group of respondents also voiced their general scepticism about the prevalent notion among the Indonesian foreign policy elite that Australia has territorial designs on the eastern part of Indonesia, particularly on West Papua. These leaders expressed their conviction that it is actually in the interest of the major powers to ensure Indonesia's territorial integrity. As one of them asserted, "I do not believe in the conspiracy theory that the major powers, like the U.S. or even Japan and Australia, actually want to break Indonesia up. I do not believe that. Because if Indonesia breaks up to become many small countries that would be more destabilizing than Indonesia as one state."[75]

In the particular case of Australia, the respondents were inclined to point to the fact that, first, Canberra has learned from its past ill-conceived and faulty involvement in Papua New Guinea, East Timor, and lately Afghanistan and Iraq and, second, that Australians are aware of the limitations of their power and capabilities. Thus, a retired high-ranking officer from the Indonesian Navy observed that "Australia does not have a design for *Papua Barat*. It has no use for Australia. Australia is big enough with small population and thus it does not need to expand its territory."[76] Similarly, a former Minister of Foreign Affairs affirmed:

> These kinds of [Australian] policies provoke us, but I do not think the government at least and most of the rational people, we do not subscribe to conspiracy theories. ... I think, on the contrary, Australia now realizes that it has a big burden in East Timor, it has a big burden in Papua New Guinea. So it will think twice to add to those burdens to have designs on West Papua.[77]

Some leaders in the "anti-conspiracy" group suggested that the notion of the Australian threat needs to be seen in the context of both Australian and Indonesian domestic politics. It was, for instance, argued that Indonesia is seen as a security threat among the Australian population

> ... because Indonesia as an issue is very easy to raise in Australia, especially before the elections. It is quite normal. So the relationship between Indonesia and Australia is very sensitive not because Australia is a military threat to Indonesia or Indonesia is a military threat to Australia. Because Indonesia does not have any military capacity or capability and from Australia there is no intention.

As to the belief among sections of the Indonesian elite that Australia might be willing to carry out a military operation against Indonesia, it was affirmed that

> ... they have the capacity but there is no intention. So it is more political in Indonesia, [particularly] among some political elites within the Parliament, and in Australia as well. ... Intelligence is very good [between] Indonesia and Australia — there is no doubt about that. And then military to military relations are also very good. So it is just political.[78]

The Place of Australia in Indonesia's *Inclusive* Foreign Policy

Since 2001, the Indonesia-Australia relationship has been characterized by an increasing diplomatic effort by both governments aimed at increasing comprehensive cooperation and enhancing mutual trust and understanding. Particularly from the interviews with senior Indonesian diplomats, it is obvious that there is a great willingness to constantly try to improve and deepen the relationship with Australia. It is clearly beyond the scope of this study to assess the degree to which other causal variables, namely economic considerations, such as an incentive of economic benefit, have encouraged the elite's effort to improve the ties with Canberra. However, it is evident that especially the senior (and more visionary) members of the Indonesian leadership consider Australia as one of the important elements in Jakarta's inclusive foreign policy. In 1996, the former Rear Admiral of the Indonesian Navy, R.M. Sunardi, asserted that "there is no doubt that cooperation between Australia and Indonesia — including security cooperation — will intensify in the future. ... Perhaps what we are looking for is not 'trust-building', but 'partnership-building' — since Indonesia has never considered Australia an enemy or a threat."[79]

While the last statement appears to be no longer valid — as demonstrated above, Australia is now seen as a potent security threat to Indonesia — what has not changed is Jakarta's desire for the intensification of security cooperation as a part of trust-building. But in this process, Australia has to do its share by dropping what the Indonesian elite views as its assertive and aggressive posture. As a former Foreign Minister observed,

> ... they have to deal with Asia, they have to deal with Indonesia, their closest neighbour, in a different way; otherwise you will get misunderstanding. So far, we are trying to understand [Australia by] organizing conferences against terrorism, about peoples' smuggling, international, trans-national crime ... We want to get Australia to cooperate with us.[80]

Acknowledging Australia's substantial humanitarian assistance in the wake of the devastating tsunami and earthquake in December 2004, a senior diplomat contended that "Aceh is a confidence-building process" and, as such, it was Canberra's step in the right direction.[81]

To get a better understanding of Australia's role in the Indonesian foreign policy elite's security considerations, we will briefly examine the Indonesian leaders' attitudes towards the concept of the East Asian Community. There were hopes that the East Asia Summit (EAS), which took place in Kuala Lumpur in December 2005, would bring the regional states closer to the establishment of the East Asian Community (EAC). This, some leaders believed, would gradually usher in a new era of close cooperation in the region akin to the European Union. One scholar went so far as to claim that "a Chinese-sponsored move to hold an East Asian summit offers the most visible expression of a trend of declining American influence in Asia."[82] The Summit in Kuala Lumpur, however, laid bare the historical rivalries and competing strategic interests of the participating countries, which originate in their respective elite's distinct worldviews.

Membership of the EAS proved to be a particularly contentious issue. On the one hand, China proposed an *exclusive* approach to membership, whereby Beijing wanted only the members of ASEAN plus China, South Korea and Japan to participate in the project. On the other, the proponents of the *inclusive* approach, particularly Japan, Indonesia and Singapore, alarmed by the vision of having the EAS dominated by China, vigorously campaigned to have India, Australia and New Zealand on board. The second, more inclusive approach finally prevailed and all three countries became members of the EAS. Here, Mohan Malik provides an explanation for the inclusive attitude: "New

Zealand, Singapore, Indonesia, Vietnam, and India are hedgers that worry more about China than America."[83] Essentially referring to the Indonesian concept of *inclusive* foreign policy, Malik also argues:

> Believing that the EAS, with more countries participating, would provide a counterbalance to China's growing influence, Japan supported equal opportunity for India, Australia and New Zealand. In this endeavour, Japan won backing from Singapore and Indonesia for its open, inclusive approach to community building by all 16 EAS members.[84]

The data available from the interviews confirm this line of argumentation. Australia's, but also Japan's and India's membership in the EAS are seen in Jakarta as desirable insofar as it provides Indonesia with a greater leverage to deal with the growing power of China and with potential Chinese expansionist aspirations. As a senior diplomat directly involved in the EAS negotiations pointed out, "Indonesia's view of the East Asian Community is an inclusive one. It is an open and inclusive one. We wish to see the participation of Australia, New Zealand and India."[85] Emphasizing the concern of the majority of the Indonesian elite that "[the EAS] will be dominated by China", another interviewed leader asserted:

> Well, we need to develop the East Asian Community but Indonesia should [also] develop relationships with India, the U.S., maintaining some levels of strategic relationship ... with Australia. Why? This is to deter China. So we have some options by including many countries. [Thus] any adventurism by China will be detrimental to China itself.[86]

On the other hand, a high-ranking diplomat affirmed that if Indonesia wants to include India, Australia and New Zealand in the EAC, "it is not to cancel or balance China," explaining that "we do not subscribe to the balance of power argument. It is about the dynamics; having India, Australia and New Zealand in EAC even by default enables ASEAN to be in the middle. Because [then] we can become like the arbitrator."[87] Whilst welcoming Australia's participation in the fledgling project of the EAC, this respondent questioned whether "Australia [actually] has a sense of community building with East Asia?"[88] He had, however, no definite answer to this question.

JAPAN

The case of Japan also illustrates how significantly elite threat perceptions can change over three decades. However, in contrast to Australia, the Indonesian foreign policy elite's view of Japan has during this period of time experienced an overall upward tendency — it has evolved from a "ambiguous threat" to an ambivalent attitude to the acute awareness that Japan is a welcome and indispensable counterweight to China's growing clout. As Leo Suryadinata observed, "in terms of Indonesian perceptions of security in a broad sense, the U.S. and Japan are the most important nations."[89]

While Weinstein's 1976 study reported that the Indonesian foreign policy elite viewed Japan "as an expansionist nation posing a threat [to Indonesia] comparable to that of China",[90] a major survey on ASEAN leaders' perceptions of Japan in 1994 presented the Southeast Asian elites' ambivalent views of the "land of the rising sun".[91] In contrast to the 1976 and 1994 studies, interviews conducted for this work revealed highly positive perceptions of Japan. None of the forty-five interviewed leaders considered the country as anything close to a "serious threat". In his perceptive study of the Indonesian elite's worldview, Weinstein aptly described the gradual change in the Indonesian leaders' attitude towards Japan. While in the 1950s only few saw any substantial conflict between Japan and Indonesia, in the early 1960s, Weinstein observed, "foreign policy elite members returned from visits to Japan 'impressed and worried.'"[92] By the early 1970s, the majority of the elite saw Japan as a "serious threat." Here, it is argued that

> [though] China was more frequently named as the principal threat, a response encouraged by the government's frequent portrayal of China as Indonesia's leading enemy, 84 per cent of the foreign policy elite members described Japan as a serious threat, whereas only 67 per cent considered the Chinese threat serious. ... [They either] singled out Japan as the principal threat, or cited Japan and China as equal dangers...[93]

The 1994 opinion poll conducted by the Japanese newspaper *The Chunichi Shimbun* analysed the ASEAN leaders' perceptions of Japan.[94] The results of the poll highlighted the elites' rather ambivalent views of Japan. While, on the one hand, out of one hundred interviewed leaders, eighty two said they liked and only three said they disliked Japan, on the other hand, 36 per cent of the Indonesian leaders thought that "Japan had not regretted enough its conduct during World War II" and 56 per cent of them were wary of Japan becoming a military giant.[95] By contrast, the interviews for this book established that a mere 4 per cent of the leaders considered Japan as the most serious state-based threat to Indonesia. This fact is also significant in light of the fact that 13 per cent and 9 per cent of respondents named Singapore and Malaysia respectively as currently the principal threat to the archipelagic nation's interests and security. It ought to be emphasized that this shift in the Indonesian elite's perceptions of Japan from negative to ambivalent to the presently very positive view has from the early 1990s coincided with Tokyo's growing assertiveness and effort to play a greater security role in the region.

This phenomenon deserves some attention. As demonstrated above, from the 1950s to the 1990s, Japan strictly adhering to its pacifist constitution and with a more passive foreign policy agenda was seen in Jakarta as a "serious threat". This section analyses the reasons as to why at present Japan's increasingly assertive foreign policy does not set alarm bells ringing in Jakarta. It will be argued that Tokyo's growing assertiveness has not raised a great concern among the Indonesian leaders because the elite now considers Japan as a lesser threat than before — particularly vis-à-vis the Indonesian leaders' deep-rooted sentiments towards what is perceived as the inherently expansionist and aggressive Chinese character and the growing projection of Chinese power and influence in regional affairs.

The Japanese "Interregnum" and Its Effects

Indonesia's political and economic relationship with Japan in the second half of the 20th century was long influenced by the events of WWII and particularly by the latter's imperialist and colonial legacy. The Japanese "interregnum", a term referring to the Japanese occupation of Southeast Asian during WWII coined by Harry J. Benda, left a long-lasting impact in the minds of the Indonesian people.[96] The dynamics of this relationship were shaped by the Indonesian foreign policy elite's unfavourable perception of the Japanese as a "crude, aggressive, and inscrutable" people.[97] Tilman claims that the Indonesians tend to take, by and large, a positive view of the consequences of the Japanese occupation during the WWII. Yet, he does not elaborate on this statement with the exception of mentioning the catalytic effect of the subjugation on the Indonesian revolution and struggle for independence.[98]

However, the Indonesian elite is not naïve and seems to be aware of the fact that the Japanese forces did not originally occupy the archipelago just to voluntarily grant it independence some three years later followed by the withdrawal of its troops. The elite clearly view the chain of events of 1942 to 1945, which culminated with the proclamation of Indonesian independence, in the broader context of the configuration of power around the world. Japan is not considered in Indonesia as a saviour, which ousted the hated Dutch colonial masters in order to altruistically liberate the Indonesian people. The three-year-long Japanese "interregnum" was described by some Indonesian officials as "worse than Dutch colonialism" that lasted some three and a half centuries.[99] Exacerbating the negative impression of Japan was the widespread perception among the elite that the Japanese people's attitude towards the rest of Asia was characterized by a sense of superiority and arrogance. Moreover, the Japanese were seen as having a cutthroat and ruthless mentality. Referring to the general conception of the Japanese mentality, Henshall asserts:

> [what] is quite distinctive about the Japanese myths is an avoidance of moral judgment as to good and evil. ... Behaviour is accepted or rejected depending on the situation, not according to any obvious set of universal principles. This is exactly what many commentators remark upon in present-day Japanese behavior. The roots of such behavior clearly run deep.[100]

"Asia's problems facing its past make it harder to face the future," argued an article published in *Newsweek* magazine pointing, among others, to what is viewed as Japan's failure to come to grips with its warmongering past.[101] The 1994 opinion poll conducted by the Japanese newspaper *Chunichi Shimbun* found lingering resentment against Japan's acts of aggression during WWII. On average 30 per cent of ASEAN leaders thought Japan had not regretted enough its acts of aggression and atrocities committed to the Indonesian people during the WWII occupation. This was in spite of the fact that Tokyo had settled war reparations with Jakarta by providing economic, financial and technological assistance and that several Japanese Prime Ministers formally expressed their regret with regards to their country's actions during WWII.[102]

The data yielded by the 2004–06 research have highlighted a significant diminution of the role of the Indonesian elite's wartime memories in shaping their perceptions of Japan. In contrast to the earlier studies from the early 1970s and 1994, during the interviews conducted as a part of this study, out of the total forty-five, only three respondents recalled and mentioned the Japanese occupation of the Indonesian archipelago during the WWII. Out of these three interviewed leaders, only one explicitly referred the perceived traditional Japanese "territorial expansion ambition" emphasizing that "history is very important" in assessing Indonesia's potential adversaries.[103]

The phenomenon of changed perceptions of Japan can be explained in terms of the generational change in the Indonesian leadership and the fading away of the feelings of hostility against the Japanese for their wartime actions. It can be reasonably assumed that the older generation of Indonesian leaders, who intimately experienced the war, felt much stronger resentment and misgiving toward Japan. Thus, in Weinstein's 1976 study, by far the largest component of the elite was the so-called Generation of 1945, which were leaders born before 1935 who "came of age politically during the 'physical revolution' from 1945 to 1949."[104] On the contrary, the smallest segment of the Indonesian foreign policy elite was the Generation of 1966, or leaders born between 1936 and 1955 who "gained [their] political identity from the struggle to depose Sukarno."[105] By contrast, in this study, the respondents from the Generation of 1945 constituted the smallest segment of the elite, whereas the largest components were the Generation of 1966 and the Generation of the 1980s (respondents born between 1956 and 1969) that made up 47 and 31 per cent of the interviewed leaders respectively. This generation change in the Indonesian leadership is one of the principal factors that account for the shift in the elite perceptions — from rather negative to relatively positive — of Japan.[106]

The Ambivalence about Japanese Economic Aggressiveness

During the tumultuous period of Guided Democracy, the relations between Indonesia and Japan were, unlike the relations with other countries belonging to the Western block, relatively close. After the 1951 San Francisco Treaty, Jakarta's negotiations with Tokyo regarding war repatriations led to an agreement in 1958 and subsequently the establishment of formal diplomatic relations. Over the next twelve years, the Japanese Government disbursed reparations funds to Indonesia and the flow continued even after the Western countries implemented a *de facto* embargo against Sukarno's regime and ceased to provide economic help to Indonesia.[107] Japan proved to be a valuable source of much-needed economic aid during the turbulent years of Sukarno's rule (particularly in the 1962–65 period).[108] Illustrative of the relatively good relationship between Jakarta and Tokyo was also the fact that Sukarno maintained personal ties with Japan. The first Indonesian President visited Tokyo a number of times and married a Japanese woman.

During the New Order regime, Indonesia's relations with Japan became closer than they had been during Guided Democracy. However, the continuing negative perceptions among Indonesian and other regional elites impeded Japan's participation in the political and security affairs of ASEAN. Although Jakarta welcomed Japan into its economic sphere, it generally rejected cooperation with Tokyo in military and political affairs. Indonesia leaders' attitude towards Japan was characterized by ambivalence. They were especially concerned about the rearmament of Japan and about its economic aggressiveness. The legacy of Japanese occupation during WWII was perhaps most felt in military circles. High-ranking military figures were apprehensive of Japanese rearmament and, more generally, there was "a great degree of uncertainty over Japan's regional military role."[109] The military establishment was very much concerned about what kinds of weapons Tokyo decided to acquire and their implications for the security of Southeast Asia. As a high-ranking military officer stated, "Japanese rearmament must be watched with great care in Southeast Asia, and particular attention should be given to the kinds of armaments they choose and what they regard as the limits of their responsibilities."[110]

Concurrently, the leaders were apprehensive of Japanese economic aggressiveness. The elite's ambivalent view on this matter was revealed in the fact that Indonesian leaders could not agree on how dangerous the Japanese economic expansionism really was and what were its implications for Indonesia. Thus, according to Weinstein, while the Indonesian elite was generally inclined to compare Japanese expansionism with the ideological and "fifth column" nature of the "China threat", some leaders were more wary of Japanese economic aggressiveness. Here, Weinstein writes:

> Japan, most agreed, wanted not only to control Southeast Asia economically but to become the hegemonic power of the region, much as the United States in Latin America. Global powers, like the United States and the Soviet Union, already have their spheres of influence; though they seek influence in Indonesia, they were said to be too "settled" to seek complete control. China, on the other hand, might desire such control but was too economically underdeveloped and beset by internal weakness to achieve it. Japan, stronger than China but weaker than the superpowers, was ripe for expansionism. [Therefore], it was frequently asserted that "Japan needs a colony".[111]

On the other hand, when Lt. General Ali Moertopo compared the "economic" threat from Japan and the "ideological" threat from China, he was much more apprehensive of the latter. Moertopo asserted that

> ... for a country like Indonesia, the economic aggressiveness of Japan should and could be channelled into a national policy for development. The case will be quite different with an aggressive ideology, for Indonesia is not only unable to absorb it, but she is not in need of a new ideology since she has already her own identity.[112]

Paradoxically, although Japan contributed a sizable bulk of the foreign direct investment to the rapid growth of the Indonesian economy, especially in the 1980s and 1990s, the negative view of the "land of the rising sun" held on among the elite well until the last decade of the 20th century. Asian countries, in particular those that experienced the ruthlessness of the Japanese occupation, were traumatized by "the second Japanese invasion" which was viewed as the latter's unscrupulous attempt at economic dominance.[113]

In 1974, the relationship between Jakarta and Tokyo reached a critical point when massive anti-Japanese street demonstrations broke out in Indonesia targeting what was perceived as Tokyo's growing economic dominance in the country. Perhaps the most serious riot known as *"Malari"* was a reaction to what was perceived as the New Order government's excessively close relationship with the ethnic Chinese conglomerates and Japanese business interests in the archipelago. In Jakarta, Japan in the role of an indispensable source of support for the Indonesia's economic development generated a peculiar mix of irritation, suspicion and fear. In 1987, Abdoel Raoef Soehoed, a prominent economist, aptly described the then prevalent perception and assessment of the Japanese:

> These fears have been kept alive, unconsciously, by the brisk and aggressive business attitudes of the present Japanese. I have tried to explain this to my Japanese friends many times, but apparently it is still not well understood, because the same attitudes seem to prevail in their own environment, a similar ruthless, competitive way of life. People are fearful of the Japanese because of their relentless way of pursuing their interest.

Concurrently, Soehoed outlined his assessment of the roots of Japanese character:

> It seems to me that there is still an undercurrent or archaic fear in the Japanese mind, bred over centuries of threat. Japan, with a very industrious and intelligent population, but which still harbours a kind of siege mentality, has to be aware of its prominent position now in the world, a prominence which brings with it responsibilities, if it is to be maintained. ... Maybe only time and closer relations [between Japan and Indonesia] will solve the problem."[114]

Changing Perceptions of Japan

Generally, the question explored during the fieldwork in Jakarta was what is the place of Japan in the Indonesian foreign policy elite's threat perceptions, at the outset of the 21st century? To what extent and how has the changing geopolitical context in this part of the world, namely the rising economic and political influence of China, affected the elite's attitude towards Japan? Initially, it needs to be pointed out that some concerns with regards to Japan have remained. For example, during the interviews, several leaders revealed their suspicion of Japan's political and economic agenda in Southeast Asia.[115] Sections of the Indonesian foreign policy elite still seem to be puzzled and feel uneasy about the so-called "second Japanese invasion" by means of unscrupulous Japanese corporations and businesspeople. A former President argued that Japan and the United States think of Indonesia as an "extracting place". The Japanese and American leaders purposely exploit Indonesia by concentrating only on extracting oil and natural resources, instead of manufacturing their products there. This "economic exploitation" constitutes the most imminent threat to Indonesia.[116]

A senior diplomat expressed his belief that Indonesia is "encircled" by Japan, Australia, Singapore and the United States. The "four points" or "four anchors", as he has termed these four countries, are of a great concern for the Indonesian foreign policy elite. According to the diplomat, "the Indonesian policy-makers and diplomats do not understand how to interpret the close cooperation between these countries; when there is an initiative by Washington, the three other countries (Singapore, Canberra and Tokyo) always support it."[117] The Indonesian leadership's wariness stems primarily from the uncertainty about, as the diplomat put it, "what will happen with the 'four anchors' in the region — will this phenomenon have some military meaning, repercussions, for Indonesia?"[118]

However, it is obvious that, rather than being concerned about the danger from Japan itself, the country's foreign policy elite is apprehensive about what the leaders refer to as "negative competition" between Japan and other major powers. Former Minister of Foreign Affairs, for example, considered Japan, along with Russia, China and the U.S. as the four main external pillars of the regional security structure. The threat for Indonesia stems from the possibility that the equilibrium of power among Japan and the three other powers breaks down and Indonesia will be forced to take sides. Such a confrontation could be spawned, for example, by a competition between Japan and China for natural resources in Southeast Asia and the control of the Straits of Malacca. It can be expected, as the former Minister asserted, that "… Beijing would gradually replace Japan in making sure that the Straits, the routes of oil, are safe for China. … I do not know … how many different things will happen, it's very difficult to predict."[119]

Referring to the elite's apprehension about a possible Cold War-like situation, in which Indonesia would be pressured to side with one of the opposing blocks in the conflict, one respondent affirmed that "… for example, if [China's] GDP increases in the next twenty years, whether they will build up their armed forces and whether there will be a competition, I mean negative competition between China and Japan related to security."[120] An IR expert with close ties to DEPLU observed that "[there] are some worries in Indonesia now that the East Asian Community is a vehicle for China and Japan to project their power not in East Asia but in Southeast Asia. So ASEAN becomes a "beautiful girl" where Japan, China and Korea will compete here in Southeast Asia." The IR expert then emphasized: "So, in order to avoid this, to reduce the negative impact of these kinds of things, we need to develop relations not only with East Asia but with India, with Australia, the EU, in order to face China."[121]

Although the negative image of Japan persists in the foreign policy elite's perception, it has largely been supplanted by a much more auspicious view. The changing perception of Japan in Indonesia is apparent, for instance, in a 1990 study, in which Sumantoro admiringly notes that the Indonesians "regard Japan as a dynamic nation. Many fantastic changes have occurred [in Japan] which no other country can manage."[122] In 1999, President Abdurrahman Wahid even called Japan "an elder brother" that had supported Indonesia during the difficult times of the 1997–98 monetary crisis.[123] In contrast to the Cold War era, current Indonesian leaders do not conceal their desire to see Japan play a greater security role in the region.

Japan: From Passive to Assertive Posture

According to a prominent scholar, the attitude towards Japan has undergone a significant change over the last six decades that span the end of the WWII and the first decade of the 21st century. Here, he raised a question: "So, when we [still] remember the bad experience under the Japanese, why do not we hate the Japanese [today]?"[124] The answer can be found in the changing geopolitical and geo-economic environment in Southeast and East Asia. The uncertainty regarding the rise of China appears to have contributed to the relative change in the Indonesian foreign policy elite's perceptions of Japan.

Tokyo renounced war after Japan's defeat in 1945 and the country's pacifist constitution prohibits it from acquiring offensive weaponry and setting its soldiers' feet on foreign soil. Yet, after the delicate process of a more than fifty-year-long gradual departure from its passive stance, Japan has now increasingly displayed a much greater assertiveness in its foreign policy agenda. This tendency became more pronounced when the Koizumi-led administration took office in 2001. Under his leadership, Tokyo set out to implement a foreign policy that would boost Japan's political, diplomatic and military influence to match its economic might. Japan's approach to the first Gulf War in 1991 was still rather tentative as Tokyo only contributed money to safeguard its oil interests in the region. Yet, in the second Gulf War in 2003, the Koizumi's Administration evolved into one of the few staunch allies of the United States in the operation aimed at toppling the Iraqi regime of Saddam Hussein. In light of the world-wide outpouring of anti-war and anti-American sentiments, in 2004 Tokyo sent to Iraq what it claimed were noncombatant troops to help in reconstructing the war-ravaged country.

Japan has proven to be increasingly assertive also in affairs affecting the Southeast Asian region. In January 2002, Tokyo proposed to establish the "Initiative for Development of East Asia" (IDEA) and the "East Asian Community" (EAC) that would include ASEAN countries, Japan, South Korea and China. This idea of an Asian version of the European Union was generally supported by all ten ASEAN states, including Indonesia. During the 2003 ASEAN-Japan Commemorative Summit, Japan joined the Treaty of Amity and Cooperation (the TAC), a non-aggression pact conceived by ASEAN in 1976. Koizumi signed the declaration of intent to join the TAC just a few weeks after China and India signed the Treaty. The TAC's signatories pledge to respect each other's sovereignty, independence and territorial sovereignty.[125]

Moreover, apart from the political and diplomatic sphere, Japan has also adopted a more assertive posture on the level of military cooperation. Tokyo became actively involved in an agreement among Asian nations to fight rampant piracy in the region.[126] In June 2005, for example, Japan dispatched a high-performance armed patrol vessel to the Malacca Strait and carried out a joint drill with the Indonesian military.[127] Generally, the palpable assertiveness of Japan has been welcomed in Southeast Asia. Indonesia, along with other ASEAN countries, has been increasingly accepting of Tokyo's expanding political and security role in Southeast Asia. Indonesian leaders seem to have been quite comfortable with Japan's rising security role, which also includes military aspects, in the region.[128]

Here, we can question why the Indonesian elite has not followed the example of the Chinese and South Korean governments, both of which have repeatedly protested about the Japanese Prime Minister's visits to a controversial war shrine and the country's failure to alter its history books that allegedly whitewash Japan's record in WWII. One interviewed leader described Japan as "more trustworthy and responsible" than China, which was also proven when "the Japanese have apologized a couple of times." The respondent concluded that "[since] the Japanese have apologized, so we are friends."[129] The Indonesian Government's divergent attitude on this issue, by contrast with Beijing's policies, can be understood in terms of the different nature of Southeast Asia's and China's historical encounters with Japan.

Having collated the historical experience of the peoples in Southeast Asia and the Chinese people in the 20th century, Sheng Lijun observed that their respective perceptions

> [are], of course, strongly coloured by history. Whereas the experience Southeast Asians had of Japanese adventurism began in 1941 and lasted for less than four years, the Chinese had chafed under [Japan] way back in 1895 when Japan forced a defeated China to cede Taiwan. Moreover, Japanese mistreatment of Southeast Asians during their occupation was not, in general, as cruel as what was meted out to the Chinese.[130]

Furthermore, he also pointed out that

> ... Japan's invasion of China was overwhelmingly directed at destroying the Chinese nation. ... By comparison, the Japanese invasion of South-East Asia was to destroy not these nations but their colonial governments. ... Japanese Premier Junichiro Koizumi's visits to the Yasukuni shrine honouring the war dead have reopened China's historical wounds again and again...[131]

Japan's gradual move away from pacifism may well turn the country into Asia's major military power. Yet, Indonesian and other Southeast Asian elites have hardly objected to Japan's growing assertiveness. An overwhelming majority of the interviewed leaders expressed a benign view of Japan. In short, in Jakarta, "the land of the rising sun" is no longer seen as a security threat to Indonesia.

The Rationale for Changing Perceptions

How can we explain this phenomenon that while during the Cold War Japan with a more passive foreign policy agenda, was viewed with apprehension in Jakarta, Japan's presently much more assertive foreign policy does not seem to be causing much alarm? Here, we can suggest an explanation: Tokyo's assertiveness has not generated a great deal of concern in Indonesia because Japan now looks less threatening than before, especially vis-à-vis the rising power of China.

Notwithstanding the existing security concerns regarding Japan outlined above, there is an increasing expectation on the part of the Indonesian elite for Tokyo to expand its influence in the region to counterbalance China.

Building on a positive view of Japan's moderate advancement of its regional policies since the 1960s, Indonesian leaders see Japan's participation in the evolving Asian security structures as fundamental to regional stability. In the words of a Minister in President Yudhoyono's government, generally the Indonesian foreign policy elite "[has] to take into account ... the growing assertiveness of Japan" along with the fact that "Japan wants to be accepted as a normal country."[132] Former President Megawati Sukarnoputri repeatedly hailed Japan as "the most important partner for ASEAN."[133]

While gradually adopting a more assertive foreign policy, it has been argued that Japan has been successfully "trying to appear as unthreatening as possible."[134] The fieldwork in Indonesia yielded some clues that help explain the positive change in the elite's perceptions of Japan. Here, we can identify three principal factors: first, Japan's sensible approach to security cooperation with ASEAN, namely its signing of the ZOPFAN Declaration and TAC Treaty; second, Tokyo's close alliance with the United States; and, third, in comparison with China, Japan's policies and intentions appear more benign.

The first factor is Tokyo's sensibly implemented policy of "security partnership" with ASEAN. Japan's accession to the TAC in December 2003 signified a deeper involvement of the country in ASEAN's political and security affairs, including military aspects. Bantarto Bandoro, an expert with the CSIS, concluded that by signing the TAC, "... it would also beef up Japan's regional security role. ... Both sides (ASEAN and Japan) are facing tremendous new geopolitical challenges ... such as terrorism and its security and economic impacts. ... This is not only good for ASEAN, but also for long-term stability and security in the region."[135] ASEAN states and Japan also, for example, agreed to work together to establish an East Asian Community, which would also include China and South Korea. Here, both Indonesian President Megawati and Japanese Prime Minister Koizumi played down criticism that Tokyo's growing assertiveness in implementing closer security cooperation with Indonesia and other ASEAN countries was a part of a strategy to counterbalance China's growing influence.[136] To this end, at least three leaders highlighted Tokyo's signing the ZOPFAN and TAC and emphasized that it is largely because of such Japanese attitudes that "Japan is not [no longer] considered a threat to Indonesia".[137] By joining both the ZOPFAN and TAC, Japan has confirmed its commitment to be "a part of the regional architecture."[138] Since the Declaration and the Treaty were signed also by India and China, as a former Foreign Minister optimistically stated, it signifies that "between these three, there must be an agreed set of guidelines, of principles, of relationships."[139]

The second factor contributing to Japan's benign image arises from its alliance with the United States. There is a sense among the members of the Indonesian foreign policy elite that Tokyo's formal, close association with Washington results in Japan's potential military or political adventurism being kept in check. They believe that as long as the "land of the rising sun" is engaged in the security alliance with the United States, there is no reason for Asian nations to be apprehensive of Japan's military capability. A prominent leader argued that the Japanese, if allowed to "get on top", are likely to become "domineering and brutal", but if the United States keeps them "under their thumb", they will remain "meek and mild-mannered".[140] Also Lam notes that "Southeast Asian states no longer have an allergic reaction to Tokyo's playing a larger political and security role in the region — insofar as it remains allied to the U.S."[141]

There is a prevailing sense that as long as it is in alliance with the United States, Tokyo could afford not to launch a full-scale militarization. China's growing military muscle and North Korea's missile test-firing have put Japan with its pacifist constitution in a complicated position. As foreign policy expert Dewi Fortuna Anwar asserted, "I think it is dilemmatic for Japan. On one hand, there is a real (military) threat, but on the other hand, Japan's move to build its military will create suspicions among neighbouring countries."[142] From the Indonesian elite's perspective, a Japan with an enhanced military capability would be detrimental to stability in East and Southeast Asia because it would only increase tension among the regional states. Conceding that "visits by Japanese leaders to the Yasukuni shrine alone can create problems," Dewi Fortuna Anwar concluded that "there would be a setback in the region if Japan built up its military."[143]

Provided that Tokyo limits the use of Japanese armed forces to UN peacekeeping operations or low-key support of the American-led military operations, such as in case of the U.S.-led military offensive against Iraq, Japan's overall benign image in Indonesia is likely to be sustained. To make up for its relative lack of military capabilities, Tokyo has been in a security alliance with Washington for more than forty years. The relationship between Japan and the United States, which is based on a very close economic and military cooperation, was further strengthened in the 1990s. It is argued that "[as] long as Japan is in the security alliance with the U.S., people aren't seriously scared or fearful of Japan's military capability."[144] Referring to the ASEAN elite's perceptions of the strategic cooperation between Tokyo and Washington, Hund concluded: "Japan's economic stability and strength is seen as a guarantee for regional economic stability. In political terms, Western-leaning Japan is seen as a counterweight to emerging China."[145]

The third factor stems from the fact that the Indonesian elite consider Japan's present policies and its perceived future intentions as more benign in comparison to those of China. Generally, there is a pronounced tendency among the leaders to juxtapose their perception of Japan to that of China. For example, one respondent, when asked about her view of China, argued that while "the word 'love' is not the right lexicon here [as] Indonesia-China relations are purely based on a pragmatic consideration", the Indonesian elite's attitude towards Japan is generally very positive.[146] The interviewed leader explained:

> Strangely enough, if we compare it with Japan, I think Indonesia and Indonesians have a more friendly attitude towards Japan (just think that Japan occupied Indonesia for three and a half years). It's because Japan brings technology, modernity and Japan has become the role model for Indonesia in terms of development. I think the lexicon "love" exists in relations with Japan.[147]

The Japanese military capability, which is regarded, in contrast to the growing Chinese military power, as weaker and not offensive, constitutes a major reason why Japan now looks less threatening than in the mid 1990s and earlier. According to Lam,

> [in] the next decade or two, the economic rise of China is unlikely to displace Japan in the region. … [the] Southeast Asian states would welcome Japan as a counterweight to China, especially when the latter is making rapid progress and emerging as a great power. … The best scenario for Southeast Asia is not "China rising, Japan declining." Ideally, it is "China rising, Japan recovering."[148]

The Indonesian foreign policy elite is not very much concerned about the Japanese military as long as it is kept in check by the military alliance with the United States. By contrast, there is no guarantee of a similar kind in the case of China's military capability. As a former high-ranking military officer argued,

> [if] it is to be seen in comparison with other states, the potential in China exists. India is preoccupied in the subcontinent of South Asia; Japan has been engaged by the presence of the U.S., which leaves China as the major power who has the potential to develop without any preoccupation in their developments.[149]

Japan in Indonesian Foreign Policy

While Tokyo has in the last few years implemented gradual moves away from pacifism, it has simultaneously succeeded in the attempt to appear as unthreatening as possible. Japan's enhanced stature in Southeast Asia does not come to be seen as a threat in the light of China's rising power. On the contrary, Indonesian leaders have hardly showed any disapproval or objections to Tokyo's growing assertiveness exactly because, as Mak and Hamzah put it, they would like to see Japan "used as a countervailing power to China's military might."[150]

Generally, the consensus among the Indonesian foreign policy elite is that, on balance, while Japan's influence in Southeast Asia had declined from the mid-1990s, China's had risen substantially.[151] Faced with the growing power of China, there is an increasing convergence of interests and common strategic outlook between Jakarta and Tokyo. Referring to the idea shared by the elites of both countries that the East Asia community building should be a more inclusive project, the Japanese Ambassador to Indonesia Yutaka Iimura stated: "Japan, Indonesia and Singapore have been looking for this inclusiveness from the beginning. And now there is an emerging consensus that this community and summit should be inclusive."[152] In the context of the uncertainty that arises from the rise of China, several leaders emphasized that there is a need for Japan to stay engaged in the security arrangements in Southeast Asia. Describing it as an "indirect psychological insurance", one leader explained: "So that is why we also want at the same time Japan to play a greater security role in East Asia and then invite India on board in the multilateral security arrangement."[153]

INDIA (VERSUS CHINA JUXTAPOSITION)

Much like the above discussed cases of Australia and Japan, the case of India also demonstrates the high degree to which elite perceptions about another state actor can change over a period of three decades. While India was all but missing in Weinstein's 1976 and Tilman's 1987 studies,[154] this research revealed the growing salience of India in the Indonesian foreign policy elite's national security considerations.

Weinstein's account of the Indonesian elite's view of India was limited to an assertion that a number of interviewed leaders "spoke of the four 'big powers' of Asia: Japan, China, India, and Indonesia," adding that "in the future there would be three 'spheres of influence' in Asia: Japan's in the north, India's in the south, and Indonesia's in Southeast Asia."[155] In contrast to the earlier studies, the respondents participating in the 2004–06 survey frequently brought up the case of India to emphasize the increasingly significant role this country plays in Indonesia's *inclusive* foreign policy. It is also important to note that no single leader identified India as a present threat to Indonesia.

During the Cold War era, whilst friendly enough owing to the deeply-entrenched historical ties, India and Indonesia saw one another as being ideologically part of the rival power bloc in the bipolar conflict. Moreover, each of the governments implemented different economic policies, reducing incentives for closer cooperation. However, as a part of the accelerating process of liberalization of the Indian economy in the 1990s, India in 1994 launched the "Look East" policy. What followed was New Delhi's conscious policy of strengthening ties with countries to the east, particularly with ASEAN countries. Today, India is one of the world's fastest growing economies, second only to China. The country now participates in the grouping's annual summit and also takes part as a full dialogue partner in the annual ASEAN Regional Forum.

Several respondents pointed out that, on the whole, there are no insurmountable obstacles for Indonesia and other regional countries in building closer ties with India. This is because, historically, mutual relations have been largely characterized by peaceful economic and cultural interactions. It was argued that the Indonesian leaders' comfort level with India is higher than with China and some other regional countries. As a senior GOLKAR official aptly stated, "[all] Chinese emperors were able to build strong military … sailing to Java in the past. [By contrast] India is not historically seen as a threat."[156]

There is a prevalent sense among the Indonesian foreign policy elite that, when compared to India, China constitutes in the long run a considerably greater security threat to Indonesia. A high-ranking diplomat observed that "India is focusing more on its domestic problems — New Delhi is preoccupied with its own region, namely Pakistan. [By contrast] China has really moved into the [Southeast Asian] region."[157] Similarly, another leader pointed out that, unlike China that has successfully extended its influence into the Southeast Asia, "India is primarily preoccupied in the subcontinent of South Asia."[158] In light of these perceptions, the elite regards China as the main external factor that needs to be constrained, and India (and Japan), whose power is seen as more benign and limited, as countries that should provide the necessary counterweight.

Indonesia has encouraged India's deeper engagement in the regional economic and security arrangements for strategic balance reasons. As former Indian foreign secretary Salman Haider pointedly notes, "… India also saw that Southeast Asia never ceased to be wary of the Chinese giant hovering above, and was thus constantly in search of a counterweight."[159] While the steadily growing cooperation between India and Indonesia, and ASEAN more generally, is seen as a welcome process in Jakarta, several members of the elite emphasized that the desirable development would be if "India will grow and become a more important country."[160] According to Subianto,

> [at] this point, some ASEAN countries view the entry of India into the whole framework of co-operation as the strategic means to balance the influence of Northeast Asian countries, which are much superior compared to those of Southeast Asia. ... It is clear that India's strategic importance in counter-balancing the overwhelming influence of Northeast Asia — China in particular, in the sub-region of Southeast Asia, remains to be seen.[161]

In short, the consensus among the respondents is that "we (Indonesia) should also increase our relationship with India"[162] because "its rise gives [us] many more options and helps establish a balance."[163]

ASEAN COUNTRIES

Jakarta's relationship with ASEAN is considered the most significant aspect of Indonesian foreign policy.[164] The survey data have revealed that a relatively large number of the country's senior leaders view some of Indonesia's neighbours as posing a great danger to the island nation's security. It is perhaps not so surprising that the United States, Australia and China are at present considered as the three greatest state-based external security threats to Indonesia. What might be of concern for the architects of the ASEAN integration process, however, is that Singapore and Malaysia rank as no. 4 and no. 5 security threats in the Indonesian elite's threat assessment, well ahead of Japan, India or the European powers. More specifically, 13 per cent of respondents identified Singapore and 9 per cent of them Malaysia as currently the principal malign factor affecting Indonesia's national interests and security.[165]

We will now set out to examine the roots of the Indonesian elite's threat perceptions of its neighbours. In terms of the factors that shape the leaders' images of other Southeast Asian states, we can identify four categories of attitudes:

- essentially conspiracy theories,
- sense of vulnerability to military invasion,

- religion-driven suspicions, and
- the "economic threat".

Indonesia and ASEAN: The Sources of Elite's Security Concerns

First, conspiracy theories seem to have traditionally played an important part in the formation of Indonesian foreign policy. More generally, deep-rooted prejudices are one of the main factors that shape the way the elite views Indonesia's neighbours. Wanandi correctly argues that "... perceptions about each other are still influenced by stereotypes and clichés, which have yet to be overcome. Indonesia sees Singapore as having a *kiasu* (self-centred and self-interested) mentality, mixed with some arrogance towards Indonesia."[166] Moreover, as a high-ranking diplomat pointed out, "in some quarters, I have to say, is inherent xenophobia or sense of over-suspicion about intentions of others."[167] Another leader agreed that "Indonesians are very good at conspiracy theories." In his view, the reason for the Indonesians' tendency to be easily influenced by conspiracy theories can be found in their historical knowledge: "We have a very strong tendency to apply our experience under the Dutch. ... So we always suspect foreign governments because of that experience. That has become an [eternal] element in our mentality."[168]

As has been pointed out, the main concern among Indonesian leaders seems to be directed at Malaysia and Singapore. Several leaders suggested that Singapore and Malaysia are two foreign powers seeking to exploit Indonesia's internal problems. These two Indonesian neighbours do not want Indonesia to be a strong country. One leader alleged that Singapore and Malaysia seek to weaken the archipelagic nation, especially by plotting to divide the Riau Province so that they can take an advantage of it. According to him, threat No. 1 to Indonesia is Singapore and no. 2 is Malaysia.[169] This case clearly illustrates the pervasive sense of Indonesia's weakness among the nation's elite. As shown earlier, the leaders are generally convinced that Indonesia is in a weaker position vis-à-vis other regional states. This is why, as a young diplomat argued, because of Indonesia's weakness, "Singapore can exploit Indonesia".[170] Another young diplomat suggested that the aim of the Singapore's government is to subdue Indonesia and thus make Indonesia its backyard or hinterland. But, according to him, "it can not be spoken openly".[171]

It could be argued that while the belief in a conspiracy theory among sections of the population is unlikely to significantly affect government policy at the elite level, it is bound to influence and potentially inflict serious damage to the state's foreign relations. Consequently, it might be of concern when a university-educated senior official of the PDI-P party and close aide to the former President Megawati Sukarnoputri asserted that Malaysia and Singapore have their missiles directed at Jakarta, Medan and other cities in Indonesia and, because of this, they pose a dire threat to the archipelagic nation's sovereignty.[172]

Malaysia, as one leader argued, attempts to break Indonesia's territorial integrity by exploiting Indonesia's internal problems, such as corruption and illegal logging in Kalimantan. Here, he explained:

> So, I think this is very dangerous. And you know exactly that the border line between Indonesia and Malaysia almost every year they move it to the south. ... According a Japanese expert who has been undertaking a research on the relationship between Dayaks in Kalimantan and Sarawak, they see that since since years ago the borderland is going to the south. The military people, because they have illegal business related to the timber, they move the borderland from the Malaysian side to the Indonesian side.[173]

Though rarely expressing its anxieties publicly, Indonesia's military establishment suspects certain elements in Malaysia of having provided tacit support for those elements involved in Indonesia's frequent regional rebellions, namely members of the GAM (*Gerakan Aceh Merdeka* — Free Aceh Movement). These suspicions stem from the awareness that Malaysian authorities did not object when some GAM activists abroad used the country and especially its capital city as a safe haven.[174] To this end, the authoritative journal *Tempo* argued that owing to these attitudes in official circles in Malaysia and also in light of the appalling mistreatment of Indonesian domestic workers and visitors in Malaysia — who are even "derogatively called *Indons* by Malaysians[175] — "perhaps we need to re-examine the relationship."[176]

Secondly, we have already highlighted the pervasive sense of weakness among Indonesian leaders. Under the Sukarno and Suharto's leadership, Indonesia was the strongest military power in Southeast Asia and, as some leaders argue, now even Singapore and the Philippines are stronger.[177] Particularly the leaders' sentiments vis-à-vis Singapore are characterized by a resentment concerning the island state's economic success because, as Jusuf Wanandi puts it,

> ... they believe it has been built on the back of Indonesian exports and resources. ... Some believe that Singaporean businesses have been too cosy with the Indonesian conglomerates that were linked to Suharto cronies. Still others feel that Singaporeans, rather than suffering and

sympathising with Indonesia during its recent years of difficulty, have
benefited at their expense.[178]

There is clearly anxiety coupled with frustration among the majority of the
Indonesian elite, in particular, about Singapore's "capacity to intervene in
Indonesian territory."[179] This perception is partially fuelled by the fact that
some maritime boundaries between the two states have not been properly
delineated. The problem is further complicated by Singapore's land reclamation
that has created some uncertainties regarding the location of the boundaries.
Referring to the elite's suspicion of Singapore's long-term intentions with
regards to the question of territorial boundaries, one leader explained that

> [the] Indonesian elite see to some extent Singapore as a problem.
> Because we still have a problem with the air space where all of the
> Indonesian aircraft flying to the northern part of Indonesia we have to
> pay to Singapore because the air is basically controlled by the Changi
> Airport. So there is a perception that it is very easy for foreign powers
> to intervene into Indonesia … because of the inability of Indonesia to
> control the airspace. … Once you enter the Indonesian territory north
> of the Equator line, then it is controlled by Singapore. So there is this
> perception about Singapore.[180]

Thirdly, a thorough evaluation of the research data has demonstrated that the
respondents' religious background substantially determines their perceptions
of other countries. This is nowhere more obvious than in the case of the
predominantly Muslim Malaysia, which has been earmarked as a security
threat to Indonesia solely by the leaders who come from non-Muslim
background. On the contrary, several Muslim leaders have named Singapore
as a threat to Indonesia. A case in point is the expressed deep suspicion of
Singapore by a senior leader of *Muhammadiyah* because of Singapore's close
military ties with Israel. There is especially a sense of irritation that Singapore
trains its soldiers in Israel. Moreover, the Muslim leader expressed his negative
attitude to Thailand and the Philippines because they are "close friends"
with the United States."[181] This case suggests that, in the future, religion as
a crucial variable might act as a "double-edged weapon" in creating benign
images among Southeast Asian states. Common culture, based on language,
ethnicity and, particularly, religion, arguably facilitates the creation of the
"we-ness" feeling, which in turn enhances an emotive affinity, shared identity
and thus benign images. Consequently, we can assume that while in some
cases religion will enhance mutual trust, in other cases it is likely to maintain
or even strengthen the mutual distrust among elites in different countries.

Finally, the most prominent source of threatening images that the Indonesia's leaders attribute to its neighbours is what they call an "economic threat". We can thus see that there has been a shift in the nature of the threat from a more conventional[182] to non-conventional threat. Again, it is mainly Singapore and Malaysia which are seen as jeopardizing Indonesia's economic interests. Several leaders have suggested that Singapore already is and might well in the future become economically an even greater threat to Indonesia.[183] Some leaders are worried, for example, that following the implementation of the U.S.-Singapore Free Trade Agreement (FTA), Indonesian products going through Singapore to the U.S. market will require a special anti-terrorism certificate. Indonesia's economic position vis-à-vis Singapore's will be further weakened, as Indonesian products will be disadvantaged vis-à-vis Singaporean products.[184]

There is also a growing concern that, as regional investors from Singapore, Malaysia and Thailand increasingly acquire strategic Indonesian assets, notably banks, the country will become more vulnerable and subject to pressures from its neighbours.[185] For example, Singapore government-owned Temasek Holdings acquired, despite pro-nationalist protests, a number of strategic assets in Indonesia particularly in the post-reform period. Former Indonesian President B.J. Habibie then referred to Singapore using highly derogatory words "*little red dot*". Drawing on this characterization, while admitting that "[though] Singapore may be small in size", Indonesian media unequivocally warned that "through Temasek Holdings Pte. Ltd., that *little red dot* is like the mouse that roared, turning giant neighbour Indonesia into one of its 'play areas'." This is why, as one article observed, "... since its early appearance in Indonesia, Temasek seems to have aroused suspicion."[186] In 2007, ten years after Temasek "shopped" for various "strategic assets that it bought at discounted prices, according to an article provocatively titled "Taming Temasek", the Indonesian KPPU (*Komisi Pengawas Persaingan Usaha* — Commission for the Supervision of Business Competition) declared that Temasek had violated the Indonesian anti-monopoly law and was thus forced to sell some of its assets in the country.[187]

The awareness of Indonesia's myriad domestic problems reinforces the elite's sense of insecurity and their view that its neighbours seek to exploit Indonesia. A further problem is the failure to conclude an extradition treaty with Singapore partially due to differences of interpretation of what should be considered as "economic criminality". Indonesian journal *Tempo* characterized Singapore as "the preferred 'country of exile for Indonesian tycoons having legal problems", while emphasizing that, according to the Indonesian Corruption Watch (ICW), there are at least ten fugitives "living comfortably in the Lion City."[188] This led one leader to express the pervasive sense among the elite that "Singapore is still a threat to Indonesian economy. Because Singapore right now is still keeping the money stolen from our country by the Chinese *konglomerat hitam*."[189] According to one leader,

> [of] course, there is a perception, it is about political interaction, economic sensitivities, of Singapore, Australia but the main security concern is still very much internal problems. ... Now we are facing economic and social crisis in Indonesia. But the main point is [that] the social capital within the Indonesian society and the economic crisis is very easy to exploit to become social unrest or political instability. That's the main problem. And I think it's very reasonable.[190]

Hence, there appears to be a clear correlation between Indonesia's economic, political and social difficulties on the one hand, and the tendency to view the outside world with suspicion and distrust.

Indonesia and ASEAN: Allaying Suspicions, Building Trust

Notwithstanding the persistent distrust towards Indonesia's neighbours, there is, however, awareness among the foreign policy elite of the necessity to "allay any left-over feelings of threat that may still exist between neighbours [in Southeast Asia]."[191] Arguing that the original ASEAN Treaty should be strengthened so that Singapore, Malaysia and Indonesia and other regional states do not feel threatened by each other, Foreign Minister Hassan Wirayuda pointed out that,

> [we] are lucky in the past thirty seven years of ASEAN's existence that we didn't have war. But when we talk about the perception of a threat, [if] you ask Singapore what it thinks of [as a] threat ... it's their immediate neighbours. ... [Until now, within ASEAN] there are more elements of competition rather than cohesion.[192]

The overwhelming majority of the elite shares the view that only if mutual suspicion and disagreements among ASEAN countries can be overcome and a common identity and the ensuing common threat perception created, will Indonesia and other regional states be able to strengthen their position vis-à-vis and thus deal with the major powers. As a former Foreign Minister observed, "[we] believe that people should get together on the basis of a common perception of their security needs, common perception of their security problems."[193] Also a senior diplomat emphasized that it is vital for

ASEAN countries to find a common ground and create the "we-feeling notion."[194] In the Indonesian case, this means that the elite must strive to allay fears of its neighbours about Southeast Asia's largest country trying to dominate the region. The diplomat argued that

> [Indonesia's foreign policy elite must be mindful of the regional environment. ... Size can be a liability and hence Indonesia has to be sensitive. Since the other countries are looking to Indonesia with suspicion, Indonesia has to exercise restraint. Indonesia has to earn leadership and to invest something into it.[195]

During the interviews, especially China was highlighted as the power that is keen to employ the "divide and rule" strategy towards ASEAN in an attempt to "dominate the grouping."[196] For a prominent policy-maker, "ASEAN is the main pillar [and] in the future when China has become powerful I agree that China will seek hegemony. We have to be careful ... we have to cooperate with China but mainly through ASEAN."[197] Indonesia's approach to the East Asian Community project offers here a useful insight into the role of ASEAN in the Indonesian elite's national security considerations. According to Subianto, "ASEAN might play its strategic interlocutory roles to striking a balanced and healthy relationship within the framework of East Asian co-operation [whereby] the latter can be pursued if ASEAN is unified..."[198]

With the ASEAN countries' mutual suspicions overcome and their threat perceptions unified, Natalegawa argues that it will be easier for Indonesia (and other ASEAN states) to manoeuvre its relationship with the major powers:

> ... we need to think beyond the "+3" countries as the constituents of the East Asia Summit by looking also at India, Australia and New Zealand. Hence, rather than looking at the ASEAN+3 as the exclusive constituting elements of the East Asia Summit, we should visualize ASEAN occupying the "hub", with three "spokes", namely the "+3" countries to its north, India to its west and Australia and New Zealand to its southeast."[199]

Underlying the view that the ASEAN states would strengthen their position vis-à-vis major powers only if they manage to overcome mutual suspicion is the following central idea: The existence of multiple external threats, which simultaneously affect several countries, generates incentives for all parties to look for ways of eliminating their common enemies and hence facilitate the mutual construction of benign images.[200]

CONCLUSION

This chapter has analysed Indonesian foreign policy elite's perceptions of Australia, Japan, India and ASEAN countries. It is apparent that the leaders' attitudes to these state actors need to be seen in the light of their primary concern about the United States and China as the two major external factors with the greatest potential to adversely affect Indonesia's national interest and security. The data evaluation has highlighted the belief among the elite that the so-called inclusive foreign policy will make it easier for Jakarta to maintain a favourable position vis-à-vis the two competing major powers and thus help Indonesia to manage its external security environment.

In the first part, we saw that, in contrast to the situation in the 1970s, Australia is at present one of the highest concerns among the elite. The Australian military involvement in East Timor in 1999 was the turning point that significantly changed the Indonesian foreign policy elite's perceptions of its southern neighbour. However, the discussion also argued that the persistent diplomatic efforts by Jakarta to improve the Indonesia-Australia relationship can be seen as a vital part of its hedging strategy aimed at eliminating potentially unfavourable implications of the growing influence of China in the region.

The second part outlined the change in the elite's perceptions of Japan from an "ambiguous threat" in the 1970s and 1980s to the present awareness that Japan is an indispensable part of Indonesia's long-term national security strategy. It highlighted the phenomenon that although Japan has in the last few years implemented a more assertive foreign policy, it has been seen in Jakarta as a lesser threat than previously when Tokyo still adhered to its pacifist Constitution. It was argued here that Japan's increasingly assertive foreign policy is welcomed by the elite insofar as Japan is considered as an important counterweight to China's expanding influence.

In the third part, the key theme was the growing importance of India in the Indonesian foreign policy elite's long-term national security considerations. It was demonstrated that, owing to largely peaceful economic and cultural interaction between these two countries, the Indonesian leaders' comfort level with India is higher than with China. And, finally, we analysed the sources of the elite's negative perceptions of Indonesia's neighbours. In particular, the data evaluation has shown that the leaders consider Singapore as no. 4 and Malaysia as no. 5 security threats to the country. Yet, the respondents simultaneously expressed a strong conviction that the countries in ASEAN need to overcome mutual suspicion and disagreements in order to create a common identity and the ensuing common threat perception, which will in turn strengthen their position vis-à-vis the major powers.

More generally, as China is seen as the principal danger in the long run and a number one external factor that needs to be constrained, Australia, Japan, India and ASEAN countries are all considered as important elements in Jakarta's hedging strategy that aims to eliminate the potentially negative implications of the rise of China. In other words, we have seen that Indonesian policymakers clearly want the country's foreign relations to remain on an open course, and remain multidirectional.

Notes

1   Interview with a former Indonesian President, Jakarta, 10 January 2005.

2   Quoted in an interview with a former Indonesian Minister of Foreign Affairs, Jakarta, 14 January 2005; the topic was also discussed during an interview with, for example, a senior Indonesian diplomat, a high-ranking official in DEPLU, Jakarta, 25 January 2005; and a CSIS-based international relations expert, Jakarta, 8 February 2005; the quotation contains author's emphasis.

3   Mohammad Hatta, "An Independent Active Foreign Policy", *Foreign Affairs*, Vol. XXXI (April 1953); also published in: Herbert Feith and Lance Castles, *Indonesian Political Thinking, 1945–1965* (Ithaca and London: Cornell University Press, 1970), p. 453.

4   Interview with a CSIS-based international relations expert, Jakarta, 8 February 2005.

5   Ibid.

6   Interview with an Indonesian expert in international relations, CSIS, Jakarta, 21 February 2005.

7   Interview with an Indonesian academic and expert in the Indonesian military, Jakarta, 24 January 2005.

8   Ibid.

9   Interview with an Indonesian scholar and IR expert affiliated with LIPI, Jakarta, 24 February 2005.

10   Samuel P. Huntington, "The Lonely Superpower", *Foreign Affairs* (March/April 1999).

11   "Indonesia and Japan: Economic and Political Relations and Implications for Southeast Asia", USINDO seminar, Washington D.C. (13 September 2004).

12   Interview with a CSIS-based international relations expert, Jakarta, 8 February 2005; the quotation contains the author's emphasis.

13   Andrew MacIntyre, "Powdered Fear and Hate", *The Australian*, 3 June 2005.

14   Paul Daley, "Breach of Trust", *The Bulletin*, 20 April 2004, pp. 36–37.

15   Interview with a senior Indonesian career diplomat, DEPLU, Jakarta, 12 January 2005.

16   Abu Hanifah, *Tales of a Revolution* (Sydney: Angus and Robertson Publishers, 1972), pp. 259–60.
17   Interview with a senior Indonesian career diplomat, DEPLU, Jakarta, 12 January 2005.
18   Interview with an Indonesian expert in international relations, CSIS, Jakarta, 21 February 2005.
19   Interview with a former Indonesian Minister of Foreign Affairs, Jakarta, 14 January 2005.
20   Among other articles, the Australia-Indonesia Security Pact was discussed in: Rizal Sukma, "Indonesia Toughens China Stance", *Far Eastern Economic Review* 159, no. 36, 5 September 1996; John McBeth, "Personal Pact: Suharto, Keating Surprise ASEAN with Security Deal", *Far Eastern Economic Review* 159, no. 1, 28 December/4 January 1996.
21   R.M. Sunardi, "Australia-Indonesia Defence Cooperation: An Indonesian Perspective", in *Indonesia: Dealing with a Neighbour*, edited by Colin Brown (St. Leonards: Allen & Unwin, 1996), p. 55.
22   Ibid., p. 57.
23   Interview with a senior Indonesian career diplomat, DEPLU, Jakarta, 12 January 2005.
24   "Isolated Indonesia Eyes Australia for Support", *Stratfor*, Stratfor Geopolitics Analysis (11 February 2002).
25   Interview with a senior Indonesian career diplomat, DEPLU, Jakarta, 12 January 2005.
26   "'Howard Doctrine' Provokes Malaysian Rage", *Asia Times Online*, 25 September 1999, <www.atimes.com> (accessed 20 April 2005).
27   Philip Bowring, "Australia: Deputy Sheriff Down Under", *International Herald Tribune*, 18 July 2003.
28   Anthony L. Smith, "Australia-Indonesia Relations: Getting Beyond East Timor", Special Assessment: Asia's Bilateral Relations, Working Paper (Honolulu: Asia-Pacific Centre for Security Studies, October 2004).
29   Interview with an Indonesian leader and academic affiliated with LIPI, Jakarta, 14 February 2005.
30   Interview with a senior Indonesian career diplomat, DEPLU, Jakarta, 12 January 2005.
31   Interview with a former Indonesian high-ranking military officer and senior diplomat, Jakarta, 14 February 2005.
32   Interview with a senior official of PDI-P, Jakarta, 22 February 2005.
33   Interview with a senior Indonesian career diplomat, Jakarta, 12 January 2005.
34   Interview with an Indonesian Army general and member of GOLKAR, Jakarta, 15 February 2005.
35   Interview with a senior member of Muhammadiyah Muslim organization, 23 February 2005.

36   For a detailed discussion on the West Papua problem, see: Richard Chauvel and Ikrar Nusa Bhakti, "The Papua Conflict: Jakarta's Perceptions and Policies", Policy Studies 5 (Washington D.C.: East-West Centre, 2004).

37   "Isolated Indonesia Eyes Australia for Support", *Stratfor*, Stratfor Geopolitics Analysis (11 February 2002).

38   Budi Setyarso et al., "Not a Total Recall", *Tempo*, 4–10 April 2006, pp. 16–17.

39   Wenseslaus Manggut and Lita Utomo, "Kicked by the Kangaroo", *Tempo*, 4–10 April 2006, pp. 12–14.

40   Interview with an Indonesian political scientist, LIPI, Jakarta, 24 February 2005.

41   Endy M. Bayuni, "Neighbourhood Security and Courtesy", *Jakarta Post*, 5 August 2006.

42   Interview with a senior Indonesian career diplomat, DEPLU, Jakarta, 12 January 2005.

43   Ibid.

44   Interview with a former Indonesian Minister of Foreign Affairs, Jakarta, 14 January 2005.

45   Interview with an Indonesian political scientist, LIPI, Jakarta, 24 February 2005.

46   Ibid.

47   Ibid.

48   Bayuni, "Neighbourhood Security and Courtesy".

49   Interview, Jakarta, 2005.

50   See also an article discussing this issue in: Daniel Novotny, "The Threat from Misperception", *Postscript* II, no. 6, a journal published by The Habibie Centre, Jakarta (June 2005).

51   According to Malaysian Prime Minister Abdullah Ahmad Badawi, Malaysia is also "constantly plagued by a perception problem, one that particularly afflicts the decision-making process of a large number of foreign investors." He characterized the perception problem among foreign investors as quite serious. Discussed in: "Malaysia — A Story Waiting to Be Told", *Straits Times*, 24 March 2005, p. 6.

52   Michelle Grattan, "Australians Grow Wary of Threat from Indonesia", *The Age*, 22 August 2004.

53   David Lague, "Australia Reconsiders Non-Aggression Pact with Asians", *International Herald Tribune*, 13 April 2005.

54   This was mentioned, for example, during the interview with an Indonesian political scientist, LIPI, Jakarta, 24 February 2005 and with a senior Indonesian career diplomat, DEPLU, Jakarta, 12 January 2005.

55   Simon Philpott, "Fear of Dark: Indonesia and the Australian National Imagination", *Australian Journal of International Affairs* 55, no. 3 (November 2001): 371.

56   Interview with an Indonesian political scientist, LIPI, Jakarta, 24 February 2005.

57 Interview wit a former Minister of Foreign Affairs, Jakarta, 14 January 2005.
58 Interview with an Indonesian diplomat, DEPLU, Jakarta, 25 February 2005.
59 Moegiadi, "Educational Links and the Dynamics of People-to-People Relations: An Indonesian Perspective", in *Indonesia: Dealing with a Neighbour*, edited by Colin Brown (St. Leonards: Allen & Unwin, 1996), pp. 135–40.
60 Interviews with young Indonesian career diplomats, DEPLU, Jakarta, 25 February 2005.
61 Interview with an Indonesian political scientist, LIPI, Jakarta, 24 February 2005.
62 Interview with a young Indonesian career diplomat, DEPLU, Jakarta, 25 February 2005.
63 Ibid.
64 Ibid.
65 Ibid.
66 Ibid; See also an editorial in: Dean Durber, "Racism within Australian Culture", *Jakarta Post*, 4 June 2005.
67 Interview with a senior Indonesian career diplomat, DEPLU, Jakarta, 12 January 2005.
68 Interview with an Indonesian expert in international relations, CSIS, Jakarta, 21 February 2005.
69 Interview with a young Muslim leader, an expert in a well-known Jakarta-based think-tank, Jakarta, 25 February 2005.
70 Interview with an Indonesian expert in international relations, CSIS, Jakarta, 21 February 2005.
71 Bayuni, "Neighbourhood Security and Courtesy".
72 Ali Alatas, *The Pebble in the Shoe — The Diplomatic Struggle for East Timor* (Jakarta: Aksara Karunia, 2006).
73 Interview with an Indonesian scholar and IR expert affiliated with LIPI, Jakarta, 24 February 2005.
74 Interview with a former Indonesian President, Jakarta, 10 January 2005.
75 Interview with an Indonesian expert in international relations, CSIS, Jakarta, 21 February 2005.
76 Interview with a former admiral of the Indonesian Navy, Jakarta, 24 February 2005.
77 Interview with a former Indonesian Minister of Foreign Affairs, Jakarta, 14 January 2005.
78 Interview with an Indonesian expert in international relations, CSIS, Jakarta, 21 February 2005.
79 Sunardi, "Australia-Indonesia Defence Cooperation: An Indonesian Perspective", p. 62.
80 Interview with a former Indonesian Minister of Foreign Affairs, Jakarta, 14 January 2005.
81 Interview with a senior Indonesian career diplomat, DEPLU, Jakarta, 12 January 2005.

82 Daniel Sneider, "Asia's Polite Reception to Bush Masks Declining U.S. Influence: Growing Regional Cooperation Threatens U.S. Pre-eminence in East Asia", Yale Global Online Magazine, 17 November 2005, <http://yaleglobal.yale. edu/display.article?id=6531> (accessed 12 April 2006).

83 Mohan Malik, "China and the East Asian Summit: More Discord than Accord" (Honolulu: Asia-Pacific Centre for Security Studies, February 2006), p. 5.

84 Ibid., p. 5.

85 Interview with a high-ranking official in DEPLU, Jakarta, 28 February 2005.

86 Interview with an Indonesian expert in international relations, CSIS, Jakarta, 21 February 2005.

87 Interview with a senior Indonesian diplomat, a high-ranking official in DEPLU, Jakarta, 28 February 2005.

88 Ibid.

89 Leo Suryadinata, *Indonesia's Foreign Policy under Suharto: Aspiring to International Leadership* (Singapore: Times Academic Press, 1996), p. 2.

90 Franklin B. Weinstein, *Indonesian Foreign Policy and the Dilemma of Dependence: From Sukarno to Soeharto* (Ithaca, New York: Cornell University Press, 1976), p. 99.

91 "Tonan Ajia no tainichikan" [Southeast Asian Perceptions of Japan], *Chunichi Shimbun*, 1 January 1995.

92 Weinstein, *Indonesian Foreign Policy and the Dilemma of Dependence*, p. 97.

93 Ibid., p. 98.

94 "Tonan Ajia no tainichikan".

95 The 1994 opinion poll was conducted by *Chunichi Shimbun* with 380 young leaders in ASEAN nations, who play leading roles in both the public and private sectors. One hundred leaders responded, out of which 42 were Thais, 25 Indonesians, 17 Malaysians, 9 Singaporeans, and 7 Filipinos. Fifty-two were male and 46 female; the average age of respondents was 36.8; For a detailed discussion on the results of the opinion poll, see: Itoh Mayumi, "Japan-Southeast Asia Relations: Perception Gaps, Legacy of World War II, and Economic Diplomacy", paper presented at the "1995 Asian Studies on the Pacific Coast (ASPAC) Conference", Pacific University, Oregon (16–18 June 1995).

96 Harry J. Benda, *The Japanese Interregnum in Southeast Asia* (New Haven: Yale University, 1968), pp. 65–79.

97 Weinstein, *Indonesian Foreign Policy and the Dilemma of Dependence*, p. 101.

98 Tilman, Robert O., "The Enemy Beyond: External Threat Perceptions in the ASEAN Region", Research Notes and Discussions Paper, No. 42 (Singapore: Institute of Southeast Asian Studies, 1984), p. 29.

99 Ibid., p. 29.

100 Kenneth G. Henshall, *History of Japan: From Stone Age to Superpower* (London: Macmillan Press, 1999), p. 3.

101 Nisid Hajari, "At War with History", *Newsweek*, 27 August 2001, pp. 1, 8–13.

[102] Mayumi, "Japan-Southeast Asia Relations".

[103] Interview with an Indonesian expert in international relations, CSIS, Jakarta, 21 February 2005.

[104] Weinstein, *Indonesian Foreign Policy and the Dilemma of Dependence*, p. 46.

[105] Ibid., p. 46.

[106] It should be noted that, in contrast to Indonesia and other Southeast Asian states, the resentment towards Japan has persisted in China and South Korea. Although there has also been a generational change at the elite level in the latter countries, two factors help explain their different perceptions about Japan's wartime actions. First, it is the fact that Japanese occupation of China and Korea lasted much longer and is said to have been characterized by much more brutal actions of the Japanese soldiers when compared with its occupation of Indonesia. Second, it is alleged that the communist regime in Beijing has deliberately drummed up the anti-Japanese sentiments among the Chinese population in order to divert its attention away from a myriad of domestic economic and social problems.

[107] Dewi Fortuna Anwar, "Indonesia's Relations with China and Japan: Images, Perceptions and Realities", *Contemporary Southeast Asia* 12, no. 3 (December 1990): 228.

[108] Mohamed Hery Saripudin, "The Effects and the Relations of Foreign Aid: A Case Study of Indonesia and Its Two Largest Donors, the United States and Japan" (MA dissertation, Saint Mary's University, Canada, 1994).

[109] J.N. Mak and B.A. Hamzah, "The External Maritime Dimension of ASEAN Security", *The Journal of Strategic Studies* 18, no. 3 (September 1995): 128.

[110] Robert O. Tilman, *Southeast Asia and the Enemy Beyond: ASEAN Perceptions of External Threats* (Boulder: Westview Press, 1987), p. 113.

[111] Weinstein, *Indonesian Foreign Policy and the Dilemma of Dependence*, p. 99.

[112] Ali Moertopo, "Indonesia in Regional and International Cooperation: Principles of Implementation and Construction", *The Indonesian Review of International Affairs* I, No. 3 and 4 (July 1972–74), pp. 6–15; cited in: op. cit., Anwar, "Indonesia's Relations with China and Japan", p. 234.

[113] Weinstein, *Indonesian Foreign Policy and the Dilemma of Dependence*, p. 101.

[114] Thee Kian Wie, ed., *Recollections: the Indonesian Economy, 1950s–1990s* (Singapore, Sydney: ISEAS and RSPAS, 2005), pp. 87–102.

[115] Itoh argues that "ASEAN elites are still haunted by past experiences with Japan's army, and have yet to forgive Japan completely." (p. 204). For more on Asian countries' views of Japan and Japanese perceptions of Asian countries, see: Mayumi Itoh, *Globalization of Japan: Japanese Sakoku Mentality and U.S. Efforts to Open Japan* (New York: St. Martin' Press, 1998).

[116] Interview with a former President, Jakarta, 10 January 2005.

[117] Interview with a senior Indonesian diplomat, Jakarta, 12 January 2005.

[118] Ibid.

[119] Interview with a former Indonesian Minister of Foreign Affairs, Jakarta, 14 January 2005.

120 Interview with an Indonesian scholar and IR expert affiliated with LIPI, Jakarta, 24 February 2005.
121 Interview with an Indonesian expert in international relations, CSIS, Jakarta, 21 February 2005; also discussed in an interview with a Minister in President Yudhoyono's cabinet, Jakarta, 28 February 2005.
122 Sumantoro, "Indonesian-Japan Relation, Experiences and Prospects", in "ASEAN-Japan Relations", an ASEAN Committee on Social Development's study (Bandung: Padjadjaran University, 1990), p. 250.
123 The Ministry of Foreign Affairs of Japan, "Visit to Japan by President Abdurrahman Wahid of the Republic of Indonesia" (Tokyo, 16 November 1999), <http://www.mofa.go.jp/announce/press/1999/11/1116.html#3> (accessed 30 May 2003).
124 Interview with an Indonesian scholar, his residence, Jakarta, 3 February 2005.
125 The Ministry of Foreign Affairs of Japan, "ASEAN-Japan Commemorative Summit — Evaluation" (Tokyo, December 2003), <http://www.mofa.go.jp/region/asia-paci/asean/year2003/summit/evaluation.html> (accessed 25 April 2005); Kornelius Purba, "East Asian Community Formed", *Jakarta Post*, 13 December 2003.
126 John F. Bradford, "Japanese Anti-Piracy Initiatives in Southeast Asia: Policy Formulation and the Coastal State Responses", *Contemporary Southeast Asia* 26, no. 3 (December 2004).
127 "Jepang Kirim Kapal Bersenjata ke Selat Malaka" [Japan Has Sent an Armed Ship to the Straits of Malacca], *Tempo Interaktif,* 6 June 2005.
128 "ASEAN-Jepang Sepakat Bahas Perdagangan Bebas", *Kompas,* 12 December 2003.
129 Interview with the director of a leading Jakarta-based think-tank, Jakarta, 6 April 2006.
130 Sheng Lijun, "Balance of Power: Great Game Plays on in Asia", *Straits Times,* 28 November 2005, p. 18.
131 Ibid., p. 18.
132 Interview with a Minister in President Yudhoyono's cabinet, Jakarta, 28 February 2005.
133 "East Asian Community Formed", *Jakarta Post*, 13 December 2003.
134 Sebastian Moffett et al, "Marching on to a New Role" in *Far Eastern Economic Review,* 15 January 2004.
135 Bandoro Bantarto is the editor of "The Indonesian Quarterly" published by the CSIS in Jakarta; Bandoro Bantarto, "Security Key Factor in Japan-ASEAN Relations", *Jakarta Post,* 4 December 2003.
136 Kornelius Purba, "East Asian Community Formed", *Jakarta Post,* 13 December 2003.
137 Interview with an Indonesian expert in international relations, CSIS, Jakarta, 24 October 2003 and 21 February 2005.

[138] Interview with a senior Indonesian diplomat, DEPLU, Jakarta, 25 January 2005.

[139] Interview with a former Indonesian Minister of Foreign Affairs, Jakarta, 14 January 2005.

[140] Quoted from: Tilman, *Southeast Asia and the Enemy Beyond*, 1987, p. 113.

[141] Lam Peng-Er, "Japan-Southeast Asia Relations: Trading Places?: The Leading Goose & Ascending Dragon", *Pacific Forum Comparative Connections* (1st Quarter 2002), <http://www.csis.org/pacfor/cc/0201Qoa.html> (accessed 2 October 2003).

[142] Quoted from: Kurniawan Hari, "Regional Security Concerns Put Japan in Dilemma", *Jakarta Post*, 10 August 2006.

[143] Ibid.

[144] Moffett et al, "Marching on to a New Role".

[145] Markus Hund, "ASEAN and ASEAN Plus Three: Manifestations of Collective Identities in Southeast Asia'" (Ph.D. dissertation, University of Trier, 2002), p. 316.

[146] Interview with a young Indonesian scholar, Singapore, 8 June 2006.

[147] Ibid.

[148] Peng-Er, "Japan-Southeast Asia Relations".

[149] Interview with a retired Indonesian Army general, presently also affiliated with a Jakarta-based research institute, Jakarta, 3 February 2005.

[150] Mak and Hamzah, "The External Maritime Dimension of ASEAN Security", p. 130.

[151] "Indonesia and Japan: Economic and Political Relations and Implications for Southeast Asia", USINDO seminar, Washington D.C. (13 September 2004).

[152] Quoted in: "RI Needs to Make Changes or It Might Be Left Behind", *Jakarta Post*, 24 May 2005.

[153] Interview with a CSIS-based international relations expert, Jakarta, 8 February 2005.

[154] Weinstein, *Indonesian Foreign Policy and the Dilemma of Dependence*; Tilman, *Southeast Asia and the Enemy Beyond*, 1987.

[155] Weinstein, *Indonesian Foreign Policy and the Dilemma of Dependence*, p. 196.

[156] Interview with an Indonesian Army general and member of GOLKAR, Jakarta, 15 February 2005.

[157] Interview with a senior Indonesian diplomat and ASEAN expert, DEPLU, Jakarta, 25 January 2005.

[158] Interview with a retired Indonesian Army general, presently also affiliated with a Jakarta-based research institute, Jakarta, 3 February 2005.

[159] Salman Haider, "India-ASEAN Strategic Partnership", *Jakarta Post*, 16 March 2005, p. 6.

[160] Interview with an Indonesian academic and expert in the Indonesian military, Jakarta, 24 January 2005; also discussed in an interview with a senior official of PDI-P, Jakarta, 22 February 2005.

161 Landry Haryo Subianto, "ASEAN and the East Asian Co-operation: Searching for a Balanced Relationship", *The Indonesian Quarterly* XXXI, no. 1 (1st Quarter 2003): 9–10.

162 Interview with an Indonesian politician, diplomat and journalist, Jakarta, 4 February 2005.

163 Interview with a journalist and chief editor of a Jakarta-based national newspaper, Jakarta, 15 February 2005.

164 "Pemilu 2004: ASEAN Harus Tetap 'Corner Stone'" [Elections 2004: ASEAN Has to Remain as a "Corner Stone"], *Kompas*, 1 April 2004.

165 Daniel Novotny, "Tear Down This 'Iron Curtain': The Exit Tax Stifles Indonesia", *Jakarta Post*, 16 January 2007, p. 6.

166 Jusuf Wanandi, "Future Challenges to Indonesia-Singapore Ties", *Jakarta Post*, 29 August 2002.

167 Interview with a senior Indonesian diplomat and ASEAN expert, DEPLU, Jakarta, 25 January 2005.

168 Interview with an Indonesian academic and economist, previously affiliated with the CSIS think-tank, Jakarta, 3 February 2005.

169 Interview with a senior Indonesian diplomat and former Ambassador, Hotel Hilton, Jakarta, 8 February 2005.

170 Interview with a young career diplomat, DEPLU, Jakarta, 2 February 2005.

171 Interview with a young career diplomat, DEPLU, Jakarta, 25 February 2005.

172 Interview with a senior official of PDI-P, Jakarta, 22 February 2005.

173 Interview with an Indonesian scholar and IR expert affiliated with LIPI, Jakarta, 24 February 2005; On the 2003 dispute between Indonesia and Malaysia, see: Derwin Pereira Devi Asmarani, "KL Played Rough with Indonesia over Islands", *Straits Times*, 29 January 2003.

174 Rizal Sukma, "U.S.-Southeast Asia Relations after the Crisis: The Security Dimension", background paper presented at "The Asia Foundation's Workshop on America's Role in Asia", Bangkok (22–24 March 2000).

175 "Trying Times in Chow Kit", *Tempo*, English Edition, 29 October 2007, pp. 12–17.

176 "Unneighborly Relations", *Tempo*, English Edition, 29 October 2007, p. 9.

177 Interview with a senior official of PDI-P, Jakarta, 22 February 2005.

178 Jusuf Wanandi and Simon Tay, "Indonesia and Singapore — Reaching Across the Divide", *Strait Times*, 6 March 2002.

179 Interview with an Indonesian academic and IR expert affiliated with the CSIS, 21 February 2005.

180 Ibid.

181 Interview with a leader of the *Muhammadiyah*, the second largest Muslim organization in Indonesia, 23 February 2005

182 There have been tense periods in the Indonesia-Singaporean relations. In 1968, for example, following an execution of two Indonesian marines-turned-saboteurs in Singapore, there was an intense sense of urgency in Indonesia to

punish Singapore for this act that was perceived as a serious insult to Indonesia's pride.

[183] Interview with an Indonesian leader and academic affiliated with a high-profile Jakarta-based think-tank, Jakarta, 17 January 2005.

[184] Interview with a senior official, a FTA negotiator, from the Department of Trade, Jakarta, 27 January 2005.

[185] Interview with a prominent Indonesian banker, vice-president of a major international banking institution, Jakarta, 2 February 2005.

[186] "Temasek: The Mouse that Roared", *Tempo*, English Edition, 15 May 2008, p. 71–73.

[187] Ibid.; "Taming Temasek", *Tempo*, English Edition, 3 December 2007, p. 9.

[188] "Safe in Singapore", *Tempo*, English Edition, 15 May 2008, p. 49.

[189] "Konglomerat hitam" is an Indonesian term for companies that practice illegal business activities. Interview with an Indonesian academic and IR expert associated with LIPI, Jakarta, 24 February 2005.

[190] Interview with an Indonesian academic and IR expert affiliated with the CSIS, Jakarta, 21 February 2005.

[191] Interview with Wirayuda in: Elisia Yeo, "When 'Forever' is a Dirty Word", *Today*, 6 October 2003, pp. 1–2.

[192] Ibid., pp. 1–2.

[193] Interview with a former Indonesian Minister of Foreign Affairs, Jakarta, 14 January 2005.

[194] Interview with a senior Indonesian diplomat, a high-ranking official in DEPLU, Jakarta, 28 February 2005.

[195] Ibid.

[196] Interview with a senior Indonesian career diplomat, DEPLU, Jakarta, 12 January 2005.

[197] Interview with a senior official of the PDI-P political party and senior member of the Indonesian Parliament (DPR), Jakarta, 23 February 2005.

[198] Subianto, "ASEAN and the East Asian Co-operation", p. 10.

[199] Natalegawa is the Director-General for ASEAN Cooperation at DEPLU; R.M. Marty M. Natalegawa, "ASEAN+3 versus the East Asia Summit", *Jakarta Post*, 8 February 2005, p. 6.

[200] Charles A. Kupchan et al., *Power in Transition: The Peaceful Change of International Order* (Tokyo: United Nations University Press, 2001), pp. 8–11.

7

THE INDONESIAN ELITE FACING A CHANGING WORLD

INTRODUCTION

In this chapter, we will attempt to address the following main question that this book tries to answer: "To what extent can the dynamics of Indonesian foreign relations in the post-Cold War period be explained in terms of the threat perceptions held by the country's foreign policy elite?" While the text aims to bring together both the theoretical and empirical aspect of this book, the discussion primarily draws on a set of assumptions and principles on which the balance of threat theory is based. In particular, this chapter aspires to prove that the dynamics of the Indonesian elite's foreign policy decision-making can be explained by means of the balance of threat concept. The theory is thus employed as an analytical tool by which to qualitatively and quantitatively evaluate the empirical findings from the 2004–06 research. As suggested in Chapter 2, one of the main arguments behind the balance of threat theory is that leaders' perceptions of a particular country always need to be placed in the broader context of the elite's worldview. Importantly, from the Indonesian perspective, both at the elite level and public at large, the country's relationship with the United States and China can be viewed in a triangular form.[1] Thus, in line with the "*mendayung antara dua karang*" thesis, it is possible to argue that we cannot understand Indonesia's approach towards the U.S. unless we place the country's relationship with the U.S. in the context of the Indonesian elite perceptions about the rise of China — and *vice versa*.

As argued in preceding chapters, a major determinant that shapes the elite's foreign policy preferences is the degree of the leaders' agreement about the nature and urgency of the threat. The elite's consensus about the threat determines what foreign policy tool will be employed to deal with a particular danger to the state's security. Consequently, to provide a better understanding of the role of elite perceptions on the foreign policy decision-making process, this chapter also addresses a second important question: "Is the Indonesian elite unanimous in its view of the world, which has been the official version and policy of the country's consecutive administrations, or is the elite divided in its foreign policy perception?"

"MENDAYUNG ANTARA DUA KARANG": THE ELITE'S "BALANCE-OF-THREAT" MODE OF THINKING

The analysis in Chapter 4 demonstrated that Indonesian leaders — especially during the George W. Bush's presidency — ranked the United States as the greatest state-based security threat. While China has progressively changed its image to appear as a benign power, the U.S. policies have been increasingly perceived as threatening. In line with the balance of threat theory, Beijing's growing projection of influence in the region is viewed positively insofar as it helps alleviate some pressure from U.S. unilateralist policies and creates greater leeway for Indonesia. Conversely, Chapter 5 highlighted the elite's deep-rooted, historically determined suspicion of China as an expansionist power with hegemonic intentions in the region. As a result, the United States is fundamentally seen — in the long run — as a guarantor of peace and stability in the region and, by extension, greater security for Indonesia. Also Tokyo's growing assertiveness, for example, has paradoxically been viewed as relatively benign and has not generated apprehension in Jakarta in part because it is considered an important check on China's growing power.

Referring to Indonesia's relations with the United States and China, which have proven to be of greatest concern among the members of the elite, there is a strong belief that in the future the archipelagic nation will increasingly have to manoeuvre between these two powers. A number of leaders pointedly used the Indonesian term "*mendayung di antara dua karang*" in reference to the authoritative article written by the first Vice-President Hatta; he made use of the expression in a 1948 speech to subtly describe the delicate state of the bi-polar Cold War era international relations.[2] It can be argued that the dynamics of contemporary Indonesian foreign policy can be understood and their future direction better predicted exactly in the context of the "row between two reefs" thesis. The idea of a (perceived) balance in the inter-state system clearly exerts a powerful affect on the elite's mode of thinking with regards to the country's national security. As Ott observed, "[Indonesia] wished to promote a geopolitical balance among the major powers that would help the countries of the region create a secure environment for economic growth."[3] Jusuf Wanandi argues that

> [in] the final analysis, ASEAN countries recognize that their security, both at home and in the region, depends on a pluralism of power. In regional terms, ASEAN needs both great powers (China and the U.S.) to be present in the region. ASEAN needs the U.S. presence to maintain a balance between the great powers in the region, and ASEAN also would like to have China incorporated in the region in cooperative security arrangements.[4]

As we have seen, the Indonesian elite welcome the rise of China insofar as it provides a greater leeway for Indonesia. According to a Minister in President Yudhoyono's Cabinet,

> [we] feel first that China is entitled to play a stronger role in East Asia. Second, that naturally must compete with Japan. It has become much more balanced from a heavily dominated American cover, American presence .... Overall, I think it helps us balancing between the United States, China, Japan and also India.[5]

Also another respondent contended that "it] will be better for us if we do not have such a powerful single superpower ... if the EU becomes very important to balance the U.S., India will grow and become a more important country..."[6] "Because the balance is important," as a retired, former high-ranking army officer suggested, "I would not mind the presence of other navies than the U.S. navy in the region."[7]

Pointing to the rise of China, an aide close to President Yudhoyono reasoned that "the more the West, and especially the U.S., pressures Jakarta, the more is China happy."[8] Another leader expressed the same idea in different words — referring to the Western governments, he argued that "they are not stupid. They know that if they press Indonesia, it will go to China, not Russia that is weak, but to China, which is powerful."[9] A former army general was also convinced that the rise of China provides Southeast Asia with a more balanced interstate system without the overwhelming predominance of the United States:

It is put in the current context in which Indonesia could be fed up in the relations with the West, especially the U.S., and Indonesia would try to find alternatives and China would be most welcome to hug and welcome. ... The more that our channels as instruments with the West, especially the U.S., are blocked, by efforts, ironically from the U.S., what else could we do? We have to find alternatives. [And] China would be an easiest alternative.[10]

As Chapter 6 showed, the elite embraces the concept of a so-called inclusive foreign policy: Indonesia should establish and maintain at least workable relations with as many states as possible, whereby the Indonesian foreign policy elite finds it important to continuously strive for the maintenance of a balance of power among all these states with the aim of creating a safe space for maneuvering for Indonesia. For example, in the context of the fear in Jakarta and more generally in other Southeast Asian capital cities that Beijing's influence is becoming too dominant in the region, Indonesia keenly supported the strategy embraced by ASEAN that insisted on including, along with China, also Japan, South Korea and India into the ASEM (Asia-Europe Meeting).[11] Yet, it is an overwhelmingly accepted view that the desirable balance in Southeast Asia cannot be achieved and sustained without the direct involvement of the U.S. in the regional security and economic arrangements. To this end, Acharya and Tan concluded that

America has long been viewed by regional governments as the region's preponderant stabilizer and "honest broker" in striking a balance against China, Japan, and other regional states. It is unlikely that this perceived value might change in the foreseeable future, particularly in the light of an ascending China.[12]

On the issue of inclusive foreign policy and the official aim of the Indonesian government to promote multilateralism in the region, one leader pointedly explained:

In the balance of power you have to have a power to deter or to make relationship in this region balanced. When you do not have that capacity, the U.S. presence is still important. ... The balance can be created by maintaining some degree of the U.S. presence. Because multilateralism is still very much experimental. Unlike in Europe, for example, you already have a lot of institutional arrangements. That's why here is very clear that multilateralism is not the guarantee at all. That's why there are lots of countries in this part of the world that still maintain bilateral relationship with the U.S. or with other external powers. Why? Because simply there is no guarantee. Multilateralism is still a baby, basically. So this is an attempt to balance.[13]

Importantly, as to the U.S. involvement in the region, the respondent also asserted:

> So it is really a delicate issue. Why? Because if you want the U.S. for instance to stay in this part of the world then you have to give some incentive. No power wants to stay if they see that this country is not interesting any more. That's why there is a trade-off between security and trade. ... What is the incentive? First, market — because if market is still open for the U.S. ... then it is easier for the U.S. government to convince the U.S. Congress that we need to stay economically and also militarily.[14]

According to the country's foremost IR expert, the Indonesian elite's attitude to the perceived balance between extraterritorial states, namely the United States and China, "... actually reflects a very strong belief in the balance of power within a multilateral arrangement. ... The basic thesis of the whole endeavor, [the foundation], has been and still is the balance of power premise."[15] On the other hand, one interviewee opposed the view that U.S. involvement in the region is through the modality of multilateral arrangements:

> The issue of the U.S. presence is related to bilateral and balance. Because most of the U.S. presence here is guaranteed by bilateral arrangements, not by multilateral arrangements. For example, the U.S.-Japan, U.S.-Thailand, U.S.-Philippines and some arrangements with Indonesia, for example, logistic and service that Indonesia provides to the U.S. ... It is not military base but if you can send signals to the U.S. that we are happy to receive you, although it is not a military base, that's fine. For example, port visits by the U.S. Psychologically![16]

This view was also shared by another leader who pointed out that "[as] you know, the ARF has become less important as a forum for balancing extra-regional powers. ... China, Korea, Japan and the U.S. are less and less inclined to use the ARF as a forum where they can match their interests."[17]

It is evident that the Indonesian elite considers the attainment of a perceived "balance between U.S., China and Japan in the region" as a principle objective of the country's foreign policy.[18] According to a former Foreign Minister, the importance of the balance has always been an inherent part of the Indonesian elite's worldview and it was also adopted by the

ASEAN grouping in the 1970s. He then explained that "[when] Indonesia and ASEAN thought the threat comes ... from the North, we do not mean China, we mean the interactions between these four countries [the United States, China, Japan and the Soviet Union] that could become a threat to the stability, peace and progress of Southeast Asia."[19] As to the idea of maintaining balance between the United States and China, the elite believe that Indonesia and, more broadly, ASEAN should be "playing an intermediate role, in the middle, mediating between [these two major powers]."[20]

Also according to a political analysis in *Kompas*, "ASEAN should always politically see China and America as strategic players to maintain the balance of power."[21] Ross argues that Washington and Beijing compete for spheres of influence in Southeast Asia, whereby continental states in the region have aligned with China and maritime states including Indonesia have aligned with the United States.[22] This perspective has been challenged by a view that ASEAN states have not aligned with either Washington or Beijing but rather have chosen to pursue a "hedging strategy". The survey data in this study suggest that the latter perspective describe the reality more truthfully. Christofferson, for example, asserts that owing to the Southeast Asian states' general distrust of great powers, they strive to achieve equidistance and maintain a perceived balance between the United States and China.[23]

While expressing the strong belief that once Indonesia recovers from its internal problems, it will enter a multi-polar world, a leader known for his close ties with the military establishment contended that

> [in] the end, it will depend on Indonesian elite to play one against the other, to get as much benefit as possible. In the past, we had only two choices, either Communist or Western countries. Now, we have many choices. Because, even though [there is] only one big superpower but there are many power centers.[24]

Thus, while an analysis characterized the so-called Jakarta-Beijing Axis as very strategic mainly because it would enhance Indonesia's bargaining power vis-à-vis the United States, it also emphasized that a healthy balance between China and America could only be achieved and maintained if Indonesia avoids anti-American sentiments and attitudes.[25] Underlying the "play-one-against-the-other" thesis is a widespread belief that the future dynamics of Indonesia's relations with the United States and China will resemble those of the Cold War era. Then, the two main rivals, the United States and the Soviet Union, competed for influence in strategically important parts of the world. As one interviewed leader argued, the principle of maintaining a (perceived) balance between the two rival superpowers underpinned the formation of Indonesian foreign policy, for example, during Sukarno's presidency and as such guided the first President's approach to resolving the West Papua issue in the early 1960 when, in his words, "Sukarno [then] managed to maneuver between the United States and the Soviet-led Communist block."[26]

Referring to the debate in Indonesia about the hidden intentions behind the U.S. help to the victims of the tsunami disaster in the province of Aceh, one respondent asserted that

> ... this controversy is a proof that the United States would like to be seen by the Indonesians as a country which is not endangering Indonesia because Indonesia has a Muslim majority. On the other hand, you see the activity of China — [also] China has tried to be nice to Indonesia; China will also strive for sympathy of Indonesia. [For America's part] it would like at least not to be seen as the enemy of Indonesia, [which will be] a kind of assurance for America that China's [influence] cannot go down to Indonesia.[27]

At least three-fourths of all interviewees agreed that Indonesia's position in the future can be compared to that of a "beautiful maid" that others try to seduce and exploit, and they largely shared a view that "strategically, the United States and China [will be] competing to have an access and sympathy of Indonesia."[28] One respondent suggested that not only Indonesia but the whole "ASEAN [grouping] becomes a 'beautiful girl'"; he predicted that, besides the United States and China, "also Japan and Korea will compete here in Southeast Asia. So, in order to avoid this, to reduce the negative impact of this kind of things, we need to develop relations not only with East Asia but with India, with Australia, the EU, in order to face China."[29]

"Indonesia will choose not to take sides, as it did before during the Cold War," concluded a USINDO-sponsored seminar on regional security.[30] In terms of the balance between the two major powers, as one leader aptly put it, [the] U.S. will be happy with that as long as we don't accommodate China too much. At the same time, China will be happy with that as long as we do not become a puppet of the U.S. So, this is a completely different set of games.[31] Ultimately, this complex situation means for Indonesia, as one of the country's foremost IR experts summed up, that

> ... we need to develop our relations with India, with Australia, with the U.S. because it is the only bargaining power for us to deal with the three big countries in East Asia. And, at the same time, we need to have a good

relationship with China and also Japan because it is the only way for us to deal with the U.S. So, now it is about how to be creative in managing all of these complex relationships for the Indonesian benefit.[32]

To conclude, the perceived equilibrium between the United States and China, the elite believes, will benefit Indonesia insofar as it will give the archipelagic nation a greater space for maneuvering between the two major powers and keep both of them at arm's length.

THE INDONESIAN ELITE'S LONG-TERM THREAT ASSESSMENT

A significant disparity exists between the Indonesian elite's present and their future, long-term threat assessment. The degree of elite consensus about the nature and urgency of the threat is crucial insofar as it determines what foreign policy tool will be employed to deal with a particular malign factor affecting the state's security. If the source of threat that the elite considers to be presently the most dangerous is identical with what it expects to be the major threat in the future, then the country's foreign relations are likely to display balancing behaviour. On the contrary, if there is a gap in perceptions or, in other words, if the elite anticipate that the most dangerous source of threat in the future will be different from the existing one, a distinct balancing behaviour against the threat presently ranked as number one is much less likely. This assumption is the starting point from which we seek to explain the seemingly ambivalent dynamics of contemporary Indonesian foreign policy. In particular, we can question why, in the light of such an overall negative attitude of the United States both at the elite level and among the Indonesian public especially during the George W. Bush Administration, most members of the foreign policy elite still consider the U.S. engagement in the region as a vital element in their country's national security.

The respondents stressed that Southeast Asia will in the future be faced with changing dynamics of international relations. Yet, as one leader affirmed, "we do not know what the policies will be beyond fifty years from now."[33] Another leader said: "We cannot make that kind of prediction based only on our own experiences. Because the world is changing ... Consider the EU, China, India, ASEAN — [there are] many unknown factors.[34] Similarly, according to Wanandi, "... there will be new uncertainties about the balance of forces and possible new alignments in the long-term in the region."[35] Whist pointing out a general sense of uncertainty about the future strategic balance among major powers in the wider region — "I do not know ... how many different things will happen, it's very difficult to predict."[36] — concurrently, the data evaluation has shed light on what the elite anticipates will be the main security threats to Indonesia within the next twenty to fifty years.

The interviewees believe that, much like during the Cold War, the way in which Indonesia manages its relationships with the United States and China, along with Japan (and perhaps India) in the next twenty to fifty years will be critical. A former Foreign Minister offered the most comprehensive explanation:

> ... to the North of us, there are four major powers. During the time of the Cold War, it was the Soviet Union, Japan, China and the U.S. ... [It] was mostly Japan and the U.S. [allied] against the Soviet Union, with China not playing a very big role yet. China was there, but China was poor, China was involved in its own problems, the Cultural Revolution and so on. So there was a kind of balance there. But these four powers [still] do have an influence on Southeast Asia. [But the threat] as we perceive it in the 1970s, is that if something breaks down in the north of us, between the four major powers, a disequilibrium starts there, a confrontation starts there for whatever reason, we will be sucked into that ... confrontation.[37]

As the former Minister of Foreign Affairs further explained, the situation after the end of the Cold War has changed as

> China took the place of the Soviet Union, more and more, China became more powerful, but it was still counterbalanced by Japan and the United States. ... There is an uneasy relationship between the four, which is moving towards a new balance of power which has not formed yet, but it is still working, it is still peaceful, but it can explode on the question of Taiwan, for example, [or] North Korea...[38]

He then predicted that, by the year 2050, "[basically], the North of Indonesia [will] still [be] very, very dangerous [since] very potentially confrontational relationships are there ... because of the four major powers. They will have an influence on our region because we are smaller and we are rich in commodities."[39]

Conversely, some other leaders expressed the hope that while major powers are at present inclined to use the divide-and-rule strategy when dealing with Southeast Asia, in the future, ASEAN will become a more cohesive and potent player. For example, "[in] the future, there will be lots of complex dynamics [and] the U.S. and Japan will also not be stationary … I am sure, in twenty, thirty years time, ASEAN will become a much more capable power. It will never be as big as China but it is not going to be a feeble country that China can easily push around.[40] From the Indonesian elite's perspective, the current tendencies on the Southeast Asia's geopolitical "chessboard" can generally be summarized as:

- China is edging closer to becoming the world's new superpower
- The United States' security role in the region continues to be very important but is not as vigorous as previously
- Japan's former dominance in the region is relatively declining.

A 2004 seminar discussing the future of Indonesian foreign relations concluded that "the full implications of these shifts remained obscured but were clearly going to be important."[41] Yet, the following analysis of the elite's long-term threat assessment demonstrates that, much like with the present threat assessment, the Indonesian leadership has a strong view of which countries will pose the most potent security threat to Indonesia within the next twenty to fifty years.

On the one hand, Chapters 4 and 5 illustrated that the elite is divided in its view about the implications of both the unilateralist policies of the United States and the rise of China. There is also a strong belief in the necessity of a closer cooperation with Beijing because this will provide a greater space for manoeuvring vis-à-vis the major (Western) powers, particularly in light of the international system heavily dominated by the United States. On the other hand, the Indonesian leaders are largely united in the view that China remains as the greater threat for Indonesia in the next twenty years and beyond. As a consequence, the interviewed leaders were convinced that the uncertainty regarding the rise of China necessitates the implementation of a contingency plan to deal with any future eventuality. Thus, while the elite's present threat assessment of the U.S. is characterized by ambivalence, by contrast, the elite is largely united in the belief that the U.S. constitutes in the long term a vital guarantee for peace and stability in the region.

While 51 per cent of interviewed leaders considered the United States and 27 per cent of them China as presently the major state-based threat to Indonesia, by contrast, Figure 7.1 demonstrates that 22 per cent of the respondents identified the United States and 49 per cent of them China as the major security threat to Indonesia within the next twenty to fifty years. This gap in the elite perceptions has a direct impact on the current course of Indonesian foreign relations. This is not to say that the elite's long-term

FIGURE 7.1
Long-Term Threat Assessment;
Based on the Research Data Evaluation

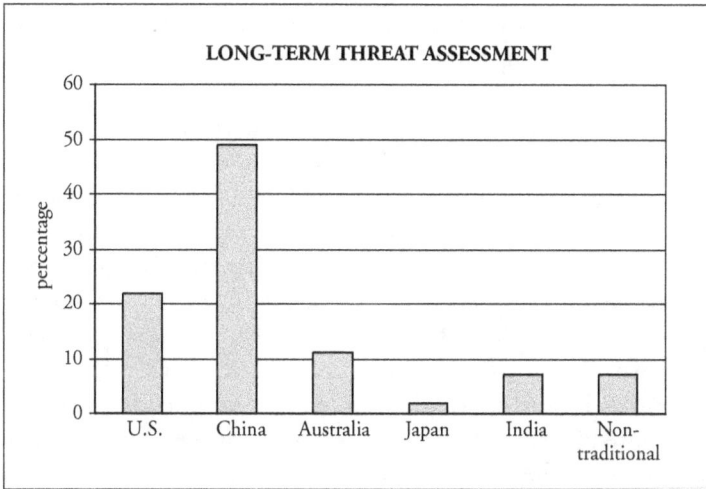

Source: Survey research conducted by the author in 2004–05.

threat assessment, or future expectations, are directly affecting Indonesia's practical, day-to-day management of its relations with China and the United States. Rather than altering Indonesia's immediate policy prescriptions toward either major power, the longer-term expectations regarding future security risks are more important insofar as they prompt the elite to carefully balance Indonesia's relations with other states as part of hedging strategy to prepare for any future undesirable course of events.

CHINA: LONG-TERM THREAT ASSESSMENT

The survey data presented above indicate that the Indonesian elite consider China the long-term number one external threat that needs to be constrained or balanced. One leader affirmed: "If you ask any man on the street now, who are they worried about, they are much more worried about the U.S., about its pre-emptive strike, unilateral doctrine, than about China. They are much more worried to be a target of Bush's foreign policy than of Beijing's foreign policy."[42] However, the leader emphasized that, in the long run "we are as much worried about China as about the U.S.!"[43] The respondents generally believe either that "China is looking into Southeast Asia with the goal to become a regional power,"[44] or that "China is going to be a major [global] power."[45] In any case, all of the interviewed leaders were convinced that "China will increase its ambition to expand its influence."[46] While pointing out that "it is normal that China is struggling for some kind of hegemony", a Muslim leader affirmed: "I can predict that in ten years from now, China will become a real competitor to Washington. ... China will be the most important country."[47]

A common theme during the series of interviews was the uncertainty regarding the rise of China owing to various factors that cannot be predicted. One respondent, for example, suggested that "there can also be some irrational behaviour in China, human factor, such as Taiwan proclaiming independence."[48] Another leader pointed out that there is a great uncertainty with respect to the social and political development inside China and this is why "we still have yet to see how the interaction between the political and economic aspects develops in China."[49] For a senior diplomat, "what is important is how authoritarian China reflects into the world order."[50] The interviewed leaders also raised questions with regard to other countries: "What about the other states? What about the EU in 30 years? Is the U.S. going to be that powerful in 30 years? What will ASEAN be like? We will not just sit and wait!"[51] From the elite's perspective, "China will be in ten years the most powerful country in Asia."[52] The most vexing uncertainty regarding China can be aptly summed up as: "Will China be a benign or assertive hegemon?"[53]

Option No. 1 — China as a Benign Hegemon

Not more than one-fifth of the interviewed leaders expect that China will be a benign hegemon. These respondents largely justify this view in terms of the liberal-idealist argument that today's increasing multidimensional economic (as well as social and ecological) interdependence will gradually diminish peoples' loyalties to their respective states, thus rendering wars irrational and obsolete.[54] The proponents of the economic interdependence theory among the elite generally do not believe that China would become a military threat for Southeast Asia. As one leader explained, "[once] you become a big economic power, interdependency between that country and other countries is also getting bigger and bigger. I do not think that in the next fifty year period there will be the way of thinking in China or in the world that a country will get natural resources or markets by war."[55]

Part of the "equation" called "economic interdependence" is the perception of China as depending on Indonesia for its consumption of oil and other mineral resources. Thus, an influential Indonesian economist and businessman asserted: "China depends on importing 30 percent of its coal consumption from Indonesia. ... As they (China) buy more and more gas and oil, importing 30 or 40 per cent of the Indonesian economy, and they cannot find a substitute, any oil and gas policy, they will make sure it will not affect them."[56] Another respondent concluded that because of China's perceived dependence on Indonesia and international markets,

> [any] adventurism by China will be detrimental to China itself. ... China really depends on international markets, so that is why it depends on the international situation. Secondly, it is also the energy. ... They need a secure international environment; they have to have good diplomatic relations with other countries.[57]

It is also argued that, ultimately, the growing economic interdependence between ASEAN countries and China will have a profound effect on each other's perceptions: "When their economies are more integrated, this will also have an impact on perceptions. ... In twenty to fifty years, the perception of threat toward China will be different — the increasing interdependence will dilute threat perceptions toward China."[58]

Several other reasons were mentioned to support the assumption that China will gradually grow into a benign hegemonic superpower. First, Indonesia and China share some of the same problems, such as the challenge of regional separatism. According to one leader, "... of course China tries to have a good relationship with ASEAN and the Pacific countries, I think, because of the Taiwan issue."[59] Second, it was argued that China cannot in the future dominate the region because "[it] can not move freely in terms of military like the United States. [Moreover] Indonesia has lots of choices today ... if China imposes sanctions on Indonesia there is still Japan, the EU and the U.S."[60] The third argument was that the economic threat from China is overstated because "the growth of Chinese economy is limited [as there is] a gap between the coastal and rural areas."[61]

The idea that Beijing would embark on expansionist policies in the future was also rejected because of the Chinese mentality or psyche. While suggesting that "it is illogical to see a threat in China's policy", a former President referred to the proponents of the "China threat" thesis that "they are wrong. They do not know the psyche of the Chinese. The psyche of the Chinese is to maintain the unity of China. ... The unity of China is number one. All policies that run against the goal of maintaining independence are abandoned."[62] And it was also argued that China will not be a threat for

Indonesia in the future because the country will change internally: "It does not make sense ... there are also internal dynamics [and] these will change China towards good."[63] Moreover, one leader affirmed that he does not consider China as a threat because "it is an Eastern nation [and thus] it is easier to discuss [with Beijing] in the Asian way."[64] All in all, these reasons outlined above led a small minority of the Indonesian leaders to conclude that "we (the Indonesians) can deal with them (the Chinese)."[65]

Option No. 2 — China as a Future Assertive Hegemonic Superpower

The majority of the respondents, including some of those who did not identify China as the future major threat, expressed wariness of that country in the long run and the impact of China's rise for Indonesia's national interest and security. When asked about the elite's long-term view of China, one leader used the following words to describe the prevalent sense in this group: "You have an alarm in your car but you will always hope that the alarm will never go off at night."[66] A number of high-profile leaders stressed that it is important not to overstate Beijing's current series of overtures to Southeast Asia and not to be deceived by its "good neighbourhood policy" towards to region. This predominant section of the elite views China's approach to its relations with Indonesia and other regional states in light of the fact that China still feels vulnerable to external pressures, namely the possibility of being contained and isolated by other countries. It was also argued that Beijing's attitude towards Southeast Asia is likely to change as soon as the regime feels confident enough to embark, both economically and politically, on a hegemonic agenda. According to a former Foreign Minister,

> [we] should not be naïve ... but right now China needs all its friends ... because it needs to catch up economically, they have still enormous problems ... We want to make it possible that China be included, not isolated ... But, of course, the possibility [for China's hegemonic ambitions] is always there. In such a big country like China, once it has the capacity, will also move to the big military power.[67]

For another leader, China will certainly use its growing clout to attempt to dominate the region "just like the U.S. [now]." He went on asserting that

> China will have hegemonic behaviour, intentions to control the region. ... Once China becomes strong enough. It is predictable. ... If Indonesia's foreign policy guy doesn't see it, he should be fired. ... The

Chinese at the moment are not strong enough to tell Indonesia [what it should do] but they will in a due course, in the next thirty to forty years.[68]

The perception that China will likely in the future behave as an expansionist power influenced also the Indonesian foreign policy elite's considerations regarding Indonesia's attitude to the East Asian Community project. As one leader pointed out, "I have been personally involved in some discussions about the East Asian Community and some of the Indonesian officials and I also personally share the view that China is really a big threat in a broader sense, economically and so on."[69]

Generally, there was a number of diverging views as to when China would become a hegemon with the capability to militarily and economically dominate the region. One respondent argued that "China will be bigger threat for Indonesia, military and economic [then the U.S.] Until now we do not know exactly what will be the policy of the Chinese government in the next twenty to fifty years, particularly post-fifty year period, when they become an economic power."[70] Conversely, another leader pointed out that "[if] Indonesia is a competitive, economic and trading power, we will solve that. … Of course, they (China) are a problem. … In ten or fifteen years, where will China be, please, there is an unfinished agenda either. Don't belittle that. It could explode![71] Then, commenting on the idea that a superpower China would impose its will on its weaker neighbours, a former President affirmed, [it] is not 100% likely. Maybe yes, in fifteen years or more [from now]."[72] In short, the majority of the Indonesian leaders believe that, as a major power, it is likely that China will seek some kind of hegemony and dominance of Southeast Asia. — "It is likely. In the end, if China becomes a major power, it is inevitable that China will be using its economic and military influence and powers in order to achieve its national interest. The question is then how are we going to reconcile those interests if those interests conflict with each other."[73] It follows that the theory prevalent among the Indonesian elite can be succinctly described as: "[Sooner or later] one day there will be *a disconnect* with China."[74]

Several respondents suggested that China's current actions and attitudes already indicate its expansionist predisposition and aggressive intentions in the future. A Muslim leader, for example, alleged: "Look at how Beijing is treating Taipei. It seems to me that Beijing is overconfident … China will have its own perspective on the region — exploiting the region."[75] Another warning sign is believed to be Beijing's territorial claims in the South China Sea and its ensuing disputes with the regional states, including Indonesia.[76] Referring to China's recent policies in the South China Sea, sometimes described as "a creeping assertiveness",[77] a former high-ranking army officer argued:

> It may not reach all the way down to Indonesia, but maybe [only] on the neighbouring states of China ... [China's actions are] an indicator or an evidence of the past Chinese assertive foreign policy. But with the opening of China maybe they come to enjoy, hey, this is good, we can pursue our national interest in a different way, although it could create clashes, conflicts of interests [with other states], it does not have to be in the same form of militaristic assertive foreign policy. ... We would have to see how things develop after they pass that strategic junction ... they can turn left, turn right, go straight ahead.[78]

Of those 49 per cent of respondents who pinpointed China as the number one factor that needs to be constrained in the long term, 14 per cent expect the threat will be in terms of a military challenge, whereas 59 per cent believe that the threat will more likely have an economic dimension. When asked about the origins of the elite's wariness about the Chinese military challenge in the future, it was argued that this continues to be fuelled by the historical perception of China as a "Middle Kingdom". Indonesia's foremost expert of China expressed his view as follows:

> Indonesian elite perceptions need to be seen in historical context. [In the past] China was a dominant power in the southern part of the globe. It always tried to subjugate countries to the south to pay tribute to the Chinese emperor. Therefore, it is believed that by building her economy and her military might China is trying to regain her superiority in the region.[79]

In light of this historical memory, the emergence of China as a second power to the United States has created a dilemma for the Indonesian elite. As the China expert explained,

> [on] the one hand, they (the Indonesian elite) are very attracted to China's power which can be also used for an aggressive foreign policy and [an exploitation] of its military might. ... But, on the other hand, the feeling of suspicion still lingers on. The Indonesian elite is still trying to guess what lies behind Chinese development of its military power.[80]

It was again this vexing uncertainty about whether a more militarily powerful China taking its place as the next superpower will be a positive factor for the regional security that lead another respondent to conclude that "... nobody is so sure that the military power China has acquired will not be used in order to put pressure on regional countries in order to pursue their (China's) national interest."[81]

The economic threat, on the other hand, can have various dimensions with one most often mentioned being China's growing dependence on the import of oil and other natural resources. Here, a former Foreign Minister observed:

> Like, for example, in the next ten or fifteen years China's search for oil will determine lots of [China's] foreign polices. They need oil. Some of it they will now do it by investing. ... Some of it is by cultivating friendships with people who have oil. But I think their foreign policy will be directed with making sure that they get this oil. And in that sense they will replace Japan in making sure that the Straits, the routes of oil, are safe for China.[82]

The members of the Indonesian foreign policy elite also, for example, expressed their concern that "in ten years *renminbi* will be at least as important as the U.S. dollar."[83] Commenting on China's future influence in Indonesia by means of its currency renminbi, one leader pledged that "We [will] not just say yes to the Chinese!"[84] Here, another respondent who is close to the military circles expressed a hope that since China is modernizing, it would not be as aggressive as it was during the Cold War. He also suggested that "[if] there will ever be threat from China in the future, not the way it was in the past. Probably, through dumping, probably, selling cheaper things to us."[85]

When asked about the perceived economic threat from China, the respondents also spoke out about a dilemma similar to that outlined above. Although the elite regards China as a long-term threat that needs to be constrained, it is concurrently aware that Indonesia desperately needs that country's massive market both for exports and investment. Concerning the dilemmatic situation facing Indonesia and Southeast Asia, in general, Marvin Ott concluded: "ASEAN saw its task vis-à-vis China as ensuring that the Southeast Asia-China economic/security competition remained a positive sum game for both. Some observers voiced doubt about the outcome because of China's continuing South-China Sea claims."[86] In short, the prevalent sense among the Indonesian elite was aptly summed up by a senior member of the Parliament who argued that Indonesia "[should] cooperate with China but also prevent China from becoming hegemonic, so that the Chinese cannot dictate their agenda."[87]

THE UNITED STATES:
LONG-TERM THREAT ASSESSMENT

There is a considerable disparity between the Indonesian foreign policy elite's present threat assessment and its future, long-term threat assessment of the United States. When discussing what the elite anticipate to be America's role in the regional security within the next twenty to fifty years, their perceptions were dominated by two themes. First, the U.S. is in the long run seen as a guarantor of peace and stability in the region as well as greater security for Indonesia. Washington's influence in the region is ultimately viewed as more benign vis-à-vis Beijing's influence, with the former being considered as an important check on China's perceived hegemonic intentions in Southeast Asia. Second, the U.S. should maintain a rather tacit security presence in the form of a psychological assurance, meaning that it is available every time its assistance is needed but concurrently should refrain from dominating regional security affairs.

The United States as a "Psychological Guarantee"

A common theme in the interviews was that it is imperative for Indonesian policy-makers and diplomats to anticipate the future course of China's foreign policy.[88] This view is also critical to understanding the elite's attitude to the United States vis-à-vis China. In the context of uncertainties regarding the rise of China, the U.S. is considered as an important and indispensable element in the elite's considerations about Indonesia's national security. As one respondent explained,

> [because] of this rise of China ... you do not know actually where China is going ... Even lots of government officials tacitly recognize that everybody would be nervous if the U.S. pulled out and then disengaged from regional politics ... [It is] because they are not sure how to respond to China and how China is going to evolve in the future. So they need it as a deterrent.[89]

There is a widespread view among the elite that the U.S. presence serves as a deterrent and "psychological assurance" — for example, one leader affirmed that "the U.S. should stay in Korea and Taiwan; otherwise Beijing would be encouraged to attack."[90] According to a retired army general, "psychologically, yes, [the U.S. presence] is a guarantee against any potential naughty intentions of major regional powers. Deterrence! It deters any potential naughty intentions of major regional powers."[91]

The Indonesian elite's long-term objective is to prevent China from dominating regional multilateral security and economic arrangements. As a senior diplomat stressed, referring to such a situation in which "China is dominating ASEAN", Indonesia must build "some means to prevent negative scenarios from happening."[92] Another respondent affirmed:

> The East Asian Community, some people said, will be dominated by China. So the point is there are some worries about the China domination economically and militarily, because it is too big. There are some worries in Indonesia now that the East Asian Community is a vehicle for China … to project their power not in East Asia but in Southeast Asia.[93]

Emphasizing that Indonesia should in the future carefully "balance the relationship with the major powers", the leader observed: "It is impossible now for us to have an exclusive relationship with China. What I mean by exclusive, we cannot exclude for example the U.S., EU and Australia."[94]

The deep-rooted perceptions about China coupled with the uncertainty regarding its rise are exceedingly important factors that shape Indonesian leaders' long-term threat assessment of the United States. Notwithstanding the recent waves of high-profile anti-American expressions in Indonesia, the U.S. is seen as an essentially benevolent, benign superpower without any territorial design and a guarantor of peace and stability in the region. It is also apparent that Jakarta and Washington share complementary strategic perspective with regards to the implications of the rise of China for the regional security. Kornelius Purba, a prominent Indonesian journalist, summed up the American perspective as: "Japan and the U.S. need a strong Indonesia because the country is expected — to a certain extent — to counter China's domination in the region. Indonesia's insistence on making the planned East Asian community more inclusive is welcomed by the two leading economies."[95] Describing the point of view of Indonesia, Marvin Ott, an American scholar, observed that "[Indonesia] would want to keep them both [the United States and Japan], in the game, but it would continue to prefer that the U.S. security support stay at arm's length, over the horizon. The ASEAN nations along with others saw a need for multilateral security arrangements."[96] These two statements from Jakarta and Washington illustrate the relative compatibility of the Indonesian and American attitudes.

"Form" versus "Substance" in Indonesia's U.S. Policy

It is obvious from the analysis in Chapter 4 that the Indonesian elite's attitude towards the United States is deeply ambivalent. On the one hand, it was demonstrated that the leaders are very concerned about some U.S. policies towards Indonesia. These were, however, associated more with President George W. Bush personally and his administration's policies than with the United States in general. In the words of one leader,

> [the] problem with the U.S. is [that] basically it is always up and down. ... If you look at the relationship between Indonesia and the U.S. from the very beginning ... it depends on certain issues basically, [and the high-profile anti-American pronouncements are] not reflecting ... the whole dimension of the relationship. Now, not only Indonesia but also many countries are sensitive to the U.S. mainly because of Bush.[97]

Concurrently, several leaders explicitly pointed out that the wave of anti-Americanism during the George W. Bush presidency is to some extent deceiving and, in essence, there is a substantial difference in the elite's attitude towards the United States and China. As one respondent put it, "[the] sensitivity of the Indonesian people towards the U.S. is not genuine — [it is] very superficial, on an ad hoc basis, [it is] on the surface and issue-based. It is different to how Indonesian people perceive China and Japan."[98] For example, the anti-American sentiments, it was argued, are not directed against the United States per se. Rather, they are driven by the belief among a section of the Indonesian population that by maintaining diplomatic relations with the U.S. and accepting the attributes of the American culture (life-style, movies, fast-food, pop-music etc.), the society had deviated from the true teachings of Islam in ethical and moral sense. According to Sukma, it is basically the same "like [when] they cannot stand a lot of prostitution, gambling and so on."[99]

Importantly, some Indonesian leaders, in particular those associated with Muslim parties and organizations, expressed during the private interviews a much more balanced and nuanced attitude towards the United States, significantly different from the attitude they are widely known to represent publicly. Thus, a member of the DPR, the Indonesian Parliament, who was otherwise exceedingly critical of Washington's policies especially following the terrorist attacks in the United States in September 2001, unequivocally claimed that "Western culture is closer to the Indonesians than the Chinese culture."[100] He then went on to argue that

> [as] to the West, in the near future, we are worried because of what America did in Afghanistan and then ... in Iraq and now ... Iran, Syria and Sudan are part of the list of the targets. It is possible that Indonesia will be the next target. But in the long term we are not worried about the

West. ... [By contrast, we are wary of China because] we have experience that the Chinese community in any country, including Indonesia, they feel they mother land is still in China.[101]

Another member of the DPR agreed that "China is going to that stage when it will try to expand its influence and hegemony. I have no doubt about that."[102]

The level of trust of the Indonesian elite, both of Muslim and non-Muslim background, toward the United States is in fact relatively high. Perhaps the most conspicuous case was a Muslim leader and prominent politician who is generally regarded as one of the main critics of the IMF's economic policies toward Indonesia and U.S.-led War on Terrorism as well as Washington's approach to the Middle East. Yet, during the interview, there was little trace of his anti-American rhetoric that he is well known for among the Indonesian public. In fact, he pointed out that America is blindly pursuing the War on Terror and, in his words, "spending its energy on Iraq and other places. ... Washington focuses too much on Muslim countries and misses the point that China is the real competitor."[103] According to him, Japan and China consolidated their economies during the Cold War arms race. Judging from the way China is treating Taiwan, it seems that Beijing is now "overconfident." He then likened the situation to a Chinese kung-fu story, whereby Beijing is now the "suhu" (the top leader in kung-fu), overconfident, looking at the U.S. who is a "drunken suhu". The Muslim leader expressed his concern that while the U.S. is fighting "the wrong war in the wrong place" and thus squandering its power, the real threat — China — is "consolidating itself while watching overseas from a distance."[104] Later, responding to the author's direct question regarding the substantial gap between his attitudes as expressed during the interview, on the one hand, and in the public, on the other, the Muslim leader explained that his public pronouncements need to be seen in the context of his role as a politician who is subject to scrutiny by his Muslim constituents.

At this point, we can again question the motives behind this two-facedness of Indonesian leaders. Since "foreign policy is a phase of domestic policy,"[105] foreign policy starts at home, and this is why not necessarily its substance but certainly its form is significantly determined by the country's political, societal and cultural conditions. In the case of Indonesia, it is particularly the country's large Muslim constituency and the nationalist ideology that has since independence significantly shaped dynamics of Indonesia's domestic politics. These two leading domestic factors in turn shape the "form" of Indonesian foreign policy towards the United States. As one respondent explained, "because [of] our strong determination to look nationalistic and also non-allied at the same time, we do not say ... in public" that we consider close political, economic and military relations with Washington as a vital element of Indonesia's national security.[106] Referring to what can be seen as a hypocritical attitude of the Indonesian elite, a former high-ranking military officer affirmed:

> To be frank, Indonesia has mostly had a double standard on [the issue of the U.S. military presence in the region]. On the political level, it would be politically incorrect to show an open gesture that we would be open for a permanent U.S. military basing. [In reality, however,] there is an expectation for the presence of ... the U.S. forces as a balancing factor. To put it in easy terms would be, yes, they should not leave the region, maybe we do not mind if you [station your troops] here and there but we cannot show a high-profile support for the U.S. But one absolute element is not in Indonesia. Not in Indonesia but somewhere else.[107]

In sum, despite the elite's current concerns about U.S. policy towards Indonesia, "the U.S. remains a guarantor of peace and stability in the region" — this is also the conclusion of similar, though limited, research conducted by the Chinese scholar Pan Yining.[108] Commenting on the Indonesian elite's fundamental attitude towards the United States, a scholar and former government official observed: "The Indonesian perspective has always been the U.S. should be 'on tap', 'not on top'. 'On tap', it means that every time you need them they should be around but they should not dominate us."[109] The leader also stressed that the U.S. role in the regional security is exceedingly important insofar as it prevents "the possible bad guys like China and Japan from coming back."[110] The Americans should "stick around" chiefly because, as a former high-ranking military official questioned: "If China has bad intentions in the future, what power can prevent China from becoming a threat?" Here, the majority of the interviewed members of the foreign policy elite had a prompt answer — it is the United States, whose "presence in the region [is seen as] the last guarantee."[111]

FACTOR NO. 1: "GEOGRAPHIC PROXIMITY"

In the following paragraphs, we are going to analyse the research data presented in this book in order to assess the degree of influence of two important factors on the Indonesian leaders' threat perceptions and, consequently, their foreign policy preferences. We will focus, in turn, on the factors of the state's geographic proximity and the leaders' religion. The explanation about the relevance of these factors is facilitated by the use of graphs.

First, we will explore the role of "geographic proximity" as a causal variable affecting the leaders' perceptions to further support the argument that the Indonesian elite's considerations underlying the foreign policy decision-making process can be explained in terms of the balance-of-threat theory. Stephen M. Walt included the state's geographic proximity, along with its aggregate power, the state's offensive capability, and the perceived aggressiveness of its intentions, as one of the main variables in the balance-of-threat theory. In his study titled *The Origins of Alliances*, based on the analysis of the Middle Eastern alliances from 1955 to 1979, Walt argued that "states are more sensitive to threats that are nearby than to dangers from far away."[112]

However, since he used the case study of the Middle East at the height of the Cold War when hard sources of power (military power) played an important role in resolving inter-state disputes, we can question the extent to which Walt's argument is still valid now in light of the increasing economic, political, cultural and environmental interdependence among different places around the world. This "complex interdependence", as Keohane and Nye call it, signifies "[a] world in which security and force matter less and countries are connected by multiple social and political relationships."[113] The analysis, which draws on a case study carried out as a part of the author's survey research in Indonesia, aims to provide a greater insight into the extent to which distance between countries matters in contemporary national security considerations. In particular, it offers an answer to the following question: *"To what extent does the factor of 'geography proximity' determines the Indonesian elite's perception about other states?"*

Elite's Attitude to Future Involvement of External Powers in Southeast Asia

The interviewees were presented with a hypothetical situation, in which he or she, in the position of a top Indonesian foreign policy-maker around the year 2030, was dealing with a particular issue that was set to affect profoundly the country's national security. By 2030, China's and India's military power-projection capability will have dramatically increased and also Japan's assertiveness will have grown exponentially. When faced with these circumstances, the respondents were asked to decide whether they would prefer the United States to continue its predominant military presence in the region or whether they would prefer the U.S. presence to be complemented or replaced by one of the three above mentioned powers. In other words, the leaders were asked to nominate an external power, whose future military

presence in the region would be least detrimental to Indonesia's national
security.

The leaders overwhelmingly preferred the U.S. military presence, as
opposed to the Chinese or other states' military presence, in Southeast Asia.
Figure 7.2 shows that while 71 per cent of respondents preferred continuing
U.S. military presence in the region, 13 per cent would welcome a combined
U.S. and Chinese military presence, 11 per cent of them would want to
see external presence of any major power in Southeast Asia, and a mere
4 per cent would like to see the Chinese military/navy to completely replace
the U.S. forces. These results can be interpreted as that the elite is highly
conscious of which state or states constitute a long-term potentially malign
factor for Indonesia's national interests and security, as much as it is aware
of the necessity to constrain the potential threat. We can thus observe the
considerable extent to which geographic proximity plays a significant role
in Indonesian foreign policy elite's threat perceptions and in turn shapes
their foreign policy preferences. When asked, a common justification for the
leaders' preference for the U.S. military presence, as opposed to the Chinese,
Indian or Japanese military presence, in Southeast Asia was the fact that the
United States is *further away*. Only one out of forty-five respondents explicitly
reasoned that "distance does not play any role today."[114]

FIGURE 7.2
Attitude to the Future Involvement of External Powers in
Southeast Asia; Based on the Research Data Evaluation

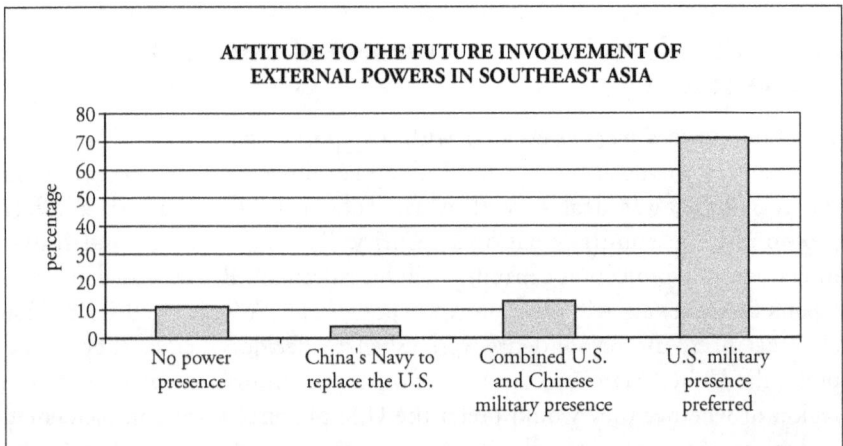

Source: Survey research conducted by the author in 2004–05.

It needs to be noted that, when first presented with the question outlined above, more than 11 per cent of the interviewed leaders initially insisted that they would never reconcile with the military presence of outside powers in the region. However, in order to be able to juxtapose the respondents' attitudes towards the major powers, they were told that "no power presence" was not on the list of possible options. One respondent observed:

> If you ask them (the Indonesian elite), would you like to see the Chinese armada or the American armada, they would not give any armada. ... My preference is nobody's predominance. I still prefer multi-polarity. ... But if they had to choose between the Americans and the Chinese, they would prefer the Americans rather than the Chinese. ... If you want to ask people, would you like to see the U.S. predominance or the Japanese predominance, the choice would be the U.S. predominance.[115]

The interviewed leader then explained: "Why? ... The U.S. is the only guy ... the only one with the blue-water navy. ... [And, most importantly,] because the Americans are further away."[116] Similarly, a senior official of the PDI-P political party argued: "The natural competitors of ours are our neighbors — China (along with India and Japan). ... We need the U.S.! ... Because of the distance, the U.S. is not really a competitor."[117]

In light of the uncertainty regarding the rise of China, according to one leader, the U.S. is expected to stay engaged in the regional security arrangements, particularly "in the ARF and also the physical presence of the U.S. in the region, either providing the maintenance facilities in Surabaya and Singapore, [which] provide an indirect psychological insurance for the stability of the region."[118] The importance of the U.S. military presence as a psychological insurance was mentioned on a couple of occasions. For example, responding to the question whether the U.S. engagement in the region is important for maintaining peace and security in Southeast Asia, a former President asserted: "The military superiority of the United States in the region is accepted. It is important — at least psychologically! I think so."[119]

Some of the other reasons mentioned for the leaders' overwhelming preference for the U.S. military presence over the Chinese or other powers' military presence were related to historical experience. A young career diplomat, for example, affirmed that he would "pragmatically choose the U.S. to stay" because the Indonesians do not have "any [similar] experience and thus no trust with China and India."[120] Another respondent juxtaposed his view of the U.S. with that of China — referring to the "historical experience with the Chinese, [particularly] during Kublai Khan", he suggested: "I think people would still prefer the U.S. navy to control the area. Because the U.S.

military until now is still perceived as *ramah*, a benevolent, friendly power. They do not have any territorial design, they do not want to occupy."[121] It is also because of historical experience that "the U.S. influence penetrating Indonesia is, in general, more acceptable"[122] and that "the U.S. is [seen as] the most effective" in maintaining the regional stability and security."[123] Suggesting that the U.S. military presence is acceptable not only for Indonesia but also for other countries in Southeast and East Asia, including China, one leader reasoned: "If you invite Japan to patrol the waters, China would protest."[124]

Finally, it ought to be again noted that even those leaders who were otherwise exceedingly critical of present U.S. policies and who exhibited a degree of distrust of America, were in the end inclined to stress their preference for military presence of the United States over other countries. Thus, one interviewee asserted that "the U.S. would [be trusted] to stay — [it is] not to be replaced by either the Chinese or the Japanese or the Indian navy."[125] A young Muslim leader who devoted most of the one-and-half hour interview to a fiery criticism of the U.S. President George W. Bush and his government's aggressive policies toward Muslim countries and its support of Israel, saying that "the U.S. will do what it can to keep Indonesia in its orbit", eventually concluded: "The U.S. navy should still better stay in the region — I would feel more comfortable than if the Chinese or Indian navy patrolled the Straits (of Malacca) and the South-China Sea."[126]

Balance of Threat Theory and the Geographic Proximity

The preceding discussion indicated that geographical proximity plays a crucial role in the Indonesian foreign policy elite's perceptions of external threats. It is evident that the leaders tend to be more sensitive to dangers that are nearby, particularly China, than to threats from far away, namely the United States. Spykman argues that "geography is the most fundamental factor in the foreign policy of states because it is the most permanent."[127] Spykman also asserted that the U.S. has the world's safest geopolitical location because it

> ... occupies a unique position in the world. ... History has treated us kindly; geography has endowed us greatly; the opportunities have been well used; and the result is that our country is today the most important political unit in the New World. ... Fronting on two oceans, the United States has direct access to the most important trading arteries of the world. [Moreover] the United States is blessed by the happy circumstance that she is a strong power between two weak powers. ... Canada and Mexico are not in a position to threaten us now and are prevented by

geography and lack of resources from ever becoming strong military powers.[128]

Commenting on the same geopolitical advantages of the U.S., some 60 years later, Brooks and Wohlforth rightly observed that "[bounded] by oceans to the east and west and weak, friendly powers to the north and south, the United States is both less vulnerable than previous aspiring hegemons and also less threatening to others."[129] In predicting the possible future dynamics of international relations in Southeast Asia, we certainly need to take the "geographic proximity" factor into consideration. In particular, it is important to assess the extent to which the Indonesian elite perceptions confirm the assumption that the United States enjoys "the world's safest geopolitical location". Because if this assumption remains substantially valid, we can reasonably expect that Indonesian and other regional governments will continue to be inclined to encourage either a physical or at least tacit presence of the U.S. in Southeast Asia and the wider region.

Walt compared in his 1990 study the geopolitical position of the United States with that of the Soviet Union. The latter, by virtue of being the largest and most powerful country on the Eurasian continent, according to Walt, "poses a significant threat to the numerous countries that lie on or near its borders." As a consequence, "Soviet relations with neighbors tend to be either imperial or hostile; the neighbors are either under de facto Soviet control or aligned with the United States."[130] By contrast, the United States has only two significantly weaker neighbours, both of whom are its allies and, more importantly, it is separated by two oceans from the other centers of power.[131] This leads Walt to argue that

> [for] the middle-level powers on Western Europe and Asia, the United
> States is the perfect ally. Its aggregate power ensures that its voice will
> be heard and its actions will be felt, and it is driven by its own concern
> for Soviet expansion to contribute substantially to its allies' defense. At
> the same time, the United States is far enough away so as not to pose a
> significant threat to these allies. Thus the United States is geographically
> isolated but politically popular, whereas the Soviet Union is politically
> isolated as a consequence of its geographic proximity to other states.[132]

Ikenberry points out that in contrast to previous hegemonic powers, the position of the United States is not geographically in close proximity to other states. Therefore, he contends, "[it is] better for states to rely on the U.S. for protection from its neighbors, than to balance against America."[133] In the former communist countries of Central and Eastern Europe, for example, this mode of thinking continues to inform the national security considerations of the regional elites. For example, Alexander Vondra, one of the most prominent Czech foreign policy-makers and thinkers in the post-Cold War era, observed: "We have never been threatened in any way by the United States. The U.S. is far from us. That is why we (the Czechs), wedged between Germany and Russia, should be really keen to maintain a special relationship (with America). The Poles, for instance, are acutely aware of this situation."[134] In the Indonesian case, it is the country's specific relationship with Vietnam and the Indonesian elite's geopolitical considerations underpinning it, which begs close scrutiny. As Suryadinata explains,

> [in] the north, the PRC has always been viewed by Indonesian leaders as an "expansionist" power and a major competitor for the role of regional leader to which Indonesia aspires. For this reason, Vietnam has been seen as a buffer against the potentially expansionist tendencies of the PRC.[135]

Following Vietnam's invasion of Cambodia in 1978, its closest Southeast Asian neighbours were increasingly apprehensive of perceived Vietnamese expansionism, which led to a convergence of interests especially between Thailand and China. In line with the geographic proximity thesis, Thailand regarded Vietnam occupying the neighboring Cambodia as a more imminent threat than China. By contrast, the New Order regime in Indonesia saw the *giant* China as a greater security threat than Vietnam. In fact, China's border war with Vietnam in 1979 further deepened the Indonesian elite's distrust of Beijing's long-term intentions in the region.[136] Despite the Suharto regime's staunch anti-communist outlook, in the case of Vietnam, this was outweighed by other considerations, notably perceived common struggle for independence and strategic concerns pertaining to Indonesia's national security and interests. The armed forces leadership and especially its commander, General Murdani, regarded Vietnam as a vital buffer against Chinese expansionism.[137] According to a former Foreign Minister, "[during] the most difficult times, we remained supporters of North Vietnam, not South Vietnam. We remained supporters of North Korea, not South Korea. … So, there is a consistency in Indonesia's foreign policy for its principles and also for its threat perceptions."[138]

This fact needs to be accentuated insofar as it sheds some light on the Indonesian foreign policy elite's broader geopolitical considerations underpinning the country's foreign policy. Despite its fierce anti-communist attitude, the New Order's political and military leadership found it desirable to extend at least a tacit backing to the communist regimes first in Northern Vietnam and later in the united Vietnam, as well as in North Korea. Apart from their respective regimes' ideology, what both these countries have in common is that they share a border with China. It has been argued that, in a broader sense, these elite's attitudes and its security considerations can be understood in terms of the traditional Javanese concept of *mandala*.

Geographic Proximity and the *Mandala* Concept

In its original Hindu meaning, the Sanskrit word "mandala" referred to "circle" or "completion" and was associated with any chart, plan or geometric pattern which represents a microcosm of the universe from the human perspective. The symmetrical geometric shape of *mandala* was designed to draw the attention towards its centre. Anderson argues that the concept of mandala has influenced traditional Javanese thought. It divided the world into two types of states: the island of Java standing in the center and Sabrang, or "overseas" meaning all non-Javanese political entities, with the latter always seen in the context of their relationship to Java. As Anderson observed, "[the] centripetality of Javanese political thinking, combined with the conceptions of graduated sovereignty sketched out above, leads logically to a specific perspective on foreign relations."[139]

Lanti and Sebastian argue here that "in significant ways, Indonesian 'national security' is understood in Javanese terms."[140] Moertono describes the concept of *mandala* as

> [a] complex of geopolitical relations, relating to boundaries and to contact with foreign countries. The doctrine emphasized the cult of expansion, a necessary spur to the struggle for existence, self-assertion and world domination, and the dynamics factor calculated to disturb the equilibrium of inter-state relations.[141]

Furthermore, he explains that

> [a] state's belligerence is in the first place directed towards its closest neighbor(s), thus making necessary the friendship of the state next to the foe, which, because of its proximity, is also a natural enemy of the foe. But if the mutual foe should be conquered, the two allies would become close neighbors, which would create a new enmity. So this circle of alignment and alienation would steadily expand until a universal peace is reached by the establishment of a world-state with a sole and supreme ruler (*chakravartin*).[142]

The concept of *mandala* teaches us that the power of the ruler/centre diminishes toward the state's periphery and it is at the point of contact with the neighbour's border where the state is the most vulnerable. The closest neighbour was traditionally seen as the a priori enemy and it was deemed as a necessity to exert the state's power against this neighbouring political entity. Consequently, as a general rule, the closer the state, the more likely it is considered as a threat to Indonesia. Commenting on the significance of geographic proximity in Indonesian elite's national security thinking, Suryadinata writes that "even a small neighboring state that is occupied or used by a major power hostile to Indonesia may be perceived as a threat."[143] This is also why one interviewed leader asserted that "Indonesia's neighbors are perceived as buffer states against China."[144] Although it has been suggested that the concept of *mandala* constitutes a distinct Indonesian international relations tradition, there is clearly a need for a detailed analysis of its relevance for the way modern Indonesia's foreign policy-making is conducted.[145] In particular, the question whether there is a correlation between the traditional Javanese political thinking, the geographic proximity factor and the present Indonesian elite's national security considerations necessitates a closer scrutiny.

As outlined in Chapters 1 and 2, adherents of the realist international relations theory would regard America's current global predominance as necessarily self-negating to the extent that it would spur other states to band together with the aim to restrain what the leaders often describe as a hegemonic power. However, the factor of geographic proximity, which is inherent to the concept of mandala, suggests that China (also, for example, Japan, Russia, India) cannot expand their influence and boost their military capabilities, without concurrently being perceived as a potent threat by their neighbours. Katzenstein and Okawara observe that "[as] has been true in Europe since 1989, in Asia-Pacific, the United States is seen as more distant and more benign than other regional powers, such as Japan and China."[146] As Brooks and Wohlforth point out,

> [politics], even international politics, is local. Although American power attracts a lot of attention globally, states are usually more concerned with their own neighborhoods than with the global equilibrium. Were any of the potential challengers to make a serious run at the United States, regional balancing efforts would almost certainly help contain them…[147]

It is worth noting that the basic assessment of the implications of China's geographic proximity to Southeast Asia had not changed in the span of six decades. In his 1942 study, Spykman accurately predicted that

> [a] modern, vitalized, and militarized China of 450 million people is going to be a threat not only to Japan, but also to the position of the Western Powers in the Asiatic Mediterranean (South-China Sea). China will be a continental power of huge dimensions in control of a large section of the littoral of that middle sea.[148]

In light of the logic underpinning the "geographic proximity" thesis, Brzezinski concluded:

> ... it would certainly be in China's own interest to exercise self-restraint in order to avoid regional fears of Chinese imperialism. That fear could generate a regional anti-Chinese coalition (and some overtones of that are already present in the nascent Indonesian-Australian military cooperation), which would then most likely seek support from the United States, Japan, and Australia.[149]

In short, we have seen that the "geographic proximity" factor shapes the Indonesian leaders' perceptions of other state actors and in turn weighs heavily into their foreign policy calculations with respect to the regional security environment.[150] And the concept of *mandala* essentially encompasses the idea behind the "geographic proximity" thesis. In line with this thesis, the Indonesian foreign policy elite will be in the long run more inclined to employ various balancing strategies against China than against the United States owing to the former state's geographic proximity to Southeast Asia.

FACTOR NO. 2: "RELIGION"

This section is concerned with the role of religion as a factor or a causal variable that affects the Indonesian leaders' perceptions. It draws attention to the phenomenon of religion as a powerful force that significantly determines people's identities and their sense of what constitutes a threat to their respective communities/nations/states. Initially, we need to emphasize that it has been a long-term policy of consecutive Indonesian Administrations to maintain an image of a religiously homogenous and cohesive political establishment. The administrations have sought to prevent any religious divide among the country's foreign policy establishment from becoming apparent. Officially, the Muslim and non-Muslim members of the elite are deemed to be unanimous in their view of the world in general, and its foreign policy perception in particular.

During the research survey in Jakarta, the author suggested to several respondents a possible religious divide among the country's foreign policy elite. All of those presented with this hypothesis strictly refused the notion of religion as playing an important role in shaping the elite's perceptions of external threats. A senior diplomat was one of the staunchest opponents of the idea of a religious divide among the elite:

> I do not quite agree with the notion that foreign policy perception has been colored by the religious theme. ... It is a dangerous over-generalization. It is factually incorrect to say that foreign policy perception in Indonesia is drawn along religious lines. ... In fact, it has been the deliberate attempt by the foreign policy establishment to make sure that religious divide, religious considerations, does not have an [impact] on our foreign policy. And we are very proud of that.[151]

The obvious question that presents itself here is to what degree is the phenomenon of religion in reality important as a causal variable in determining the Indonesian elite's threat perceptions? And, ultimately, is the country's elite unanimous in its view of the world, which has been the official policy of Indonesian political establishment, or is the elite divided in its foreign policy perception?

In his study *The Clash of Civilizations*, Huntington posits that "of all the objective elements (blood, language, religion, way of life) which define civilizations ... the most important usually is religion; ... people who share ethnicity and language but differ in religion may slaughter each other."[152] He furthermore contends that "religion is not a 'small difference' but possibly the most profound difference that can exist between people." As a result, he presents an argument that warfare between various political entities is "greatly enhanced by beliefs in different gods."[153] However, other scholars disputed Huntington's "Clash of Civilizations" thesis, which is based on the assumption that since international relations are increasingly reconfigured along cultural (understand principally religious) lines, conflicts are more likely to occur between states of different civilizations. For example, Henderson and Tucker concluded in their study that "...contrary to the primary assumptions of Huntington's clash of civilizations thesis, civilization difference is not significantly associated with an increased likelihood of interstate war..."[154]

To this end, we will now examine the research data to establish the extent to which Indonesian leaders' religious identity influences their attitudes towards other countries. In other words, rather than focusing on the causal relationship between the leaders' religion and the international conflict, meaning interstate wars, we will analyse the impact of the leaders' religious beliefs on their perceptions of other countries, particularly the United States and China. According to Henderson and Tucker, "... the most propitious path in this regard is to examine systematically the role of cultural variables on the process of elite decision-making. Their most obvious role in political outcomes is to provide a context for foreign policy decision-making."[155] For the purpose of this analysis, religion as a cultural variable will be divided into two categories: first, members of the foreign policy elite of Muslim background and, second, members of non-Muslim background. This categorization will facilitate the assessment of the pattern and degree of religious divisions among the Indonesian leadership.

There are few studies that have examined the role of religious identity in shaping public opinion of other countries. An opinion analysis by the U.S. Department of States, for example, targeted urban Malaysians to find out about their views of the United States and its policies. The most significant finding was that the perceptions of the U.S. among the urban Malaysians run along religious lines. Commenting on the divergent images of the U.S. between the Muslims and non-Muslims, the analysis concluded that

> ... the country's Muslims [have] a basic belief that the U.S. is hostile to Islam — a belief which colors their bottom-line judgments across a wide range of issues, from American society to American foreign policy. But non-Muslims, lacking this basic mistrust of American intentions, tend to look at the same range of issues and see positives. ... Less trustful of U.S. intentions, Muslims gravitate toward negative views of the U.S. on a range of issues.[156]

Consequently, whereas 77 per cent of the Muslims, who are virtually all ethnic Malays, had an unfavourable opinion of the U.S., 69 per cent of the non-Muslims, who are primarily people of Chinese and Indian descent, had a favourable view of that country.[157]

Another research, conducted by the Washington D.C.-based Pew Research Centre, also revealed a strong division along religious lines among the Lebanese population in their views of the U.S.-led anti-terrorism campaign: while 88 per cent of Muslims in that country were opposed and 11 per cent of them supported the U.S. anti-terrorism effort, 33 per cent of Christians opposed and 60 per cent of them supported the war on terrorism.[158] Also views among the Lebanese population about China becoming as military powerful as the United States are strongly colored by religious beliefs. Whereas 53 per cent of Muslims view this scenario positively, 55 per cent of Christians in Lebanon think that a China equal in military strength to the U.S. is a development with negative implications.[159]

The series of interviews the author conducted in Indonesia has revealed a similar situation as in the studies outlined above. A detailed analysis of the Indonesian foreign policy elite present and future, long-term threat assessment shows that the leaders' views are fundamentally divided along the lines of their religious identity. It is obvious from Figures 7.3 and 7.4 that there is a significant gap between the perceptions of the leaders coming from Muslim and non-Muslim background especially in the case of the United States. As was illustrated in preceding chapters, members of the elite coming both from the Muslim and the non-Muslim background share certain basic negative perceptions of some U.S. foreign policies and critical concerns about America's style of interaction with the rest of the world.

However, the Muslim and non-Muslim respondents had conspicuously divergent impression of America's real intentions. On the one hand, the non-Muslims displayed overall trust in the U.S. long-term intentions with regards to Indonesia with only a handful of them being drawn to the negative images about America; on the other hand, the Muslim leaders' perception of the U.S. was characterized by a considerable mistrust owing to their basic conviction that America is intrinsically hostile to Islam. A case in point is, for example, the considerable difference between the Muslim and non-Muslim group's attitude to Israel. A senior official of non-Muslim background from the Department of Trade criticized the Indonesian Government policy of not diplomatically recognizing the state of Israel, asserting that "what the Bible said is that Israel will survive because it will be supported by foreign powers."[160] By contrast, for example one Muslim leader claimed he was suspicious of Singapore's intentions because of the country's close military ties with Israel.[161]

Thus, the perception that the U.S. is anti-Islam in nature affects the Muslim leaders' emotional disposition towards America and in turn negatively colours their judgments across a wide range of issues pertaining to that country. The negative impression among the Muslim respondents of America is often the result of what they perceive as Washington's hostile policies towards other, particularly Muslim, countries, rather than being framed in terms of the security threat the U.S. poses directly to Indonesia. By contrast, since the non-Muslim leaders' perception of the United States lack this basic mistrust and suspicion, which is coloured by the religious aspect, they are inclined to view the same issues in a positive light. Figure 7.3 illustrates that

FIGURE 7.3

The Greatest Present External Threat to Indonesia: Muslim versus Non-Muslim Dichotomy; Based on the Research Data Evaluation

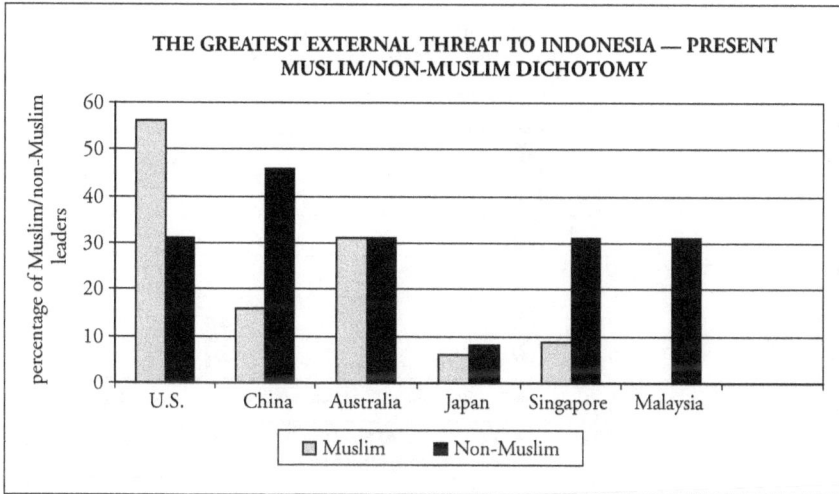

THE GREATEST EXTERNAL THREAT TO INDONESIA — PRESENT
MUSLIM/NON-MUSLIM DICHOTOMY

Source: Survey research conducted by the author in 2004–05.

there is a gap between the Muslim and non-Muslim respondents' present threat assessment with regards to the U.S.: almost twice as many Muslim leaders as non-Muslim ones consider America as presently the most serious security threat to Indonesia. Figure 7.4 then provides more support to the assumption that religion constitutes the essential filter in the Indonesian foreign policy elite's views of the United States: none of the non-Muslim respondents was concerned about America and its policies in the future, whereas about one third of the Muslim respondents identified the U.S. as a long-term threat to Indonesia. It can thus also be argued that this fact confirms the earlier presented claim about the relative superficiality of the elite's anti-American and anti-Western sentiments.

A detailed analysis based on Figures 7.3 and 7.4 demonstrates that the leaders' religious identity significantly influenced also their perceptions of other countries. It can be assumed that, owing to the Muslim respondents' deep mistrust of the U.S. intentions, which is coloured by religion, considerably less Muslim leaders than non-Muslim ones regard China as the number one external factor that needs to be constrained. In other words, since religion is an important aspect of the elite worldview through which the leaders' perceptions are "filtered", by virtue of being less trustful of the United States,

FIGURE 7.4
**The Elite Future, Long-Term Threat Assessment: Muslim versus
Non-Muslim Dichotomy; Based on the Research Data Evaluation**

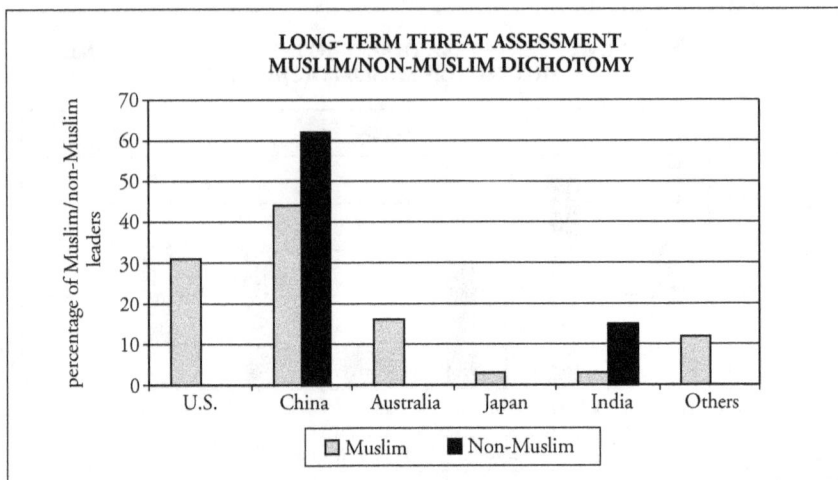

Source: Survey research conducted by the author in 2004–05.

the Muslim respondents tended to gravitate toward negative views of the
U.S. more than in the case of China. Moreover, the fact that 31 per cent of
leaders in both religious groups consider Australia as presently a serious threat
to Indonesia indicates that their security concerns with regards to Indonesia's
southern neighbour cut across the religious divisions. The Indonesian elite's
wariness of Australia's intentions with regard to West Papua thus does
not appear to be significantly influenced by the religious aspect. On the
other hand, in light of the finding that only Muslim respondents regarded
Australia as a threat in the long run, it is apparent that this view was strongly
coloured by the leaders' religious identity. We may interpret this as that, by
and large, the elite is fairly optimistic about the country's future relationship
with Australia. Finally, a similar conclusion can be applied to Malaysia, a
predominantly Muslim country, which was identified as a security threat to
Indonesia only by non-Muslim respondents.

On the role of religion and religious affiliation in the foreign policy
formation, Azyumardi Azra writes: "One has to admit that one of the
most obvious features of Islamic politics in Southeast Asia, particularly in
Indonesia and Malaysia, is conflict and fragmentation among political elite."[162]

All in all, we have found that the phenomenon of religious beliefs can be considered a leading causal variable affecting the Indonesian elite's attitudes. The discussion has highlighted a substantial gap between the Muslim and non-Muslim members of the foreign policy elite in terms of their worldview as well as their perceptions about other countries. The finding that the Indonesian leadership is divided in its general outlook on international relations along religious lines also essentially challenges the carefully maintained image of religiously homogenous and cohesive Indonesian foreign policy establishment that is united in its threat perceptions.

CONCLUSION:
THE QUESTION OF THE ELITE CONSENSUS

This chapter has brought together both the theoretical and the empirical aspect of this study. The key two themes running through the discussion have been that, first, the Indonesian elite's considerations underlying the foreign policy decision-making process exhibit a distinct inclination to operate along the lines of the balance of threat concept and, second, the Indonesian leadership is fundamentally divided in its foreign policy perceptions.

First, we have found that the concept or idea of a perceived/imaginary balance in the inter-state system constitutes a foundation of the Indonesian elite's mode of thinking with regards of the country's national security. In particular, China and the United States are considered strategic players, whereby Indonesia (and other ASEAN states) — in light of the *"row between two reefs"* concept — should play an intermediate, mediating role and maintain a (perceived/imaginary) equilibrium between these two major powers. This balance is seen as important insofar as it will provide Indonesia with a leeway, a safe space for maneuvering.

Second, this chapter has elaborated the phenomenon of elite agreement (or disagreement) about the nature and urgency of the threat. The discussion accentuated the high degree to which the elite's perceptions of external threats are diffused and complex. One important factor, which determines how the elite perceptions of external threats affect the present and future direction of Indonesia's foreign relations, is the disparity between the leaders' present and future, long-term threat assessment. We have seen that while at present the elite consider the U.S. as the main security concern, it concurrently believes that in twenty years and beyond China will be the most serious security threat to Indonesia. Hence, the Indonesian elite is forced to deal with this dichotomous situation in the context of the "*mendayung antara dua karang*" concept.

The role of geographic proximity has proved to be a potent factor that shapes the elite's threat perceptions. The data revealed the Indonesian elite's overwhelming preference for the U.S. military presence in the long run, as opposed to the Chinese, Indian or Japanese military presence, in the region. This clearly illustrates the elite's awareness of which state actors constitute a potentially malign factor for Indonesia's national interests and, in line with the balance-of-threat concept, their appreciation of the necessity to eliminate, or balance, this potential threat. One of the most frequent explanations for the leaders' preference for the U.S. navy's presence in the region was the fact that "the Americans are further away". This finding unequivocally confirms Walt's argument that "geographic proximity" informs elite perceptions and suggests that the role of the United States as an important guarantor of regional security is likely to be sustained in the long run.

Chapters 2 and 3 drew attention to one of the main contributions of this study, which is its attempt to enhance the balance-of-threat theory's explanatory power by putting more emphasis on the degree of elite cohesion and the leaders' consensus about the nature and urgency of the threat. It could be argued that against the backdrop of Indonesia's competitive and pluralist democratic environment in the *reformasi* period, there is a low degree of elite cohesion and hence the leaders are badly divided in their basic attitudes and perceptions. Walt claims that "disagreements about policy usually rest on the more fundamental disagreements about the basic forces that shape international outcomes."[163] This discussion focused on the elite's religious/cultural division that contributes the elite's polarization and ensuing disagreements with regard to national security. It has effectively challenged the carefully maintained image of a religiously homogenous and cohesive Indonesian foreign policy establishment united in its threat perception. At present, it is basically impossible to identify one dominant and paramount security concern that outweighs the others by a wide margin. Though being a source of the most serious state-based security concern, neither the United States, nor China has yielded more than 51 and 49 per cent of respondents respectively.

In his 1971/1972 study, Weinstein tackled the factor of the elite consensus about the direction of Indonesian foreign policy when he concluded that "... to the degree that political power in Djakarta becomes more diffuse and political competition is restored, one may expect increasing challenges to Indonesia's foreign policy of development."[164] Undoubtedly, the same factor needs to be taken into account in any analysis of how perceptions of external threats among the present Indonesian leadership weigh into the foreign policy-making process. To this end, an article analysing contemporary Indonesian foreign policy argued:

> The problem is in the internal policies. The policy-makers are split, the elite as a whole is not solid. This is because of bureaucratic constraints and also because Indonesia's internal policies have no clear vision. The political outputs are often different and contradictive, notably between the Foreign Department, and the Directorate of Trade and Industry.[165]

To conclude, this chapter has provided an explanation for the state of contemporary Indonesian foreign policy that was by some diplomats and scholars characterized as "untidy, illogical and messy" and "haphazard, lacking priorities". We have found here that there is a considerable disagreement among central Indonesian decision-makers about how to rank dangers to the state's security in terms of their nature and urgency which leads to the low consensus in the elite's foreign policy preferences. As we had argued earlier, this is the result of, first, the existence of a diversity of ideational influences that has generated disparate elite views about what constitutes Indonesia's national interest and how to defend it; and, second, a growing complexity of the international system that gives rise to perceived multiple threats which are increasingly multi-sourced, multi-dimensional and multi-layered by nature. Most importantly, this low level of elite consensus in turn contributes to the current state of the foreign policy that appears ambivalent, short of purpose and lacking priorities.

Notes

[1] Irman Lanti, "Indonesia in Triangular Relations with China and the United States", in *China, the United States, and Southeast Asia: Contending Perspectives on Politics, Security, and Economics*, edited by Evelyn Goh and Sheldon W. Simon (New York: Routledge, 2008), pp. 128–41.

[2] Muhammad Hatta, *Mendayung antara Dua Karang* [Rowing between Two Reefs] (Jakarta: NV Bulan Bintang, 1988.

[3] Quoting from Marvin Ott's speech at: "Indonesia and Japan: Economic and Political Relations and Implications for Southeast Asia", USINDO seminar, Washington D.C. (13 September 2004).

[4] Jusuf Wanandi, "ASEAN's China Strategy: Towards Deeper Engagement", *Survival*, No. 3 (Autumn 1996), p. 127.

[5] Interview with a Minister in President Yudhoyono's cabinet, Jakarta, 28 February 2005.

6   Interview with an Indonesian academic and expert in the Indonesian military, Jakarta, 24 January 2005.

7   Interview with a former admiral of the Indonesian Navy, Jakarta, 24 February 2005.

8   Interview with a senior Indonesian diplomat, Jakarta, 24 October 2004.

9   Interview with a former admiral of the Indonesian Navy, Jakarta, 24 February 2005.

10 Interview with a retired Indonesian Army general, presently also affiliated with a Jakarta-based research institute, Jakarta, 3 February 2005.

11 Wahyu Dhyatmika, "Mendayung di antara Banyak Karang" [Rowing among Many Reefs], *Tempo*, 2 November 2008.

12 Amitav Acharya and See Seng Tan, "Betwixt Balance and Community: America, ASEAN and the Security of Southeast Asia", *International Relations of the Asia-Pacific* 6, no. 1 (February 2006): 38.

13 Interview with an Indonesian expert in international relations, CSIS, Jakarta, 21 February 2005.

14 Ibid.

15 Interview with a CSIS-based international relations expert, Jakarta, 8 February 2005.

16 Interview with an Indonesian expert in international relations, CSIS, Jakarta, 21 February 2005.

17 Interview with a Minister in President Yudhoyono's cabinet, Jakarta, 28 February 2005.

18 Interview with a senior official of PDI-P, Jakarta, 22 February 2005.

19 Interview with a former Indonesian Minister of Foreign Affairs, Jakarta, 14 January 2005.

20 Interview with a Minister in President Yudhoyono's cabinet, Jakarta, 28 February 2005.

21 "Pemilu 2004: ASEAN Harus Tetap 'Corner Stone'" [Elections 2004: ASEAN Has to Remain as a "Corner Stone"], *Kompas*, 1 April 2004.

22 Robert S. Ross, "The Geography of Peace", *International Security* 23, no. 4 (Spring 1999): 84–86.

23 Gaye Christofferson, "The Role of East Asia in Sino-U.S. Relations", *Asian Survey* 42, no. 3 (May/June 2002).

24 Interview with an Indonesian academic and expert in the Indonesian military, Jakarta, 24 January 2005.

25 "Poros Jakarta-Peking: Siapa Takut" [Axis Jakarta-Beijing: No Need to Worry], *Gatra* 51, no. XII (8 November 2006): 18–19.

26 Interview with an Indonesian journalist, Singapore, 4 November 2008.

27 Interview with an Indonesian academic and expert in the Indonesian military, Jakarta, 24 January 2005.

28 Ibid.

29   Interview with an Indonesian expert in international relations, CSIS, Jakarta, 21 February 2005.

30   "Indonesia and Regional Security", USINDO Security Workshops I, Washington D.C. (9 May 2001).

31   Interview with an Indonesian academic and expert in the Indonesian military, Jakarta, 24 January 2005.

32   Interview with an Indonesian expert in international relations, CSIS, Jakarta, 21 February 2005.

33   Interview with an Indonesian scholar and IR expert affiliated with LIPI, Jakarta, 24 February 2005.

34   Interview with an Indonesian academic and expert in the Indonesian military, Jakarta, 24 January 2005.

35   Jusuf Wanandi, "Changes in the Political Role of the TNI", in "Joint Public Forum on Indonesia: The First 100 Days of President Megawati, Political and Economic Perspectives", organized by ISEAS (Singapore) and CSIS (Jakarta), Singapore (1 November 2001).

36   Interview with a former Indonesian Minister of Foreign Affairs, Jakarta, 14 January 2005.

37   Ibid.

38   Ibid.

39   Ibid.

40   Interview with an Indonesian leader and academic affiliated with LIPI, Jakarta, 14 February 2005.

41   "Indonesia and Japan: Economic and Political Relations and Implications for Southeast Asia", USINDO seminar, Washington D.C. (13 September 2004).

42   Interview with an Indonesian leader and academic affiliated with LIPI, Jakarta, 14 February 2005.

43   Ibid.

44   Interview with a senior Indonesian career diplomat, DEPLU, Jakarta, 12 January 2005.

45   Interview with an Indonesian leader and academic affiliated with LIPI, Jakarta, 14 February 2005.

46   Interview with a senior official of the PDI-P political party and senior member of the Indonesian Parliament (DPR), Jakarta, 23 February 2005.

47   Interview with an Indonesian politician and leader of a Muslim organization, Yogyakarta, 2 March 2005.

48   Interview with an Indonesian expert in international relations, CSIS, Jakarta, 21 February 2005.

49   Interview with a retired Indonesian Army general, presently also affiliated with a Jakarta-based research institute, Jakarta, 3 February 2005.

50   Interview with a senior Indonesian career diplomat, DEPLU, Jakarta, 12 January 2005.

51 Interview with an Indonesian leader and academic affiliated with LIPI, Jakarta, 14 February 2005.

52 Interview with a senior official of the PDI-P political party and senior member of the Indonesian Parliament (DPR), Jakarta, 23 February 2005.

53 Interview with a retired Indonesian Army general, presently also affiliated with a Jakarta-based research institute, Jakarta, 3 February 2005.

54 For a detailed analysis on the issue of economic interdependence, see: Robert O. Keohane and Joseph S. Nye Jr., *Power and Interdependence*, 2nd edition (New York: Harper Collins Publishers, 1989); Robert O. Keohane and Joseph S. Nye Jr., "Power and Interdependence in the Information Age", *Foreign Affairs* 77, no. 5 (September/October 1998).

55 Interview with an Indonesian scholar and IR expert affiliated with LIPI, Jakarta, 24 February 2005.

56 Interview with an Indonesian executive officer who is working for an U.S.-based major private financial institution, Jakarta, 2 February 2005.

57 Interview with an Indonesian expert in international relations, CSIS, Jakarta, 21 February 2005.

58 Interview with a leader and academic affiliated with the LIPI, Jakarta, 10 December 2004.

59 Interview with an Indonesian scholar and IR expert affiliated with LIPI, Jakarta, 24 February 2005.

60 Interview with an Indonesian journalist, a foreign relations commentator, Jakarta, 21 February 2005.

61 Interview with a senior official of PDI-P, Jakarta, 22 February 2005.

62 Interview with a former Indonesian President, Jakarta, 10 January 2005.

63 Interview with an Indonesian academic and former cabinet minister, Singapore, 15 April 2005.

64 Interview with a senior member of *Muhammadiyah* Muslim organization, 23 February 2005.

65 Interview with an Indonesian politician, diplomat and journalist, Jakarta, 4 February 2005.

66 Interview with a senior Indonesian career diplomat, DEPLU, Jakarta, 12 January 2005.

67 Interview with a former Indonesian Minister of Foreign Affairs, Jakarta, 14 January 2005.

68 Interview with an Indonesian executive officer who is working for an U.S.-based major private financial institution, Jakarta, 2 February 2005.

69 Interview with an Indonesian expert in international relations, CSIS, Jakarta, 21 February 2005.

70 Interview with an Indonesian scholar and IR expert affiliated with LIPI, Jakarta, 24 February 2005.

71 Interview with an Indonesian politician, diplomat and journalist, Jakarta, 4 February 2005.

72 Interview with a former Indonesian President, Jakarta, 10 January 2005.
73 Interview with a CSIS-based international relations expert, Jakarta, 8 February 2005.
74 Interview with an expert on Indonesian foreign policy, Singapore, 15 May 2006.
75 Interview with an Indonesian politician and leader of a Muslim organization, Yogyakarta, 2 March 2005.
76 Interview with a CSIS-based international relations expert, Jakarta, 8 February 2005.
77 Ian James Storey, "Creeping Assertiveness: China, the Philippines and the South-China Sea Dispute", *Contemporary Southeast Asia* 21, no. 1 (April 1999).
78 Interview with a retired Indonesian army general, presently also affiliated with a Jakarta-based research institute, Jakarta, 3 February 2005.
79 An Indonesian scholar and the country's foremost expert on China, Jakarta, 3 July 2006.
80 Ibid.
81 Interview with a CSIS-based international relations expert, Jakarta, 8 February 2005.
82 Interview with a former Indonesian Minister of Foreign Affairs, Jakarta, 14 January 2005.
83 Interview with a journalist and chief editor of a Jakarta-based national newspaper, Jakarta, 15 February 2005.
84 Ibid.
85 Interview with an Indonesian academic and expert in the Indonesian military, Jakarta, 24 January 2005.
86 Quoted from: "Indonesia and Japan: Economic and Political Relations and Implications for Southeast Asia", USINDO seminar, Washington D.C. (13 September 2004).
87 Interview with a senior official of the PDI-P political party and senior member of the Indonesian Parliament (DPR), Jakarta, 23 February 2005.
88 Interview with an Indonesian expert in international relations, CSIS, Jakarta, 21 February 2005.
89 Interview with a CSIS-based international relations expert, Jakarta, 8 February 2005.
90 Interview with an Indonesian politician and leader of a Muslim organization, Yogyakarta, 2 March 2005.
91 Interview with a retired Indonesian army general, presently also affiliated with a Jakarta-based research institute, Jakarta, 3 February 2005.
92 Interview with a senior Indonesian career diplomat, DEPLU, Jakarta, 12 January 2005.
93 Interview with an Indonesian expert in international relations, CSIS, Jakarta, 21 February 2005.
94 Ibid.

95   Kornelius Purba, "Celebrating 16 Years of Normalized Ties between China, Indonesia", *Jakarta Post* (8 August 2006).

96   Quoting from Marvin Ott's speech at: "Indonesia and Japan: Economic and Political Relations and Implications for Southeast Asia", USINDO seminar, Washington D.C. (13 September 2004).

97   Interview with an Indonesian expert in international relations, CSIS, Jakarta, 21 February 2005.

98   Ibid.

99   Interview with Rizal Sukma in "Perspective: Iraq-U.S.-Indonesia", Radio Singapore International, 8 February 2003.

100   Interview with a member of DPR, Indonesian Parliament, for the National Mandate Party (PAN), Jakarta, 7 February 2005.

101   Ibid.

102   Interview with a senior official of the PDI-P political party and senior member of the Indonesian Parliament (DPR), Jakarta, 23 February 2005.

103   Interview, 2005.

104   Interview, 2005.

105   Charles A. Beard, *Foreign Policy for America* (New York: Alfred A. Knopf, 1940); Stelios Stavridis and Christopher Hill, eds., *Domestic Sources of Foreign Policy: West European Reactions to the Falklands Conflict* (Oxford: Berg Publishers, 1996); Rizal Sukma, *Islam in Indonesian Foreign Policy* (London, New York: RoutledgeCurzon, 2003).

106   Interview with a CSIS-based international relations expert, Jakarta, 8 February 2005.

107   Interview with a retired Indonesian army general, presently also affiliated with a Jakarta-based research institute, Jakarta, 3 February 2005.

108   Quoting Pan Yining from: "Report on Discussion: Indonesia's Perceptions of China and the U.S. Security Roles in East Asia", *Postscript* III, no. 3 (Jakarta: The Habibie Center, March 2006): 30–34.

109   Interview with an Indonesian leader and academic affiliated with LIPI, Jakarta, 14 February 2005.

110   Ibid.

111   Interview with a former Indonesian high-ranking military officer and senior diplomat, Jakarta, 14 February 2005.

112   Stephen M. Walt, *The Origins of Alliances* (London, Cornell University Press, 1990), p. 276.

113   Keohane and Nye, "Power and Interdependence in the Information Age", p. 34.

114   Interview with an Indonesian journalist, a foreign relations commentator, Jakarta, 21 February 2005.

115   Interview with an Indonesian leader and academic affiliated with LIPI, Jakarta, 14 February 2005.

116   Ibid.

117 Interview with a senior official of the PDI-P political party and senior member of the Indonesian Parliament (DPR), Jakarta, 23 February 2005.

118 Interview with a CSIS-based international relations expert, Jakarta, 8 February 2005.

119 Interview with a former Indonesian President, Jakarta, 1 March 2005.

120 Interview with a young Indonesian career diplomat, DEPLU, Jakarta, 25 February 2005.

121 Interview with an Indonesian scholar and IR expert affiliated with LIPI, Jakarta, 24 February 2005.

122 Interview with an Indonesian expert in international relations, CSIS, Jakarta, 21 February 2005.

123 Interview with an Indonesian leader, diplomat and scholar, Jakarta, 23 February 2005.

124 Interview with an Indonesian expert in international relations, CSIS, Jakarta, 21 February 2005.

125 Interview with a young Indonesian career diplomat, DEPLU, Jakarta, 25 February 2005.

126 Interview with a young Muslim leader, an expert in a leading and respected Jakarta-based think-tank, Jakarta, 25 February 2005.

127 Nicholas J. Spykman, *America's Strategy in World Politics: The United States and the Balance of Power* (New York: Harcourt, Brace and Company, 1942), p. 41.

128 Ibid., pp. 43, 59–60.

129 Stephen G. Brooks and William C. Wohlforth, "American Primacy in Perspective", *Foreign Affairs* 81, no. 4 (July/August 2002): 24.

130 Walt, *The Origins of Alliances*, p. 276.

131 Kupchan and Adler conclude that "[...] balancing against American power [is unlikely] to provoke a countervailing coalition. The United States is separated from both Europe and Asia by large expanses of water, making American power less threatening." For more, see: Charles A. Kupchan et al., *Power in Transition: The Peaceful Change of International Order* (Tokyo: United Nations University Press, 2001), p. 3.

132 Walt, *The Origins of Alliances*, pp. 276–77.

133 John G. Ikenberry, ed., *America Unrivalled: The Future of the Balance of Power* (Ithaca, New York: Cornell University Press, 2002), p. 17.

134 Alexander Vondra became the country's Minister of Foreign Affairs in 2006. Quoted and translated from: *Magazin Patek — Lidove Noviny*, No. 2, Prague, 9 January 2004.

135 Leo Suryadinata, *Indonesia's Foreign Policy under Suharto: Aspiring to International Leadership* (Singapore: Times Academic Press, 1996), pp. 2–3.

136 Leszek Buszynski, "China and the ASEAN Region", in *China as a Great Power: Myth, Realities and Challenges in the Asia-Pacific Region*, edited by Stuart Harris and Gary Klintworth (New York: St. Martin's Press, 1995), pp. 164–65.

137 Heath McMichael, "Indonesian Foreign Policy: Towards a More Assertive Style", Australia-Asia Papers No. 40 (Nathan: Griffith University, February 1987), pp. 4–5.

138 Interview with a former Indonesian Minister of Foreign Affairs, Jakarta, 14 January 2005.

139 "The Idea of Power in Javanese Culture" in Benedict R. O'G Anderson, *Language and Power: Exploring Political Cultures in Indonesia* (Ithaca, New York: Cornell University Press, 1990), p. 43.

140 Irman G. Lanti and Leonard C. Sebastian, "Perceiving Indonesian Approaches to International Relations Theory", *International Relations of the Asia Pacific*, manuscript (currently under review, forthcoming).

141 Soemarsaid Moertono, *State and Statecraft in Old Java*, Cornell Modern Indonesia Project Monograph Series (Ithaca, New York: Cornell University, 1968), p. 71.

142 Ibid., p. 71.

143 Suryadinata, *Indonesia's Foreign Policy under Suharto*, p. 2.

144 Interview with an Indonesian leader and academic affiliated with a high-profile Jakarta-based think-tank, Jakarta, 17 January 2005.

145 Anderson, *Language and Power: Exploring Political Cultures in Indonesia*, p. 43; Lanti and Sebastian, "Perceiving Indonesian Approaches to International Relations Theory".

146 Peter J. Katzenstein and Nobuo Okawara, "Japan, Asian-Pacific Security, and the Case for Analytical Eclecticism", *International Security* 26, no. 2 (Winter 2001/02): 156.

147 Brooks and Wohlforth, "American Primacy in Perspective", p. 24.

148 Spykman, *America's Strategy in World Politics*, p. 469.

149 Zbigniew Brzezinski, *The Grand Chessboard: American Primacy and Its Geostrategic Imperatives* (New York: Basic Books, 1998), p. 188.

150 Shannon Tow, "Southeast Asia in the Sino-U.S. Strategic Balance", *Contemporary Southeast Asia* 26, no. 3 (December 2004): 436–37.

151 Interview with a senior Indonesian diplomat, DEPLU, Jakarta, 28 February 2005.

152 Samuel P. Huntington, *The Clash of Civilizations and the Remaking of World Order* (New York: A Touchstone Book, Simon & Schuster, 1997), p. 42.

153 Ibid., p. 254.

154 Errol Anthony Henderson and Richard Tucker, "Clear and Present Strangers: The Clash of Civilizations and International Conflict", *International Studies Quarterly* 45, no. 2 (June 2001): 334; see also: Quansheng Zhao, "Asian-Pacific International Relations in the 21st Century", *Journal of Strategic Studies* 24, no. 4 (December 2001).

155 Ibid., p. 334.

156 Department of State — Office of Research, "Religion is the Essential Filter in Urban Malaysian Views of the U.S.", Opinion Analysis (Washington D.C., 19 October 2005).

157 Ibid.
158 "U.S. Image Up Slightly, But Still Negative: American Character Gets Mixed Reviews", *The Pew Global Attitudes Project*, The Pew Research Centre (24 June 2005).
159 "Views of China", *The Pew Global Attitudes Project*, The Pew Research Centre (June 2005).
160 Interview with a senior official from the Indonesian Department of Trade, Jakarta, 2 February 2005.
161 Interview with a leader of the *Muhammadiyah*, the second largest Muslim organization in Indonesia, 23 February 2005.
162 Azyumardi Azra, "Islam in Southeast Asia: Between Tolerance and Radicalism", Muis Occasional Papers Series, Paper No. 5, Majlis Ugama Islam Singapura, Islamic Religious Council of Singapore (2008), p. 5.
163 Stephen M. Walt, "International Relations: One World, Many Theories", *Foreign Policy*, No. 110 (Spring 1998), p. 29.
164 Franklin B. Weinstein, "The Indonesian Elite's View of the World and the Foreign Policy of Development", *Indonesia*, Cornell Modern Indonesia Project, No. 12 (October 1971), p. 131.
165 "Pemilu 2004: ASEAN Harus Tetap 'Corner Stone'".

8

CONCLUSION

THE SUMMARY OF FINDINGS

The Indonesian foreign policy elite's strategic thinking about the country's foreign relations and how to achieve maximum security for Indonesia in the post-Cold War period have been to a great extent in line with the precepts of the balance-of-threat theory. However, we have found that the balance-of-threat theory is capable of explaining Indonesia's foreign policy dynamics provided it extends the analysis beyond the elite's threat perceptions by putting more emphasis on the degree of the elite's consensus about the threat.

Although the interviewed members of the Indonesian elite ostensibly declared that they generally regard threats to the country's national interest that are internal in origin as more dangerous and serious than external threats, it should not be by any means interpreted as that the leaders are not concerned about the more traditional state-based security threats. In fact, the elite perceives both the United States and China as the two most potent state-based external factors with the potential to endanger Indonesia's national interests and security. From the perspective of many Indonesians, both at the elite level and public at large, Indonesia's relationship with the "incumbent" and the "rising" superpower can be viewed in a triangular form. On the one hand, among all state actors, the interviewed leaders identified the United States during the George W. Bush's Administration as the most significant malign factor affecting Indonesia's national security. China's growing influence is at present seen quite positively for it enhances multipolarity in the international system and eases the pressure especially from what is widely considered as an excessive, ubiquitous power of the United States. Concurrently, however,

China is seen as the principal danger in the long run and a number one external factor that needs to be constrained.

The Indonesian leaders are convinced that, in light of the uncertainty about how China will use its power in the future, it is absolutely vital for Indonesia to hedge its relations with China. The elite's main security concern is about the trajectory the rising might of China will follow in the future, namely the prospect of facing a giant with hegemonic intentions at its doorstep. In the words of a French scholar, "the [vexing] question is not whether China is rising, but whether the rise will be peaceful."[1] Or as Dewi Fortuna Anwar put it: "Is [China] a wolf in sheep's clothes?"[2] This uncertainty then contributes to the fact that, despite the present high-profile hostile anti-American sentiments, the U.S. is in the long run seen as a benevolent and friendly power without any territorial design. The U.S. is seen as "the last guarantee" and its security role as the indirect psychological insurance for the stability of the region.

The discussion in this book has highlighted the marked difference in Indonesian leaders' attitudes towards the U.S. and China. The negative impression and sensitivity towards America, especially during the 2001–08 period, can be characterized as issue-based and superficial — it is evident that it is the Bush Administration's overtly assertive and unilateralist policies that were the main source of the threatening appearance of the United States. Then the arrival of the new Obama Administration has generated considerable optimism in Jakarta in the potential and prospects for continual and substantial improvement in Indonesia-U.S. relations. There is a general sense among the Indonesian foreign policy elite that, in terms of their long-term goals and strategic objectives, Indonesia under President Yudhoyono and the United States under President Obama's leadership are despite occasional lapses moving in much the same direction. By contrast, the elite's attitude toward China is clearly a much more persistent phenomenon — the deep-rooted perceptions of China (and Japan, for that matter) have their origin in the long history of mutual interaction coupled with the country's geographic proximity. The data collected can be interpreted as that while China is seen in the long term as the principal specific threat, the Indonesian leadership views the United States as less serious ill-defined non-specific insecurity. Importantly, as demonstrated in Chapter 7, while the negative perception of the U.S. during Bush's presidency was strongly "coloured" by religion, the persistent anxiety about the China threat comes from all sections of the elite.

Drawing on these data concerning the Indonesian elite's threat perceptions, this book has also identified the main factors contributing to the current state of Indonesian foreign policy, which is sometimes described as ambivalent or "haphazard and lacking priorities"'. Moreover, it addressed the argument that Indonesia did not follow the scenario expected by classical realists because it did not display, both during the New Order regime and after the fall of President Suharto, a balancing behaviour aimed at diffusing Washington's influence in the region. This state of the Indonesian foreign policy can be regarded as a reflection of the following factors.

First, it is the combination of the diversity of ideational influences that has generated a plurality of disparate worldviews among the elite and the leaders' sense of vulnerability in the face of the growing complexity of international relations in which, from the Indonesian leaders' perspective, the threats are increasingly multi-sourced, multi-dimensional and multi-layered by nature. Further complicating the whole picture is the finding that the majority of the interviewed leaders claimed to be actually more concerned about internal threats, such as economic depression, secessionist movements or ethnic-religious conflicts, than external threats. In other words, as was also demonstrated throughout this study, the elite is well aware that many external threats have their origins within the country, namely in its internal weakness. There is thus an increasingly blurred boundary between external and internal threats. It follows that, psychologically, the elite's sense of internal weakness encourages the leaders' constructions of external vulnerabilities and in turn sustains the "Hostile World" image.

Second, these factors described above in turn give rise to the elite's polarization. The relatively low level of the elite's consensus is particularly revealed in the substantial disagreement among the Indonesian leadership on their rankings of external threats from the most to the least dangerous for Indonesia's national security and interests; the disparity of views about the nature of the threat and how to deal with it; and the significant disparity between the elite's present and the future, long-term threat assessment. As outlined in Chapters 4 and 5, though being considered as the foremost external threats (one at present and one in the long-term) that need to be constrained, neither the U.S. nor China has yielded more than 51 and 49 per cent of all respondents respectively. Moreover, it needs to be stressed that a number of respondents identified more than one security concern; 58 per cent of the total number of respondents identified more than two countries that they were particularly wary of.

The degree of the leaders' consensus about the nature and urgency of the threat is a crucial aspect of the foreign policy decision-making process insofar as it is a major determinant shaping the elite's foreign policy preferences. The elite's agreement about the threat determines what foreign policy tool will be employed to deal with a particular danger to the state's security. As argued in

Chapter 2, the greater the consensus across all sections of the foreign policy elite, the more likely it is that the country will display a balancing behaviour against another state to deal with the security threat. Conversely, with the currently more diffused political power in Jakarta — in contrast to Suharto-dominated government — and with the greater disagreement among the central decision-makers about what the national security and interests and the dramatically changing international context demand, Indonesian foreign policy appears as ambivalent or "haphazard and lacking priorities".

THE FINDINGS AND INDONESIA'S FUTURE FOREIGN RELATIONS

One of the key messages with a special relevance for today's policy-makers that underlies the discussion in this book is related to the basic logic inherent in the balance-of-threat theory: a state whose actions appear (more) threatening runs the risk of having to face a hostile security alliance, as for example China experienced during the Cold War, or generate obstacles in exerting political and economic influence, a situation, which has lately to some extent constrained the scope and effectiveness of the United States' foreign policy.[3]

The changing dynamics in the relationships between Indonesia on the one side, and China and the United States on the other, illustrate the significance of this issue. China has managed the makeover of its image in the past several years that its policy toward Indonesia has been characterized as "sophisticated and well executed as to be 'a thing of beauty'".[4] Consequently, neither Indonesia, nor its neighbours, seems to be considerably alarmed by the dramatic rise of its power and influence. By contrast, the U.S. policies principally defined by unilateralism and the War on Terrorism often aroused suspicion, irritation and concern among the regional states. This unfavourable image, it is assumed, has instigated adverse effects for the U.S. security policies and business interests in Southeast Asia and thus is in danger losing its influence in the region.[5]

It could be argued that the preceding findings offer an insight into the future dynamics of interstate relations in Asia. The Indonesian elite's thinking about international relations envisages the existence of a distinct balance of power system to some extent resembling the bipolar Cold War conflict in which the main "poles" will be the United States and China. The elite expects that Indonesia, as Southeast Asia's largest and most powerful state, is a keystone country that will in the future be courted by both the United States and China whereby both Washington and Beijing will seek to gain influence in Jakarta. With both these major powers headed for an increasing strategic competition, there is a widespread sense that Indonesia and other regional states will face pressure to take sides. In these circumstances, the elite embraces a two-pronged approach to the country's foreign policy designed to achieve a maximum security for Indonesia in the long run: first, to maintain a (perceived) balance both between the United States and China as well as more generally among all other state actors by carefully implementing an inclusive foreign policy; and, second, to encourage Washington's engagement in Southeast Asia.

The prevalent sense among the Indonesian leadership is that it is principally the United States that serves as an indispensable stabilizing and balancing element in the regional security structures — each of the other major powers, including China, are important but dispensable elements in the system. While seeking a closer engagement with Beijing in the future, Jakarta will concurrently balance China's growing clout by tacitly backing the U.S. military presence in the region, endorsing the ARF security framework and encouraging other powers, namely Japan and India, to greater involvement in regional affairs. The Indonesian elite is also anxious to prevent China from dominating the emerging East Asian Community. This was manifested recently in Indonesia's determined push for the inclusion of India and Australia into the emerging structures of EAC. In other words, the Indonesian decision-makers believe that peace and stability of the region can be upheld if the long-term security strategy involves a multilateral security dialogue with the ASEAN-centred community formation and the U.S.-preponderance.

In the future, Indonesia is very unlikely to accept a predominance or hegemony of either China or the United States. The Indonesian elite can be expected to seek equable relations with Washington and Beijing by way of a continuous equidistant manoeuvring between the two powers that will enable it to maintain a desirable and delicate U.S.-Sino regional balance. To use Tow's words, the Indonesian elite will "seek to enhance [Indonesia's] manoeuvrability and anticipate that the Sino-U.S. relationship will afford them sufficient strategic latitude to do so."[6] Underlying this notion of balance is the idea that Jakarta will promote Indonesia's interests by building relations with both the United States and China, although it might sometime cooperate with either of them on an issue-by-issue basis. By attempting to balance the two major powers off each other, Indonesia can also gain economic and military benefits from both while preserving its autonomy. In line with the "*bebas aktif*" principle of the Indonesian foreign policy, the elite will not enter into any formal alliance with either Washington or Beijing. However, Jakarta can be expected to expand its relations with either the United States or China ad hoc based on the perceived shared interest even if it meant advancing their common interest vis-à-vis the third power.

In light of the "*mendayung antara dua karang*" thesis and the logic of the balance-of-power theory, there are two possibilities as to what course Indonesian foreign policy will follow in the future. The first is that China will carry on with its current strategy of acting moderately and calmly, slowly expanding its sphere of influence by means of its *soft power* (exemplified by the growing cultural ties) while stressing the "win-win" approach to economic cooperation. In this case, notwithstanding its advantage stemming from America's separation from Asia by large expanses of water (the "geographic proximity" factor), which makes its power generally appear less threatening than China's, if Washington does not want to see its influence in the region marginalized, it will have to respond in kind, also treading carefully and conducting a nuanced policy fine-tuned to the region. Conversely, a break-down in China's economic machine with the ensuing social unrest or a rise of chauvinistic nationalism could dramatically change the dynamics driving China's foreign relations, prompting the country to adopt a more aggressive posture against its neighbours. A China that pushes its weight around the region and frightens its neighbours will naturally face the prospect of a balancing process. In this case, the United States along with other major powers, namely Japan, India and Russia, joined by middle powers including Indonesia, will come together to constrain China's emerging power. Unless the United States is perceived as a direct, imminent threat to Indonesia's independence, China is destined to remain for the long run, owing to its geographic proximity coupled with the centuries-long interaction between the indigenous Indonesians and the ethnic Chinese people, the principal source of concern for the Indonesian elite.

There is, however, a number of unknown factors that will in the future shape and reshape the Indonesian elite perceptions. For example, international politics has not been significantly affected only by the re-emergence of China but also the other teeming Asian giant India on the world stage. How these two ancient civilizations shape and reshape the Southeast Asian security architecture in the coming decades and, particularly how Indonesian elite views India's security role in the wider region, will be very important. Perhaps most importantly, perceptions tend to change over time. While it needs to be acknowledged that the Indonesian perception of China has changed considerably from the late 1980s from a wholly negative one to a much more favourable one, the data have indicated that a fundamental change in perceptions has not taken place. Rather than the perception of China itself, what has changed is the Indonesian strategy in dealing with this perceived threat. During the New Order regime, Indonesia sought to insulate itself from and contain the China threat. This book has shown that the Indonesian elite, though still considering China as a threat (and an opportunity), now prefers no longer to keep the threat away but to deal with China as a friend and employ an engagement strategy to embrace this perceived threat. This is arguably an ongoing process during which the elite perceptions of China can still change in either direction.

Another unpredictable factor is how the Indonesian elite respond to pressure to take sides in the strategic competition between the U.S. and China. The Indonesian Government will likely be increasingly vulnerable to pressure from Beijing especially in relation to Jakarta's acquiescence to the U.S. military presence in the region, which is seen as a vital element in the strategy of dealing with the rise of China. Thus, with China's growing regional economic importance, the challenge for Indonesia will be to sustain the U.S. presence while simultaneously avoiding antagonizing Beijing. It is still difficult to predict how Jakarta will handle the problem of maintaining the perceived balance between the two major powers in case Washington and Beijing drift further apart on some major issues, such as a possible confrontation over Taiwan. These circumstances, as described and analysed above, necessitate a careful management of Indonesian foreign relations.

Notes

[1]   Jérome Monod, "The Chinese Are Coming. Let's Greet Them.", *International Herald Tribune*, 17 May 2005 <http://www.iht.com/articles/2005/05/16/opinion/edmonod.php> (accessed 25 May 2006).

[2]   Cited from: "Indonesia's Perceptions of China and U.S. Security Roles in East Asia", seminar organized by The Habibie Centre, Jakarta (16 February 2006).

[3]   Evelyn Goh, "Hegemonic Constraints: The Implications of 11 September for American Power", *Australian Journal of International Affairs* 57, no. 1 (April 2003).

[4]   "China-Indonesia Relations and Implications for the United States", USINDO Report, presented at the USINDO-GWU joint conference (Washington D.C., 7 November 2003).

[5]   Ibid.

[6]   Shannon Tow, "Southeast Asia in the Sino-U.S. Strategic Balance", *Contemporary Southeast Asia* 26, no. 3 (December 2004): 453.

GLOSSARY

ENGLISH AND INDONESIAN TERMS

Abangan
Referring to nominal Muslims, often with syncretic beliefs and preferring Islamic mysticism to the *Sharia*.

Bangsa
race, nation (the bangsa Cina)

Binnenlandsch Bestuur
Interior Administration, the European civil service (BB) in colonial Java

Constructivism
or social constructivism; one of the theoretical approaches in international relations that focuses on human consciousness and its role in international life

Demokrasi Terpimpin
Guided Democracy

Hard power
a term used in the study of international relations; a theory that describes using economic and military means to influence other political actors' interests and behaviour

Hoofdenscholen
Chief's schools set up by the Dutch to educate the natives in general and also more specialized bureaucratic skills.

Indo
an individual of Indonesian-European origin, Eurasian.

International relations
1. a branch of political science that is concerned with foreign affairs of and relations among states within the international system;
2. foreign affairs, relations among countries

Liberalism	a theory in the field of international relations that, first, considers state preferences, rather than state capabilities, to be the primary determinant of state behaviour; and, second, views interaction between states as not limited to the political/security but also economic/cultural
Lebensraum	a term especially used in Nazi Germany that refers to additional territory deemed necessary to a nation, for its continued existence or economic well-being
Keturunan	term that refers to the ethnic Chinese.
Kiyayi	respected elder men, particularly of Islamic learning
Konfrontasi	or confrontation; it was Sukarno's response to the formation of Malaysia, comprising Malaya, Sabah, Sarawak and Singapore
Kraton	palace, residential compound of ruler
Krisis moneter	monetary crisis in Indonesia after 1997
Ksatriya	knight-like figure in Indian or Javanese tradition; in Indian tradition referred to the second highest group in the occupational division in the classical Indian society. It comprised of kings, warriors, governmental bureaucrats and other individuals who represented power.
Madrasah	a Muslim boarding school
Malari	the Indonesian acronym for the "Disaster of 15 January"
Mandala	referred, in its original Hindu meaning, to "circle" or "completion"; it was associated with any geometric pattern which represents a microcosm of the universe from the human perspective

Masyumi	moderate Muslim party with somewhat pro-Western orientation, banned by Sukarno in 1960
Muhammadiyah	the second largest Islamic organization in Indonesia
Nasakom	*Nasionalis, Agama* dan *Komunis*; a concept first introduced by President Sukarno with the purpose to unify into one ideological front different competing groups on the Indonesian political scene
Opleidingscholen voor Inlandsche Ambtenaren	OSVIA, or Training School for Native Officials
Orde Baru	New Order, the term used for the regime of Indonesian President Suharto in the period of 1967–98
Pancasila	the philosophical basis of the Indonesian state that is embodied in its five "pillars"
Pangreh Praja	"Rulers of the realm", Java's colonial native civil service in the areas under direct Dutch rule
Pegawai negeri	public servant
Pejabat	generally, refers to high-ranking government official
Pekerjaan halus	a "soft job" that involves working in the office
Penguasa	individuals or a group of people wielding political power
Penghijauan	"greenization", a term describing the process in the 1970s and 1980s when an increasing number of more devote Muslims were entering the ranks of the hitherto Christian and Muslim *abangan*-dominated Indonesian armed forces
Pesantren	a Muslim school in Indonesia operated by religious leaders

Pribumi	native
Priyayi	aristocrat or official, member of the governing elite of Java, or referring to characteristics of that class
Realism	a set of theories in international relations that share a common assumption that the primary motivation behind states' behaviour is the desire for military and economic power or security, rather than ideas and ethics
Renminbi	the Chinese currency
Reformasi	refers to the political and social reform following the fall of President Suharto in 1998
Santri	devout Muslim, self-consciously non-syncretic
Soft power	a term used in the study of international relations. It is a theory that refers to power that comes from history, culture and diplomacy
Structural realism	or neorealism; a theory of international relations that argues in favor of a systemic approach to IR analysis and that views the international structure as acting as a constraint on state behaviour
Tanah asli	motherland
Wong cilik	common people; often used to compare the common people with the elite
Warga Negara	non-indigenous citizens, an official Indonesian

ABBREVIATIONS

ABRI	Angkatan Bersenjata Republik Indonesia, or Indonesian Armed Forces
ACFTA	ASEAN-China Free Trade Agreement
AFTA	ASEAN Free Trade Area
APEC	Asia Pacific Economic Cooperation
ARF	ASEAN Regional Forum
ASEAN	Association of Southeast Asian Nations
ASEAN+3	A regular series of meetings at the cabinet and head-of-government levels between the ten ASEAN countries and Japan, China, and Korea.
ASEM	Asia-Europe Meeting
BAIS	*Badan Intelijen Strategis*, Strategic Intelligence Body
BAKIN	*Badan Koordinasi Intelijen Negara*, State Intelligence Co-ordinating Body
BPI	*Badan Pusat Intelijen*, Central Intelligence Board
BPS	*Badan Pusat Statistik*, the Indonesian Central Statistic Bureau
CIA	Central Intelligence Service
CSIS	Centre for Strategic and International Studies
DEPLU	*Departemen Luar Negeri*, Ministry of Foreign Affairs
DPR	*Dewan Perwakilan Rakyat*, House of Representatives of the Republic of Indonesia
EAC	East Asian Community
EU	European Union
FEER	Far Eastern Economic Review
GAM	Gerakan Aceh Merdeka, or Free Aceh Movement
GESTAPU	an acronym of *Gerakan September Tiga Puluh*, or September Thirtieth Movement; an ambiguous and abortive leftist coup on 1 October 1965, which brought the end of Indonesia's Guided Democracy

	period and led to the instalment of the New Order regime
GOLKAR	*Partai Golongan Karya*, or Functional Groups; political party established during Suharto's New Order regime
HANKAM	*Departemen Pertahanan Keamanan*, Ministry of Defence and Security
ICMI	*Ikatan Cendekiawan Muslim Indonesia*, or Indonesian Moslem Intellectuals Association
ICG	International Crisis Group, an organization based in Brussels
IGGI	Inter-Governmental Group on Indonesia
IMF	International Monetary Fund
IR	international relations
JI	*Jemaah Islamiya*; a militant Islamist group active in several Southeast Asian
KADIN	*Kamar Dagang dan Industri*, Chamber of Commerce and Industry
LIPI	*Lembaga Ilmu Pengetahuan Indonesia*, or Indonesian Institute of Sciences
MPR	*Majelis Permusyawaratan Rakyat*, or Indonesia's People's Consultative Assembly
NEFOS	New Emerging Forces, an acronym used by President Sukarno
NGO	non-governmental organization
NU	*Nadathul Ulama*, Muslim Teachers' Party
OIC	Organization of Islamic Conference
OLDEFOS	Old Established Forces, an acronym used by President Sukarno
OPEC	The Organization of the Petroleum Exporting Countries
OPM	*Organisasi Papua Merdeka*, Free Papua Movement
OSVIA	*Opleidingscholen voor Inlandsche Ambtenaren*, or Training School for Native Officials
PAN	*Partai Amanat Nasional*, or National Mandate Party
PKI	*Partai Komunis Indonesia*, or the Indonesian Communist Party
PKS	*Partai Keadilan Sejahtera*, or Prosperity and Justice Party
PNI	*Partai Nasional Indonesia*, Indonesian National/Nationalist Party
PPP	*Partai Persatuan Pembangunan*, or United Development Party

TAC	a nonaggression pact, one of the most important ASEAN documents, in which the members pledge respect for each other's independence, sovereignty and territorial integrity.
TNI	*Tentara Nasional Indonesia,* or National Army of Indonesia
UN	United Nations
VOC	*Verenigde Oostindische Compagnie*, United (Dutch) East India Company 1602–1800
ZOPFAN	Zone of Peace, Freedom and Neutrality

BIBLIOGRAPHY

Books and Publications

Aandstad, Stig Aga. "Surrendering to Symbols: United States Policy towards Indonesia 1961–1965". Ph.D. dissertation, Department of History, University of Oslo, Spring 1999.

Acharya, Amitav. *Constructing a Security Community in Southeast Asia: ASEAN and the Problem of Regional Order*. London: Routledge, 2001.

———. *The Quest for Identity: International Relations of Southeast Asia*. Oxford: Oxford University Press, 2000.

Adams, Cindy. *Sukarno: An Autobiography*. Hong Kong: Gunung Agung, 1965.

Adhitama, Toeti, F.R. Dalrymple et al. *Sekar Semerbak: Kenangan untuk Ali Moertopo* [Fragrant Flower: In Memoriam of Ali Moertopo]. Jakarta: Centre for Strategic and International Studies, 1985.

Adler, Emanuel and Michael Barnett, eds. *Security Communities*. Cambridge: Cambridge University Press, 1998.

Agung, Ide Anak Agung Gde Agung. *Twenty Years Indonesian Foreign Policy, 1945–1965*. The Hague: Mouton & Co., 1973.

Ahn, Byong-Man. *Elites and Political Power in South Korea*. Cheltenham and Northampton: Edward Elgar Publishing, 2003.

Alagappa, Muthiah, ed. *Asian Security Practice: Material and Ideational Influences*. Stanford: Stanford University Press, 1998.

Alatas, Ali. *The Pebble in the Shoe —The Diplomatic Struggle for East Timor*. Jakarta: Aksara Kurnia, 2006.

Allison, John M. *Ambassador from the Prairie: Or Allison in Wonderland*. Boston: Houghton Mifflin, 1973.

Anderson, Benedict R.O'G. *Imagined Communities: Reflections on the Origin and Spread of Nationalism*. London: Verso, 1983.

———. *Language and Power: Exploring Political Cultures in Indonesia*. Ithaca: Cornell University Press, 1990.

Ang, Ien. *On Not Speaking Chinese: Living between Asia and the West*. London: Routledge, 2001.

Anwar, Dewi Fortuna. *Indonesia at Large: Collected Writings on ASEAN, Foreign Policy, Security and Democratization*. Jakarta: The Habibie Center, 2005.

Axelrod, R., ed. *Structure of Decision*. Princeton: Princeton University Press, 1976.

Ayoob, Mohammed and Chai-Anan Samudavanija, eds. *Leadership Perceptions and National Security: The Southeast Asian Experience*. Singapore: Institute of Southeast Asian Studies, 1989.

Azar, Edward E. and Chung-in Moon, eds. *National Security in the Third World: The Management of Internal and External Threats*. Aldershot: Edward Elgar, 1988.

Baliga, Bantval Mohandas. "The American Approach to Imperialism in Southeast Asia: The Attitude of the United States Government in the Philippines, Indo-China and Indonesia, 1945–1958". Ph.D. dissertation, Southern Illinois University of Carbondale, 1961.

Barnes, Barry. *The Nature of Power*. Cambridge: Polity Press, 1988.

Baylis, John and Steve Smith. *The Globalization of World Politics: An Introduction to International Relations*. Oxford: Oxford University Press, 2001.

Beard, Charles A. *Foreign Policy for America*. New York: Alfred A. Knopf, 1940.

Beeson, Mark, ed. *Bush and Asia: America's Evolving Relations with East Asia*. London: Routledge, 2006.

———. *Contemporary Southeast Asia: Regional Dynamics, National Differences*. New York: Palgrave, Macmillan, 2004.

Bell, Roger, Tim McDonald, and Alan Tidwell, eds. *Negotiating the Pacific Century: The "New" Asia, the United States, and Australia*. St. Leonards: Allen & Unwin, 1996.

Benda, Harry J. *The Japanese Interregnum in Southeast Asia*. New Haven: Yale University, 1968.

Benton, Gregor and Hong Liu. *Diasporic Chinese Ventures: The Life and Work of Wang Gungwu*. London: RoutledgeCurzon 2004.

Berger, Peter L. and Thomas Luchmann. *The Social Construction of Reality: The Treatise in the Sociology of Knowledge*. Baltimore: The Penguin Press, 1966.

Bertrand, Jacques. *Nationalism and Ethnic Conflict in Indonesia*. Cambridge: Press Syndicate of the University of Cambridge, 2004.

Bo, Zhiyue. *China's Elite Politics: Political Transition and Power Balancing*. Singapore: World Scientific, 2007.

Boeke, J.H. *The Evolution of the Netherlands Indies Economy*. New York: Institute of Pacific Relations, 1946.

Bond, George C. and Angela Gilliam, eds. *Social Construction of the Past: Representation as Power*. London: Routledge, 1994.

Bouma, G. *The Research Process*. Melbourne: Oxford University Press, 1996.

Bourchier, David and Vedi R. Hadiz, eds. *Indonesian Politics and Society: A Reader*. London: RoutledgeCurzon, 2003.

Brook, Timothy and Andre Schmid, ed. *Nation Work: Asian Elites and National Identities*. Ann Arbor: University of Michigan Press, 2000.

Brown, Colin, ed. *Indonesia: Dealing with a Neighbour*. St. Leonards: Allen & Unwin, 1996.

Brown, Colin. *A Short History of Indonesia: The Unlikely Nation?* Crows Nest: Allen & Unwin, 2003.

Brown, Michael E. et al., eds. *The Rise of China.* Cambridge: The MIT Press, 2000.

————. *The Perils of Anarchy: Contemporary Realism and International Security.* Cambridge: The MIT Press, 1995.

————. *Theories of War and Peace.* Cambridge: The MIT Press, 1998.

Brunnell, Frederick P. "The Kennedy Initiatives in Indonesia, 1962–1963". Microfilm. Ph.D. dissertation, Cornell University, 1969.

Bryman, Alan. *Social Research Methods.* London: Oxford University Press, 2004.

Brzezinski, Zbigniew. *The Geostrategic Triad: Living with China, Europe, and Russia.* Washington, D.C.: CSIS Press, 2001.

Brzezinski, Zbigniew. *The Grand Chessboard: American Primacy and Its Geostrategic Imperatives.* New York: Basic Books, 1998.

Budiman, Arief, ed. *Politik Luar Negeri Indonesia Dewasa Ini.* Jakarta: Yayasan Indonesia, 1972.

Bull, Hedley. *The Anarchical Society: A Study of Order in World Politics.* London: The Macmillan Press, 1983.

Burton, J.W. *International Relations: A General Theory.* Cambridge: The University Press, 1967.

Buttinger, Joseph. *Vietnam: The Unforgettable Tragedy.* London: Andre Deutsch, 1977.

Buzan, Barry. *People, States and Fear: The National Security Problem in International Relations.* Sussex: Wheatsheaf Books, 1983.

Camilleri, Joseph A. *Southeast Asia in China's Foreign Policy.* Singapore: Institute of Southeast Asian Studies, 1975.

Campbell, David. *Writing Security: United States Foreign Policy and the Politics of Identity.* Minneapolis: University of Minnesota Press, 1992.

Carlton, Eric. *The Few and the Many: A Typology of Elites.* Brookfield: Ashgate Publishing, 1996.

Carr, E.H. *The Twenty Years' Crisis 1919–1939.* London: Macmillan, 1939.

Carter, Lauren. "The Ethnic Chinese Variable in Domestic and Foreign Policies in Malaysia and Indonesia". M.A. dissertation, Simon Fraser University, 1995.

Case, William. *Politics in Southeast Asia: Democracy of Less.* Richmond: Curzon Press, 2002.

Chase, Robert, Emily Hill, and Paul Kennedy, eds. *The Pivotal States: A New Framework for U.S. Policy in the Developing World.* New York: W.W. Norton & Company, 1999.

Chawla, Sudershan, Melvin Gurtov, and Alain-Gerard Marsot, eds. *Southeast Asia under the New Balance of Power.* New York: Praeger, 1974.

Chow, Paula, K. and Gregory C. Chow, eds. *Asia in the Twenty-First Century: Economic, Socio-Political, Diplomatic Issues.* Singapore: World Scientific, 1997.

Cohen, Bernard C. *The Press and Foreign Policy*. Princeton: Princeton University Press, 1963.

Cohen, Saul B. *Geography and Politics in a Divided World*. London: Methuen, 1964.

Conboy, Kenneth and James Morrison. *Feet to Fire: CIA Covert Operations in Indonesia, 1957–1958*. Annapolis: Naval Institute Press, 1999.

Corbett, Julian. *Some Principles of Maritime Strategy*. Annapolis: U.S. Naval Institute Press, 1988.

Cox, Michael, John Ikenberry, and Takashi Inoguchi, eds. *American Democracy Promotion: Impulses, Strategies and Impacts*. Oxford: Oxford University Press, 2000.

Crawford, June et al. *Emotion and Gender: Constructing Meaning from Memory*. London: Sage, 1992.

Crouch, Harold. *Army and Politics in Indonesia*. Ithaca: Cornell University Press, 1978.

Damono, Sapardi Djoko. *Priayi Abangan: Dunia Novel Jawa Tahun 1950-an* [Priayi Abangan: The World of Javanese Novel in 1950s]. Yogyakarta: Bentang, 2000.

Dane, Francis C. *Research Methods*. Pacific Grove: Brooks/Cole, 1990.

Davidson, James W., William E. Gienapp, Christine L. Heyrman, Mark H. Lytle, and Michael B. Stoff. *Nation of Nations: A Narrative History of the American Republic*. New York: McGraw-Hill Publishing Company, 1990.

Deutsch, Karl W. *Nationalism and Social Communication: An Inquiry into the Foundations of Nationality*. New York: The Technology Press of the Massachusetts Institute of Technology and Wiley, 1953.

Djalal, Hasjim. *Preventive Diplomacy in Southeast Asia: Lessons Learned*. Jakarta: The Habibie Centre, 2002.

Djojohadikusumo, Sumitro. *Indonesia Dalam Perkembangan Dunia: Kini dan Masa Datang* [Indonesia in World's Development: At Present and in the Future]. Jakarta: Penerbit LP3ES, 1976.

Duchacek, Ivo D. *Power Maps: Comparative Politics of Constitutions*. Santa Barbara: ABC-Clio, 1973.

Dupont, Alan. *East Asia Imperilled: Transnational Challenges to Security*. Cambridge: Cambridge University Press, 2001.

East, M.A., S.A. Salmore, and C.F. Hermann, eds. *Why Nations Act*. Beverly Hills: Sage, 1978.

Easter, Gerald M. *Reconstructing the State: Personal Networks and Elite Identity in Soviet Russia*. Cambridge: Cambridge University Press, 2000.

Eldersveld, Samuel. *Political Elites in Modern Societies: Empirical Research and Democratic Theory*. Ann Arbor: University of Michigan Press, 1989.

Elson, R.E. *Suharto: A Political Biography*. Cambridge: Cambridge University Press, 2001.

Emmers, Ralf. *Cooperative Security and the Balance of Power in ASEAN and the ARF*. London: RoutledgeCurzon, 2003.

Emmerson, Donald K. *Indonesia's Elite: Political Culture and Cultural Politics.* Ithaca: Cornell University Press, 1976.

Fairbank, John F. *Dějiny Číny* [The History of China]. Prague: Nakladatelství Lidove Noviny, 1998.

Falkowski, Lawrence, ed. *Psychological Models in International Politics.* Boulder: Westview Press, 1979.

Farrell, R. Barry, ed. *Approaches to Comparative and International Politics.* Evanston: North-Western University Press, 1966.

Fealy, Greg. "The Release of Indonesia's Political Prisoners: Domestic versus Foreign Policy, 1975–1979". Working Paper 94, Monash University, 1994.

Feith, Herbert and Lance Castles. *Indonesian Political Thinking, 1945–1965.* Ithaca: Cornell University Press, 1970.

Feith, Herbert. *The Decline of Constitutional Democracy in Indonesia.* Ithaca: Cornell University Press, 1962.

Fiske, Susan T. and Susan E. Taylor. *Social Cognition.* Boston: Addison-Wesley, 1984.

Fitzgerald, C.P. *The Southern Expansion of the Chinese People: The Southern Fields and Southern Ocean.* Canberra: Australian National University Press, 1972.

Flint, David. *The Twilight of the Elites.* North Melbourne: Freedom Publishing, 2003.

Forrester, Geoff, ed. *Post-Suharto Indonesia: Renewal or Chaos?* Bathurst: Crawford House Publishing, 1999.

Forrester, Geoff and R.J. May, eds. *The Fall of Soeharto.* Bathurst: Craford House, 1998.

Freedman, Amy L. *Political Participation and Ethnic Minorities: Chinese Overseas in Malaysia, Indonesia, and the United States.* New York: Routledge, 2000.

Foucault, Michael. *The Will to Knowledge.* London: Penguin, 1990.

———. *Discipline and Punish: The Birth of the Prison.* New York: Random House, 1995.

Foucault, Michael and Paul Rabinow, eds. *Ethics: Subjectivity and Truth.* New York: New Press, 1998.

Gaddis, John Lewis. *Strategies of Containment; A Critical Appraisal of Post-war American National Security Policy.* New York: Oxford University Press, 1982.

Gardner, Paul F. *Shared Hopes, Separate Fears: Fifty Years of U.S.-Indonesian Relations.* Oxford: Westview Press, 1997.

Garry, Rodan, Kevin Hewison, and Richard Robison, *The Political Economy of Southeast Asia: An Introduction.* Melbourne: Oxford University Press, 1997.

Geertz, Clifford. *The Religion of Java.* Chicago: The University of Chicago Press, 1976.

Goh, Evelyn and Sheldon W. Simon. *China, the United States, and Southeast Asia: Contending Perspectives on Politics, Security, and Economics.* New York: Routledge, 2008.

Goldstein, Judith and Robert O. Keohane, eds. *Ideas and Foreign Policy.* Ithaca: Cornell University Press, 1993.

Gong, Gerrit W. *Memory and History in East and Southeast Asia: Issues of Identity in International Relations*. Washington, D.C.: The CSIS Press, 2001.

Goodman, S.G. and Gerald Segal, eds. *China Rising: Nationalism and Interdependence*. London: Routledge, 1997.

Greif, Stuart William. *Indonesians of Chinese Origin: Assimilation and the Goal of "One Nation — One People"*. New York: The Professors World Peace Academy, 1988.

Guoxing, Ji and Hadi Soesastro, eds. *Sino-Indonesian Relations in the Post-Cold War Era*. Jakarta: Centre for Strategic and International Studies, 1992.

Gungwu, Wang. *The Chinese Overseas: From Earthbound China to the Quest for Autonomy*. Cambridge: Harvard University Press, 2000.

Gurtov, Melvin. *China and Southeast Asia, the Politics of Survival: A Study of Foreign Policy Interaction*. Baltimore: Johns Hopkins University Press, 1975.

Hanifah, Abu. *Tales of a Revolution*. Sydney: Angus and Robertson Publishers, 1972.

Harris, Stuart and Andrew Mark, eds. *Asia-Pacific Security: The Economics-Politics Nexus*. Sydney: Allen & Unwin, 1997.

Harris, Stuart and Gary Klintworth, eds. *China as a Great Power: Myth, Realities and Challenges in the Asia-Pacific Region*. New York: St. Martin's Press, 1995.

Harsono, Ganis. *Recollections of an Indonesian Diplomat in the Sukarno Era*, edited by C.L.M. Penders and B.B. Hering. St. Lucia: University of Queensland Press, 1977.

Hatta, Mohammad. *Bung Hatta's Answers*. Singapore: Gunung Agung, 1981.

———. *Indonesian Patriot: Memoirs*, edited by C.L.M. Penders. Singapore: Gunung Agung, 1981.

Hatta, Muhammad. *Mendayung antara Dua Karang* [Rowing between Two Reefs]. Jakarta: NV Bulan Bintang, 1988.

Hefner, Robert W. *Civil Islam: Muslims and Democratization in Indonesia*. Princeton: Princeton University Press, 2000.

Hein, Gordon Robert. "Soeharto's Foreign Policy: Second-Generation Nationalism in Indonesia". Ph.D. dissertation, University of California, 1986.

Henshall, Kenneth G. *History of Japan: From Stone Age to Superpower*. London: Macmillan Press, 1999.

Hess, Gary R. *The United States' Emergence as a Southeast Asian Power, 1940–1950*. New York: Columbia University, 1987.

Hill, Hal, ed. *Indonesia's New Order: The Dynamics of Socio-Economic Transformation*. St. Leonards: Allen & Unwin, 1994.

Hobden, Stephen and John M. Hobson, eds. *Historical Sociology of International Relations*. Cambridge: Cambridge University Press, 2002.

Hoffmann, Stanley. *The State of War*. New York: Praeger, 1965.

Holsti, K.J. *International Politics: A Framework for Analysis*. Englewood Cliffs: Prentice-Hall, 1995.

Houseman, Gerald L. *Researching Indonesia: A Guide to Political Analysis.* New York: The Edward Mellen Press, 2004.

Hund, Markus. "ASEAN and ASEAN Plus Three: Manifestations of Collective Identities in Southeast Asia?". Ph.D. dissertation, University of Trier, 2002.

Huntington, Samuel P. *The Clash of Civilizations and the Remaking of World Order.* New York: Touchstone, 1997.

Ikenberry, G. John. *America Unrivalled: The Future of the Balance of Power.* Ithaca: Cornell University Press, 2002.

Isakovic, Zlatko. *Introduction to a Theory of Political Power in International Relations.* Vermont: Ashgate Publishing Company, 2000.

Itoh, Mayumi. *Globalization of Japan: Japanese Sakoku Mentality and U.S. Efforts to Open Japan.* New York: St. Martin' Press, 1998.

Jackson, Karl D. and Lucian W. Pye. *Political Power and Communication in Indonesia.* Berkeley: University of California Press, 1978.

Jacques, Hersh. *The USA and the Rise of East Asia since 1945: Dilemmas of the Post-War International Political Economy.* New York: St. Martin's Press, 1993.

Jan, George P. *International Politics of Asia: Readings.* Belmont: Wadsworth Publishing Company, 1969.

Jervis, Robert. *Perception and Misperception in International Politics.* Princeton: Princeton University Press, 1976.

Jeshurun, Chandran, ed. *China, India, Japan, and the Security of Southeast Asia.* Singapore: Institute of Southeast Asian Studies, 1993.

Johnston, Alistair Iain and Robert S. Ross, ed. *Engaging China: The Management of an Emerging Power.* London: Routledge, 1999.

Jones, Matthew. *Conflict and Confrontation in Southeast Asia, 1961–1965: Britain, the United States and the Creation of Malaysia.* Cambridge: Cambridge University Press, 2002.

Jones, Palfrey Howard. *Indonesia: The Possible Dream.* Jakarta: Gunung Agung, 1980.

Kahin, Audrey R. and George McT. Kahin. *Subversion as Foreign Policy: The Secret Eisenhower and Dulles Debacle in Indonesia.* Seattle: University of Washington Press, 1995.

Kahin, George McT. *Nationalism and Revolution in Indonesia.* Ithaca: Cornell University Press, 1969.

Kahn, Joel S., ed. *Southeast Asian Identities: Culture and the Politics of Representation in Indonesia, Malaysia, Singapore, and Thailand.* Singapore: Institute of Southeast Asian Studies, 1998.

Kapstein, Ethan B. and Michael Mastanduno, eds. *Unipolar Politics: Realism and State Strategies after the Cold War.* New York: Columbia University Press, 1999.

Katzenstein, Peter J., ed. *The Culture of National Security: Norms and Identity in World Politics,* New York: Columbia University Press, 1996.

Katzenstein, Peter J. and Allen Carlson, eds. *Rethinking Security in East Asia: Identity, Power and Efficiency.* Stanford: Stanford University Press, 2004.

Kegley, Charles W., Jr., ed. *Controversies in International Relations Theory: Realism and the Neoliberal Challenge*. New York: St. Martin's Press, 1995.

Kennan, George. *American Diplomacy, 1900–1950*. Chicago: University of Chicago Press, 1951.

Kennedy, Paul. *The Rise and Fall of the Great Powers: Economic Change and Military Conflict from 1500 to 2000*. New York: Random House, 1987.

Keohane, Robert O., ed. *Neorealism and Its Critics*. New York: Columbia University Press, 1986.

Keohane, Robert O. *After Hegemony: Cooperation and Discord in the World Political Economy*. New Jersey: Princeton University Press, 1994.

———. *International Institutions and State Power: Essays in International Relations Theory*. Nashville: Westview, 1989.

Keohane, Robert O. and Helen V. Milner, eds. *Internationalisation and Domestic Politics*. Cambridge: Cambridge University Press, 1996.

Keohane, Robert O. and Joseph S. Nye. *Power and Interdependence*. New York: Harper Collins Publishers, 1989.

Kibbe, Jennifer Dale. "Presidents as Kingmakers: United States Decisions to Overthrow Foreign Governments". Ph.D. dissertation, University of California, 2003.

Kissinger, Henry. *Diplomacy*. New York: Simon & Schuster, 1994.

Kivimaki, Timo Antero. "Distribution of Benefits in Bargaining Between a Superpower and a Developing Country: A Study of Negotiation Processes between the United States and Indonesia". Ph.D. dissertation, University of Helsinki, 1993.

Kivimaki, Timo Antero. *U.S.-Indonesian Hegemonic Bargaining: Strength of Weakness*. Aldershot: Ashgate Publishing, 2003.

Knorr, Klaus Eugen, ed. *Historical Dimensions of National Security Problems*. Lawrence: University Press of Kansas, 1976.

Kupchan, Charles A., Emanuel Adler, Jean-Marc Coicaud, and Yuen Foong Khong. *Power in Transition: The Peaceful Change of International Order*. Tokyo: United Nations University Press, 2001.

Lampton, David M. *Same Bed, Different Dreams: Managing U.S.-China Relations, 1989–2000*. Berkeley: University of California Press, 2001.

Legge, J.D. *Sukarno: A Political Biography*. New York: Praeger, 1972.

Leifer, Michael. *Indonesia's Foreign Policy*. London: Allen & Unwin, 1983.

———. *ASEAN and the Security of Southeast Asia*. London: Routledge, 1989.

———. *Dictionary of the Modern Politics of Southeast Asia*. London: Routledge, 1995.

———. *Singapore's Foreign Policy: Coping with Vulnerability*. London: Routledge, 2000.

Levine, Alan J. *The United States and the Struggle for Southeast Asia, 1945–1975*. Westport: Praeger, 1995.

Lindsey, Tim and Helen Pausacker. *Chinese Indonesians: Remembering, Distorting, Forgetting*. Singapore: Institute of Southeast Asian Studies, 2005.

Liska, George. *Nations in Alliance: The Limits of Interdependence*. Baltimore: Johns Hopkins Press, 1968.

Lovell, David W. *Asia-Pacific Security: Policy Challenges*. Singapore: Institute of Southeast Asian Studies, 2003.

Lowry, Robert. *The Armed Forces of Indonesia*. St. Leonards: Allen & Unwin, 1996.

Lu, Soo Chun. "United States Relations with Indonesia, 1953–1961". Ph.D. dissertation, Ohio University, 1997.

Mackinder, Halford J. *Democratic Ideals and Reality*. New York: Henry Holt and Company, 1942.

Maddison, Angus, D.S. Prasada Rao, and William F. Shepherd, eds. *The Asian Economies in the Twentieth Century*. Cheltenham: Edward Elgar, 2002.

Mahan, A.T. The *Problem of Asia and Its Effect upon International Policies*. London: Sampson Low, Marston & Company, 1900.

Maliki, Zainuddin. *Agama Priyayi: Makna Agama Di Tangan Elite Penguasa* [Priyayi Religion: Meanings of Religion in Elite's Hand]. Yogyakarta: Pustaka Marva, 2004.

Malone, David M. and Yuen Foong Khong, eds. *Unilateralism and U.S. Foreign Policy: International Perspectives*. London: Lynne Rienner Publishers, 2003.

Martin, Edwin W. *Southeast Asia and China: The End of Containment*. Boulder: Westview Press, 1977.

Mayers, Ramon H. *A U.S. Foreign Policy for Asia: The 1980s and Beyond*. Stanford: Hoover Institution Press, 1982.

Maynard, Harold Ward. "A Comparison of Military Elite Role Perceptions in Indonesia and the Philippines". Ph.D. dissertation, The American University, 1976.

McCabe, Ina Baghdiantz, Gelina Harlaftis, and Ioanna Pepelasis Minoglou, eds. *Diaspora Entrepreneurial Networks: Four Centuries of History*. Oxford: Berg, 2005.

McIntyre, Angus. *The Indonesian Presidency: The Shift from Personal toward Constitutional Rule*. Lanham: Rowman & Littlefield Publishers, 2005.

McMahon, Robert J. *Colonialism and Cold War: The United States and the Struggle for Indonesian Independence, 1945–49*. Ithaca: Cornell University Press, 1981.

———. *The Limits of Empire: The United States and Southeast Asia since World War II*. New York: Columbia University Press, 1999.

McMahon, Robert James. "The United States and Decolonization in Southeast Asia: The Case of Indonesia, 1945–1949". Ph.D. dissertation, The University of Connecticut, 1977.

McMichael, Heath. *Indonesian Foreign Policy: Towards a More Assertive Style*. Australia-Asia Papers No. 40, Nathan: Griffith University, 1987.

Mearsheimer, John J. *The Tragedy of Great Power Politics*. New York: W.W. Norton, 2001.

Moertono, Soemarsaid. *State and Statecraft in Old Java: A Study of the Later Mataram Period, 16th to 19th Century.* Ithaca: Cornell University Press, 1968.

Morgenthau, Hans J. *Politics among Nations: The Struggle for Power and Peace.* New York: Alfred A. Knopf, 1985.

———. *Scientific Man versus Power Politics.* Chicago: The University of Chicago Press, 1967.

Mortimer, Rex. *Indonesian Communism under Sukarno: Ideology and Politics, 1959–1965.* London: Cornell University Press, 1974.

Mozingo, David. *Chinese Policy toward Indonesia 1949–1967.* London: Cornell University Press, 1976.

Mrázek, Rudolf. *Jihovýchodní Asie ve světové politice 1900–1975* [Southeast Asia in World Politics, 1900–1975]. Prague: Publishing House Svoboda, 1980.

———. *Sjahrir: Politics and Exile in Indonesia.* Ithaca: Cornell University Press, 1994.

———. *The United States and the Indonesian Military 1945–1965: A Study of an Intervention.* Volume I and II. Prague: Oriental Institute in Academia Publishing House, 1978.

Mrázek, Rudolf, Dagmar Ansárí, Jan Bečka et al. *USA a jihovýchodní Asie po druhé světové válce* [The U.S. and the Southeast Asia after the WWII]. Prague: Academia Publishing House, 1978.

Najjarine, Karim. "Australian Policy towards Indonesia 1965–72: An Archival Study". Ph.D. dissertation, University of Western Sydney, 2004.

Nordholt, Schulte N.G. *State-Citizen Relations in Suharto's Indonesia: Kawula-Gusti.* Rotterdam: Erasmus University, 1987.

Nordholt, Schulte and Jan Willhelm. *The Myth of the West: America as the Last Empire.* Translated by Herbert H. Rowen. Michigan: William B. Eerdmans Publishing Company, Grand Rapids, 1995.

Nursam, M., ed. *Surat-Surat Pribadi Soejatmoko kepada Presiden (Jenderal) Soeharto,* [Personal Letters of Soejatmoko to President (General) Soeharto]. Jakarta: Yayasan Soejatmoko dan PT Gramedia, 2002.

Nye, Joseph S., Jr. *Bound to Lead: The Changing Nature of American Power.* New York: Basic Books, 1991.

———. *Soft Power: The Means to Success in World Politics.* New York: Public Affairs, 2004.

Parker, W.H. *Mackinder: Geography as an Aid to Statecraft.* Oxford: Clarendon Press, 1982.

Peacock, James L. *Muslim Puritans: Reformist Psychology in Southeast Asian Islam.* Berkeley: University of California Press, 1978.

Pempel, T.J., ed. *The Politics of the Asian Economic Crisis.* Ithaca: Cornell University Press, 1999.

Penders C.L.M., ed. *Milestones on My Journey: The Memoirs of Ali Sastroamijoyo, Indonesian Patriot and Political Leader.* St. Lucia: University of Queensland Press, 1979.

Philpott, Simon. *Rethinking Indonesia: Postcolonial Theory, Authoritarianism and Identity*. New York: St. Martin's Press, 2000.

Pringle, Robert. *Indonesia and the Philippines: American Interests in Island Southeast Asia*. New York: Columbia University Press, 1980.

Punch, Keith F. *Survey Research: The Basics*. London: Sage Publications, 2003.

Rabasa, Angel and Peter Chalk. *Indonesia's Transformation and the Stability of Southeast Asia*. Santa Monica: RAND, 2001.

Raffles, Thomas S. *The History of Java*. Volume II. London: Black, Parbury, and Allen, 1817.

Ramage, Douglas E. *Politics in Indonesia: Democracy, Islam and the Ideology of Tolerance*. London: Routledge, 1995.

Reeve, David. *Golkar of Indonesia: An Alternative to the Party System*. Singapore: Oxford University Press, 1985.

Ricklefs, M.C. *A History of Modern Indonesia since c.1200*. 3rd Edition. Houndmills: Palgrave, 2001.

Robertson, Beth M. *Oral History Handbook*. 4th Edition. Adelaide: Oral History Association Australia, 2000.

Robinson, Richard and Vedi R. Hadiz. *Reorganising Power in Indonesia: The Politics of Oligarchy in an Age of Markets*. London: Routledge Curzon, 2004.

Roces, Mina. *Recording Voices: Oral History and the Interview*. A Study Kit. Sydney: UNSW, 2004.

Ross, Robert S., ed. *East Asia in Transition: Toward a New Regional Order*. New York: An East Gate Book, 1995.

Ross, Robert S. *Negotiating Cooperation: The United States and China, 1969–1989*. Stanford: Stanford University Press, 1995.

Rosser, Andrew. *The Politics of Economic Liberalisation in Indonesia: State, Market and Power*. Richmond: Curzon Press, 1992.

Rossi, Peter H., James D. Wright, and Andy B. Anderson, eds. *Handbook of Survey Research*. Orlando: Academic Press, 1983.

Rotberg, Robert I. and Theodore K. Rabb, eds. *The Origin and Prevention of Major Wars*. New York: Cambridge University Press, 1989.

Rotter, Andrew J. *The Path to Vietnam: Origins of the American Commitment to Southeast Asia*. Ithaca: Cornell University Press, 1987.

Rumley, Dennis, Tatsuya Chiba, Akihiko Takagi, and Yoriko Fukushima. *Global Geopolitical Change and the Asia-Pacific: A Regional Perspective*. Brookfield: Ashgate Publishing Company, 1996.

Said, Edward W. *Orientalism*. London: Penguin, 2003.

Said, Salim. *Legitimising Military Rule: Indonesian Armed Forces Ideology, 1958–2000*. Jakarta: Pustaka Sinar Harapan, 2006.

Saripudin, Mohamad Hery. "The Effects and the Relations of Foreign Aid: A Case Study of Indonesia and Its Two Largest Donors, the United States and Japan". M.A. dissertation, Saint Mary's University, 1994.

Scalapino, Robert A. *Major Power Relations in Northeast Asia*. Washington: University Press of America, 1987.

Scalapino, Robert A., Seizaburo Sato, and Jusuf Wanandi. *Internal and External Security Issues in Asia*. Berkeley: University of California, 1986.

Schwarz, Adam and Jonathan Paris, eds. *The Politics of Post-Suharto Indonesia*. New York: Council on Foreign Relations Press, 1999.

Scott, John, ed. *The Sociology of Elites*. Brookfield: Edward Elgar Publishing, 1990.

Silverman, David, ed. *Qualitative Research: Theory Method and Practice*. Second edition. London: SAGE Publications, 2004.

Skinner, Quentin et al. *Great Political Thinkers*. Oxford: Oxford University Press, 1992.

Snyder, Jack. *Myths of Empire: Domestic Politics and International Ambition*. Ithaca: Cornell University Press, 1991.

Soeharto. *Soeharto, My Thoughts, Words and Deeds: An Autobiography*. As told to G. Dwipayana and Ramadhan K.H., edited by Muti'ah Lestiono. Jakarta: Citra Lamtoro Gung Persada, 1991.

Soesastro, Hadi and A.R. Sutopo, ed. *Strategi dan Hubungan Internasional: Indonesia di Kawasan Asia-Pasifik* [Strategy and International Relations of Indonesia in the Asia-Pacific Region]. Jakarta: Centre for Strategic and International Studies, 1981.

Spiegel, Steven. *The Other Arab-Israeli Conflict: Making America's Middle East Policy from Truman to Reagan*. Chicago: University of Chicago Press, 1985.

Spykman, Nicholas J. *America's Strategy in World Politics: The United States and the Balance of Power*. New York: Harcourt, Brace and Company, 1942.

Spykman, Nicholas J. and Hellen R. Nicholl, eds. *The Geography of the Peace*. New York: Harcourt, Brace and Company, 1994.

Stavridis, Stelios and Christopher Hill, eds. *Domestic Sources of Foreign Policy: West European Reactions to the Falklands Conflict*. Oxford: Berg Publishers, 1996.

Steinbruner, John. *The Cybernetic Theory of Decision: New Dimensions of Political Analysis*. Princeton: Princeton University Press, 1974.

Stuart-Fox, Martin. *A Short History of China and Southeast Asia: Tribute, Trade and Influence*. Crows Nest: Allen & Unwin, 2003.

Sudarsono, Juwono. *Surviving Globalisation: Indonesia and the World*. Jakarta: The Jakarta Post, 1996.

Suh, J.J., Peter J. Katzenstein, and Allen Carlson. *Rethinking Security in East Asia: Identity, Power, and Efficiency*. Stanford: Stanford University Press, 2004

Suleiman, Satyawati. *Concise Ancient History of Indonesia*. Jakarta: The Archaeological Foundation, 1974.

Sukma, Rizal. *Indonesia and China: The Politics of a Troubled Relationship*. London: Routledge, 1999.

Sukma, Rizal. *Islam in Indonesian Foreign Policy*. London: RoutledgeCurzon, 2003.

Suryadinata, Leo. *Indonesia's Foreign Policy under Suharto: Aspiring to International Leadership*. Singapore: Times Academic Press, 1996.

―――. *Pribumi Indonesians, the Chinese Minority, and China: A Study of Perceptions and Policies*. Singapore: Heinemann Asia, 1986.

―――. *Dilema Minoritas Tionghoa*. Singapore: Heinemann Educational Books, 1982.

―――. *The Chinese Minority in Indonesia: Seven Papers*. Singapore: Chopmen Enterprise, 1978.

Suryadinata, Leo, ed. *Ethnic Chinese as Southeast Asians*. Singapore: Institute of Southeast Asian Studies, 1997.

―――. *Southeast Asian Chinese and China: The Politico-Economic Dimension*. Singapore: Times Academic Press, 1995.

―――. *The Ethnic Chinese in the ASEAN States: Bibliographical Essays*. Singapore: Institute of Southeast Asian Studies, 1989.

Suryadinata, Leo, Evi Nurvidya Arifin, and Aris Ananta, *Indonesia's Population: Ethnicity and Religion in a Changing Political Landscape*. Singapore: Institute of Southeast Asian Studies, 2003.

Suryakusuma, Julia I. *Sex, Power and Nation: An Anthology of Writings 1979–2003*. Jakarta: Metafor Publishing, 2004.

Sutherland, Heather. *The Making of a Bureaucratic Elite: The Colonial Transformation of the Javanese Priyayi*. Singapore: Heinemann Educational Books, 1979.

Sutter, Robert G. *China's Rise in Asia: Promises and Perils*. Lanham: Rowman & Littlefield Publishing Group, 2005.

Tarling, Nicholas, ed. *The Cambridge History of Southeast Asia*. Cambridge: The Press Syndicate of the University of Cambridge, 1999.

Taylor, Jay. *China and Southeast Asia: Peking's Relations with Revolutionary Movements*. New York: Praeger, 1976.

Taylor, Jean Gelman. *Indonesia: Peoples and Histories*. New Haven: Yale University Press, 2003.

Taylor, Peter J. *Political Geography, World-Economy, Nation-State and Locality*. New York: Longman Group UK, 1989.

Tellis, Ashley J. and Michael Wills, eds. *Strategic Asia 2004–05: Confronting Terrorism in the Pursuit of Power*. Seattle: National Bureau of Research, 2004.

Thakur, Ramesh and Edward Newman, eds. *Broadening Asia's Security Discourse and Agenda: Political, Social, and Environmental Perspectives*. Tokyo: United Nations University Press, 2004.

Thucydides. *History of the Peloponnesian War*, translated by Rex Warner. London: Penguin Books, 1972.

Tilman, Robert O. *Southeast Asia and the Enemy Beyond: ASEAN Perceptions of External Threats*. Boulder: Westview Press, 1987.

Van Niel, Robert. *The Emergence of the Modern Indonesian Elite*. Chicago: Quadrangle Books, 1960.

Vasquez, John A. *The Power of Power Politics: A Critique*. London: Frances Pinter, 1983.

Vasquez, John A. and Colin Elman, eds. *Realism and the Balancing of Power: A New Debate.* Upper Saddle River: Prentice Hall, 2002.

Vaughn, Sandra Yvonne. "Chambers Foreign Aid: Its Impact on Indonesian Political Development 1950–1972". Ph.D. dissertation, Howard University, 1978.

Vickers, Adrian. *A History of Modern Indonesia.* Cambridge: Cambridge University Press, 2005.

Wadsworth, Yoland. *Do It Yourself Social Research.* Sydney: Allen & Unwin, 1997.

Walt, Stephen M. *The Origins of Alliances.* London: Cornell University Press, 1990.

Waltz, Kenneth W. *Man, the State, and War.* New York: Columbia University Press, 1959.

––––––. *Theory of International Politics.* Boston: Addison-Wesley Press, 1979.

Ward, Robert E. and Roy C. Macridis, ed. *Modern Political Systems: Asia.* Englewood Cliffs: Prentice-Hall, 1963.

Wardaya, F.X. Baskara T. "A Cold War Shadow: United States Policy toward Indonesia, 1953–1963". Ph.D. dissertation, Marquette University, 2001.

Weinstein, Franklin B. *Indonesian Foreign Policy and the Dilemma of Dependence: From Sukarno to Soeharto.* Ithaca: Cornell University Press, 1976.

Weissman, Steve, ed. *The Trojan Horse: A Radical Look at Foreign Aid.* Palo Alto: Ramparts Press, 1975.

Wendt, Alexander. *Social Theory of International Politics.* Cambridge: Cambridge University Press, 1999.

Wie, Thee Kian, ed. *Recollections: The Indonesian Economy, 1950s–1990s.* Institute of Southeast Asian Studies, Singapore, 2005.

Willison, Malcolm. "Leaders of Revolution: The Social Origins of the Republican Cabinet Members in Indonesia, 1945–55". M.A. dissertation, Cornell University, 1958.

Wilson, Greta O., ed. *Regents, Reformers and Revolutionaries: Indonesian Voices of Colonial Days, Selected Historical Readings 1899–1949.* Honolulu: The University Press of Hawaii, 1978.

Wong, John. *The Political Economy of China's Changing Relations with Southeast Asia.* London: Macmillan, 1984.

Woods, Ngaire, ed. *Explaining International Relations since 1945.* New York: Oxford University Press, 1996.

Wriggins, Howard W. *The Ruler's Imperative: Strategies for Political Surviving in Asia and Africa.* New York: Columbia University Press, 1969.

Wurfel, David and Bruce Burton, eds. *The Political Economy of Foreign Policy in Southeast Asia.* Basingstoke: Macmillan, 1990.

Yahuda, Michael B. *The International Politics of Asia-Pacific: 1945–1995.* London: Routledge, 1996.

Yee, Herbert and Ian Storey, eds. *The China Threat: Perceptions, Myths and Reality.* London: RoutledgeCourzon, 2002.

Zweigenhaft, Richard L. and William G. Domhoff. *Diversity in the Power Elite: Have Women and Minorities Reached the Top?* New Haven: Yale University Press, 1998.

Academic Articles

Acharya, Amitav. "Reordering Asia: 'Cooperative Security' or Concert of Powers?" IDSS Working Paper No. 3, Singapore, July 1999.

———. "Will Asia's Past Be Its Future?" *International Security* 28, no. 3 (Winter 2003/04).

Acharia, Amitav and Barry Buzan. "Why Is There No Non-Western IR Theory? An Introduction". *International Relations of the Asia-Pacific* 7, no. 3 (2007).

Acharya, Amitav and Richard Stubbs. "Theorizing Southeast Asian Relations: An Introduction". *The Pacific Review* 19, no. 2 (June 2006).

Acharya, Amitav and See Seng Tan. "Betwixt Balance and Community: America, ASEAN and the Security of Southeast Asia". *International Relations of the Asia-Pacific* 6, no. 1 (2006).

Anwar, Dewi Fortuna. "Indonesia's Relations with China and Japan: Images, Perceptions and Realities". *Contemporary Southeast Asia* 12, no. 3 (December 1990): 225–46.

Azra, Azyumardi. "Islam in Southeast Asia: Between Tolerance and Radicalism". Muis Occasional Papers Series, Paper No. 5, Majlis Ugama Islam Singapura (Islamic Religious Council of Singapore), 2008.

Ba, Alice D. "China and ASEAN: Renavigating Relations for a 21st-Century Asia". *Asian Survey* XLIII, no. 4 (July/August 2003).

Bachtiar, Harsja W. "The Religion of Java: A Commentary". *Madjalah Ilmu-Ilmu Sastra Indonesia* 5, no. 1 (1973): 85–115.

Baker III, James A. "America in Asia: Emerging Architecture for a Pacific Community". *Foreign Affairs* 70, no. 5 (Winter 1991/92).

Bandow, Doug. "Needless Entanglements: Washington's Expanding Security Ties in Southeast Asia". Policy Analysis No. 401, Cato Institute, Washington, D.C., 24 May 2001.

Baswedan, Anies Rasyid. "Political Islam in Indonesia: Present and Future Trajectory" *Asian Survey* 44, no. 5 (September/October 2004).

Bell, Coral. "American Ascendancy and the Pretence of Concert". *The National Interest*, no. 57 (Fall 1999).

———. "East Timor, Canberra and Washington: A Case Study in Crisis Management". *Australian Journal of International Affairs* 54, no. 2, July 2000.

Benda, Harry J. "The Pattern of Administrative Reforms in the Closing Years of Dutch Rule in Indonesia". *Journal of Asian Studies* 25, no. 4 (August 1966).

Bernstein, Richard and Ross H. Munro. "China I.: The Coming Conflict with America". *Foreign Affairs* 76, no. 2 (March/April 1997).

Bradford, John F. "Japanese Anti-Piracy Initiatives in Southeast Asia: Policy Formulation and the Coastal State Responses". *Contemporary Southeast Asia* 26, no. 3 (December 2004): 480–505.

Brands, H.W. "The Limits of Manipulation: How the United States Didn't Topple Sukarno". *Journal of American History* 76, no. 3. (December 1989).

Brecher, Michael et al. "A Framework for Research on Foreign Policy Behaviour". *Journal of Conflict Resolution* 13, no. 1 (March 1969).

Brooks, Stephen G. and William C. Wohlforth. "American Primacy in Perspective". *Foreign Affairs* 81, no. 4 (July/August 2002).

Brzezinski, Zbigniew. "Selective Global Commitment". *Foreign Affairs* 70, no. 4. (Fall 1991).

Calder, Kent E. "Asia's Empty Tank". *Foreign Affairs* 75, no. 2 (March/April 1996).

Carothers, Thomas. "Promoting Democracy and Fighting Terror". *Foreign Affairs* 82, no. 1 (January/February 2003): 84–97.

Chauvel, Richard and Ikrar Nusa Bhakti. "The Papua Conflict: Jakarta's Perceptions and Policies". Policy Studies 5, East-West Centre, Washington, D.C., 2004.

Chase, Robert S., Emily B. Hill, and Paul Kennedy. "Pivotal States and U.S. Strategy". *Foreign Affairs* 75, no. 1 (January/February 1996).

Cheng, Joseph Y.S. "Sino-ASEAN Relations in the Early Twenty-first Century". *Contemporary Southeast Asia* 23, no. 3 (December 2001): 420–51

———. "China's ASEAN Policy in the 1990s: Pushing for Regional Multipolarity". *Contemporary Southeast Asia* 21, no. 2 (August 1999): 176–204.

Chomsky, Noam. "Indonesia, Master Card in Washington's Hand" *Indonesia* 66 (October 1998): 1–6.

Christensen, Thomas J. "China, the U.S.-Japan Alliance, and the Security Dilemma in East Asia". *International Security* 23, no. 4 (Spring 1999).

Christofferson, Gaye. "The Role of East Asia in Sino-U.S. Relations". *Asian Survey* 42, no. 3 (May/June 2002).

Cohen, R. "Threat Perception in International Crisis". *Political Science Quarterly* 93, no. 1 (1978).

Conable, Barber B., Jr. and David M. Lampton. "China: The Coming Power". *Foreign Affairs* 70, no. 5 (Winter 1992/93).

Copeland, Dale C. "The Constructivist Challenge to Structural Realism: Book Review". *International Security* 25, no. 2 (Fall 2000).

Crawford, Neta C. "The Passion of World Politics". *International Security* 24, no. 4 (Spring 2000).

Crowe, William J., Jr. and Alan D. Romberg. "Rethinking Security in the Pacific". *Foreign Affairs* 70, no. 2 (Spring 1991).

Dewit, David. "Common, Comprehensive and Cooperative Security". *The Pacific Review* 7, no.1 (1994).

Djalal, Hashim. "Policy Issues in U.S.-Indonesia Relations". *Indonesian Quarterly* 23, no. 2 (1995).

Djiwandono, J. Soedjati. "Great Power Relations in the Pacific: Their Impact on U.S.-Indonesian Relations". *Indonesian Quarterly* 14, no. 3 (1986).

Drake, Earl. "Indonesia and China: Old Habits and New Internationalism". *The Pacific Review* 4, no. 3 (1991).

Dupont, Alan. "Indonesian Defence Strategy and Security: Time for a Rethink?", *Contemporary Southeast Asia* 18, no. 3 (December 1996): 275–97.

Dzung, Dang Vu. "A New Balance of Power in Asia-Pacific: Implications for ASEAN's Posture". Research Paper. Weatherhead Center for International Affairs, Harvard University, May 2000.

Emmers, Ralf. "The Influence of the Balance of Power Factor within the ASEAN Regional Forum". *Contemporary Southeast Asia* 23, no. 2 (August 2001): 275–91.

Emmerson, Donald K. "Will Indonesia Survive?". *Foreign Affairs* 79, no. 3 (May/June 2000).

Fordham, Benjamin. "The Politics of Threat Perception and the Use of Force: A Political Economy Model of U.S. Uses of Force, 1949–1994". *International Studies Quarterly* 42, no. 3 (1998).

Foyle, Douglas C. "Public Opinion and Foreign Policy: Elite Beliefs as a Mediating Variable". *International Studies Quarterly* 41, no. 1 (1997).

Friedberg, Aaron L. "Ripe for Rivalry: Prospects for Peace in a Multipolar Asia". *International Security* 18, no. 3 (Winter 1993/94).

———. "Europe's Past, Asia's Future?" SAIS Policy Forum Series, No. 3 (October 1998).

Ganesan, N. "ASEAN's Relations with Major External Powers". *Contemporary Southeast Asia* 22, no. 2 (August 2000): 258–78.

———. "The Collapse of Authoritarian Regimes in Indonesia and Thailand: Structural and Contextual Factors". *Brill* 32, no. 1 (2004): 1–18.

Geertz, Clifford. "Book Review: Robert Van Niel, The Emergence of the Modern Indonesian Elite, Book Review". *American Anthropologist* 63, no. 3 (June 1961).

Glaser, Charles L. "The Security Dilemma Revisited". *World Politics* 50, no. 2 (October 1997).

Goh, Evelyn, ed. "Betwixt and Between: Southeast Asian Strategic Relations with the U.S. and China". IDSS Monograph No. 7, Institute of Defence and Strategic Studies, Singapore, 2005.

Goh, Evelyn. "Hegemonic Constraints: The Implications of 11 September for American Power". *Australian Journal of International Affairs* 57, no. 1 (2003).

———. "Meeting the China Challenge: The U.S. in Southeast Asian Regional Security Strategies". Policy Studies 16, East-West Centre, Washington, D.C., 2005.

Goodman, David S.G. "Are Asia's 'Ethnic Chinese' a Regional-Security Threat?". *Survival* 39, no. 4 (Winter 1997/98).

Hatta, Mohammad. "An Independent Active Foreign Policy". *Foreign Affairs* XXXI (April 1953).

Henderson, Errol Anthony and Richard Tucker. "Clear and Present Strangers: The Clash of Civilizations and International Conflict". *International Studies Quarterly* 45, no. 2 (June 2001).

Hermann, Richard. "The Power of Perceptions in Foreign-Policy Decision-Making: Do Views of the Soviet Union Determine the Policy Choices of American Leaders?". *American Journal of Political Science* 30, no. 4 (December 1986).

Herrmann, Richard. "The Empirical Challenge of the Cognitive Revolution: A Strategy for Drawing Inferences about Perceptions". *International Studies Quarterly* 32, no. 2 (1988): 175–203.

Herrmann, Richard, James F. Voss, Tonya Y.E. Schooler, and Joseph Ciarrochi. "Images in International Relations: An Experimental Test of Cognitive Schemata" *International Studies Quarterly* 41, no. 3 (1997): 403–33.

Herz, John H. "Idealist Internationalism and the Security Dilemma". *World Politics* 2, no. 2 (January 1950).

Holsti, Ole R. and James N. Rosenau. "The Structure of Foreign Policy: Attitudes among American Leaders". *Journal of Politics* 52, no. 1 (February 1990).

Hopf, Ted. "The Promise of Constructivism in International Relations Theory". *International Security* 23, no. 1 (Summer 1998).

Howell, Julia Day. "Sufism and the Indonesian Islamic Revival". *The Journal of Asian Studies* 60, no. 3 (August 2001).

Huntington, Samuel P. "The Clash of Civilizations?". *Foreign Affairs* 72, no. 3 (Summer 1993).

———. "The Lonely Superpower". *Foreign Affairs* 78, no. 2 (March/April 1999).

Hwang, Jihwan. "Rethinking the East Asian Balance of Power: Historical Antagonism, Internal Balancing, and the Korean-Japanese Security Relationship". *World Affairs* 166, no. 2 (Fall 2003).

Ikle, Fred Charles and Terumasa Nakanishi. "Japan's Grand Strategy". *Foreign Affairs* 69, no. 3 (Summer 1990).

Inoguchi, Takashi and Edward Newman. "Introduction: 'Asian Values' and Democracy in Asia". Proceedings from the conference "'Asian Values' and Democracy in Asia". Hamamatsu, Shizuoka, Japan, 28 March 1997.

Lee, Jae-Hyung. "China's Expanding Maritime Ambitions in the Western Pacific and the Indian Ocean". *Contemporary Southeast Asia* 24, no. 3 (December 2002): 549–68.

Jamhari. "Javanese Islam: The Flow of Creed". *Studia Islamika: Indonesian Journal for Islamic Studies* 9, no. 2 (2002).

Jervis, Robert. "Cooperation under the Security Dilemma". *World Politics* 30, no. 2 (January 1978).

Kang, David C. "Getting Asia Wrong: The Need for New Analytical Frameworks". *International Security* 27, no. 4 (Spring 2003).

————. "Hierarchy, Balancing, and Empirical Puzzles in Asian International Relations". *International Security* 28, no. 3 (Winter 2003/04).

Katzenstein, Peter J. and Nobuo Okawara. "Japan, Asian-Pacific Security, and the Case for Analytical Eclecticism". *International Security* 26, no. 2 (Winter 2001/02).

Keohane, Robert O. and Joseph S. Nye, Jr. "Power and Interdependence in the Information Age". *Foreign Affairs* 77, no. 5 (September/October 1998).

————. "Power and Independence Revisited". *International Organization* 41, no. 4 (Autumn 1987).

Kivimaeki, Timo. "Strength of Weakness: American-Indonesian Hegemonic Bargaining". *Journal of Peace Research* 30, no. 4 (November 1993).

Kivimaeki, Timo. "U.S.-Indonesian Relations during the Economic Crisis: Where Has Indonesia's Bargaining Power Gone?". *Contemporary Southeast Asia* 22, no. 3 (December 2000): 527–49.

Klare, Michael T. "The New Geography of Conflict". *Foreign Affairs* 80, no. 3 (May/June 2001).

Koentjaraningrat. "Review of the Religion of Java". *Madjalah Ilmu-Ilmu Sastra* [Magazine of Literature] I, no. 2 (1963).

Koong, Pai Ching. "Southeast Asian Countries' Perceptions of China's Military Modernization". Conference Paper. The Sigur Centre, The George Washington University, Washington, D.C., 1998.

Kuik, Cheng-Chwee. "The Essence of Hedging: Malaysia and Singapore's Response to a Rising China". *Contemporary Southeast Asia* 30, no. 2 (2008): 159–87.

Kusumaatmadja, Mochtar. "Indonesia-United States Bilateral Relations". Indonesian Quarterly XIV, no. 3 (1986).

Larson, D.W. "The Role of Belief Systems and Schemas in Foreign Policy Decision-Making". *Political Psychology* 15, no. 1 (March 1994).

Legro, Jeffrey W. and Andrew Moravcsik. "Is Anybody Still a Realist?". *International Security* 24, no. 2 (Fall 1999).

Leifer, Michael. "The ASEAN Peace Process: A Category Mistake". *The Pacific Review* 12, no. 1 (1999).

————. "The ASEAN Regional Forum". Adelphia Paper 302. Oxford: Oxford University Press, 1996).

Liddle, William R. "The Islamic Turn in Indonesia: A Political Explanation". *The Journal of Asian Studies* 55, no. 3 (August 1996).

Lieberthal, Kenneth. "A New China Strategy: The Challenge". *Foreign Affairs* 74, no. 6 (November/December 1995).

Lipski, Seth and Raphael Pura. "Critical Countries: Indonesia: Testing Time for the 'New Order'". *Foreign Affairs* 57, no. 1 (Fall 1978).

Little, Richard. "Rethinking the Dynamics of the Balance of Power". Conference Paper. Annual meeting of the International Studies Association, Hilton Hawaiian Village, Honolulu, 5 March 2005.

Mackinder, Halford J. "The Geographical Pivot of History". *Geographical Journal* *XXIII* (1904).

Mak, J.N. and B.A. Hamzah. "The External Maritime Dimension of ASEAN Security". *The Journal of Strategic Studies* 18, no. 3 (September 1995).

Malik, Mohan J. "Dragon on Terrorism: Assessing China's Tactical Gains and Strategic Losses After 11 September". *Contemporary Southeast Asia* 24, no. 2 (August 2002).

Maoz, Zeev. "The Controversy over the Democratic Peace". *International Security* 22, no. 1 (Summer 1997).

Mastanduno, Michael. "Preserving the Unipolar Moment: Realist Theories and U.S. Grand Strategy after the Cold War". *International Security* 21, no. 4 (Spring 1997).

Mayumi, Itoh. "Japan-Southeast Asia Relations: Perception Gaps, Legacy of World War II, and Economic Diplomacy". Conference Paper. The 1995 Asian Studies on the Pacific Coast Conference, Pacific University, Forest Grove, 16–18 June 1995.

McMichael, Heath. "Indonesian Foreign Policy: Towards a More Assertive Style". Australia-Asia Papers No. 40. Nathan: Griffith University, February 1987.

McVey, Ruth. "Redesigning the Cosmos: Belief Systems and State Power in Indonesia". NIAS Reports No. 14. Copenhagen: Nordic Institute of Asian Studies, Copenhagen, 1998.

Mearsheimer, John J. "Back to the Future". *International Security* 15, no. 1 (Summer 1990).

Midlarski, Manus I. "The Impact of External Threat on States and Domestic Societies". *International Studies Review* 5, No. 4 (December 2003).

Moertopo, Ali. "Future Indonesian-U.S. Relations: A View from Jakarta". *Pacific Community: An Asian Quarterly Review* 7, no. 4 (July 1976).

Nairn, Allan. "U.S. Support for the Indonesian Military: Congressional Testimony". *Bulletin of Concerned Asian Scholars* 32, nos. 1–2 (January/June 2000).

Ness, Peter Van. "Alternative U.S. Strategies with Respect to China and the Implications for Vietnam". *Contemporary Southeast Asia* 20, no. 2 (August 1998).

Nye, Joseph S., Jr. "Limits of American Power". *Political Science Quarterly* 17, no. 4 (2002/03).

―――. "The Decline of America's Soft Power". *Foreign Affairs* 83, no. 3 (May/June 2004).

Novotny, Daniel. "Indonesia's Elite: Media as a Source of Threat in the Information Era". Conference Paper. "Media and Identity in Asia" Conference, Curtin University of Technology, Miri, Malaysia, 15–16 February 2006.

―――. "The Threat from Misperception". *Postscript* II, no. 6 (June 2005).

Peffley, Mark and Jon Hurwitz. "International Events and Foreign Policy Beliefs: Public Response to Changing Soviet-U.S. Relations". *American Journal of Political Science* 36, no. 2 (May 1992).

Peou, Sorpong. "Realism and Constructivism in Southeast Asian Security Studies Today: A Review Essay". *The Pacific Review* 15, no. 1 (2002).

Perwita, Anak Agung Banyu. "Security Sector Reform in Indonesia: The Case of Indonesia's Defence White Paper 2003". *Journal of Security Sector Management* 2, no. 4 (December 2004).

Philpott, Simon. "Fear of Dark: Indonesia and the Australian National Imagination". *Australian Journal of International Affairs* 55, no. 3 (November 2001).

Porter, Donald J. "Citizen Participation through Mobilization and the Rise of Political Islam in Indonesia". *The Pacific Review* 15, no. 2 (2002).

Putnam, Robert. "Diplomacy and Domestic Politics: The Logic of Two-Level Games". *International Organization* 42, no. 3 (Summer 1988).

Robinson, Richard. "Toward a Class Analysis of the Indonesian Military Bureaucratic State". *Indonesia* 25 (April 1978).

Roggeveen, Sam. "Towards a Liberal Theory of International Relations". *Policy*. The Centre for Independent Studies (Autumn 2001).

Rose, Gideon. "Neoclassical Realism and Theories of Foreign Policy". *World Politics* 51, no. 1 (October 1998).

Ross, Robert S. "China II.: Beijing as a Conservative Power". *Foreign Affairs* 76, no. 2 (March/April 1997).

―――. "The Geography of Peace". *International Security* 23, No. 4 (Spring 1999).

Roy, Denny. "Current Sino-U.S. Relations in Strategic Perspective". *Contemporary Southeast Asia* 20, no. 3 (December 1998).

―――. "The Foreign Policy of Great-Power China". *Contemporary Southeast Asia* 19, no. 2 (September 1997).

Rustow, A. Dankwart. "Realignments in the Middle East". *Foreign Affairs* 63, no. 3 (1984).

Scalapino, Robert A. "China and the Balance of Power". *Foreign Affairs* 52, no. 2 (January 1974).

Schweller, Randall L. "Unanswered Threats: A Neoclassical Realist Theory of Underbalancing". *International Security* 29, no. 2 (Fall 2004).

Segal, Gerald. "Does China Matter?". *Foreign Affairs*. (September/October 1999).

Shuja, Sharif M. "The Historical Myopia of International Relations". *Contemporary Review* 278 (January 2001).

Siegel, Lenny. "Riches of the East: U.S. Interests in Indonesia". *Southeast Asia Chronicle*, No. 63 (July/August 1978).

Simon, Sheldon W. "ASEAN Strategic Situation in the 1980s". *Pacific Affairs* 60, no. 1 (1987).

―――. "Is There a U.S. Strategy for East Asia?". *Contemporary Southeast Asia* 21, no. 3 (December 1999).

Singh, Bhubhindar. "ASEAN's Perception of Japan: Change and Continuity". *Asian Survey* 42, no. 2 (March/April 2002).

Singh, Bilveer. "The Challenge of Militant Islam and Terrorism in Indonesia". *Australian Journal of International Affairs* 58, no. 1 (March 2004).

Skinner, William G. "Change and Persistence in Chinese Culture Overseas". *Journal of the South Seas Society* 16 (1960).

Smith, Anthony L. "A Glass Half Full: Indonesia-U.S. Relations in the Age of Terror". *Contemporary Southeast Asia* 25, no. 3 (December 2003): 449–72.

———. "Australia-Indonesia Relations: Getting Beyond East Timor". Special Assessment: Asia's Bilateral Relations, Asia-Pacific Centre for Security Studies, Honolulu, October 2004.

———. "Indonesia's Foreign Policy under Abdurrahman Wahid: Radical or Status Quo State?". *Contemporary Southeast Asia* 22, no. 3 (December 2000): 498–26.

Smith, Steve. "Wendt's World". *Review of International Studies* 26, no. 1 (2000).

Snyder, Glenn H. "Mearsheimer's World — Offensive Realism and the Struggle for Security". *International Security* 27, no. 1 (Summer 2002).

Soemardi, Soelaeman. "Some Aspects of the Social Origins of the Indonesian Political Decision-Makers". *Transactions of the Third World Congress of Sociology*. International Sociological Association, 1956.

Soesastro, Hadi. "After the Resumption of Diplomatic Relations: Aspects of Sino-Indonesian Economic Relations". *Indonesian Quarterly* 19, no. 3 (1991).

Soroka, Stuart N. "Media, Public Opinion, and Foreign Policy". *Harvard International Journal of Press-Politics* 8, no. 1 (Winter 2003).

Storey, Ian James. "Creeping Assertiveness: China, the Philippines and the South China Sea Dispute". *Contemporary Southeast Asia* 21, no. 1 (April 1999): 95–118.

———. "Indonesia's China Policy in the New Order and Beyond: Problems and Prospects". *Contemporary Southeast Asia* 22, no. 1 (April 2000): 145–74.

Stuart-Fox, Martin. "Southeast Asia and China: The Role of History and Culture in Shaping Future Relations". *Contemporary Southeast Asia* 26, no. 1 (April 2004): 116–39.

Subianto, Landry Haryo. "ASEAN and the East Asian Co-operation: Searching for a Balanced Relationship". *The Indonesian Quarterly* XXXI, no. 1 (1st Quarter 2003).

Sukma, Rizal. "Recent Developments in Sino-Indonesian Relations: An Indonesian View". *Contemporary Southeast Asia* 16, no. 1 (June 1994): 35–45.

———. "Islam and Foreign Policy in Indonesia: Internal Weaknesses and the Dilemma of Dual Identity". Working Paper No. 11. The Asia Foundation's Project on Domestic Dynamics of Foreign Policy in Asia, September 1999.

———. "The First Sino-Indonesian Conference: Building a New Mutual Understanding". *Indonesian Quarterly* 19, No. 3 (1991).

———. "U.S.-Southeast Asia Relations after the Crisis: the Security Dimension". Background paper. The Asia Foundation's Workshop on America's Role in Asia, Bangkok, 22–24 March 2000.

Suryadinata, Leo. "The Chinese Minority and Sino-Indonesian Diplomatic Normalization". *Journal of Southeast Asian Studies* 12, No. 1 (March 1981).

Sutherland, Heather. "The Priyayi". *Indonesia* 19 (1975).

Taliaferro, Jeffrey W. "Security Seeking under Anarchy: Defensive Realism Revisited". *International Security* 25, No. 3 (Winter 2000).

Tan, Paige Johnson. "Navigating a Turbulent Ocean: Indonesia's Worldview and Foreign Policy". *Asian Perspective* 31, no. 3 (2007).

The Editors. "Current Data on the Indonesian Military Elite". *Indonesia* 75 (April 2003).

Tilman, Robert O. "The Enemy Beyond: External Threat Perceptions in the ASEAN Region". Research Notes and Discussion Paper No. 42. Singapore: Institute of Southeast Asian Studies, 1984.

Tomaka, Joe et al. "Cognitive and Physiological Antecedents of Threat and Challenge Appraisal". *Journal of Personality and Social Psychology* 73, no. 1 (January 1997).

Tow, Shannon. "Southeast Asia in the Sino-U.S. Strategic Balance". *Contemporary Southeast Asia* 26, no. 3 (December 2004).

Turner, Sarah. "Speaking Out: Chinese Indonesians after Suharto". *Asian Ethnicity* 4, no. 3 (October 2003).

Van der Kroef, Justus M. "National Security, Defence Strategy and Foreign Policy Perceptions in Indonesia". *Orbis* 20, no. 2 (Summer 1976).

———. "Normalizing Relations with China: Indonesia's Policies and Perceptions". *Asian Survey* 26, no. 8 (1986).

Vatikiotis, Michael R.J. "Catching the Dragon's Tail: China and Southeast Asia in the 21st Century". *Contemporary Southeast Asia* 25, no. 1 (April 2003): 65–78.

Walt, Stephen M. "Beyond bin Laden". *International Security* 26, no. 3 (Winter 2001/02).

———. "International Relations: One World, Many Theories". *Foreign Policy*, No. 110 (Spring 1998).

Waltz, Kenneth. "Globalisation and American Power". *The National Interest*. (Spring 2000).

Wanandi, Jusuf. "Indonesia: Domestic Politics and Foreign Policy". Conference paper. The Third U.S.-ASEAN Conference "ASEAN in the Regional and International Context", Chiang Mai, 7–11 January 1985.

Wanandi, Jusuf and Hadi Soesastro. "Indonesian Security and Threat Perceptions". Conference paper. The Pacific Forum Symposium "National Threat Perceptions in East Asia/Pacific'", Waikola, Hawaii, 6–8 February 1982.

Weinstein, Franklin B. "The Indonesian Elite's View of the World and the Foreign Policy of Development". *Indonesia* 12 (October 1971).

———. "The Uses of Foreign Policy in Indonesia: An Approach to the Analysis of Foreign Policy in the Less Developed Countries". *World Politics: A Quarterly Journal of International Relations* XXIV, no. 3 (April 1972).

Wendt, Alexander. "Anarchy is What States Make of It: The Social Construction of Power Politics". *International Organization* 46, no. 2 (Spring 1992).

Whiting, Allen S. "ASEAN Eyes China: The Security Dimension". *Asian Survey* XXXVII, no. 4 (April 1997).

————. "Reflections on 'Misunderstanding' China". Seminar paper. The 2001 Annual Gaston Sigur Memorial Lecture, The George Washington University, Washington, D.C., 15 March 2001.

Xinbo, Wu. "U.S. Security Policy in Asia: Implications for China-U.S. Relations". *Contemporary Southeast Asia* 22, no. 3 (December 2000).

Yahuda, Michael. "Europe and America in Asia: Different Beds, Same Dreams". Seminar Paper. The Sigur Center for Asian Studies, The George Washington University, Washington, D.C., 10 October 2003.

Yamazaki, Masakazu. "Asia, a Civilization in the Making: East Asia, the Pacific, and the Modern Age". *Foreign Affairs* 75, no. 4 (July/August 1996).

Yergin, Daniel, Dennis Eklof, and Jefferson Edwards. "Fuelling Asia's Recovery". *Foreign Affairs* 77, no. 2 (March/April 1998).

Zakaria, Fareed. "Realism and Domestic Politics: A Review Essay". *International Security* 17, no. 1 (Summer 1992).

Zhao, Quansheng. "Asian-Pacific International Relations in the 21st Century". *Journal of Strategic Studies* 24, no. 4 (December 2001).

Relevant Journals and News Agencies

Agence France Presse (period of 1999–2006)
Australian Journal of International Affairs
Asia Times Online (period of 2005–06)
Asian Survey
Asian Wall Street Journal
Asahi Shimbun
Bali Post (period of 2003–06)
BBC
China Quarterly
Contemporary Southeast Asia
Far Eastern Economic Review (FEER)
Foreign Affairs
Foreign Policy
Gatra
Geopolitics
Harvard Magazine
International Economy
International Security
Jawa Post
Kompas
Lidove Noviny
Newsweek (period of 1990–2006)
Nihon Kezai Shimbun
Rakyat Merdeka
Republika

Sinar Harapan
Survival
Tempo (period of 1999–2006)
The Australian (1999–2006)
The Bulletin
Chunichi Shimbun
The Economist (period of 1995–2006)
International Herald Tribune
Jakarta Post (period of 1990-2008)
Pacific Review
Straits Times (period of 1995-2008)
Time International (period of 1990–2006)
U.S. News & World Report (period of 2004–05)
World Politics

Other Sources

"A Chronology of Indonesian History", Jakarta, published by Departemen Penerangan (Department of Information), 1960.

"Books for Breakfast Program", an interview with Joseph S. Nye, organized by Carnegie Council, 2004, transcript accessible online at <http://www. carnegiecouncil.org/viewMedia.php/prmTemplateID/8/prmID/4466>.

"ASEAN — Japan Relations", ASEAN Committee on Social Development's study, Bandung, Padjadjaran University, 1990.

Chair, Independent Task Force on Southeast Asia sponsored by the Council on Foreign Relations "Memorandum to the President", in The United States and Southeast Asia: A Policy Agenda for the New Administration, 2001, accessible online at <http://www.cfr.org/>.

"China and the Idea of an East Asian Community", a seminar organized by the CSIS, Jakarta, 18 January 2005, accessible online at <http://www.csis.or.id/tool_print. asp?type=events&mode=past&id=51>.

"Foreign Relations of the United States" (FRUS), U.S. Department of State, available online at <http://www.state.gov/r/pa/ho/frus/>.

"Indonesia's Perceptions of China and U.S. Security Roles in East Asia", seminar organized by The Habibie Centre, Jakarta, 16 February 2006

"Information Revolution Impacts International Relations and Security", an International Conference jointly organized by the Centre for Security Studies (CSS) at the Swiss Federal Institute for Technology (ETH) Zurich and the Comparative Interdisciplinary Studies Section (CISS) of the International Studies Association (ISA), Lucerne, Switzerland, 23–25 May 2005.

"Mempertahankan Tanah Air Memasuki Abad 21" [Defending the Homeland at the Start of the 21st Century], Indonesia's Defence White Paper 2003.

"Mengenal Kabinet RI Selama 40 Tahun Indonesia Merdeka", Jakarta, Kreasi Jaya Utama, 1986.

"The Policy of the State Defence and Security of the Republic of Indonesia",
    Indonesia's Defence White Paper 1995, Jakarta, Ministry of Defence and
    Security, 17 August 1995.
<http://www.asianresearch.org> (*Association for Asian Research*).
<http://www.gwu.edu> (*The National Security Archive*, The George Washington
    University).
<http://www.stratfor.com> (Stratfor).
<http://ww.wsws.org> (World Socialist Web Site).
<http://yaleglobal.yale.edu/> (Yale Global Online Magazine).

INDEX

A

Aandstad, Stig Aga, 111
abangan class, 69, 74, 78, 79, 93n37, 97n102, 145
Abdullah Ahmad Badawi, 291n51
Abu Ghraib prison, 146
Aceh
    alleged external involvement in, 103, 283
    in U.S.-Indonesian relations, 103, 136
    non-governmental organizations and, 103, 152, 254, 256
    tsunami relief efforts in, 156, 159, 264, 305
ACFTA (ASEAN-China Free Trade Agreement), 177, 215–16
Acharya, Amitav, 37, 302
Adler, Emanuel, 343n131
Afghanistan. *See* U.S. wars in Iraq and Afghanistan
Aidit, Dipa Nusantara, 109, 113
Al Qaeda, 141
Al-Azhar University, 75
Alagappa, Muthiah, 8
Alatas, Ali, 81
Albright, Madeleine, 125
All-Indonesian National Importers Congress, 204
Anderson, Benedict R. O'G., 42, 327

anti-American sentiment
    educational background and, 75
    George W. Bush and, 5, 130–31, 306, 318
    in U.S.-Indonesia relations, 6
    Indonesian politics and, 144–45
        issue-based, 153–59
    surveys of, 5, 103–4
    war on terrorism and, 136–41
Anwar, Dewi Fortuna
    on China, 185, 227–28, 347
    on Indonesia's foreign policy dilemma, 3
    on Japan's foreign policy dilemma, 277
    on perceptions in foreign policy, 34, 64
    on U.S.-Indonesia relations, 105
APEC (Asia-Pacific Economic Cooperation) forum, 132
ARF (ASEAN Regional Forum)
    China and, 177, 225, 226, 350
    declining importance of, 303
    Indonesia in, 19
    United States in, 104, 323
ASEAN (Association of Southeast Asian Nations)
    during Cold War, 117
    East Asian Community and, 248
    free trade agreements, 177, 215–16
    historical factors, 18, 46

Indonesian relations with, 19,
    281–87
military cooperation, 51n23, 219
perceptions of, 11, 12, 307–8
relations with China, 224–26, 227,
    311
relations with Japan, 266, 268, 269,
    276, 294n115
relations with other powers, 301,
    302, 304, 305
relations with United States, 160
ASEAN Economic Community, 218
ASEAN+3, 19, 226, 287
ASEM (Asia-Europe Meeting), 302
Asian financial crisis (1997–98), 103,
    125, 126, 128, 187, 214, 273
Asian-African Summit, 6, 177
Australia
    Cold War threats to, 23
    East Timor and, 151, 253, 262
    in East Asian Community, 7, 228,
        248, 264, 350
    Indonesian ambassadors to, 88,
        256
    military cooperation with Indonesia,
        251, 329
    movement of capital to, 207
    perceptions of, 11, 103–4, 143,
        177–79, 250–65, 334
    relations with China, 216
    relations with Indonesia, 176, 220,
        250–65, 317
    relations with Southeast Asia, 249,
        287, 305
    relations with United States, 124,
        253, 272
    tsunami relief effort, 264
    wars in Afghanistan and Iraq, 253,
        262
Australian Embassy bombing, 154
Australian National University, 257
Awaluddin, Hamid, 149
Azra, Azyumardi, 334

B
Baashir, Abu Bakar, 140
Bachit, Sutrisno, 127
Badan Pusat Statistik (BPS), 96n97
Bakrie, Aburizal, 128
balance-of-threat theory, 8, 37–46,
    300. *See also* Walt, Stephen M.
Bali, 149, 154
Bandoro, Bantarto, 276
Bandung, 6, 152, 177
Bangkok, 142
Barnes, Barry, 30–31
Bayuni, Endy M., 261
Beard, Charles A., 45
Benda, Harry J., 267
Bertrand, Jacques, 204
Bin Laden, Osama, 139, 140, 156
Binnenlandsch Bestuur, 70
Boeke, J.H., 18
Borobudur, 142
Brecher, Michael, 36
Brooks, Stephen G., 325, 328
Bryman, Alan, 87
Brzezinski, Zbigniew, 329
Buchori, Mochtar, 75
Buddhism, 80, 202, 237n154
Budiman, Arief, 201, 206
Bull, Hedley, 29, 40
Burma, 23, 214
Bush, George W.
    anti-American sentiment and, 5,
        130–31, 306, 318
    Bin Laden and, 139
    Indonesians' perception of, 123,
        153–54, 160, 300, 309, 324,
        346
    popularity in Asia, 165n94
    pre-emptive strike doctrine, 133, 253
    relations with Islamic world, 141
    unilateralism, 6, 19, 132, 225, 347
    war on terrorism, 136
Buttinger, Joseph, 30
Buzan, Barry, 33, 62–63

C

Cabinet, 67

Cairo, 75

Cambodia, 191, 214, 326

Camdessus, Michael, 125

Canada, 324

Carr, E.H., 25, 27

Carter, Jimmy, 165n94

Castles, Lance, 78

Catholicism, 78, 80

Central Europe, 89, 325

Centre for Strategic and International
    Studies (CSIS)
  in sample selection, 87, 88
  interviews, 116, 124, 140, 182,
    186, 213, 276
  staff profile, 80

Cepu Block oilfield, 127–28

Chanda, Nayan, 121

Changi International Airport, 284

Cheney, Dick, 127

Cheng Ho, 221

China
  Cold War and, 6, 179, 212, 319
  East Asian Community and, 264,
    274, 276
  economic growth and reform,
    177, 193–94, 196, 200, 211,
    240n214
  economic links with Southeast Asia,
    249
  energy demand, 310–11
  historical patterns of power, 7, 179,
    228, 314
  historical relations with Indonesia,
    108, 184, 188–91, 221, 280
  Indonesian name for, 183–84
  Indonesian response to rise of, 11,
    205, 223, 273, 346–47
  military growth and presence, 44,
    211, 213, 221, 227, 278, 321
  multilateral approach, 132
  projections for future, 308, 309–15
  regional response to rise of, 5, 6–7,
    19, 47, 287
  relations with other powers,
    272–73, 294n106
  relations with United States, 115,
    116–17, 222
  stereotyped views of, 181–87
  territorial claims, 176, 209, 220,
    313–14
  threat perceptions of, 104, 105,
    114, 131, 174–229

Chou En Lai, 195

Christofferson, Gaye, 304

Chunichi Shimbun, 266, 268, 293n95

CIA (Central Intelligence Agency),
    108, 110, 112, 138, 140

Clash of Civilizations, 330

Clinton, Bill, 120, 121–22, 123, 132,
    165n94, 225

Clinton, Hillary, 160

CNN, 148, 150

Cold War
  China and, 6, 179, 212, 319
  domestic politics during, 109–10
  end, 121
  foreign policy during, 9–10, 64,
    216, 280
  foreign policy elite during, 9–10,
    117
  India during, 280
  Japan during, 275, 319
  Middle East during, 37, 39
  model for future situation, 300, 304
  power balance during, 37, 38, 150,
    257
  U.S. policies during, 23, 29–30,
    113
  U.S.-Indonesian relations during,
    6, 122

Communist Party of Indonesia. *See*
    PKI (Partai Komunis Indonesia)

Confucianism, 80, 186

constructivism, 42–43

Cornell University, 74
corruption, 35–36, 89, 283, 285–86
Cotan, Imron, 151
Crawford, June, 32, 33, 34
Czech Republic, 89, 326

D

Dahana, A., 116, 204
Damono, Sapardi Djoko, 71
Darul Islam, 199
Dayaks, 283
Demokrasi Termimpin, 66, 109, 192,
    269
Deng Xiaoping, 115, 131, 164n58,
    177, 196, 197, 200
Department of Foreign Affairs. *See*
    DEPLU (Departemen Luar
    Negeri Republik Indonesia)
Department of Information, 186
Department of Trade and Industry,
    87, 215
DEPLU (Departemen Luar Negeri
    Republik Indonesia)
  characterization of staff, 65, 73, 81,
      251, 258
  interviews, 86, 133, 136, 142, 145
  role in foreign policy-making, 67,
      215
  role in sample selection, 87
Deutsch, Karl W., 42
Dharmala Group, 207
Djalal, Hashim, 240n214
Dole, Bob, 135
DPR (Dewan Perwakilan Rakyat), 64,
    67, 88, 120, 151, 318
Dupont, Alan, 24
Dutch colonial era
  Chinese community during, 183,
      201, 203
  in relations with China, 237n153
  Japanese occupation and, 267–68
  origins of present elite class, 68,
      70–72, 80

E

East Asia Summit (EAS), 264, 287
East Asian Community (EAC)
  ASEAN and, 273, 287
  China and, 177, 228, 264, 313,
      317, 350
  more inclusive vision of, 7, 264
  other multilateral initiatives and,
      19, 226, 274, 276
  United States and, 5
East Timor
  Australian military involvement in,
      11, 151, 252, 253, 262
  non-governmental organizations in,
      254, 261
  United States and, 103, 121, 136,
      224
Eastern Europe, 89, 224, 325
Egypt, 75
Eisenhower, Dwight D., 23, 108,
    111–12
Elson, R.E., 192–93
Emmerson, Donald K., 69
Enlightenment, 44
European Union (EU)
  absence in study, 250
  as balancing power, 301, 305, 311,
      317
  in foreign policy elite's worldviews,
      105
  military supplies from, 224
  model for East Asian Community,
      274
  norm-building power, 146
ExxonMobil, 126–28

F

Fealy, Greg, 193, 234n104
Feith, Herbert, 65, 66, 67, 68, 78
Fiske, Susan T., 36
Fitzgerald, C.P., 184
Foot, Rosemary, 41
Ford Foundation, 74

foreign policy elite. *See also* Indonesian
    foreign policy
  defining, 65–68
  education, 73–77, 111, 143, 156–58,
    258–59
  heterogeneity of background, 9, 12,
    68–83
  Islamic groups within, 65, 69–70,
    78
  lack of consensus, 13, 63–65,
    335–37
  lack of reading habit, 76–77
  links with press and academia, 68,
    135
  methods for studying, 81–82,
    83–90
  non-Muslim minority, 128, 141,
    284
  perceptions of China, 10, 174–229,
    300–315
  perceptions of Japan, 265–79
  perceptions of United States, 10,
    103–60, 190, 198, 316–35
  personality factor, 63
  preference for liberal approach,
    20–21
  view of itself, 17
Foucault, Michel, 58n145
France, 124
Free Aceh Movement (GAM), 283
Free Papua Movement (OPM), 151,
  254
Freedman, Amy L., 237n159

G
Gaduh, Arya B., 213
GAM (Gerakan Aceh Merdeka), 283
Garuda hijacking (1981), 141–42
Geertz, Clifford, 69, 73, 78, 79
Germany, 326
GESTAPU coup, 113
Glassner, Barry, 88
Goldstein, Judith, 33

Golkar, 80, 88, 108, 146, 253, 280
Gong, Gerrit W., 188
Gorbachev, Mikhail, 197
Guided Democracy, 66, 109, 192, 269
Gus Dur. *See* Wahid, Abdurrahman

H
Habibie Centre, 87, 88
Habibie, B.J., 105, 122, 127, 185,
  285
Hadiz, Vedi R., 89
Haider, Salman, 280
Hambali, 140
Hamzah, B.A., 279
Hanifah, Abu, 79, 107, 111, 203, 251
Hanoi, 221
Harvard University, 74
Hashim, Wahid, 81
Hatta, Mohammad
  "rowing between two reefs"
    metaphor, 300
  attitude to the West, 107
  on Indonesian foreign policy, 248
  on international relations theory, 24
  Sukarno and, 111, 112, 113
  views on education, 72
Haz, Hamzah, 138, 169n170
Hefner, Robert W., 96n83
Hein, Gordon Robert, 64
Henderson, Errol Anthony, 330–31
Henshall, Kenneth G., 268
Heryanto, Ariel, 200
Hindu-Buddhist tradition, 69, 78
Hinduism, 80, 202
Ho Chi Minh, 30, 54n69, 161n13,
  187
Hobbes, Thomas, 25, 40, 52n42
Holsti, Ole R., 26, 85
Hong Kong, 207
Hopf, Ted, 42
Howard, John, 74, 252, 253, 254–55,
  256, 257
human rights, 121, 146

Hund, Markus, 277
Huntington, Samuel P., 18, 249, 330
Hussein, Saddam, 274

I

Ibrahim, Marwah Daud, 127
IDSS (Institute for Defence and
    Strategic Studies), 88
Iimura, Yutaka, 279
Ikenberry, John G., 325
IMET (International Military
    Education and Training), 120
IMF (International Monetary Fund),
    103, 125, 126, 128–29, 151, 319
India
    in Asia-Europe Meeting, 302
    in East Asian Community, 7, 228,
        248, 264–65, 287, 350
    military power, 321, 328
    perceptions of, 11, 12, 226, 279–81
    regional response to rise of, 47, 301
    relations with other powers, 223,
        280, 305, 351
    signing of Treaty of Amity and
        Cooperation, 276
Indochina, 29–30
Indonesia. *See also* Dutch colonial era;
    Indonesian economy; Indonesian
    foreign policy; Indonesian
    military; Indonesians
    education in, 63, 72, 94n50
    political and social transformation,
        64
    population, 67
    Revolution of 1945-49, 106, 107,
        269
    social structure, 69–70, 78
    streams of political thought, 78–79
    war on terrorism and, 136–44, 154
Indonesian Association of Muslim
    Intellectuals (ICMI), 127, 144
Indonesian Corruption Watch (ICW),
    285–86

Indonesian Democratic Party —
    Struggle, 88, 127, 210, 253, 283,
    323
Indonesian economy. *See also* Asian
    financial crisis (1997–98)
    China and, 214, 215
    Chinese community and, 203–4,
        210
    Japan and, 270–71
    national image and, 149–50
    resource-based, 272, 311
    rupiah, 125
    U.S. and IMF intervention, 125–29
Indonesian foreign policy. *See also*
    foreign policy elite
    "hostile world" image, 9, 348
    "Pretty Girl Analogy," 9, 84, 122,
        216–17, 260, 273, 305
    characterizations of, 4, 337, 347–48
    democratic processes and, 9, 61–62
    domestic politics and, 109–13,
        319–20
    mandala concept in, 327–29
    national interest and, 63
Indonesian Institute, 87, 88
Indonesian military
    actions in East Timor, 224, 252
    cooperation with Australia, 251, 329
    cooperation with Japan, 274
    make-up of leadership, 80–81,
        97n102
    perceptions of China, 213, 218–22
    perceptions of Vietnam, 326
    pro-U.S. stance, 135
    state of navy, 261
    vs. DEPLU personnel, 73–74
    vs. PKI, 109, 110, 113, 175
    within foreign policy elite, 67, 73
Indonesians. *See also* *abangan* class;
    Muslim community; *priyayi* class;
    santri class
    anti-Chinese pogroms, 6, 176
    anti-Japanese protests, 271

Chinese community, 6, 80, 176, 192, 193, 195, 200–210
Christian community, 78, 80, 81, 256
communist threat and, 198
foreign policy and, 63, 66, 90
Islamization, 97n114, 144
religion, 80, 82–83, 94n56, 202
Initiative for Development of East Asia (IDEA), 274
Inter-Governmental Group on Indonesia (IGGI), 113
International Criminal Court, 131
international relations. *See also* balance-of-threat theory; power; realist theory of international relations
  constructivism in, 41–44
  domestic politics and, 23, 44–46
  elite decision-makers and, 34–36, 46–48
  human nature and, 24–27, 42, 47
  national interest in, 62–63
  role of emotion in, 32–34
  threat perception in, 7–8, 31, 38–39, 62
Iran, 318
Iraq. *See* U.S. wars in Iraq and Afghanistan
Isamuddin, Riduan, 140
Islam, 80, 137, 202, 210, 237(nn153, 154), 318. *See also* Muslim community
Israel, 137, 284, 332
Itoh, Mayumi, 294n115

J
Jackson, Karl D., 82
Jakarta, 159, 176, 283
Jakarta Post, 88
Jamhari, 79
Japan
  East Asian Community and, 264, 265

  in Asia-Europe Meeting, 302
  Indonesian ambassador to, 207
  military assertiveness, 270, 273–74, 277–78, 300, 321, 328
  perceptions of, 11–12, 143, 186, 262, 265–79
  projections for future, 307, 308, 311
  relations with China, 187, 222, 294n106, 301
  relations with other powers, 198, 223, 225, 253, 272, 351
  relations with Southeast Asia, 249, 266, 273, 276, 277, 305
  relations with United States, 30, 303
  travel advisories, 149
  United Nations and, 147
Java
  Chinese naval expedition to, 184, 189, 190
  Dutch civil service training, 71
  ethnic Chinese in, 203
  Hindu courtly culture, 69, 186, 237n154
  in mandala concept, 327
  PKI strongholds in, 193
  religion in, 79
  social elite, 78
  social unrest and terror attacks, 142, 149
Java Sea, 134, 255
Jemaah Islamiyah (JI), 138, 140
Jervis, Robert, 77
Johnston, Alastair Iain, 51n24
Jones, Sidney, 149, 152

K
Kahin, George McTurnan, 65, 66
Kalimantan, 283
Kalla, Jusuf, 128
Kang, David C., 19, 37
Katzenstein, Peter J., 328

Kennedy, John F., 54n69, 109, 175
Keohane, Robert O., 28, 148, 321
Kiemas, Taufik, 135
kiyayi class, 69, 78
Koizumi, Junichiro, 273–74, 275, 276
Komando Jihad, 142, 199
Kompas, 88, 159, 304
Konfrontasi, 175
Korea. *See* North Korea; South Korea
KPPU (Komisi Pengawas Persaingan Usaha), 285
kraton aristocracy, 70, 78
Kuala Lumpur, 221, 264
Kublai Khan, 189–90, 323
Kupchan, Charles A., 343n131
Kusumaatmadja, Mochtar, 81
Kyoto Agreement, 131

L
Lam Peng-Er, 277, 278
Lanti, Irman G., 64, 117, 211, 327
Laos, 191
Lebanon, 331–32
Leifer, Michael, 47, 113, 186
Lenin, Vladimir Il'ich, 44
Leninism, 79
liberalism, 72
Liddle, William R., 74, 145
Liem corporation, 207
LIPI (Lembaga Ilmu Pengetahuan Indonesia), 87, 88, 140, 143, 198, 227
Lippo Group, 207
Lowry, Robert, 213
Lubis, Zulkifli, 112
Luhulima, C.P.F., 118

M
Machiavelli, Niccolò, 25, 38
MacIntyre, Andrew, 192, 250
Mackie, Jamie, 192
Madjid, Nurcholish, 94n56
madrasah, 75, 142

Majapahit Empire, 186
Mak, J.N., 279
Makassar Sea, 255
Malacca Straits, 272, 274, 324
Malaya, 23
Malaysia, 12, 217, 281–83, 285, 331, 334
Malik, Adam, 81
Malik, Mohan, 264–65
Maliki, Zainuddin, 97n114
Maluku Sea, 255
Mao Zedong, 197, 198, 208
Maritime Identification Zone, 255, 256, 260
Marriott Hotel bombing, 154
Marx, Karl, 44
Marxism, 72, 79
Mastanduno, Michael, 24, 41
Masyumi, 112, 113
Maulani, Lieutenant-General Zen, 133, 138
McAllister, Ian, 257
McIntyre, Angus, 110
McMichael, Heath, 187
McVey, Ruth, 77, 95n82
Mearsheimer, John J., 25
Medan, 176, 283
media coverage
    image of Indonesia and, 257
    influence on elite and public opinion, 76–77
    of fall of Abdurrahman Wahid, 135
    scrutiny of government policies, 63
    threat perception and, 28, 31, 46
    U.S. control of, 146, 147–51
Medina, 75
Mehden, Fred von der, 83
Merdeka, 206
Mexico, 324
Middle East, 37, 39, 45–46, 119, 225, 319, 321
Military Academy, 81
Miller, Jody, 88

Ministry of Foreign Affairs. *See*
    DEPLU (Departemen Luar
    Negeri Republik Indonesia)
MIT (Massachusetts Institute of
    Technology), 74
Moertono, Soemarsaid, 327
Moertopo, Ali, 80, 182, 201, 270
Morgenthau, Hans J., 21–22, 25, 28,
    34
Mortimer, Rex, 111
Mozingo, David, 202, 203, 237n153
Muhammadiyah, 140, 198, 213, 254,
    284
Mulia, Siti Musdah, 145
Murdani, General Leonardus
    Benyamin, 326
Muslim community
    differences within, 127
    education, 74–75
    influence on foreign policy, 319–20
    radical groups within, 137–38,
        170n197
    social class and, 69–70
Muslim Crescent Star Party (PBB), 120

N
Nasution, General Abdul Haris, 109,
    111, 196
Natalegawa, Marty, 146, 287
National Mandate Party, 88, 127, 139,
    140
National Security Archive, 151
Natsir, Mohammad, 94n50
Natuna Islands, 176, 209, 220–21,
    251
nepotism, 89
Netherlands, 106, 150, 210, 251
New Guinea, 150. *See also* Papua New
    Guinea; West Papua
New Order regime. *See also* Suharto
    domination by Suharto, 64, 66
    ethnic Chinese community and,
        204, 206

relations with China, 192, 198–200,
    326, 352
relations with Japan, 269, 271
relations with United States, 103,
    113–15
support for communist regimes,
    326–27
use of communist threat, 193,
    198–99, 208
New Zealand
    during Cold War, 23
    in East Asian Community (EAC),
        7, 228, 248, 264–65, 287
    in Indonesian outlook, 249
    relations with Australia, 255
Newsweek, 268
NGOs (non-governmental
    organizations), 103, 122, 123,
    152–53, 254, 255, 261
North Korea, 139, 185, 277, 307, 326
Nye, Joseph S., Jr., 28, 29, 31, 148,
    321

O
Obama, Barack, 5–6, 104, 120, 159,
    160, 347
Okawara, Nobuo, 328
Opleidingscholen voor Inlandsche
    Ambtenaren (OSVIA), 71
OPM (Organisasi Papua Merdeka),
    151, 254
Origins of Alliances, 8, 37, 39, 45, 321
Ott, Marvin, 179, 301, 315, 317
Outer Island rebellions, 107, 108,
    110, 190–91

P
Pakistan, 142, 280
Palar, Lambertus Nicodemus, 106
Palestine, 148
PAN (Partai Amanat Nasional), 88,
    127, 139, 140
Pan Yining, 320

Pancasila, 126, 199
Pangestu, Mari, 216
Pangreh Praja, 70, 72
Papua New Guinea, 256, 262
PBB (Partai Bulan Bintang), 120
PDI-P (Partai Demokrasi Indonesia
    Perjuangan), 88, 127, 210, 253,
    283, 323
Peacock, James L., 79
pejabat, 61
Peou, Sorpong, 41
pesantren, 75
Pew Global Attitudes survey, 5, 137f,
    154f, 155f, 157f, 158f, 178f
Pew Research Centre, 130, 153, 177,
    331
Philippines, 26, 88, 105, 283, 284,
    303
Philpott, Simon, 258
piracy, 147, 274
PKI (Partai Komunis Indonesia)
    Mohammad Hatta and, 107
    Suharto's assessment of, 193, 205
    Sukarno and, 109, 110, 112, 113,
        199
    support from China, 175, 192, 195,
        196, 198
PKS (Partai Keadilan Sejahtera), 75,
    127, 159
Plato, 44
Portugal, 210
power
    in realist theory, 21–22, 27–28
    information and, 28–29, 123, 146,
        147–51, 257
    norm-building, 146
    soft *vs.* hard, 29, 123
    subjective appraisals of, 40, 43,
        58n145
    vs. threat perception, 31
PPP (Partai Persatuan Pembangunan),
    88, 138
priyayi class, 9, 69–73, 78, 80, 97n114

Prosperous Justice Party, 75, 127, 159
Protestantism, 78, 80
Purba, Kornelius, 317
Putnam, Robert, 66

R
Radjasa, Hatta, 127
Raffles, Sir Thomas Stamford, 79
Rais, Amien, 119–20, 127, 128, 176,
    205, 252
Reagan, Ronald, 165n94
realist theory of international relations
    applicability to Asian states, 17–19,
        23–24, 37, 52n36
    assumptions, 32, 42
    balance-of-power concept, 4, 22,
        36–37
    China's rise and, 6–7
    defined and analysed, 21–23,
        24–27, 39–40, 51n24
    failure to model Indonesian policies,
        4–5, 179
    Indonesian disavowal of, 20
Reformasi era, 201, 204, 336
religion. *See also individual religions*
    in Australia and eastern Indonesia,
        256
    in Java, 79
    in race relations, 202, 203
    in shaping worldview, 33, 77,
        329–35
    in Southeast Asian interstate
        relations, 284
    in the *priyayi* concept, 69
Riau Islands, 220
Riau Province, 282
Robinson, Richard, 89
Robison, Richard, 73
Roosevelt, Franklin D., 106, 161n13
Rosenau, James N., 36
Ross, Robert S., 304
Russia, 250, 251, 272, 326, 328,
    351

S

Said, Edward W., 13n7
Said, Salim, 80, 81, 129
Samson, Allan A., 83
San Francisco Treaty, 269
santri class, 69, 70, 74, 78, 79, 93n38,
    97n114
Sarawak, 283
Saudi Arabia, 75
Schweller, Randall L., 48
Sebastian, Leonard C., 327
September 11 terrorist attacks, 130,
    132, 136, 318
Shanghai, 216
Shann, Keith, 17
Sheng Lijun, 275
Siddiq, Mahfudz, 159
Simandjuntak, Djisman, 249
Sinar Harapan, 88
Singapore
    Chinese naval expeditions, 221
    East Asian Community and,
        264–65
    foreign policy, 47, 253, 272
    military, 134, 332
    perceptions of, 12, 260, 281–86
    piracy issue and, 147
    relations with the U.S., 26, 285, 323
    tensions with Indonesia, 297n182
Singhasari, 189
Sjahrir, Sutan, 113, 120
Sjarifuddin, Amir, 107
Skinner, William G., 201, 237n154
Smith, Anthony L., 138, 253
Snyder, Jack, 45
Socialist Party of Indonesia, 113
Soedjatmoko, 33
Soehoed, Abdoel Raoef, 271
Soerjogoeritno, Soetardjo, 254
Soesastro, Hadi, 186, 222
Soroka, Stuart N., 76
South China Sea, 176, 213, 220, 222,
    251, 313, 324

South Korea
    absence in study, 250
    in Asia-Europe Meeting, 302
    in East Asian Community, 264,
        274, 276
    relations with ASEAN, 273, 305
    relations with China, 185, 294n106
    relations with United States, 117,
        316
Soviet Union
    collapse, 121, 131, 197, 200, 249
    during Cold War, 19, 304, 307
    geopolitical position, 325
    relations with Indonesia, 109, 111
    relations with other powers, 198
    threat perceptions of, 37, 38, 114,
        177, 196
Spiegel, Steven, 32
Spratly Islands, 220, 251
Spykman, Nicholas J., 31, 324, 329
Stanford University, 74
Steinbruner, John, 36
Stratfor, 135
Stuart-Fox, Martin, 7, 179, 180, 183,
    202
Subianto, Landry Haryo, 281, 287
Sudan, 318
Sudarman, Suzie, 219
Sudarsono, Juwono, 127, 184, 254,
    256, 261
Suharto
    anti-communist outlook, 192, 196,
        326
    Clinton Administration's criticism
        of, 121
    fall of, 124, 177
    influence on foreign policy, 16, 24,
        34, 64, 66, 122, 248–49
    Islamization policies, 144
    manipulation of public opinion,
        90
    military leadership under, 80, 283
    ministers, 74

relations with China, 183–84,
    191–94, 196, 197, 212, 213,
    251
relations with United States, 113,
    115, 126
Sukarno
    decree on religion, 80
    fall of, 192
    Guided Democracy, 109, 192
    influence on foreign policy, 16, 24,
        26, 65, 248
    leadership style, 72
    manipulation of public opinion, 90
    military power under, 283
    nationalist, anti-Western attitudes,
        107, 162n34, 175, 186
    on international relations, 47
    proclamation of independence, 187
    relations with China, 175–76, 192,
        195, 199
    relations with Japan, 269
    relations with United States,
        109–13, 114
    West Papua and, 150–51, 251,
        305
    worldview, 33, 79, 109–13
Sukarnoputri, Megawati, 135, 140,
    145, 262, 276, 283
Sukma, Rizal, 99n130, 109, 129, 180,
    191, 210, 318
Sulawesi, 108
Sumantoro, 273
Sumargono, Ahmad, 120
Sumatra, 108
Sunardi, R.M., 28, 251, 263
Surabaya, 104, 323
Suryadinata, Leo, 65, 81, 205, 266,
    326, 328
Suryakusuma, Julia I., 105, 150
Sutherland, Heather, 69, 72
Sutjipto, Widodo Adi, 254
Syahrir, Sutan, 113
Syria, 318

T
TAC (Treaty of Amity and
    Cooperation), 224, 225, 226,
    274, 276
Taiwan
    ASEAN and, 311
    China's growing confidence and,
        313, 319
    Japan and, 275
    potential flashpoint, 307, 310
    United States and, 117, 222, 316
Tan See Seng, 302
Tanjung, Akbar, 252
Taylor, Susan E., 36
Tellis, Ashley J., 137
Temasek Holdings, 285
Tempo, 283, 285
Thailand
    Chinese community in, 203
    currency, 125
    during Cold War, 23
    relations with China, 214, 326
    relations with Indonesia, 88, 217,
        285
    relations with United States, 284, 303
    terrorism and, 140, 141
    threat perception, 31–34, 39–41,84,
        143, 336
Tilman, Robert O., 35, 67, 267, 279
Toha, Abdillah, 127
Tomaka, Joe, 32
Tow, Shannon, 350
Truman, Harry, 161n13
tsunami, 156, 264, 305
Tucker, Richard, 330–31
Turner, Sarah, 210

U
U.S. State Department Human Rights
    Report, 146
U.S. wars in Iraq and Afghanistan
    anti-American sentiment and, 103,
        130, 136, 144–45

Australian involvement, 253, 262
effectiveness of, 54n62
in U.S.-Indonesian relations, 5,
    108, 133–34, 139, 318
Japanese involvement in, 274, 277
United Development Party, 88, 138
United Kingdom, 106, 147, 254
United Nations, 106, 130, 146–47,
    151, 222, 247, 251
United States Military Academy at
    West Point, 74
United States of America. *See also*
    anti-American sentiment;
    U.S. wars in Iraq and
    Afghanistan
  "four anchors" leadership, 253,
      272
  Cold War strategies, 19, 23, 29–30
  domestic situation, 29, 45–46, 119
  economic links with Southeast Asia,
      249
  Indonesian ambassadors to, 74, 88
  Islamic world and, 137–38, 148,
      331–33
  military presence in region, 44,
      51n23, 117, 134, 308, 321,
      323
  movement of capital to, 207
  norm-building power, 123, 146
  Outer Island rebellions and, 107,
      108, 110, 190–91
  post-Cold War strategies, 121
  projections for future, 316–35
  relations with China, 55n79, 115,
      116–17, 222, 223, 225
  relations with Indonesia, 5–6, 65,
      74, 75, 219, 224
  relations with Japan, 274, 277
  relations with Singapore, 26, 253,
      272, 285
  relations with the Philippines, 26
  rise in 19th century, 30, 38
  superpower status, 54n64, 124, 249

support for Indonesian
    independence, 251
tsunami relief effort, 156, 157f,
    159, 305
unilateralism, 11, 19, 121, 123,
    130, 222
war on terrorism, 54n62, 103, 123,
    132, 136–44, 319
Universitas Gadjah Mada, 88
University of California Berkeley, 74,
    119
University of Chicago, 74
University of Indonesia, 88, 219
University of New South Wales,
    98n125
USINDO, 305

V
Vietnam, 187, 191, 217, 265, 326
Vietnam War, 29–30, 54n69, 119,
    191, 251
Vondra, Alexander, 326

W
Wahid, Abdurrahman
  ethnic Chinese community and, 206
  father of, 81
  foreign policy under, 176, 215,
      229n10, 273
  resignation, 134–35
  war on terrorism and, 138
Walt, Stephen M.
  attitude to constructivism, 43
  balance-of-threat theory, 8, 37–41,
      42
  on geographic proximity, 321, 325
  on link between theory and policy,
      17
  on U.S. politics, 45–46
Waltz, Kenneth W., 4, 5, 24, 25, 26,
    42
Wanandi, Jusuf, 104, 114, 182, 282,
    283, 301, 306

Weinstein, Franklin B.
countries excluded in study, 250,
279
on attitudes to China, 175–76, 177,
208
on attitudes to Chinese Indonesians,
205
on attitudes to Japan, 266, 269, 270
on attitudes to the United States,
110, 114
on degree of elite consensus, 336
study of foreign policy elite, 9–10,
66, 216
Wendt, Alexander, 34, 42–43
West Papua
Australia and, 11, 252, 253,
254–58, 261, 262, 334
Sukarno and, 150–51, 251, 305
United States and, 103, 107, 109,
136, 150, 152
Western Europe, 30, 38, 89, 301, 325
Westphalia, Treaty of, 21
Whiting, Allen S., 221
Wilson, Greta O., 72
Wirayuda, Hassan, 138, 286
Wirjosandjojo, Sukiman, 108

Witoelar, Wimar, 159
Wohlforth, William C., 325, 328
World Wide Web, 148

Y
Yani, General Ahmad, 175
Yasukuni shrine, 275, 277
Yogyakarta, 106, 162n16
Yogyakarta, Sultan of, 112
Yudhoyono, Susilo Bambang
cabinet members, 124, 143, 187,
196, 223, 276, 301
education, 120
foreign affairs and, 64
leadership style, 65
relations with United States, 104,
120, 160, 347
Sidney Jones travel ban and, 152

Z
Zheng Bijian, 231n32
Zheng He, 221
Zhou Enlai, 195
Zhu Rongji, 225
ZOPFAN (Zone of Peace, Freedom
and Neutrality), 224, 225, 276

NOTE ON THE AUTHOR

Dr Daniel Novotny is an Endeavour Research Fellow at the Monash European and EU Centre, Monash University in Melbourne. He specializes in international relations of Southeast Asia, Asian elite perceptions and foreign policy — theory and practice, security and contemporary geopolitical developments in the Asia-Pacific, and EU's foreign policy strategy in Asia. In 1998–2000, he was an aide in the Political Department of The Office of the President of the Czech Republic. Since writing his Ph.D. at the University of New South Wales, Sydney, he coordinated a special research project on the "EU-India relations" for the Czech Ministry of Foreign Affairs. He has also been affiliated with the Prague-based think-tank Association for International Affairs and as a Visiting Research Fellow with the Singapore-based RSIS and ISEAS institutes and The Habibie Centre in Jakarta. Apart from his academic endeavours, he has produced several dozens of short documentaries covering the Asia-Pacific region as an associate freelance correspondent for The Czech Television (ČT). He is married with two children.

www.ingramcontent.com/pod-product-compliance
Lightning Source LLC
Chambersburg PA
CBHW021844020426
42334CB00013B/175